CANADA LOOKS SOUTH

In Search of an Americas Policy

Recent events in the Western hemisphere have led to a dramatic shift in the strategic and political importance of Latin America. But with relations still cool between the United States and Cuba, and Venezuela becoming more distant every day, there is considerable potential for Canada – with its long-standing commitment to constructive engagement – to forge mutually beneficial relations with these nations as well as rising industrial and economic players such as Mexico and Brazil.

In *Canada Looks South*, experts on foreign policy in Canada and Central America provide a timely exploration of Canada's growing role in the Americas and the most pressing issues of the region. Starting with the historical scope of the bilateral relationship, the volume goes on to cover such subjects as trade engagement, democratization, and security. As current and future Canadian governments embrace expanding linkages with this region, this collection fills a significant gap in scholarship on Canadian-Latin American relations.

PETER MCKENNA is professor and chair of the Department of Political Science at the University of Prince Edward Island.

Canada Looks South

In Search of an Americas Policy

EDITED BY PETER MCKENNA

UNIVERSITY OF TORONTO PRESS
Toronto Buffalo London

ISBN 978-1-4426-4206-5 (cloth)
ISBN 978-1-4426-1108-5 (paper)

Printed on acid-free, 100% post-consumer recycled paper with
vegetable-based inks.

Library and Archives Canada Cataloguing in Publication

Canada looks South : in search of an Americas policy / edited by
Peter McKenna.

Includes bibliographical references and index.
ISBN 978-1-4426-4206-5 (bound). – ISBN 978-1-4426-1108-5 (pbk.)

1. Canada – Foreign relations – Latin America.   2. Latin America –
Foreign relations – Canada.   I. McKenna, Peter, 1961–

FC244.L3C353 2012   327.7108   C2012-904969-7

This book has been published with the help of a grant from the Canadian
Federation for the Humanities and Social Sciences, through the Awards to
Scholarly Publications Program, using funds provided by the Social
Sciences and Humanities Research Council of Canada.

University of Toronto Press acknowledges the financial assistance to its
publishing program of the Canada Council for the Arts and the Ontario
Arts Council.

 Canada Council   Conseil des Arts
for the Arts   du Canada   ONTARIO ARTS COUNCIL
CONSEIL DES ARTS DE L'ONTARIO

University of Toronto Press acknowledges the financial support of the
Government of Canada through the Canada Book Fund for its publishing
activities.

For Aline and Jessica

Contents

Acknowledgments

I would like to thank the University of Toronto Press, especially Daniel Quinlan, for believing in this project from the beginning and for offering kind support along the way. The copy editor also merits considerable credit for improving the style and presentation of the work. Any errors of commission or omission rest entirely with myself. Each of the contributors deserves high praise and thanks for responding positively and patiently to my many emails. A huge thank-you to John Kirk, my long-time friend and mentor, for being the gifted life teacher that he is. A special note of gratitude to my colleagues and friends at the University of Prince Edward Island (UPEI), who have provided me with a wonderful working environment. Last, but certainly not least, I would like to acknowledge my family for their unstinting love and support. Without them, I would not be able to do the kind of work that I love to do.

Preface

As a full-fledged member of the Organization of American States (OAS) since 1990, Canada cannot simply insulate itself from significant developments in this hemisphere (witness the 2009 coup in Honduras, Mexico's bloody drug war, or Cuba's internal political and economic status). Official Ottawa will invariably be called upon to respond in some fashion. In fact, other countries in the region look to Canada and want to hear what it has to say about the region's most pressing issues and challenges. But if our voice is to be heard, our presence felt, and our influence exercised, Canada's actions have to speak louder than its flowery words. To do that, though, the Canadian government needs to muster up the requisite political will and resources (including bureaucratic support), to learn from past experiences, to grasp the essence of key issues and core bilateral relationships, and to craft a comprehensive and coherent Americas policy. The insights that are contained within this collection of essays will certainly be indispensible in this regard.

Fifty years ago, the countries of Latin America and the Caribbean were largely an afterthought for Canadian governments and policy makers. Rights-abusing military regimes, stagnating and closed economies, abject poverty, and growing indebtedness confined them to the margins of Canada's external relations. Indeed, Canadian foreign service officers once dreaded being assigned to an inter-American desk or bureau position and studiously avoided diplomatic postings to the region itself. All of that has changed considerably in the intervening years. To be sure, Canada has once again rediscovered the Americas in the 2000s as a core plank in the conduct of Canadian foreign policy.

Not surprisingly, then, the idea for this book has been rattling around in my mind for several years now. I still vividly recall, when he was discussing a crucial part of Canada's newly minted Latin American strategy in 1989, former secretary of state for external affairs Joe Clark saying that 'Canada's joining of the OAS represents not so much a decision to become a member of an organization as it does a decision to become a partner in this hemisphere. For too long, Canadians have seen this hemisphere as our house; it is now time to make it our home.'[1] Two weeks earlier, former prime minister Brian Mulroney, at a meeting of hemispheric leaders in Costa Rica – where he formally announced Canada's decision to finally join the hemisphere's principal political forum – argued that 'hemispheric cooperation is integral to Canada's interests and the OAS holds the key to that cooperation. Canada's presence here today signals a new departure in our relations with Latin America. We recognize that our interests are directly engaged here. We will no longer stand apart.'[2] Ever since Canada took its long-empty seat at the OAS in January 1990, there has been a real need for a comprehensive assessment of Canada's relationship with the Americas. Some twenty years later, this would seem to be an opportune time to do so.

Prime Minister Stephen Harper's pledge to make hemispheric affairs 'a critical international priority for our country' has made the need for careful reflection more palpable.[3] As Harper's former chief spokesperson, Dimitri Soudas, remarked in July 2009: 'Our government is strengthening its development assistance programs in the Americas because this is our neighbourhood, where we have significant interests and the ability and influence to make a difference. Our assistance is helping to build the basis for sustainable prosperity and security and strengthening democracy and the rule of law.'[4] The governing Harper Conservatives have obviously borrowed from the party's past focus on the region, but it appears to be proceeding in the absence of a clear Americas vision for going forward.[5] Part of Harper's tepid approach to the Americas could have been a function of his tenuous minority government situation. But with his garnering of a majority government in May 2011, his government would be well advised to continue to sharpen its focus on cultivating, broadening, and deepening its engagement in the region within an all-encompassing strategy and policy menu.[6] To the surprise of some, Harper did not take the opportunity at the VI Summit of the Americas in Cartagena, Colombia in mid-April 2012 to reconfigure and relaunch his Americas gambit, by spelling out specific policy priorities, initiatives, and spending commitments.[7]

Of course, Canada's involvement with Latin America and the Caribbean did not begin with Brian Mulroney or Stephen Harper. As the so-called 'Gringos from the Far North,' as historian Jack Ogelsby once aptly described Canadians, we have had an on-again, off-again relationship with the inter-American community.[8] In fact, former prime minister Pierre Trudeau singled out Latin America as a key region in his 1970 foreign policy review document *Foreign Policy for Canadians*. Always actively searching for counterweights to the preponderance of U.S. power, Trudeau sought to diversify our political and commercial relations (in the manner of the Third Option) with the major players in the hemisphere. Additionally, former prime minister Jean Chrétien made the Americas a central part of his government's foreign policy thrust. Not only did Canada host a series of major hemispheric conferences (including the April 2001 Summit of the Americas in Quebec City), meetings, and sporting events, but Chrétien also brought his patented 'Team Canada' trade missions to Latin America and the Caribbean.

The media in Canada periodically cover, though often in a cursory nature, sundry developments with an inter-American twist.[9] We hear about a military-backed coup in Honduras, efforts to reintegrate Cuba into the OAS, Colombia's disturbing human rights record, and the imposition of visa requirements on Mexican citizens. (What we hear less about is the fact that Canada has had a long-standing requirement for visitors' visas for all of the countries of South and Central America.) But there is only fleeting coverage of the growing saliency of the Americas to Canada's external relations, the $150 billion worth of Canadian investment in the area (three times what Canadians invest in Asia, making it the region's third-largest investor), our increasing trade ties (where Canada is pursuing bilateral trade deals with a number of countries in the region), and the fact that Latin Americans make up one of the largest groups of new immigrants to this country (11 per cent).[10] Accordingly, very few Canadians, especially since the signing of the North American Free Trade Agreement (NAFTA) in 1993, have ever bothered to look beyond Mexico.

Thankfully, that is now changing – and, indeed, it must change as the twenty-first century unfolds. In terms of two-way trade alone, the overall tally has jumped from $11.5 billion in 1997 to a whopping $51 billion in 2010 – dramatically increasing by more than 50 per cent over the last five years alone.[11] (In terms of official development assistance, Canada earmarked some $492 million to the Americas in 2007–8.)[12] Canadians need to wake up to the reality that their future is inextricably tied to Latin America and the Caribbean.[13] The Chinese have obviously realized this, as they have significantly enhanced their presence throughout the Americas. Ottawa can ill-afford to sit idly by while other countries (including the U.S.) seek to deepen their footprint in the hemisphere. It is hoped, then, that this volume will serve as a call-to-action and a sort of policy handbook and roadmap for Canadians within and without government. It will certainly be instructive for the governing Conservatives (and any future governing party) as they move forward under a majority government.[14]

To begin, though, it is not exactly clear why the Stephen Harper government sought to broaden and deepen Canada's relationship with the Americas in 2006–7.[15] Harper himself had said precious little over his political career about foreign affairs, let alone anything specifically involving the Americas. It is also very doubtful that public opinion in Canada pushed the governing Conservatives to embrace the Americas.[16] Granted, there had been some noise emanating from civil society about revitalizing our interest in Latin America and the Caribbean, but they were not particularly loud voices.[17] Moreover, there was a feeling among some in the 'attentive public' that Canada stood a real chance of playing an influential role in the region.[18] Paul Heinbecker, Canada's former ambassador to the UN, speculated that it had something to do with the incoming Harper Conservatives wanting to clearly differentiate themselves from previous Liberal governments: 'The reasoning process did not appear to be much more complicated than a determination that, if the Liberals "did" Africa, the Conservatives would "do" Latin America,' he argued.[19] But according to long-time Latin America hand John Graham, the initial foundation for constructing an Americas strategy had been in place before the Conservatives came into office in early 2006 – as contained in a letter by the transition team to incoming foreign affairs minister Peter MacKay.

At first glance, there is always the possibility – though incontrovertible evidence is sparse – that the George W. Bush White House put the Americas bug in Harper's ear for their own reasons. The argument goes something like this: since Bush had mostly neglected Latin America throughout his entire first administration, he hoped that Harper's renewed engagement in the Americas would help to smooth things over with the region's disgruntled political leaders. But according to a WikiLeaks cable dated 15 April 2009, issued by a political counsellor at the U.S. embassy in Ottawa after discussing the matter with Canada's then director general for Latin America and the Caribbean James Lambert, Harper's focus on the region came out of extensive talks with former Australian prime minister John Howard, a close confidante of

Harper's. As the leaked cable explains: 'Harper had long been favorably impressed by Australia's ability to exert outsized influence with the U.S. in particular – and other powers as well – by emphasizing its relations in its own neighborhood, observed Lambert, who added that PM Harper hoped to gain similar benefits for Canada by increased attention to Latin America and the Caribbean.'[20] It could also have had something to do with a carry-over from the previous Conservative government of Brian Mulroney – who, after all, had brought Canada into the OAS in 1990 – and who at one time had the ear of Prime Minister Harper.[21] Latin America and the Caribbean would also provide something else for the government to talk about, and thus additional foreign policy cover, should things go terribly wrong in war-torn Afghanistan.

It is equally plausible to understand Harper's Americas thrust primarily within the context of investment and trade promotion and diversification (as the string of free trade pacts with various countries would seem to confirm).[22] While it is true that two-way trade is not huge by any measurement, it is growing, and future projections for growth are encouraging. This is particularly true in the case of Canada's mining footprint in Latin America, where hundreds of Canadian companies ply their trade (and where the value of their investment tops $57 billion).[23] And as Yasmine Shamsie and Ricardo Grinspun point out: 'Given that many of these companies are based in western Canada, where the Harper government draws its strongest support, it is not a stretch to suggest that it is attending to the interests of this corporate constituency.'[24]

If it is not already clear in official Ottawa why Latin America should be a core focus of Canadian foreign policy, it is hoped that the contents of this book will clarify things significantly. Indeed, the overarching thrust of this collection is to examine in detail the growing and deepening Canadian links with the southern hemisphere (where some 4 million Canadians visited in 2007). However, there is no one theoretical model or perspective that connects the various chapters into a single tapestry, as it brings together a diverse collection of scholars. As is often the case in edited volumes, each contributor has incorporated his or her own particular theoretical analysis. There is no attempt, then, to break new theoretical ground in the study of Canadian foreign policy toward the Americas. The major intellectual challenge here was to provide greater understanding and context of hemispheric affairs, to single out important political actors and opinion makers, and to offer insightful analysis and explanation of the major policy drivers or determinants that will shape and inform future policy-making decisions toward the region. To be sure, there is an effort here not only to make general policy recommendations for the present Conservative government, and future governments, to do something with respect to Latin America and the Caribbean, but for it to do something very specific from a policy-making standpoint.

This book first seeks to paint the broad strokes of Canada's past and present relationship with the Americas. It then moves on to examine some of the key overarching issues for the Canadian government – namely, trade promotion, democratization, and hemispheric security. That discussion is followed by several individual case studies on Canada's various bilateral relationships throughout the region as a whole (space limitations do not permit an in-depth investigation of every country in the hemisphere). The book concludes with some general observations about the state of Canadian/inter-American affairs and restates some of the key policy recommendations for fashioning a comprehensive Americas policy.

There is little doubt that Canada's future economic, political, and security objectives are in play in the Americas – especially since it is our geographic home and the place where many of our core foreign policy interests are directly affected.[25] Moreover, Canada has a tremendous opportunity, as a leading member of the OAS, to really 'punch above its weight' in the Americas. And there is no better time to do so as U.S. president Barack Obama – who visited the region in March 2011 – moves to position the United States in a more favourable light in the hemisphere. After all, we have many natural advantages that are simply not available to the U.S. (including no historical baggage of intervention and a general perception of having no hidden agenda), and this puts us in an enviable position to capitalize on strengthening our hemispheric linkages. (It is also true that Canada's enhanced role in the Americas could pay important diplomatic dividends in Washington as well.)[26] But to do so effectively and prudently, politicians and policy makers in Ottawa need to craft a well-thought-out plan of action or strategy. It is my hope that this book will go some way toward accomplishing that crucial policy objective.

NOTES

1 Government of Canada, 'Notes for Remarks by the Secretary of State for External Affairs, The Right Honourable Joe Clark, at the Meeting of the

Council of the Organization of American States,' *Statement*, 13 November
1989, 1.

2 Office of the Prime Minister, 'Notes for an Address by The Right Honourable Brian Mulroney – Meeting of Hemispheric Leaders,' 27 October 1989, 5.

3 As the chair of the June 2010 G8 meeting in Huntsville, Ontario, Prime
Minister Harper took it upon himself to invite three leaders from the
Americas for 'outreach sessions': Bruce Golding from Jamaica, René
Préval from Haiti, and Álvaro Uribe from Colombia. See Campbell Clark,
'"Outreach" invitees share Harper's foreign policies,' *Globe and Mail*, 14
June 2010, A8. Further emblematic of Canada's increased activity in the
Americas was a busy August 2009 for the Conservative government – with
Prime Minister Harper visiting both Mexico and Panama, then interna-
tional trade minister Stockwell Day undertaking a trade mission to Brazil
and Ecuador, and minister of state for the Americas Peter Kent participat-
ing in high-level OAS delegations to Honduras. Following the April 2009
Summit of the Americas meeting in Trinidad and Tobago, the Harper government promulgated its approach to the Americas in a single document.
See Government of Canada, *Canada and the Americas: Priorities and Progress*
(Ottawa: Her Majesty the Queen in Right of Canada, 2009), 1–22. In early
2012, minister of state for foreign affairs (Americas) Diane Ablonczy visited Cuba, Peru, and Central America.

4 Quoted in Doug Saunders, 'Second Wave of Financial Crisis Coming,
Brown Warns,' *Globe and Mail*, 8 July 2009, A1.

5 See Tim Harper, 'Canada's Voice Fading in the Americas,' *Toronto Star*, 21
June 2011, A7. Moreover, a late 2010 internal report by DFAIT's office of
the inspector-general noted that the Conservative government's Americas strategy was poorly supported and mostly superficial. Because of
a scarcity of financial resources, it was exceedingly difficult to put the
elements of the strategy into place. One of the report's findings was
especially pointed: 'Most Canadian embassies in the region have limited
staff and resources to provide meaningful follow-up or effective support
for programming, resulting in a threat of decreased credibility rather than
increased visibility for Canada.' Quoted in Jennifer Ditchburn, 'Harper's
Americas Strategy Falling Short: Internal Review,' *Waterloo Region Record*,
17 March 2011, A12. There was also news in May 2011 that Canada's main
think tank on relations with the Americas – the Canadian Foundation for
the Americas (FOCAL) – was on the brink of closure in the absence of
federal government funding. As one FOCAL research fellow commented:
'If you look at the funding that the Asia Pacific Foundation gets, there's
just no comparison even though Latin America represents a far greater
proportion of Canadian trade and investment that Asia does. They should

be doubling, tripling, quadrupling their budget. It shows a great deal of nearsightedness.' Jennifer Ditchburn, 'Funding Squeeze Threatens Think-Tank,' *Chronicle Herald*, 30 May 2011, C4. It subsequently closed its doors for good in September 2011.

6 His August 2011 visit to the region – which included stops in Brazil, Colombia, Costa Rica, and Honduras – was a good start. The long-awaited visit to Brazil was especially important, and the prime minister should be commended for this move (even if it was four or five years late in coming). But it will not amount to much if it is not followed up by a deep and sustained political commitment to the Americas as a whole – and not just those countries with which we have negotiated comprehensive free trade pacts. As one (magazine) editorial in Canada pointed out: 'And yet there is a specific slant to Canada's engagement in the region. The overarching themes are democracy and free trade. In the prime minister's view, the two go hand-in-hand and those countries he has visited before or will be visiting this time around either agree with the ideal or – in the case of the Caribbean Community – have been encouraged to do so. The flipside is that those countries that don't embrace such ideals are ignored or viewed with more than a little animosity.' 'Real Americas Engagement,' editorial, *Embassy Magazine*, 10 August 2011, 6.

7 See Jennifer Ditchburn, 'PM to Unveil New Plan to Re-engage Americas,' *Chronicle Herald*, 23 March 2012, A12, and Mark Kennedy, 'Division on Cuba Ends Summit of Americas on Frosty Note,' *Ottawa Citizen*, 16 April 2012, A1.

8 See J.C.M. Ogelsby, *Gringos from the Far North: Essays in the History of Canadian-Latin American Relations 1866–1968* (Toronto: Macmillan, 1976), and Stephen J. Randall, 'Canadian Policy and the Development of Latin America,' in Norman Hillmer and Garth Stevenson (eds.), *Foremost Nation: Canadian Foreign Policy and a Changing World* (Toronto: McClelland and Stewart, 1977), 202–29.

9 In May 2011, Canada's national newspaper, the *Globe and Mail*, ran a three-part series on Canada's expanding linkages with Latin America under its 'Our Time to Lead' frame. In a front-page editorial, it went on to observe: 'Yet our government's attention to Mexico and the region is fitful, and Canadians' deeper understanding of Mexico (beyond its beaches) is lacking.' 'The Canadian Quotient: On the World Stage and at Home,' editorial, *Globe and Mail*, 24 May 2011, A1.

10 From a voluntary donor standpoint, Ottawa earmarked some $525 million to the OAS and other hemispheric partners, placing Canada at the top overall for 2008, just ahead of the United States. See John Graham, 'Cana-

dian Policy in the Americas: Between Rhetoric and Reality – A Needless Distance,' in Fen Osler Hampson and Paul Heinbecker (eds.), *Canada among Nations 2009–2010: As Others See Us* (Montreal: McGill-Queen's University Press, 2010), 103–12. See also Jonathan Manthorpe, 'Latin America Rivals Asia as Canadian Partner,' *Vancouver Sun*, 30 May 2011, C10.

11 See Brian Morton, 'Trade with the Americas up 50 Per Cent in Five Years,' *Vancouver Sun*, 27 May 2011, C2.

12 Government of Canada, *Canada's Engagement in the Americas* (Ottawa: Department of Foreign Affairs and International Trade, 2011), 2. Canada has an extensive network of people-to-people contacts with the Americas, including some eighty academic agreements between Canadian universities and colleges and their counterparts in the wider region.

13 For a sharply differing view, see Jean Daudelin, 'Canada and the Americas: A Time for Modesty,' *Behind the Headlines* 64, no. 3 (May 2007): 1–28.

14 In a May 2011 address to the Forum on Canada-Latin American Relations, minister of state for foreign affairs (Americas and consular affairs) Diane Ablonczy indicated that the Harper government still considered the region a key priority and that it would be working harder to sharpen its focus on the Americas. 'The Americas is a region where we have extensive ties, where we can and do make a difference,' she said. See Morton, 'Trade with the Americas.' However, Ablonczy failed to re-emphasize Canada's commitment to the Americas at her first OAS General Assembly in El Salvador in early June 2011 (and the Harper government neglected to mention its Americas focus in its June 2011 Throne Speech). On a more positive note, PM Harper did manage to undertake an official visit to Costa Rica in early August 2011 (and made a quick one-day visit to Chile after the April 2012 Summit of the Americas in Colombia ended).

15 From previous interviews with interested observers, it is known that then foreign affairs minister Peter MacKay was canvassing widely in the summer of 2006 on whether Canada should strengthen its ties with the region. But if we know anything about the Harper government after more than six years in office, it is that nothing happens from a policy-making standpoint without Stephen Harper himself wielding the pen and paper. To the Conservative government's credit, Harper reintroduced the staffing position of an assistant deputy minister for the Americas to shepherd through Canada's Americas strategy. To offer assistance, there has also been a reshuffling of other staffing elements, but no additional personnel resources.

16 According to a March 2011 Leger Marketing survey, 49 per cent of Canadians believed that Latin America was important to Canada, while 42 per cent viewed it as 'not too important' or 'not at all important.' Victor

Armony and Jack Jedwab, 'Canadians Largely Indifferent to Latin America and the Caribbean,' *FOCALPoint* 10, no. 6 (July–August 2011): 3.

17 One should not discount the impact of bureaucratic elements within the government itself – especially the Department of Foreign Affairs and International Trade – pushing for a greater Canadian presence in the Americas. This kind of pressure emanating from the bureaucracy was certainly present in Canada's decision to join the OAS in 1990 and the Mulroney's government's subsequent focus on Latin America and the Caribbean. See Peter McKenna, 'Canada Joins the OAS: Anatomy of a Decision,' in Jacques Zylberberg and Francois Demers (eds.), *America in the Americas* (Laval: Les Presses de l'Université Laval, 1992), 253–69, and McKenna, 'Canada's Policy toward Latin America: A Statist Interpretation,' *International Journal* 49, no. 4 (Autumn 1994): 929–53.

18 Graham, 'Canadian Policy in the Americas,' 105.

19 Paul Heinbecker, *Getting Back in the Game: A Foreign Policy Playbook for Canada* (Toronto: Key Porter Books, 2010), 197.

20 WikiLeaks, 'Viewing cable 09OTTAWA291, Canada and the Americas' (released 11 July 2011), 1.

21 One should remember that Mulroney's finance minister, Michael Wilson, was also Harper's top diplomat in Washington. On this point, see Les Whittington, 'PM Sees Payoff in Adding Americas to Foreign Agenda,' *Toronto Star*, 22 June 2007, A14. In addition, Derek Burney, who headed Harper's transition team, was at one time Mulroney's chief of staff.

22 See Thomas Walkom, 'PM's Interest in Latin America Easily Explained,' *Toronto Star*, 26 July 2007, A10.

23 See Karyn Keenan, 'Canadian Mining: Still Unaccountable,' *NACLA Report on the Americas* (May/June 2010), 30, and Liisa L. North, 'Bad Neighbours,' *Canadian Dimension* 45, no. 1 (January/February 2011): 19–23.

24 See Yasmine Shamsie and Ricardo Grinspun, 'Missed Opportunity: Canada's Re-engagement with Latin America and the Caribbean,' *Canadian Journal of Latin American and Caribbean Studies* 35, no. 69 (Summer 2010): 186.

25 By way of illustration, Canada now has some sixty-eight trade commissioners for Latin America and only twenty-five for the entire African continent. See Campbell Clark, 'Africa Sets Its Eyes on a Brighter Future, but Canada's Vision Is as Murky as Ever,' *Globe and Mail*, 12 May 2010, A1.

26 Former Canadian diplomat Colin Robertson makes this same point in his piece, 'Embracing the Americas, Starting with Mexico,' *Policy Options* (May 2011): 40–4.

CANADA LOOKS SOUTH

In Search of an Americas Policy

1 Introduction
Canada and the Americas:
There's Still Much to Discover

JAMES ROCHLIN

Changing hegemonic structures have largely shaped Canada's historical evolution in the Americas, with hegemony defined as a confluence between the forces of ideas, institutions, and capabilities in a largely consensual context.[1] That is, Canada's place within a world order defined by the United Kingdom and then the United States provided the framework for Canadian policy from the dawn of the twentieth century until the beginning of the third millennium. The twenty-first century ushered in an era of post-hegemony, a tectonic conceptual shift to which Ottawa has not yet adjusted. Indeed, rather than redefining a policy commensurate with a vastly altered global landscape during the first decade of the new millennium, at its worst Canada seemed to behave as an echo chamber of Washington's now outdated and polarizing Cold War policies. There is a place for something old and something new – Canadian policy makers should revisit the country's traditional and favoured role as a peacebuilder and as a beacon of conflict resolution. To accomplish that, Ottawa requires independent and creative thinking that can help bridge the great ideological divide that has plagued the Americas.

Let us begin with a brief overview of Canada's historical relations with the region before shifting to a predominant focus on the country's post-NAFTA role in the Americas. Canada had important and growing economic interests in Latin America near the turn of the twentieth century, but Ottawa's relations with the region were constrained. Part of this had to do with the fact that Canada lacked autonomy from England in the foreign policy realm until the 1926–31 period and the culmination of the Statute of Westminster. Following that epoch, the country's relations with Latin America were symbolized by Canada's predicament vis-à-vis the Pan American Union, the precursor to the Organization of American States (OAS). Canada wanted 'in,' but the U.S. was suspicious of Ottawa's strong ties to the fading hegemon of the United Kingdom, thereby dashing Canada's hopes for a stronger role in hemispheric affairs.

Ironically, the tables turned following the Second World War and the ascension of the United States to superpower status. With the UK war-ravaged and in decline, Washington was now anxious for a stronger Canadian role in the hemisphere and welcomed the country's presence at the OAS. But the world order had shifted considerably, with the global south representing a target area for superpower competition in their Great Contest between two rival systems of production – Soviet-styled communism versus American capitalism. With Latin America solidly within the U.S. sphere of influence, a stake the U.S. had claimed with the promulgation of the 1823 Monroe Doctrine, the OAS became a vehicle for Washington's anti-communist crusades. Against such a backdrop, Ottawa resisted pressure to join the hemispheric organization for fear of pronounced friction with the U.S. Instead of blaming Soviet and later Soviet-Cuban subversion for strategic troubles in the hemisphere, which underpinned Washington's approach, Ottawa maintained throughout the Cold War that inequitable distributions of wealth combined with pronounced social injustice were the bases of strategic problems in the Americas. While the U.S. remained clearly dominant in Latin America, Washington was not hegemonic in the Americas in the sense that the consensual aspect of hegemony was largely absent. The U.S. relied on inordinate force to discipline its Latin American subordinate states, with many of these led by brutal military governments until the early 1980s. While Canada pursued growing economic interests in the Americas, against such a backdrop it never fully engaged politically in Latin America.

A major shift occurred in Canada, and at the level of the world order, beginning in the late 1960s and stretching into the next decade. With the lost war in Vietnam, growing global economic competition, and the termination of the Bretton Woods system, as well as the Soviet achievement of nuclear parity with the U.S., among other issues, the government of Pierre Trudeau attempted to craft a foreign policy for Canada that was decidedly independent from American policy. The result was the so-called 'Third Option,' where Canada placed Latin America among the top destinations for the enhancement of Canadian foreign policy and trade diversification. Beyond growing economic ties, among the prominent results of that policy was that Canada joined the OAS as a permanent observer, Trudeau made some high-profile trips to Cuba (and China) as a means of flaunting Canada's newfound independence, and the country accepted about 7,000 mostly socialist refugees in the wake of the U.S.-supported coup that installed General Augusto Pinochet in Chile in 1973. Although the Third Option did not succeed as a general global policy for Canada, clearly this was a turning point for the country and thrust it into Latin American affairs like never before. As we shall see, the general framework for the Third Option is something Ottawa should consider revisiting at the beginning of the twenty-first century.

Although the context changed significantly in the 1980s, this period hosted another incremental jump that deepened Canada's role in the hemisphere. This decade witnessed the dawn of unfettered capitalism, or neoliberalism.[2] Latin American nationalism was almost obliterated during this era and would not appear again until the election of Venezuela's Hugo Chávez in 1998. The crushing debt crisis of the 'lost decade' resulted in the imposition of a harsh form of Reaganomics in Latin America through the instrument of a resurrected International Monetary Fund (IMF). The material basis of most regional states was transformed to meet the needs of U.S.-centred transnational capital. Welfare was cut, limits to foreign investments were nearly erased, protectionist policies disappeared, while military force was fortified to subdue the social outcries against neoliberal pain that was promised to produce long-term gain. While Canada was vulnerable to Latin American debt, the general effect was that Canadian economic links to the region were fortified as Canada underwent its own period of neoliberal transformation beginning with the Progressive Conservative government of Brian Mulroney. This marked the beginning of an ideological convergence in the Americas that was underpinned by prevailing neoliberal structures and that would last until the new millennium. This restructuring paved the way for NAFTA and for a series of bilateral trade agreements pursued by Canada in Latin America.

The second theme of the 1980s was the end of Cold War guerrilla warfare and the withering of options for armed revolution, with Central America representing the epitome of the trend. The Nicaraguan Revolution of 1979, and strong guerrilla movements in El Salvador and to a lesser extent in Guatemala, were snuffed out by U.S. forces during Washington's second cold war with the Soviet Union. Legitimate and historical rebukes against U.S. policies that clearly did not benefit the

majority population, beautifully documented in Walter LeFeber's *Inevitable Revolutions*,[3] were buried under a wave of military force that at
times was declared illegal under international law, as was the case with
the U.S.-created *contra* paramilitary forces in Nicaragua. Under difficult circumstances, Canada made its mark with its support for peaceful conflict resolution mechanisms such as the Contadora Initiative and
subsequent peacekeeping operations that would stretch into the 1990s.
Ottawa's role in conflict resolution was appropriate given Canada's
even-handed approach to Latin America up to the 1970s. As we shall
see, in order for Canada to regain a crucial role in conflict resolution in
the new millennium, an independent foreign policy for the region will
need to be formulated.

While the Reagan Doctrine succeeded at forcefully receding revolutionary agendas in Central America, Washington was able to manipu-
late to its interests the political economies of most other Latin American
states through the enhanced power of finance capital within the context
of the aforementioned debt crisis. At the same time, Canada and the
U.S. had negotiated the Canada–United States Free Trade Agreement
in 1988, which became the precursor for NAFTA in 1994. Let us examine how these forces have played out, and how dramatic shifts in the
world order during the new millennium require innovative and more
independent policy toward the Americas on the part of Ottawa.

The 1990s

Ideological Harmonization

Notwithstanding a couple of potholes in the road during the 1990s, the
political atmosphere of Latin America during this era was just what
Ottawa hoped it would be when Canada decided to join the OAS in
1990. We saw that Ottawa had been reluctant to join the OAS during
the Cold War because it preferred not to get involved in feuds between
the United States and various factions of Latin America. This was especially the case during a period when Canada viewed the roots of turmoil in the region to be profound socio-economic inequity and political
exclusion, rather than Washington's propensity to blame trouble in Latin America on Soviet-Cuban subversion. But that scenario evaporated
in the 1990s. This was the era of T.I.N.A., to use one of the favourite
phrases of Cold Warrior Margaret Thatcher – There Is No Alternative.

It was a relatively short-lived period of perceived nirvana in the story of Canada's relations with the Americas.

Bounded by the fall of the Soviets and the advent of 9/11, this brief epoch of the world order celebrated U.S. supremacy and a New World Order (NWO) whereby Washington took the global lead in democratic consultation with other powers through multilateral institutions such as the United Nations. Ideologically, neoliberalism ruled the day. Socialism was deemed to have perished along with the Soviets everywhere but Cuba.[4] And even this island of.U.S. resistance was forced to experiment with more market-friendly manoeuvres such as a reliance on global tourism at a time when Havana was faced with no other choice than to reinvent the country's economy. Beginning with the Mulroney era, Canada had embraced neoliberal economics through the disbanding of many crown corporations and its newfound embrace of globalization and free trade agreements. In terms of the political economy of the hemisphere, then, there was little to argue about. Overall, this era was just what Ottawa had hoped the Americas would be from an ideological standpoint – mostly, a friendly and agreeable neighbourhood.

Institutions and Conflict Resolution

At the level of global institutions, not only was the United Nations resuscitated under the regime of the NWO, but the emergence or fortification of regional frameworks for political economy and security matters became the norm. Europe witnessed the birth of the European Union and the less-than-sturdy Conference on Security and Cooperation in Europe (CSCE). In the Americas, the OAS was revived both by Canada's late-for-dinner membership in 1990 and by an ideological coherence in Latin America that precluded polarization. In the realm of trade, this decade witnessed the birth of Mercosur in 1991 and NAFTA in 1994. At the time, these regional FTAs were viewed as the likely foundation for an emerging free trade agreement that would encompass most, if not all, of the Americas (known as the Free Trade Area of the Americas). Along with membership in the OAS, Canada's role in NAFTA implied a generally deepening engagement with Latin America as a whole.

In terms of global institutions and inter-American security, Canada participated in various United Nations peacekeeping missions in Central America throughout the 1990s to clean up the remnants of Cold

War conflicts, with the focus upon El Salvador and Guatemala. Canada also contributed to peacekeeping missions in Haiti beginning in 1996, as a prelude to a deeper involvement in that country in the new millennium.[5] Overall, this relatively brief and very mellow transition period from one world order to the emerging outlines of a new one meant that there was no better time for Canada to be a 'joiner' in global and hemispheric institutions.

Economic and Military Forces

In terms of material capabilities, the United States reached its pinnacle of economic and military supremacy during this period. There was no obvious competitor on the economic front. While China was growing, it had not yet reached the status of economic superpower that it would enjoy in the subsequent decade. And when the West bothered to acknowledge China's stupendous annual growth rates, typically the directive role of the state in the country's political economy was ignored or downplayed. Instead, the Chinese case was celebrated as just another example of the world's embrace of the market principles established and promoted by the United States. Things looked so good for the U.S. that some suggested the history of ideas reached the end of the line with the attainment of American-bred capitalism and (neo) liberal democracy.[6] Within such a context, Ottawa sought to entrench its ties to the United States first through the Canada-U.S. Free Trade Agreement and then through NAFTA. And given that the world seemed to be tilting to three economic regions, Canada's growing role in the Americas seemed more important than ever.[7]

Although Canada's trade and investment with Latin America grew during the 1990s, in proportional terms this uptick was quite modest. Canada's investment in Mexico grew from .25 per cent of total Canadian foreign direct investment abroad in 1990 to .59 per cent in 2000; in South and Central America, Canadian investment grew from 2.4 to 4.9 per cent during that period. Exports to Latin America and the Caribbean shrank from 1.5 per cent of Canada's global total in 1994 to 1 per cent in 2000, while imports crept up from 1.7 to 1.9 per cent during that period. Canadian exports to Mexico remained largely unchanged from .48 per cent in 1994 to .49 per cent in 2000, though imports increased from 2.2 per cent of Canada's global total to 3.3 per cent during that period.[8] Overall, the perception of Canada's growing economic relations with Latin America loomed larger than actual material growth.

In terms of global military or strategic capabilities, the U.S. lacked a formidable challenger in the 1990s, though celebrated organic intellectuals such as Samuel Huntington devoted themselves to the problem of manufacturing enemies.[9] In the Americas, Canada no longer had to manage the implications of Washington's anti-communist crusades and devoted resources to UN campaigns for reconciliation in Central America, as noted. With regard to serious insurgencies during the 1990s, Peru's Sendero Luminoso had been snuffed out by 1992. In Mexico, there was initial alarm when the Zapatista rebels of Chiapas appeared on NAFTA's birthday – especially during the first twelve days or so of the struggle, during which the EZLN clung to a Cold War mentality and aimed to march to Mexico City in an effort to defeat the military and take control of the government.[10] But, after being encircled and militarily neutralized by the Mexican army after less than two weeks of combat, Subcomandante Marcos and other Zapatista leaders thought on their feet and quickly switched to a postmodern approach that rebuked their now unachievable goal of taking the state. These photogenic, warm, and fuzzy guerrillas shared nothing with the sheer terror launched by the Sendero Luminoso guerrillas in the late 1980s and early 1990s, or with the nationalized civil wars in Central America during the 1980s. For Canada, the Zapatista insurgency did not represent a serious strategic concern.

In terms of insurgency, the real threat during the 1990s was Colombia's increasingly violent and narco-fuelled imbroglio involving the Fuerzas Armadas Revolucionarias de Colombia (FARC) and the Ejército de Liberación Nacional (ELN) on the left, the Autodefensas Unidas de Colombia (AUC) on the right, and the notoriously corrupt and abusive Colombian state. That problem had been all but ignored by the U.S. until 1998, when the FARC achieved the acquisition from the Colombian government of a piece of territory the size of Switzerland. It took another two years for the U.S. to implement Plan Colombia (PC). The escalation of narcotrafficking during this era represented an important turning point in hemispheric security.[11] Illicit drug trafficking grew in tandem with the more porous borders implied by globalization, trade blocs, and in Eurasia, by the loosening of border security in the former Soviet bloc. For Canada, its effects were felt domestically with the escalation of cocaine and crack use. This correlated with increased crime and rising levels of HIV, with a stark illustration of the crisis expressed regularly on Vancouver's East Hastings Street.[12]

Despite the relative tranquillity of the 1990s, looking back one can discern clear glimmers of problems that would transform into full-blown crises in the new millennium, and which would frame Canada's relations with the Americas during that same period. For example, outrage among global Islam regarding Muslim genocide in Bosnia in the early 1990s, and al-Qaeda's coordinated attacks against U.S. embassies in four Eastern African countries in 1998, were early manifestations of an explosion of global tension that was unleashed with 9/11 and the subsequent U.S.-led invasions of Iraq and Afghanistan. Those events preoccupied Washington and the administration of George W. Bush, with Latin America effectively placed on the back burner of U.S. global affairs.

In the Americas, existing security issues such as the Colombian insurgency and regional narcotrafficking ballooned into major strategic concerns during the first decade of the new millennium. These were expressed in Washington's Plan Colombia and through a drug war in Mexico where more people have perished annually from narco-warfare than from the insurgency in Colombia. As we shall see, both those crises have had implications for Canadian foreign policy. In Venezuela, explosive anti-neoliberal frustrations expressed in 1989's *Caracazo* riots paved the way for the election in 1998 of Hugo Chávez, who would emerge as Latin America's most significant anti-American maverick since Fidel Castro. And while the 1990s were hailed as the golden era of neoliberalism, serious cracks in the model appeared not only in Venezuela but through a series of debt and currency crises. As Walter Wriston noted in his influential *The Twilight of Sovereignty*,[13] by the 1990s speculative capital had trumped the 'real' economy to the point that by the mid-1990s, about 90 per cent of global trade was speculative rather than in goods and services, the inverse of the proportion just prior to the collapse of Bretton Woods in 1971. The ferociously punitive effects of 'hot money' were unleashed on Mexico during the 1994–5 peso crisis. These pernicious forces subsequently caught fire through the currency crises that commenced in Asia in 1997, spread to Brazil in 1998, and then triggered the economic collapse and radicalization of Argentina between 2000 and 2001.

The New Millennium

Ideological Forces

The world order was once again transformed dramatically after the

9/11 attacks in 2001. While the U.S. had received unequivocal sympathy from almost all major states in the wake of the attacks, the global tone began to tilt away from the Bush Doctrine's unilateralism and condescension that was most clearly expressed in the 2003 invasion of Iraq. Preoccupied by Iraq and increasingly Afghanistan-Pakistan, the U.S. during the first decade of the new millennium generally ignored Latin America and failed to comprehend a rising tide of anti-Americanism in the region that proved to be the most intense in the history of Washington's relations with the Americas. That trend was compounded by increasing Chinese investment in Latin America toward the end of the decade, and by China's provision of a highly successful model of a statist political economy that contrasted sharply with U.S.-inspired neoliberalism, which was globally rebuked after the financial crisis that emerged in 2007–8.

While the era of neoliberal dominance has ended amid sharp criticism of the model in many parts of Latin America, it contributed in a positive way to market efficiency, reductions in bureaucratic red tape, and to a clearer orientation for the region vis-à-vis the forces of globalization. It is also important to underscore that democratic structures in Latin America appeared alongside the emergence of neoliberalism in the early 1980s. Military generals who ran up debt prior to 1982 preferred to go back to the barracks and let civilian politicians face the heat of public wrath in countries such as Argentina and Brazil. Throughout the late 1980s and most of the 1990s – until the election of Hugo Chávez in 1998 – leftist candidates were precluded from electoral victory within the context of TINA. From the perspective of the U.S., then, during that era democracy in Latin America was viewed as safe to the extent that a rightist candidate was virtually assured of an election victory. As we saw, Ottawa enjoyed the ideological homogeneity of the 1990s and presumably projected that this trend would spill into the new decade. That view propelled Canada's support for democratic structures as it hosted the 2001 Summit of the Americas in Quebec City, where Peruvian politicians pressed for the establishment of the Inter-American Democratic Charter that was signed in Lima in September 2001.[14] The charter celebrated 'respect for human rights ... periodic, free, and fair elections ... and the separation of powers and independence of the branches of government.'[15] Despite the election of Chávez and Nestor Kirchner in Argentina, signatories to the Charter did not anticipate that radical revolutions would transpire not through guerrilla movements – as they had in Cuba and Nicaragua – but through the ballot box as the decade progressed. Examples include not only subsequent re-elections of Chávez and the Kirchners, but the election in 2005 of Bolivia's Evo Morales, of Nicaragua's Daniel Ortega and Ecuador's Rafael Correa in 2006, Jose Mujica of Uruguay, Mauricio Funes of El Salvador in 2009, and Ollanta Humala of Peru in 2011.

For the United States, then, democracy in the Americas could no longer be associated with mom and apple pie, and in some cases turned out to be a Frankenstein's monster. Against the backdrop of neoliberal fatigue and the rising levels of economic inequity it ushered in, charismatic politicians on the left (the so-called 'Pink Tide') were able to mobilize the majority populations of Latin America who were poor and disenfranchised from the benefits of rightist models of political economy. The U.S. obviously felt threatened by radical democracy in the Americas. The Bush administration supported an unsuccessful coup against Hugo Chávez in 2002 that removed him from power for a couple of days, and which more importantly served to radicalize the Chávez government into one of the world's most audible proponents of anti-Americanism. And despite a campaign that sloganeered 'Change We Can Believe In,' the Barack Obama administration in 2009 essentially supported a military coup against Honduran president Manuel Zelaya by legitimizing presidential elections in November 2009 that had been held in its wake.

Democracy, as it turned out, had triggered ideological polarization in the Americas, and in some cases generated a political headache for Canada. For example, Canada's minister of state for the Americas at the time, Peter Kent, made comments that attempted to straddle the line between the U.S. and most of Latin America regarding the Honduran coup and the subsequent election in November 2009. Kent noted, on the one hand, that 'Canada is disappointed with the lack of progress on the implementation of the Tegucigalpa-San José Accord … Unfortunately, this meant that Canada could not provide support to the electoral process' that was boycotted by both the OAS and the UN.[16] On the other hand, echoing statements made the previous day by Kent's U.S. counterpart, Arturo Valenzuela, that the elections represented a 'very important first step for Honduras,'[17] Kent called the elections 'an important step in moving out of the current political impasse.'[18]

This was not the first time during the new millennium that the widening ideological gulf in the Americas created pressure for the Stephen Harper government. While the Harper government's 2009 *Canada and the Americas – Priorities and Progress* noted that the prime minister's truncated 2007 tour of the Caribbean and South America 'launched a new beginning for Canada's engagement of the western hemisphere,'[19] it seemed more like a blast from the Cold War past that Ottawa hoped it would never have to revisit when it entrenched its interests in the Americas during the 1990s. During his visit to Chile in 2007 to celebrate the tenth anniversary of Canada's free trade agreement with the country, Harper was interpreted by the media and an assortment of academics to utter a thinly veiled attack on Hugo Chávez when he criticized those who wished 'to return to the syndrome of economic nationalism, political authoritarianism and class warfare.'[20]

While failing to build bridges or to promote conflict resolution with Venezuela or other Latin American countries that had moved to the hard left, the Harper government seemed to adopt a polarized position that toed the U.S. line not only with its scathing reference to Venezuela but with regard to his visit to just one other country besides Chile during his trip – Colombia. By that time, Colombia was the only major power in South America to continue its embrace of neoliberalism while simultaneously transforming into the bastion of U.S. military power in South America through the $6-billion-plus Plan Colombia. Despite being the most dangerous place on the planet for members of labour unions, and the almost constant scandals linking the Álvaro Uribe government to narco-funded paramilitary organizations responsible for much of the country's human rights abuses,[21] the Harper government heaped praise upon Colombia and proceeded to sign a free trade agreement with the country in 2008, which took effect 15 August 2011.

The prime minister's visit to Colombia and his government's reference to its 'long democratic tradition,'[22] despite the notoriously murderous politics in the country, on the one hand, and its apparent demonization of Chávez, on the other, rendered Ottawa as an echo chamber of U.S. policy that only entrenched the acute political polarization in the region. In the Colombia-Venezuela case, that polarization is particularly worrisome since it is undergirded by an intense arms race – a point to which we shall return. One can indeed make a strong argument that Canada can help improve the Colombian situation by engaging the country, and working with it to improve human rights and so on. The same is true of Venezuela – where Canada can help resolve hemispheric tension by winning Venezuela's confidence, rather than rebuking it. Both sides need to be played evenly, in sharp contrast to actual Canadian policy. Overall, for the first time in the history of the country's relations with Latin America, Canada under the Harper government actually fanned the flames of ideological polarization in the Americas rather than attempting to douse them.

While the ideological gulf between left and right is perhaps more pronounced in the Americas than any other region of the world, significant epistemological issues and fissures in the hemisphere have been increasingly emphasized by proponents of the postmodern approach in Latin America. The emergence of the Zapatistas in 1994 introduced the world's first postmodern guerrillas that promoted identity politics, network organization, strategic exploitation of the time-space compression, indigenous epistemes, and complexity through its emphasis on the biosphere.[23] All of those themes and others related to the 'Revolution in Military Affairs' have affected Canada's interests in Latin American security, as we shall see. Further, Colombian-born Arturo Escobar released an important work in 1995 that redefined the politics of development beyond the spectrum of left and right. Instead, Escobar emphasized local empowerment and decision making as well as the celebration of local epistemological approaches to the worn notion of development, which was invented by Harry Truman in 1949 as a means of fighting communism in the Third World.[24] Thus, important epistemological shifts have occurred which frame Canadian interests in the region's critical security and 'development.'

The Politics of Institutions in the Americas

Canada's most important institutional commitments in the hemisphere are expressed through its roles in the OAS, NAFTA, the North American Aerospace Defense Command (NORAD),[25] and the United Nations. As we noted in the previous section, the Democratic Charter of the OAS is perhaps the component of the institution that has most served to revitalize it in the first decade of the new millennium. Democracy has empowered populations that historically have been excluded throughout the hemisphere, but its achievements are uneven and it still remains vulnerable, as the Honduran example demonstrated in 2009. Although the OAS faces limits, it remains a crucial forum for potential conflict resolution in the hemisphere. It will remain an important multilateral venue for Canada, which was the second-largest contributor to the OAS in 2009, paying 13 per cent of the institution's total contributions.

Let us turn now to Canada's role in the hemisphere's economic organizations. It is ironic that NAFTA, the institution that in the 1990s was viewed as key to cementing Canada's growing role in the hemisphere, appeared to be so vulnerable by 2011. Economist Joseph Stiglitz argues that Mexico was one of the countries most ravaged by the post-2007 economic crisis due to its profound economic dependence on a depleted United States.[26] This has affected not only exports and investments, but remittances as well. While the U.S. has fortified its frontier with Mexico to repel would-be migrants, Canada imposed on 14 July 2009 a visa requirement for Mexicans wishing to travel to Canada. Ottawa defended the action by noting that Canada had received about 9,400 refugee claims by Mexicans between 2005 and 2009, and that it rejected 90 per cent of these. Beyond those problems, Mexico has been debilitated by an escalating drug war in the northern and Pacific coast regions of the country, as traffickers feud over routes to feed the cravings of northern nostrils and veins.[27] Finally, in terms of the new hierarchy of states that has emerged in the hemisphere by 2011, Mexico has lost its place to Brazil as the leader of Latin America. This is largely due to the harmonization of Mexico's political economy with the United States, in contrast to Brazil's more independent stance that has underpinned its aspiration to achieve the status of a major global power. So far it appears that Mexico played a losing bet when it gambled that entrance into NAFTA was the country's ticket to first-world status. The politics of the trade bloc have soured to a degree that was unfathomable when it was first negotiated in 1994.

While Canada had imagined in the 1990s that regional trade blocs such as NAFTA would blossom into a large Latin American trade region, that presumption has not materialized. Instead, a pronounced and sometimes bitter ideological gulf in the Americas has precluded hemispheric economic integration. With regional agreements harder to achieve, Canada instead has created a series of bilateral FTAs with Chile, Colombia, Peru, and others. Overall, the politics of inter-American institutions have proven to be more complicated than Ottawa had imagined in the early 1990s.

The New Landscape of Economic Forces

There have been three interrelated trends with regard to productive forces in the Americas at the dawn of the new millennium. The first was the emergence of a commodity boom, especially with regard to energy resources. It primarily fed the U.S. real estate bubble of the early to middle part of the decade and grew more reliant on China during the middle and later part of the decade. The second significant transformation, both at the level of the world order and in the Americas, was indeed the rising presence of China in a political sense and perhaps as an exemplary model of political economy. Finally, many key Latin American states witnessed revolutionary transformations in state structure from being a transmission belt for transnational capitalism under neoliberalism to a statist and re-distributionary model that shuns U.S. dominance. But the post-2007 financial crisis opened the door for further and major transformations in the near future, as states on both the left and the right attempt to fend off the challenges associated with a shrinking global economy. That is, by 2011, both leftist and right-wing governments looked vulnerable in the face of global economic weakness. Let us explore the impact of these trends upon Canada's role in the Americas.

The radicalization that has taken place in some Latin American states has been fuelled by a commodity boom that endowed newborn socialist states with fresh wealth to redistribute. Nowhere has this been clearer than in Venezuela, though its obvious impact also has been apparent in other countries such as Bolivia and Ecuador. While many countries in the region also benefited from a boom in the mining sector, the preciousness of petroleum meant special political empowerment in Venezuela, whose proven oil reserves that are concentrated in the Orinoco basin are among the largest in the world. The price of oil shot up from about $10 a barrel when Chávez came to power in 1998, to around $150 a barrel in 2008. Like him or not, Chávez paved the way for a redefined model of the state that featured strong government intervention and a relatively large 'government take' in the extractive sector. The Venezuelan president raised royalties in the oil patch from 1 per cent in 2004, to 16.6 per cent in 2005 and 33 per cent in 2006. The total 'government take' in Venezuela was about 86 per cent by the end of the decade.[28] Governments in Ecuador and Bolivia followed Chávez's lead and joined a global trend whereby 77 per cent of world oil was produced by state-owned companies by 2007.

Much of the growing investment in Venezuela, and in Latin America more generally, has emanated from China. Chinese trade with the region increased at an annual rate of 30 per cent between 2001 and 2008, ballooning from $15 billion to $140 billion during that same period.[29] Chinese foreign investment, located primarily in the extractive sector, escalated at an annual rate of 60 per cent between 2000 and 2008, to reach $52.2 billion in 2008. Chinese companies invested another $15 billion in 2010 largely through mergers and acquisitions, with about 90 per cent of this in the commodity sector. While the U.S. remains the dominant economic presence in the region, the growth of the Chinese role is enormous and has significant political and economic implications. China's statist model of development has been viewed sympathetically in much of the region. In the region's leftist countries, it was hoped that growing Chinese influence would offset both U.S. political and economic power. That trend toward statism in Latin America, especially vis-à-vis the extractive sector, has also had important implications for Canada since its economic presence in Latin America leans heavily toward that sector.[30]

In Venezuela, Petro-Canada had partnered in a 50-50 arrangement with ExxonMobil for a project regarding development in the La Ceibe block near Maracaibo. In 2007, President Chávez required all private corporations to assume minority holdings in oil production, with PDVSA possessing at least a 60 per cent majority stake. The Chávez government also expressed its preference for dealing with state-owned oil companies, rather than privately owned entities such as Petro-Canada. ExxonMobil pulled out after a feud with the government that also involved its interests in the Orinoco region. When its partnership with ExxonMobil dissolved, Petro-Canada did not find a suitable role in the country's oil sector. Venezuela's oil minister announced that 'Petro-Canada has decided on the culmination of its participation in its business in the country and compensation has been agreed upon between the companies that has already been accepted by both parties.'[31] Canadian Embassy officials in Venezuela privately indicated that they felt 'burned' by the Chávez government.[32] This also explains, in part, Canada's love affair with Colombia that blossomed after Prime Minister Harper's 2007 visit there. Colombia, a veritable magnet for transnational capital, may have the lowest royalty rate in the world for petroleum production, which falls on a sliding scale between 5 and 25 per cent. Its royalties on the mining sector are also comparatively low.[33]

Finally, the global economic crisis that began in 2007, and which initially emanated from the United States, dealt a serious blow to Washington's credibility as an economic leader. A vital component of a hegemon's chassis is to showcase a model of political economy to which others wish to aspire. Many states in Latin America clearly grew weary of the U.S. neoliberal model long before the crisis of the U.S. economy post-2007. But the collapse of that model seemed to reaffirm and fortify growing doubts regarding U.S. leadership in the hemisphere. The escalating debt crisis in the US, which flirted with debt default as borrowing reached 100 per cent of its GDP by August 2011, must seem bitterly ironic to many Latin Americans who endured harsh U.S.-inspired austerity measures during their own debt crises in the 1980s and early 1990s.

The Military Strategic Landscape

Fresh strategic challenges were ushered in alongside the ideological and economic chasms that emerged in Latin America at the beginning of the third millennium. There have been four broad issues at play. First has been the reappearance of coups in Latin America. Second, there has been a remarkable arms race in the region, most alarmingly between Colombia and Venezuela. Next, Brazil is clearly poised to be a dominant military power in South America. Finally, the Revolution in Military Affairs has found numerous expressions throughout the region. Given Canada's historic role in inter-American conflict resolution – as evidenced through the bridging role it played between Cuba and the U.S. during the Cold War and through its multiple roles in resolving conflict in Central America and Haiti – it is within this realm that Canada may be able to make its most significant contribution in the Americas.

We observed two attempted coups during the first decade of the millennium – the failed attack against Chávez in 2002 and the 'successful' one in its ALBA sister state of Honduras in 2009. Clearly, the achievement of democratic structures in the Americas cannot be taken for granted, and these may face further attempts at military usurpation during an era of severe economic challenges. This is an area where Canada has professed strong interests, ones that were directly or indirectly challenged by the United States in the two cases noted above.

The ideological rivalry between Colombia and Venezuela is accompanied by a multi-billion-dollar arms race. Colombia has emerged as a formidable military base for U.S. interests in South America. This entails over $6 billion associated with Plan Colombia that was initiated in 2000, and the agreement between Colombia and the U.S. in 2009 for the transfer of a major military base that President Rafael Correa evicted from Manta, Ecuador to a series of seven bases in Colombia. Chávez has not been shy about his intent to match penny for penny U.S. military investment in Colombia with arms purchases from Russia. Venezuela received approximately $4.4 billion in arms purchases principally from Russia between 2005 and 2009, and signed an agreement in September of 2009 for an additional $2.2 billion in Russian military equipment. Canada already has important interests in Colombia, where a free trade agreement was negotiated in 2008. It would be extremely useful if Ottawa crafted ways to build confidence with the Chávez government, thereby paving the way for Canada's role as a strong promoter of conflict resolution. It is not clear how much longer Chávez can govern – his diagnosis with cancer in 2011 and his continuing health struggles in mid-2012 may weaken him politically in a way that Washington and his local opponents never could. Should he succumb to illness, the Venezuelan president will have to groom a charismatic successor if the Bolivarian Revolution is to continue. Given the context of existing polarization in the country, political tensions in Venezuela are likely to mount if the president is perceived by his opponents as weak. Canada can play an important role in conflict resolution if it has the respect of competing stakeholders in the country – something it has not yet achieved.

Let us turn to Brazil, which is by far the largest arms purchaser in South America and the only major arms maker in the region. It purchased $23.3 billion worth of arms in 2008 according to SIPRI, with Colombia purchasing $9 billion and Venezuela $3.31 billion. Brazil accounted for 48 per cent of all arms purchases for Latin America during that year.[34] Brazil has been the key player in the construction of the twelve-country UNASUR (Unión de Naciones Suramericanas), a strategic conflict resolution institution that has pushed the U.S. and Canada out of the security equation. The country clearly is headed for a hegemonic role in South America. Given this trend, Canada needs to redouble its efforts to fortify relations with Brazil, and this must evolve as a centrepiece of Canada's Americas policy.[35]

Finally, and quite broadly, the Revolution in Military Affairs (RMA) is reflected in Latin America in numerous ways. The RMA can be viewed as a synergistic bundle of concepts that is marked by technological change, social reorganization, and sometimes by a new system of thought, among other features.[36] It deserves serious attention and comprehension so that crucial strategic issues can be addressed successfully. One of the key components of the RMA is the blurring distinction between crime and warfare, and nowhere is this clearer than in Mexico's drug war, the imbroglio in Colombia where insurgents on both the left and the right are funded through narco-dollars, and on the streets of Canadian cities where drug-related crime and health issues are emerging as important public policy issues.[37] Another manifestation of the RMA is the link between identity politics and strategic affairs.

Examples abound, and include an array of issues ranging from the contested atmosphere in Bolivia that pits the largely indigenous highlands against the mestizo and wealthy petro-provinces of the lowlands, to the feminists' rightful outrage regarding uninvestigated murders of hundreds of Mexican sex trade workers in Ciudad Juárez and elsewhere. Further, key organizational shifts in the realm of strategy include the implications of network formation. In Venezuela, for example, given the unsuccessful coup attempt and Chávez's subsequent distrust of the army, the president created a grass-roots network of localized militias in the form of Bolivarian circles, building upon the network structure that the EZLN had used to project peaceful and global struggle for their plight in Mexico since 1994. Another key component of the new security landscape is a focus on ecocide, with the biosphere representing an important reflection of the concept of complexity that is central to the RMA. Nowhere is this clearer than in Ecuador, whose Amazonian region is host to perhaps the worst petro-related ecocide in the Americas.[38] In neighbouring Colombia, Plan Colombia has been an essential experiment for Washington's manipulation of the RMA featuring privatized war, ultra-surveillance, the blur of crime and war, and the recasting of former communist adversaries as terrorists. One could go on with many other examples, but the point is that the presence of the RMA is clear. Understanding its influence is key to war and peace in the Americas.

A Crucial Juncture

There have been two major turning points in the last four decades regarding Canada's growing role in Latin America. First was the Trudeau government's nod toward the Americas in the late 1960s and early 1970s as part of the broader Third Option formula to diversify trade and investment away from the U.S. The second occurred during the early 1990s when Canada entered the OAS as a full member and subsequently became part of NAFTA. As we enter the second decade of a new millennium, we have reached another threshold that is framed by drastic changes in what has become a post-hegemonic world order. Given this new context, Ottawa's tendency especially during the Harper government to echo U.S. policy in Latin America represents a dangerous and irresponsible path that needs to be replaced by thoughtful and creative directions.

Canada has made mixed and incremental progress toward a stronger role in Latin America since the early 1990s. In the economic realm, Canadian exports to Latin America (excluding Mexico) have remained flat at 1.5 per cent of the country's total exports between 1994 and 2007, but imports from the region have doubled to 3.4 per cent of Canada's total during that period. With respect to Mexico, both Canada's exports and imports have doubled to 1.1 per cent and 4.2 per cent of the country's totals between 1994 and 2007. The realm of foreign investment has not been particularly promising. Canadian foreign direct investment in South America has fallen from 4.9 per cent of the country's total to 3.9 per cent between 1995 and 2008, while investment in Mexico has remained flat at .6 per cent of the total during that period.[39] Between 2009 and 2010, Canadian direct investment decreased a slight .5 per cent in Mexico and fell more than 60 per cent in Venezuela, while Canadian direct investment increased over 43 per cent in Colombia, 25 per cent in Argentina, and 13 per cent in Brazil. Most of those increases have occurred in the extractive sector, where Canada's economic influence is most strongly felt in the region.

Overall, in a proportional sense, some economic progress has been achieved, but this appears to be dwarfed by the context of Canada's overwhelming economic dependence upon the U.S. Politically, we have seen that Canada has established a stronger profile in the region in the post-NAFTA period. This has been expressed, for example, through its activities in the OAS, its support for democratic structures, and its crucial role in Haiti (which is analysed later in this volume). But that sense of progress has been limited by the Harper government's tendency to mimic the most pernicious aspects of U.S. policy to Latin America, and its penchant toward exacerbating regional polarization rather than contributing to conflict resolution. Overall, the 'new beginning' promised by Ottawa's *Canada and the Americas: Priorities and Progress* was rote and failed to recognize tectonic transformations in the world order and in the Americas.[40]

What are the options for Canada? Although the New World now seems newer than ever, three rather traditional themes have proven to be quite resilient and deserve consideration as a possible centrepiece for a refashioned Canadian policy toward the Americas. First, despite the profundity of transformations globally and regionally, democracy is not likely to go out of style. Canada will win the support of Latin America's majority population by working to enhance democratic structures and by supporting their outcome regardless of its ideological implications. Unwavering support for the will of the majority is a primary ingredient for the cultivation of regional political respect that will underpin Canada's economic and security interests in Latin America.

Second, tolerance and respect for varied democratic outcomes will fortify Canada's traditional penchant for conflict resolution. Given the intensified ideological polarization in Latin America, the rising tenor of anti-Americanism, and a growing regional potential for class warfare against the backdrop of global economic crisis, the promotion of conflict resolution is more important than ever. Given Canada's past roles in helping to resolve disputes involving Cuba and Central America, Ottawa has a strong foundation upon which to draw. To assume a position as a leading protagonist of serious conflict resolution, Canada will need to formulate an even-handed policy that is respected by regional actors as fair and independent. That kind of respect cannot be achieved quickly. It takes longer to build lasting friendships than to make enemies. There is no better opportunity or role for Canada in the Americas than to evolve as the leading proponent of regional conflict resolution.

Third, support for democratic structures and for resolving escalating regional conflict will provide a better context for Canadian economic interests in Latin America. The promotion of corporate social responsibility should receive priority treatment in a reformulated Canadian policy to the region. This is especially relevant for Canada's extractive sector, which has strong interests in Latin America. Critics have observed 'the Canadian government's flat-out refusal to impose any kind of human rights standards on Canadian companies' actions outside Canada,' despite such recommendations from the parliamentary Standing Committee for Foreign Affairs and from other groups.[41] When Canadian companies are perceived to be involved in human rights abuses, as was the case in late 2009 when a Mexican activist who had protested against Canada's Blackfire gold mine in Chiapas was murdered, the reputation of the country's mining sector is tarnished and may inhibit further economic prospects. In a globalized world, and in a region such as Latin America that has become more suspicious of the dark side of transnational corporations, an enhanced platform of corporate responsibility will serve well Canada's economic, political, and security interests in Latin America.

Simply put, Canada is still in the process of discovering the Americas. Incremental but generally steady progress has been made, especially since the formulation of the Trudeau government's Third Option. While the original manifestation of that policy never reached its lofty objective, perhaps Ottawa should dust it off and have another look.

This is especially the case in a post-hegemonic world where rising powers such as China require more attention and where the politics of Latin America have been redefined in a democratic but revolutionary way to shed the exploitative and authoritarian yoke that was so dominant during the Cold War.

NOTES

1 This was the argument of Rochlin's *Discovering the Americas: The Evolution of Canadian Foreign Policy towards Latin America* (Vancouver: UBC Press, 1994).

2 Arguably the best definition and analysis of neoliberalism is provided in David Harvey's *A Brief History of Neoliberalism* (London: Oxford, 2005). A brief definition is provided on page 2, with the historical context found throughout the book. He notes on page 2: 'Neoliberalism is in the first instance a theory of political economic practices that proposes that human well-being can best be advanced by liberating individual entrepreneurial freedoms and skills within an institutional framework characterized by strong private property rights, free markets, and free trade. The role of the state is to create and preserve an institutional framework appropriate to such practices. The state has to guarantee, for example, the quality and integrity of money. It must also set up those military, defence, police, and legal structures and functions required to secure private property rights and to guarantee, by force if need be, the proper functioning of the markets.'

3 See Walter LeFeber, *Inevitable Revolutions* (New York: Norton, 1983).

4 Canada's relations with Cuba are well covered by John Kirk and Peter McKenna, 'Stephen Harper's Cuba Policy: From Autonomy to Americanization?' *Canadian Foreign Policy* 15, no. 1 (Spring 2009): 21–39.

5 For a discussion of Canada's role in various international institutions as they relate to Latin America in the 1990s, see Stephen Randall and Jillian Dowding, 'Canada, Latin America, Colombia, and the Evolving Policy Agenda,' *Canadian Foreign Policy* 14, no. 3 (Fall 2008): 29–46.

6 The loudest voice in this regard was Francis Fukuyama, 'The End of History?' *National Interest* 16 (Summer 1989): 3–18.

7 For a discussion of Canada's economic relations with the region during the late 1990s, see Peter McKenna, 'Canada's Southern Exposure,' *Hemisphere: A Magazine of the Americas* 8, no. 3 (Fall 1998): 26–9.

8 Statistics Canada, 'Canadian Exports,' 'Canadian Imports,' 'Canadian Direct Investment Abroad, Table 376-0051,' web-generated charts.

9 See Samuel Huntington, 'The Clash of Civilizations,' *Foreign Affairs* 72, no. 3 (1993): 22–49.

10 See James Rochlin, *Redefining Mexican Security: Society, State and Region under Nafta* (Boulder: Lynn Rienner, 1997), and *Vanguard Revolutionaries in Latin America: The Cases of Peru, Colombia and Mexico* (Boulder: Lynne Rienner 2003).

11 See James Rochlin, 'The Revolution in Military Affairs, Plan Colombia and the FARC,' *Review of International Studies*, 37, no. 2 (Spring 2011): 715–40.

12 James Rochlin, 'Canada, Narcotrafficking and Streams of Power,' *Canadian Foreign Policy* 7, no. 1 (Fall 1999): 109–46. See also Ian Bailey and Wendy Stueck, 'Vancouver Losing Fight with Gangs, Mayor Says,' *Globe and Mail*, 5 March 2009, A4, and Colin Freeze and Marina Jimenez, 'Mexico's Drug War Becomes Canadian Security Issue,' *Globe and Mail*, 5 March 2009, A4. For a critique of the Harper government's approach to the so-called 'war on drugs,' see Peter McKenna, 'Time to Call Off Canada's Drug War,' *Toronto Star*, 9 May 2012, A23.

13 Walter Wriston, *The Twilight of Sovereignty* (New York: Replica, 1997).

14 Max Cameron has done much important work in the area of Canada and democracy in Latin America. See, for example, Max Cameron and Catherine Hecht, 'Canada's Engagement with Democracies in the Americas,' *Canadian Foreign Policy* 14, no. 3 (Fall 2008): 11–28.

15 Organization of American States, 11 September 2001, *Inter-American Democratic Charter* (Lima, Peru), http://www.oas.org/charter/docs/resolution1_en_p4.htm (accessed 2 December 2009).

16 Foreign Affairs and International Trade Canada, 'Minister of State Kent Calls for Peaceful Elections in Honduras,' press release, 27 November 2009.

17 United States Department of State, 'Briefing on the Honduran Elections,' Arturo Valenzuela, 30 November 2009, http://www.state.gov/p/wha/rls/rm/2009/132777.htm (accessed 3 December 2009).

18 Foreign Affairs and International Trade Canada, 'Minister of State Kent Calls for Peaceful Elections in Honduras.'

19 Government of Canada, *Canada and the Americas – Priorities and Progress* (Ottawa, 2009), 1.

20 As reported by CBC, '"Nonsense" to Believe Latin America Faces only 2 Political Choices: PM,' CBC News Online (17 July 2007), http://www.cbc.ca/news/world/story/2007/07/17/harper-chile.htlm.

21 For a broad discussion of these themes, see James Rochlin, *Social Forces and the Revolution in Military Affairs: The Cases of Colombia and Mexico* (New York and London: Palgrave Macmillan, 2008).

22 The quote is from Peter Kent, Minister of State for Foreign Affairs, Foreign

Affairs and International Trade Canada, 'Notes for an Address by the Honourable Peter Kent, Minister of State of Foreign Affairs (Americas), at the 50th Annual Meeting of the Inter-American Development Bank' (30 March 2009), 1.

23 See Rochlin, *Social Forces and the Revolution in Military Affairs*.

24 See Arturo Escobar, *Encountering Development: The Making and Unmaking of the Third World* (New Jersey: Princeton University Press, 1995).

25 Government of Canada, *Canada First Defense Strategy* (Ottawa: May 2008).

26 Juan Antonio Zuniga and Roberto Gonzales Amador, 'Se despeno 10.3% en abril-junio, reporta el Inegi,' La Jornada Online, 21 August 2009, http://www.jornada.unam.mx/2009/08/21/economia/024n1eco.

27 See Rochlin, *Social Forces and the Revolution in Military Affairs*, especially chapters 5–7.

28 Interview by author with Pedro León, general manager, New Business Orinoco Oil Belt, PDVSA, 17 September 2007, Caracas.

29 Joshua Goodman, 'China Plans More Trade, Investment in Latin America, Zhou Says,' Bloomberg, 28 March 2009, http://www.bloomberg.com/apps/news?pid=newsarchive&sid=aEK3kCAe9wew.

30 For a good overview see Liisa North, Timothy Clark, and Viviana Patroni (eds.), *Community Rights and Corporate Responsibility: Canadian Mining and Oil Companies in Latin America* (Toronto: Between the Lines, 2006).

31 Associated Press, 'Petro-Canada Joins Oil Companies Abandoning Venezuela,' CNBC Online, 27 June 2007, http://www.cnbc.com/id/19468283/Petro_Canada_Joins_Oil_Companies_Abandon-ing_Venezuela.

32 Interview by author with officials at the Canadian Embassy in Caracas who wish to remain anonymous, 22 May 2009.

33 For a broader discussion of this, see Escuela Nacional Sindical, 'La Minería en Colombia,' August 2011, www.ens.org.

34 Mark Bromley, 'Arms Transfers to the Americas,' *SIPRI Background Paper* (Solna, Sweden: Stockholm International Peace Research Institute, June 2009), 1–8.

35 An excellent piece in this regard is Paul Haslam and Edison Rodriguez Barreto, Jr, 'World's Apart: Canadian and Brazilian Multilateralism in Comparative Perspective,' *Canadian Foreign Policy* 15, no. 1 (Spring 2009): 1–20.

36 For a broader discussion of the Revolution in Military Affairs, see Rochlin, *Social Forces and the Revolution in Military Affairs,* chapter 1.

37 See Colin Freeze and Marina Jiménez, 'Mexico's Drug War Becomes Canadian Security Issue,' *Globe and Mail*, 5 March 2009, A4.

38 See, for example: James Rochlin, 'Development, the Environment and

Ecuador's Oil Patch: The Context and Nuances of the Case Against Tex-
aco,' *Journal of Third World Studies* 28, no. 2 (Fall 2011): 11–39, and Suzana
Sawyer, 'Empire/Multitude – State/Civil Society,' *Social Analysis* 51, no. 2
(2007): 64–85.

39 Statistics Canada, *Foreign Direct Investment, 2009* (Ottawa: Queen's Printer,
2009).

40 Government of Canada, *Canada and the Americas*, 1.

41 Quote from Todd Gordon and Jeffrey Webber, 'Imperialism and Resistance:
Canadian Mining Companies in Latin America,' *Third World Quarterly* 29,
no. 1 (2008): 69. See also Advisory Group Report, *National Roundtables on
Corporate Responsibility and the Canadian Extractive Industry in Developing
Countries* (Ottawa: March 2007).

2 The Most Challenging of Links?
   Canada and Inter-American Security

HAL KLEPAK

This chapter will argue that while Canada has developed an interest in inter-American security affairs that goes far beyond anything the country's government was considering in 1989 when it decided to join the Organization of American States (OAS), this does not mean that such an interest has been clearly understood, followed consistently, or easily sustained over the ensuing two decades. While it is generally argued that the connection has been *relatively* easy to develop in economic and political terms, in the defence and security area this has not been the case. This is not to say that the relationship does not exist or that it is not worthy of sustaining, but it does mean that it has been a difficult one to establish and to continue with consistency and a sense of purpose. And it will also be suggested that few in Ottawa understood the complexities of inter-American security when the first decisions to engage in it were taken.

In order to do this we will make a short overview of the Canadian relationship with Latin America before the Second World War, when relations were established between Ottawa and several regional states, and follow this with a look at the developments between the early 1940s and the historic decision to join the OAS in late 1989. We can then assess what has happened since the formation of that relationship. At all times, emphasis will be placed on the defence and security side of the connection.

Introduction: How Did We Get Where We Are?

While Canada was, of course, part of the Americas long before it finally decided it was in the late 1980s, it is easy to exaggerate the impact of this on Canadians' view of themselves or where they fit into the international scene before this period. While the long-standing French presence in northern North America tended to make at least some francophone Canadians comfortable with the idea of their actually belonging to their geographical space, English-speaking Canadians were usually more comfortable with the thought that they were part of a vast and powerful British imperial system which could guarantee their cultural, political, social, and even economic future despite the asymmetries of North American political and military conditions.[1]

As innumerable Canadian historians and political scientists have pointed out, Canada was able to hide behind British power, especially naval strength, as no other neighbour of that country was able to do and thus to develop the nation without undue outside interference. While Mexico lost roughly half of its national territory in its first half-century of independence, and Haiti, Nicaragua, the Dominican Republic, Panama, Costa Rica, El Salvador, Cuba, Honduras, and briefly even the British possessions of Bermuda and the Bahamas, saw United States official and 'filibustering' invasions on many occasions, British North America saw Canadian and imperial forces beat off the many similar state and state-sponsored attempts to seize the country in the first hundred years of U.S. independence.[2]

Canadians watched with horror as other neighbours of the U.S. suffered that country's invasions and military interventions and occupations while they themselves slowly built first a deterrent system and then a modus vivendi with their huge rival and partner in North America.[3] Indeed, such was the success of these positive trends that the two countries were eventually to build one of the closest bilateral relationships in the world.[4]

This context meant that there was precious little interest at any time in Canada in seeing the model of U.S. relationships with its neighbours applied south of the Rio Grande also established to the north. Mutual respect, especially after the Washington Treaty of 1871, and even a formal alliance in the First World War, became the general rule in the bilateral relationship even if this was not always the case, while to the south Washington behaved with a mixture of benign neglect and powerful military action which might have made many more formal imperial powers blush in their own spheres of influence.[5] Canadians remained steadfast in their view that the U.S. should not be encouraged in any way to see its northern neighbour in ways similar to their southern counterparts, and Ottawa was secretly pleased that both in the Department of State and the Department of Defense in Washington, Canada was for long squarely 'in' Europe and the British Empire and Commonwealth and not seen to be part of the rest of the Americas.

This did not mean that there was no Canadian relationship with Latin America before the Second World War. New France (1608–1759) had maintained reasonably close connections and trade with the French West Indies and, as the only part of the French empire with a reasonably large white population, often provided troops and resources for the defence of the French islands there.[6] British Canada after 1759, basking in the benefits of British naval power and imperial trade, was able to strengthen links with the south even further, although this was usually limited by Spanish mercantilist policies in Madrid's own empire. And when the Reciprocity Treaty with the U.S. was clearly on its way to oblivion in 1866 after Britain and Canada's perceived backing of the South in the U.S. Civil War, the colonies founding the new Dominion the next year sent a trade mission to Latin America even before the new nation took off in order to try to find trading links that might reduce the impact of the end of the agreement with Washington.

It is important to note, however, that this trade mission found little positive on its trip. Mexico was in the throes of civil war and foreign invasion; Cuba was about to have its first independence war and was simmering with discontent; Haiti was a disaster on all fronts; and generally the region appeared to the mission members to offer little potential to aid the new Dominion with its trade troubles.[7] And thus the long, seemingly permanent tradition of small trade levels with Latin America began for Ottawa. While those depressing figures, normally hanging around the two or three percentage mark of total international trade, remained the rule in peacetime, it should be noted that these totals were still often impressive if U.S. percentages of Canadian trade are taken into account as leaving in recent decades very little for the rest of the world at large.

What was more important and impressive was investment. Canadian expertise in many areas of development meant that the country was superbly placed, especially given its links to the mother country and British capital, to move into the investment field in Latin America. And move in it did, early and powerfully, by the late 1890s.[8] This trend continued up to the Great Depression of 1929 and started afresh after the Second World War.

Political connections were slower to develop. Under France, the Family Compact, the Bourbon alliance between the courts of Spain and

France that endured for so much of the eighteenth century, ensured some linkages between French and Spanish colonies in the Americas. Indeed, the death of Canada's arguably finest general ever, Sieur Le Moyne d'Iberville, in Havana in 1706, was testimony to that defence connection.[9] But continued Spanish rule in most of the hemisphere meant that a British Canada was unlikely to have much political connection at all with 'Latin' America even though the ancient British alliance with Portugal meant some stronger connections at times with Brazil.

Indeed, Cuban complications led to the closing off of the most potentially influential breakthrough of the British Empire in Latin America when the British, having taken the western and most developed part of the island in 1762 as part of the extraordinary amphibious operations of the Seven Years' War that also delivered Canada itself into London's care, yielded it up at war's end. This was done, at least in part, because, having already absorbed 70,000 French Catholics in the North, the British Empire was in no position to easily do the same with almost a million more Spanish subjects of similar religion and loyalty in the South.[10] Cuba proved too large a pill to swallow even for the massively growing British-American empire, and it would be another half-century before other possibilities on this scale were to present themselves.[11]

When independence movements rocked Spanish America in the early years of the next century, there was little involvement by British North America save for attempts to share general British economic penetration of the area. British political penetration accompanied this process, but direct Canadian involvement was small except when complications arising from Anglo-American rivalry there raised their heads, as they did, for example, in the diplomatic moves preceding the U.S.-Mexican War of 1846–8, known in this country as the Oregon Crisis, in various U.S. official and unofficial efforts to acquire Cuba from Spain throughout the century, and in bilateral conflict in Central America.[12]

That rivalry ensured for a long time after Dominion status in 1867, when Canada was not included in most multilateral political agendas in the hemisphere. This became especially true as U.S. adoption of pan-American ideas in late century saw Canada excluded from the movement that, by 1910, led to something of a Pan American Union (PAU) as being merely a Trojan horse of British power within what Washington chose to call the 'American family of nations.'[13] While Latin Americans increasingly tended to seek exactly such a horse in order to reduce U.S. relative power in the region, the United States was successful in keeping it from the door whenever the issue of Canada taking a greater role in hemispheric affairs arose.[14]

This state of affairs was reinforced by the fact that Canada, until the late 1920s, did not benefit from the Statute of Westminster and did not have its own diplomatic representation abroad – although this would begin to change in 1927 with the opening of a legation in Washington.[15] The reluctance of Prime Minister Mackenzie King, head of government for the second time from 1935 until 1948, to broaden too quickly Canada's international linkages (and especially commitments) ensured that Canada's political presence in Latin America remained limited and that as British influence waned during and after the First World War, so did Canada's.

As with the First World War, so with the Second, as Canada saw its trade with Latin America from 1939 onward go from under 3 per cent to over 6 per cent of total trade. Unfortunately, this did not really reflect a permanent trend but rather the effects of distortions in normal hemispheric and world trade caused by the Royal Navy blockade of continental Europe and the German U-boat campaign against Britain and the Commonwealth.

But the idea of having direct diplomatic relations with selected Latin American states at this stage came to make some sense to Mackenzie King. The end of Canadian missions in The Hague, Paris, Rome, Tokyo, and Geneva as a result of the war and Nazi conquests had freed up a number of diplomats for reassignment. The cost of establishing relations with selected Latin American countries was thus reduced. When this was combined with what was hoped would be a permanent change in Canadian exports to the region, arguments for giving some further priority to Latin America began to carry more weight. Thus by midwar, missions were approved for Mexico, Argentina, Brazil, and Cuba, and relations with other Latin American countries were soon to come.

Formally, if indirectly, most nations of Latin America were now 'allies' of Canada's. For even before the United Nations arrangements for the war were fully in place, most of these countries were allies of the U.S. in light of their engagements at the Rio conference of February 1942 as well as many of their bilateral commitments to that country; Canada was also, after Pearl Harbor, an ally of the U.S. While this had been briefly the case in the First World War, it had had no real impact on public opinion, bilateral commitments, or even any major economic implications.[16] In the Second World War, Canada began to accept more fully that it was an 'American' nation, and allied status moved this acceptance along even if the direct connections this arrangement made were not numerous.[17] This was not discouraged by the mother country, and indeed in the defence field London had asked Canada to help by garrisoning a number of colonial dependencies in the West Indies in order to free up regular British troops for the war effort closer to home. Canada had done the same with the Royal Canadian Regiment sent to Bermuda during the First World War but this deployment had done nothing to strengthen defence relations with Latin America. The same was to prove true of the southern deployments during the Second World War.[18]

The end of the war dashed the hopes of most of those wishing to see a rapidly developing Canada–Latin American relationship: Canada–Latin America trade eased back to its usual near 3 per cent of total trade level; Canadian investment, while still present, generally looked for easier pickings closer to home; and the United States's rejection of Mackenzie King's at best lukewarm wartime flirtation with Pan American Union membership all spelled the end of the speedy developments of 1939–45. Canadians had noticed that almost everyone but the U.S. had welcomed a Canadian interest in PAU membership but the rebuff had pushed traditional Canadian thinking back to the fore: a Latin American link promised little gain for Canada and much potential difficulty for the bilateral relationship with its huge neighbour. Then the onset of the Cold War, and its return to strong-arm tactics by the United States in its normal dealings with its infamous 'backyard,' led to even less Canadian interest in a connection especially in the defence field.

While Prime Minister John Diefenbaker early on in his government (1957–63) did again flirt with the idea of a stronger connection with the region as part of his desire to diversify trade away from the United States, this hope also flickered and died in the light of continuing trends in two-way trade figures. Despite a visit to Mexico that seemed to herald new times, the wider initiative disappeared as did the inter-American elements of it, and Canadian-U.S. bickering over how to handle the Cuban Revolution was merely the most visible element of differences over policies to the region between the two North American capitals.

In the Cold War the bedrock of Canadian foreign and defence policy had become alliance with the United States and membership in the North Atlantic Treaty Organization (NATO), that magical alliance for Canadians that permitted the 'multilateralization' of Canadian security and defence relations with the United States instead of the horrifying prospect of bilateral defence accords alone between the giant and the pygmy.[19] Nothing that threatened this comfort zone would long be considered by Canadian policy makers, and too great a Latin American connection appeared on too many occasions to do just that.

U.S. military interventions in Latin America had generally been unpopular with the Canadian public, and for obvious reasons, although it must be said that many Canadian investors joined their British colleagues in welcoming some U.S. interventions during the 'dollar diplomacy' days prior to 1934 and the establishment of the Good Neighbor Policy by President Franklin Roosevelt.[20] It was well known that Canadian public opinion would continue to decry such actions on the part of the U.S. and that Ottawa would then be walking a tightrope between public opinion at home and keeping the favour of Washington when such events occurred. But this had been largely a forgotten difficulty for the two decades 1934–54, when the new policy not only eschewed interventions but harvested the benefits of such non-intervention in the exceptional Latin American backing for the U.S. after it was attacked at Pearl Harbor in 1941.[21] The Cold War put paid to this policy as Washington backed military coups and authoritarian governments across the region especially after the success of the Cuban Revolution in 1959. Latin America was far from a Canadian priority, and a military link there seemed to most Canadians who thought about it to be a potential nightmare.

Soon after his arrival in power in 1968, however, Prime Minister Pierre Trudeau began a major study and then revision of Canadian foreign policy that was to have as a significant component yet another attempt at reversing the main trends in national trade of the twentieth century, especially the drift towards U.S. dominance. A 'Third Option' that called for diversification of trade as the key for national independence gave Latin America an important place in future goals where such diversification was concerned.[22] While rejecting full membership in the OAS, Canada did become a formal observer with that body in 1972, and bilateral relations were stepped up with a number of countries in the region. Two of the main reasons for holding off from actually joining were the perceived need to sign the Inter-American Treaty of Reciprocal Assistance (the Rio Pact of 1947), a collective security agreement that would have made Canada a direct ally of the U.S. in the Latin American region, and the feeling that Canada would have to reject Cuba's socialist government and work to unseat it if it joined. Neither of these was deemed acceptable to public opinion in Canada.[23] But as Brian Stevenson argues convincingly, the Cuban question also focused

Canadian attention on Latin America as nothing else had done, and even when Trudeau was annoyed by Havana, he remained close to it, its leader, and its problems.[24]

Latin America did not remain anything like a priority for Ottawa, however, even under Trudeau, and when Ottawa opted a few years later to quietly remove its observer to the OAS from a permanent presence in Washington and return him home it caused hardly a ripple of public or press comment. A more forward policy towards Latin America brought simply too little gains and too many political and diplomatic headaches to be palatable at the time.

The Late 1980s: Change Is in the Air

When the Liberal government was replaced by a Conservative one in 1984, it came in the form of what many felt would be the most pro-United States prime minister in Canadian history. Brian Mulroney won the election promising that the relationship with the U.S. would be back as the priority in Canadian foreign policy and that cooperation with that power would be the linchpin of our policy in the future.[25] Like Mexico, and in the face of trade trends that brought the U.S. to some 80 per cent of total Canadian exports for the first time and meant that a real North American market had been created, like it or not, Canada abandoned schemes like the Third Option and accepted that dependence on the U.S. was inevitable. Fearful of rising U.S. protectionism in this context, Mulroney abandoned the historic nationalist positions of his party and began negotiations for a free trade arrangement with Washington.[26] The decision divided the country as rarely before, but by 1988 free trade with the U.S. was a fact. On a wider Latin American level this first step was to lead to free trade with Mexico only six years later and many other agreements of this kind with Latin American nations in the years to follow.

The next year Mulroney announced in Costa Rica that in January 1990 Canada would join the OAS as a full-fledged member. The country was truly broadening its inter-American links in ways unheard of up to this time. It should be noted that this did not entail, at least in theory, any security commitments as Ottawa formally eschewed the Rio Pact and did not join the Inter-American Defense Board, the Inter-American Defense College, the conferences of commanders of Armies, Navies and Air Forces, or the rest of the accords and institutions of what is termed the inter-American security system.[27] This will be discussed in greater detail later on. The first real military deployments ever made by Canada to the region were equally taking place at roughly the same time. The Central American civil wars that ravaged El Salvador, Guatemala, and Nicaragua for some time but were most noticed in Canada in the 1980s had led to a level of interest in the region unknown before. Dozens of NGOs were deployed to the area and Canadian foreign assistance began to consider it a priority. And the aid Ottawa gave went to both the rightist governments of El Salvador and Guatemala on the one hand and to the leftist government of Nicaragua, as well as to NGOs throughout the region.

During the 1988–9 period, and in the absence of the United States as the decisive and unwelcoming key player in the Americas – brought on by the crisis of the Reagan government occasioned by, among other things, the Iran-Contragate Scandal – the United Nations (UN) was allowed a first opportunity ever to play a major role in Latin America. Backing local and regional efforts to find a way to bring peace to Central America, the UN organized observer missions to both the region (ONUCA) and specifically to El Salvador (ONUSAL) in 1989 and 1992 respectively.[28] It called on Canada to help, and Ottawa eventually provided not only the largest contingent and a helicopter squadron but also the commander to the first mission; it became a major contributor to the second as well. And then the usual UN 'mission creep' ensured that the roles of those troops, naval vessels, and aircraft were expanded as greater support for the peace process grew. For the first time, hundreds of Canadian Forces personnel were to serve in and get to know a part of Latin America proper, and not just as a British Commonwealth country or ally.

The lack of knowledge of Spanish among serving members became obvious to the Canadian Forces as soon as they began to deploy. Equally it was clear that local knowledge of the region, despite some very recent Central American immigration to Canada caused by the civil wars, was not by any means easy to come by.[29] The few Spanish speakers in the CF were usually winkled out from their units in order to provide a minimum linguistic presence. This was eased by the fact that the mission needed air, naval, and land forces personnel and not just the traditional soldiers.

At roughly the same time, the Mulroney government proved to be one of the most adamant in the United Nations on how to handle the successive military governments coming into power in Haiti in the wake of the end of the Duvalier dictatorship there. Several HMC ships

were dispatched by the navy to maintain a watch on, and then a blockade of, the island and enforce a UN embargo on trade with those governments in the early 1990s. This was the first time the Canadian Navy
had been involved in such an intrusive mission in the region since one
of the country's destroyers briefly landed sailors in El Salvador to protect British subjects during the troubles in that country in the 1930s.

Thus, it could no longer be said that Canada was not a player in issues
of security and defence in the region. Instead it had acted with vigour
in what was increasingly seen as 'its hemisphere' and had done so in
specifically military ways. Latin American nations, which had long
wished for another 'northern' presence in the region, were generally
very pleased to see this trend. When the first ambassador to the Organization of American States made his maiden speech at the institution's
headquarters in Washington, it was greeted by delighted applause by
almost all the delegations. And the mention in the speech of the need to
reincorporate as soon as possible Cuba, 'excluded' in 1962 under dubi-
ous conditions, received the almost unanimous support of those same
nations. It left the U.S., still arguing defence considerations, the odd
member state opposed to such a move. It was clear that things had dramatically changed for Canada.

Reluctance Still on Defence and Security

Few nations had noticed, however, that the Canadian commitment to
hemispheric security had been so small despite its formal signature
of the Charter of the OAS. Not only did Ottawa not agree to sign the
Rio Pact, but it also placed 'reservations' on its adherence to the 1948
Charter respecting Chapters V and VI, which reiterated the collective
security commitments of the Pact and which, like that accord, would
have committed Canada to the territorial defence of all the other signatories – that is, virtually the entire hemisphere. Given serious outstanding problems between the United Kingdom and Argentina, Guatemala
and Belize, a member of the Commonwealth with quite strong ties
to Canada, and among many of the actual signatories of the Rio Pact
itself, Ottawa was in no mood to give collective security guarantees to
anyone.[30]

Equally, what little debate there had been in Canada on the wisdom
of joining the OAS had frequently commented negatively on the Pact,
collective security in the Americas in general, the overwhelming dominance of the U.S. in the defence arrangements of the hemisphere, and

what many saw as the unsavoury character of the armed forces of the region. Since the decision was also taken not to join the Commanders' Conferences of the Armies, Air Forces and Navies of the Americas, nor to send officers to the Inter-American Defense Board or students to the Inter-American Defense College, nor even to take part in inter-American military exercises, it was not difficult to see that Canada wished to distance itself in a major way from the institutional life of the military dimension of the region despite its overall interest in other fields.

Those security connections were indeed dominated by the United States, and thus Canada was far from certain whether it wanted much to do with them. Canadians had become quite reassured in terms of their sovereignty and independence concerns by their Commonwealth experience historically as well as their recent and current conditions enjoyed in NATO. The relationship with the United Kingdom had evolved well from Ottawa's experience and it was not at all unusual in recent decades to have British troops under Canadian command instead of the former colonial experience of almost always being the *commanded* instead of the *commander*. A Canadian general had, at one point, even commanded a British division in the British Army of the Rhine, and the military connection was in general one of mutual respect and admiration.

In NATO, the United States was by far the most important country in the alliance, but there were several other major players as well, including the UK, France, and Germany. Fewer than half of the general or flag-officer commands of the alliance were held by United States officers. And it was in no way unusual to have U.S. personnel serving under those of other NATO nations. Likewise, the majority of the institutions of the alliance were located in countries other than the U.S.

In that sense, the inter-American security system had evolved to look on paper more like that of the Warsaw Pact than NATO – especially its emphasis on U.S-brokered bilateral arrangements with over a dozen countries in the region. In the formal sense, there was the 1947 Rio Pact, the central element of the arrangement but supported by the OAS Charter's Chapter V and VI of the following year and by the wartime but still surviving Inter-American Defense Board – the longest-standing international defence institution in the world dating back to 1942. These basic accords had been given 'muscle' and reality by the Mutual Assistance Pacts (MAPs) signed bilaterally by Washington and most Latin American capitals in the years during or after the Korean War of 1950–3 (much like the Warsaw Pact bloc of countries). Under them, the United States had permanent access to many bases as well as to strategic minerals and agricultural products (at special prices) in time of conflict in exchange for Latin American access to cheap U.S. equipment, armaments, and training establishments.[31] Given the smaller armed forces of many of these nations, U.S. military engagement was widespread in the region and took on, in many cases, a dominant role in the defence affairs of these same countries.

When the Cuban Revolution won victory from the corrupt and sanguinary U.S.-backed regime of Fulgencio Batista in January 1959, it quickly showed that it was serious in ending the lengthy domination of the island by the United States and implementing a social program of vast consequences. Washington was not slow in mobilizing the inter-American security system to prevent the drive for fundamental change in Havana from succeeding.[32] And the U.S. insisted with the majority of its MAP partners that they turn from their preference for training in traditional defence to an emphasis on counter-insurgency (COIN). Specialist teams of 'Green Beret' and other COIN instructors were sent to several of the countries of the region and were accompanied by enormous increases in funding for these and related initiatives.

At the same time, an Inter-American Defense College was set up to train officers for staff positions in hemispheric institutions that the U.S. wished to be established along the collective security lines of NATO. Multinational exercises of naval, air, and even army units were begun on an annual basis, and the series of armed forces commanders' conferences that are still in place was started for the majority of navies, armies, and air forces in the hemisphere. This expansion of the system retained and reinforced the elements that most troubled Canada. For once again, all institutions and coordinating efforts were Washington-based and reflected directly and constantly utterly total U.S. domination, a situation with which Canada was neither comfortable nor accustomed in its international defence affairs.

Washington was interested in Canada coming into any of these arrangements it wished. But Ottawa saw Cuba in a greatly different light and kept the door open to the island and its new leftist regime. In any case, Prime Minister John Diefenbaker shared with most NATO leaders the view that an isolated Castro would merely drive him into the arms of the Soviet Union.[33] And, in general, what happened next worried Canada greatly as U.S.-supported or even -sponsored coups removed from power government after government in the region if they were felt to be 'soft on communism' and replaced them with what

are generally agreed to have been the most savage authoritarian governments in the sad history of the region since independence.[34] There
was to be little enough interest in Canada in close relations with any
of this. And if the Mulroney government could look to the 'return' of
democracy in the region and its growing stability and prosperity in the
late 1980s as reasons to join the OAS, improvement was not seen as in
any way obvious in the security domain.

This was the background to the reticence of the country to get involved
in any major way with defence affairs when it joined the OAS in 1990.
The government had set as its priorities for development assistance as
well as wider policy towards the region as support for development,
democracy, and peace. If Canada was truly, in external affairs minister
Joe Clark's words, to make the Americas not merely 'its house' but also
'its home,' then the hemisphere would have to be prosperous, democratic, and peaceful. Otherwise, Canadians would not adjust to a region
in which they felt neither at home nor particularly drawn towards.[35]

These three pillars of Canadian policy were enunciated repeatedly
from 1989 to 1991, but their security implications had not yet sunk in.
The discomfort with the realities of civil-military relations in so many
regional countries, and with U.S. military dominance in all of them
(even Cuba in an indirect if dire way), kept Canada firmly away from
deeper involvement. As senior officials dealt with and visited the region
in ever greater numbers, however, the real situation in these countries
began to become evident.

There could be no sustained development in the region unless there
was security both internally and externally. The state of domestic
security was in most countries a source of enormous concern, and the
increasing role of illegal drugs as a destabilizing factor within these
nations was a fact that could not be ignored, especially as Canada's
great neighbour declared the 'war on drugs' in 1986 and stated that
the scourge was now their main security and defence threat.[36] Vast
amounts of money were spent on non-productive military and police
efforts that did not bring much in the way of development. And foreign
investment was not attracted to insecure places; without that investment, development of the region was merely a dream. Thus, development was linked with security in the most direct of ways, and slowly
the Canadian International Development Agency (CIDA) was forced to
accept this state of affairs. So, too, were politicians close to these issues.

Likewise, democracy could not advance properly in the 1990s unless
the thorny issues of security and civil-military relations were first tack-

led. Even though most countries now had at least formally democratic governments, they still in most cases faced security concerns that forced them to use their armed forces excessively, thus ensuring their role and power in society grew to unwise levels. Those forces were without question the most powerful, respected, relatively honest, ubiquitous, flexible, capable, and permanent institution of most of these states, and they automatically found themselves being asked to undertake tasks that corrupt, inefficient, underpaid, underequipped, and undertrained police forces could not. This subsequently moved into such areas of national life as diverse as border control, transport of crops to market, prison guarding, intelligence gathering, anti-drugs and anti-illegal immigration activities, anti-gang violence operations, airport security and control, police training and command, and a host of others across the region.[37]

The civil-military relations aspects of this problem are legion. These roles necessarily led to a dominance in funding, cabinet influence, popular respect, state presence, and many other areas that were dangerous for democracy and the proper functioning of a democratic state.[38] And it was not necessarily the case that these militaries all wished for such roles. However, with weak civil societies and public services, and other security services without funds, prestige, or efficiency, the armed forces filled gap after gap in countries with major security problems. Thus, ignoring security and defence matters had a direct impact on the anchoring of democracy, another principal pillar of Canadian policy in the Americas.

Finally, the question of a region of peace to call our own was even more directly related to matters of defence and security than the other two pillars of Ottawa's policy towards the region. As we have seen, there are any number of hemispheric disputes regarding borders, maritime and other jurisdictions, ideology, and other matters. Since the Second World War, in this region of relative peace, there have been wars between El Salvador and Honduras, Argentina and the United Kingdom, and Ecuador and Peru; military interventions by the United States across the Caribbean and Central America; and militarized diplomatic disputes in many places, notably those between Guyana and Venezuela, Cuba and the U.S., Argentina and Chile, Honduras and Nicaragua, Colombia and Venezuela, Guatemala and Belize, and, most recently, in the Ecuador-Colombia border region.[39]

Traditional strategic balances of power have helped reduce the frequency of open conflicts, but they reflect the lack of mutual confidence among countries which like to talk of a 'Latin American common-wealth' but where the reality of such a description is not quickly visible to the careful observer.[40] The long-standing balances of power between Argentina and Brazil, between Venezuela and Colombia, and between Peru and Chile have been in place since shortly after independence and were still in place when Canada joined the OAS in 1990.

U.S. reluctance to have conflict in its own backyard has also acted to put a lid on the more open forms of inter-American dispute. Equally important has been the sheer difficulty of waging war in the majority of border areas of this region of vast rivers, high mountains, great jungles, and resulting poor communications. Be that as it may, the region may be one of relative peace but it is most definitely not a 'region of peace.' Most armed forces prepare for possible wars with neighbours, how-ever remote the possibility, and some also use their militaries in distinct deterrent roles vis-à-vis other members of the hemisphere.

Tellingly, Canada soon found that all three of its policy pillars towards the region were distinctly linked to defence and security. Just as important, Latin Americans looked to Canada for assistance in just those areas. To the surprise of many Canadians, Latin American nations tended to see Canada as having distinct comparative advantages in the defence and security field. For a start, it was not the United States. That is to say, it did not bring to defence and security cooperation the bag-gage or history that working with that superpower usually did, espe-cially in this region of the world.

In addition, Canada had armed forces which were internationally linked and respected, modern, and accustomed to international cooper-ation, with vast United Nations peacekeeping experience accumulated, and with strong credentials in democracy and civil-military relations, all things most Latin American countries wanted for their own mili-tary establishments.[41] Moreover, the asymmetries between regional forces and those of the United States did not apply in relations with the Canadian Forces, which in size and budgets did not differ so much from many others in the region. Problems were similar, including those of administration and keeping up in a field where military technol-ogy was advancing at a great pace and the costs of not falling behind seemed prohibitive.

Even in the police field, the prestige and regard of the Royal Cana-dian Mounted Police (RCMP) are simply exceptional throughout Latin America, and nations there keen on police modernization and general improvement look to the RCMP as a model of great interest. To some extent this is also reflected in a lesser but extant interest in the Canadian Security and Intelligence Service (CSIS).

Canada, then, was of great interest to Latin America in the specific fields of security and defence and was soon asked to assist in a wide range of areas even when it showed no acute interest to do anything of the sort. But as the recognition of the importance of these fields grew in Ottawa, the first steps towards new policy initiatives eventually took place. At the OAS General Assembly in Nassau in 1991, Canada agreed to take a greater role in what was variously termed 'democratic' or 'cooperative security.'[42]

Within a couple of years, Canada had opened its first defence attaché office ever in Mexico City, responsible also for Cuba and most of Central America. It had also sent students on a trial basis to the Inter-American Defense College in Washington, continued and expanded its Central American deployment, increased its peacekeeping operations along-side Latin American armed forces, and sent observers to the command-ers' conferences of American armies, navies, and air forces. In addition, it had beefed up assistance, including diplomatic involvement, in the peaceful resolution of disputes in Central America, and had become even more engaged in impoverished Haiti.

The mid-1990s saw this effort continued and strengthened under the Liberal government of Jean Chrétien. Canada spent money in efforts to assist some Latin American nations to modernize their forces – espe-cially in the administration-of-defence domain. Ottawa also spear-headed an attempt to make progress in the field of confidence-building measures among all the nations of the region. And the now-active mem-ber of the OAS became a major pillar of that institution's new support for its erstwhile Unit for the Promotion of Democracy (UPD). More dra-matic was the Canadian military deployment to Haiti in 1994, a move which was to see Canada become the most important contributor to that force as well as the provider of its commander, and where the RCMP and other Canadian police forces played a major security role beyond the strictly military one. On the diplomatic front, Ottawa took an active part in efforts to push forward the Guatemalan peace process, which culminated in an end to that civil conflict in 1996. And a second defence attaché office opened in Buenos Aires, reflective of the increased connec-tion with Argentina in multilateral arms control forums and in peace-keeping operations worldwide. The office in the southern cone of South America also permitted a closer link with Chile, whose armed forces were recognized as the most professional in the region.

Canada also became a firm supporter of the U.S. initiative for a series of Defence Ministerials of the Americas (held generally every two years in a specific country of the Americas), the first one hosted in Williamsburg, Virginia in 1995 and then after the 1996 one in Bariloche, Argentina. This was to be the one meeting where ministers of defence of the Americas could meet reasonably frequently, get to know one another, and discuss wider security challenges face to face.

During this period, the Canadian government pressed for two major objectives in the arms control and disarmament field: the Ottawa Treaty banning landmines and the adoption of 'human security.' As the basis for Canada's foreign and security policies, defence diplomacy in the region was more intense than any had ever imagined it becoming before.[43] In the first area, success was virtually complete as Canada's foreign minister Lloyd Axworthy achieved 100 per cent support for the treaty from those Latin American countries that did not have a major immediate defence problem that would make it impossible for them to sign. Only the United States stood aloof from the treaty, arguing that its worldwide commitments did not allow for such a stand and that especially in Korea its defence posture depended on landmines in order to deter North Korean attack on the South. Politics makes strange bedfellows, and the only other country in the Americas to refuse was Cuba, whose deterrent stance vis-à-vis the United States is totally dependent on its ability to deploy landmines to key beach landing areas and potential parachute drop zones. Even there, however, Canada could take heart as the Cubans went out of their way to say that as soon as the U.S. policy bent on destroying the regime ended, they would be in a position to revise their stance and adopt what they otherwise would have signed happily.

In the second area, the drift of events was different. While the United States opposed the idea of human security, as did most traditional Latin American armed forces and defence ministries, the idea gained some ground in more reformist governments. By the time of a conference to discuss the future of security in the Americas in 2003 in Mexico City, a number of Latin American governments had adopted elements of the thinking behind the idea in their approaches to defence. Curiously, Canada had by then become involved in more difficult traditional defence issues, especially those around being the neighbour of the United States in the wake of the terrorist bombings in New York and Washington in September 2001, and had with time moved away from its firm backing of the human security concept. Still, Canadian defence diplomacy had made a mark in the region.

Canada was by now deeply involved in hemispheric defence. Its Military Training and Assistance Programme (MTAP) was steadily extended to more countries in the region, and Latin America and the Caribbean became the second most important destination for such assistance after the Partnership for Peace nations of the former Warsaw Pact and USSR. Indeed, as money became less necessary for that part of the world, it was the Western hemisphere that received most of the new surplus. Canada put officers from Latin America and the Caribbean on courses for language training useful for UN operations and trained them in peacekeeping at the Pearson Peacekeeping Centre (PPC) in Nova Scotia and at more hands-on military centres at Canadian Forces Base Kingston.[44] Latin American officers from a variety of countries joined their Commonwealth Caribbean neighbours at junior staff schools and senior staff colleges in Canada. And civilians from these countries were also brought to the PPC. And such was the continuing growth of the Canadian Army link with the region's armies, in every case the influential 'senior service' of those countries, that the commander of the Canadian Army appointed a special adviser on Latin American defence in 2000 to help his staff with issues coming out of those connections.

Over the same period the Canadian Forces set up further defence attaché offices in Brasilia and Bogotá, and General Rick Hillier, then army commander, hosted the Conference of Commanders of the Armies of the Americas in Ottawa in 2003 as the Forces expanded the reach of the MTAP to most Latin American armed forces. Senior officers meanwhile visited a number of countries in the region – especially Chile and Brazil – and substantive staff and political-military talks were begun with a variety of nations.

In 2008, Canada hosted its first Conference of Defence Ministers of the Americas (CDMA) at Banff. The United States, Argentina, Colombia, Brazil, Chile, and even the small countries of Ecuador and Nicaragua had done so, and it was apparent that it really was Canada's turn to host. But the growing tensions in the hemisphere made this a difficult task for DND, unaccustomed to the ins and outs of hemispheric defence relations and especially lacking in linguistic skills to hold something of the size and importance of the conference. And while the divisions in the hemisphere were visible from the number of ministers not present, the conference was held and most observers thought that, given the unfavourable context, it had to be considered a success.

By 2009, the long-awaited Canadian Defence Attaché office in

Havana was set up. Ottawa had been concerned about U.S. reactions to such a move, but eventually the decision was taken.[45] In fact, the Canadian defence connection with Cuba dated back to the late 1980s, when members of the National Defence College visited the island on two occasions. Following these visits, Cuban military education teams came to Canada to study military education and training in the Canadian Forces and visited National Defence Headquarters, the NDC, the Royal Military College, the Collège militaire royal de Saint-Jean, and other educational and training installations. The Cuban Colegio de Defensa Nacional, the senior national defence education centre, was set up to some extent along the Canadian NDC model in the early 1990s. And senior DND civilian and military officials spoke at the Cuban College in the subsequent years.

Canadian diplomats, DND officials, and professors attended conferences and gave talks at Cuba's new defence think tank, the Centro de Educación e Información de la Defensa (Centre for Defence Education and Information – CEID) throughout the first years of the new century. They had already had connections with the island's other defence think tank, the Centro de Estudios sobre Desarme y Seguridad Internacional (Centre for Disarmament and International Security Studies – CEDSI) for some time. The new attaché's office in Havana could now work to anchor these connections even further.

Frustrations

Although Canadians often find it hard to understand fully, the nation does truly count for something in the Americas. With a population behind not only the United States but also Brazil, Mexico, Argentina, and Colombia, Canada's economy is only marginally less modern and sophisticated than that of the U.S. and, in terms of size, the second or third largest in the hemisphere. Our political connections with the United Nations, the Commonwealth, la Francophonie, the OECD, Asia-Pacific, the OAS, and so many other multilateral organizations make us uniquely linked to the world in a way not enjoyed by any Latin American country.

Thus, when Canada speaks it is listened to with considerable attention in the Americas, which is not usually the case in other regions of the world. The hemisphere wishes to know where Canada stands on issues of the moment and wants to influence that position. This was confirmed by the fact that Latin American nations had diplomatic and consular offices in Ottawa, Montreal, and Toronto decades before Canada reciprocated. And now it is reflected in the ways in which Latin American diplomats seek out Canada for its thinking on the major issues of the day. This means that when we take a decision, it is noted far and wide. And changes from traditional Canadian policy stances on matters of the day are quickly taken note of and commented upon.

This importance is, of course, all to the good in terms of influence and shaping of contexts to the benefit of Canadian exporters and investors. But it is more nuanced when it comes to the feeling Latin Americans sometimes have that Canada can somehow replace the United States with aid, investment, interest, equipment, and the like. This is especially true of defence and security, a field where politics has primacy like so few others.

Latin American and Caribbean ministers of defence tend to have lists of things they would like Canada to provide for them. The U.S. has long had this same problem, but ideological, financial, congressional/ political, and other constraints have made it more difficult in recent years for it to play the dominant role it enjoyed for so many decades, essentially since the 1930s until the end of the century. And while it is still unquestionably the country with the most military influence in the region, it is no longer alone (i.e., China is seeking to carve out a position for itself in the hemisphere).[46] The French in Brazil, a variety of players in Venezuela, and others playing some role elsewhere, have meant that U.S. absolute dominance has slipped markedly although not in ways that threaten its overall position.

It is difficult for Latin Americans to imagine that the Canadian Forces are just over 65,000 (all ranks) for a country of well over 30 million people; that it does not have an aircraft carrier; that it has an aging fleet of fighter and search and rescue aircraft; and that it possesses very limited strategic lift capacity. Nor can they understand the overstretch problems of the Canadian Army involved in keeping fewer than 3,000 troops on the ground in Afghanistan. Instead, they often assume that if Canada does not show great interest in helping out with their security needs it is because we are not concerned enough rather than the usual Canadian Forces situation that we do not have the resources to do so. This has led to much disappointment in regional armed forces circles over the years since Ottawa began to show more keenness on hemispheric security problems.

Regrettably, Canadian rhetoric has not helped with this situation. After a slow start, Canada began to be very strident about the need for more effort in the regional defence and security field. It trumpeted the advantages of disarmament, arms reductions, confidence-building measures, cooperative and then human security, de-mining, a more relevant and efficient IADB, interoperability for regional armed forces in case of needs abroad, and democratic control over the military. But it did not have the actual resources to carry through with any concrete or substantial support for these generally laudable objectives. In the words of many of the region's military officers and diplomats today, 'Canada talks loudly but carries a small stick.'[47] Raising hopes that one cannot actually fulfil is a major hazard for Canadians in inter-American defence and security affairs.

Another frustration is with regard to a point made above about nineteenth-century Canadian relations with the region. Canada now wants to be part of the hemisphere in the defence field as it is in the economic, social, and political areas. But it wants to do so in ways that do not encourage Washington to see the relationship with Canada only through such a hemispheric prism. It is a constant of Canadian policy in the region to push for inter-American approaches to matters of concern and less so for sub-regional and other strategies that would see Canada not fully involved because it is so far away and on 'the other side' geographically *behind* the U.S. But on matters where U.S. policy in the bilateral area is likely to be affected by such a hemisphere-wide approach to the detriment of Canadian interests, particularly if these interests are in the field of defence and security, Canada will not see things in this same wider context.

In this sense the U.S. State Department's 1998 'move' of Canada from the Western European section of the ministry to the Western Hemisphere, while logical in a geographical sense, could not be seen with particular favour in Ottawa by those with a keen strategic or even historical sense. The classic example of the problem arose with Mexico in the wake of 11 September 2001.

The Mexican approach to defence cooperation with the U.S., with the notable exception of the Second World War where its effort was impressive indeed, has historically been of distrust. The loss of half the country's territory in the nineteenth century has meant that even today, although now only in the most formal of senses, the official main threat, for which Defence Plan No. 1 is maintained, is still the U.S. This is, of course, not really the case, especially since the days of the Zapatista uprising of early 1994, where cooperation between the two nations has been impressive even in the defence field, and needless to say in economic affairs with NAFTA as well.[48] And such bilateral cooperation was greatly beefed up after the terrorist attacks of 2001.

For a brief period, Mexico sought a trilateral approach to a sort of North American defence and security cooperative arrangement or even the extension of NORAD to include the three countries. While Canada might have backed such a move in an earlier period, and had done so recently, the terrifying lessons of 2001, when the border was closed and so many restrictions put on the bilateral Canada–U.S. commercial relationship in the wake of 11 September, ensured that the last thing Ottawa sincerely wished for was to see in future cases of similar things happening, a U.S. knee-jerk reaction that treated the borders with both Mexico and Canada in the same way. Canada worked hard to ensure that after the 9/11 tragedy the U.S. would have no cause for complaint about the quality or level of Canadian cooperation and would thus eschew any future approach that would treat the two countries the same. Canada had six decades of experience of effective defence alliance and slowly but surely built up a mutual trust in defence and security with its southern neighbour – while Mexico could claim no such comparable historical record. Indeed, Canadians may take in multilateralism with their mothers' milk but that does not mean that in the Americas they will always believe in it as the best solution for them.

A third and powerful frustration from Canada's standpoint is the tendency of Latin American nations to agree to do things which in fact they have no intention of doing. The region is raft with accords, treaties, declarations, memoranda of understanding, agreements, and every sort of public statement among nations. But the percentage of them which were *lettre morte* at or just after birth is to northern nations quite extraordinary. But in the defence and security field one should be careful about jumping to conclusions here. In general, that seeming lack of Latin American seriousness may reflect very serious political considerations indeed.

The fact is that the inter-American system's asymmetries and differences of fundamental views mean that the idea of cooperation on common goals and threats is often easier said than done. Since, while there is often true agreement in the Americas about the things which ought in the best of all worlds to be done, there is rarely real agreement among all these countries as to the priority one should assign to each of these things much less the approach one should use in dealing with them. The most powerful examples of this in the security field at the moment are illegal immigration and the anti–illegal narcotics efforts, both of which are seen as security problems in the hemisphere but for which little agreement of substance has been forthcoming, reflecting these widely divergent views on the source of the problems and how best to deal with them.[49]

If at the highest and earliest level one does not concur on anything more than listing the problems that everyone agrees are problems, the prospects for meaningful cooperation may not be all that great. And when ideological divides come in to threaten even further what little consensus there may be, the prospects are dimmer still. Thus a country like Canada, newly arrived and accustomed to NATO or Commonwealth levels of basic agreement on goals, however imperfect they may be, finds it difficult to understand the problem by simply proposing what appear to Ottawa to be minor efforts at coordination of effort, interoperability, effective use of resources, and the rest. Frustrations also arise on this score from Latin American diplomats and military officers who find it difficult to believe that Canadians do not understand the real problem and that they are so naive at times, that they do not sense that the best approach may well be 'if it's broke, don't fix it,' because its being broken is exactly the objective of some members of the inter-American system.[50]

Present Challenges

The principal Canadian challenge for defence policy towards the Americas is to find ways, within reasonable political and financial costs, to help advance our national goals in the hemisphere: creating a prosperous region with which we can trade and invest, furthering that region's elusive quest for effective democracy, and anchoring peaceful relations among its nations. This, of course, is a tall order. It is also important to remember that while our policy on these issues dovetails in public stances with that of the United States on many matters, it does not coincide with Washington on either all of its objectives or on the means to achieve them.

This is both Canada's principal advantage and its principal handicap. The fact that Canada has not always followed the U.S. lead on major issues in the past and present – principally in its Cuba policy and on matters as thorny as how to treat the Nicaraguan Sandinista Revolution, what to do about the Central American civil wars, how to perceive and deal with the recent drift to the left in the region, and what to single out as the major causes of unrest and instability there – has meant that

Ottawa enjoys a legitimacy in the south of the hemisphere utterly lost by Washington since the end of the Good Neighbor Policy in 1954.[51]

While Canada is not a formal ally of the United States in the hemisphere's affairs south of the Rio Grande, it is that country's close ally in many parts of the world and in the northern part of the Americas its closest collaborator. It is difficult for Canada to resist U.S. pressure to make the two nations' approaches to the region as a whole since Washington often sees Canadian legitimacy in the area as a potential aid in its own attempts to get certain things done, especially in defence and security, where Ottawa's comparative advantages are tangible. The U.S. is Canada's most important trading partner and is its major source for investment as well. And as mentioned, our policy objectives, as least on the public level of declaratory policy, do seem to aim at the same ends.

Accordingly, it is vital for the successful achievement of those shared objectives that Canadian efforts be seen as properly Canadian and not merely those resulting from U.S pressures. An approach showing that Canada continues to understand the very special moment that Latin America is passing through as its democracies try to find their feet is crucial for the creation of a regional environment that lacks confrontation and excessive ideological bombast and the dangers for peace that such a context presents.

Canada is well placed to play this interlocutory role and thereby move forward towards achieving its overall hemispheric goals. And defence policy is even better placed to help in this because in the security field, until recently, the region was less divided than in the economic or political spheres.

There is more of a need for dialogue in the region than ever before, given the recent stresses caused by the ideological chasm that has opened between reformist and conservative governments in the region. It is vital not to shut off discussion at such a dangerous juncture. It is worth recalling that Canada is appreciated across the spectrum of regimes as a country of openness and democratic pluralism that has become especially tuned to the need for building bridges and not tearing them down when things begin to go badly. The northern nation's success in building a social democratic system essentially accepted by all its political parties, along the British and now European continental models, is acknowledged and generally applauded in Latin America. Ottawa has traditionally understood excesses on the left as a reaction to long-standing excesses on the right, and the need to leave those excesses, on whatever side of the ideological divide, as much behind us as possible in the search for sustainable development and enduring peace.

The Canadian Forces are a superbly developed asset in such a drive to find moderation. They are closely tied to those of the United States but also have proud traditions and links with those of the United Kingdom. They are NATO and United Nations forces and reflect that experience in peace enforcement and peacekeeping roles at this time and in the past.[52] They have been, and currently are, deeply involved in development and nation-building tasks in several parts of the world and here in our own hemisphere in earthquake-ravaged Haiti in early 2010 (where Canada deployed an unprecedented range of military assets). They are no longer strangers to the region, and their linguistic capabilities, while still very limited, are much greater than they were even a short time ago.

Conclusions

Canada did not understand the full implications of becoming a partner in defence and security when it 'joined' the Americas over two decades ago. The learning process involved has been a challenging and often frustrating one since that time – with disappointment a frequent result both from the Canadian and Latin American sides. But these frustrations and misunderstandings can dissolve over time.

It does appear, however, that the country is now 'in' the region as a full-fledged partner and that this situation is going to continue. And it also appears that Ottawa now understands that there can be no 'pick and choose' approach to what we want to deal with in the hemisphere and what we do not. The reality is that the region will not become a prosperous, peaceful, and democratic 'home' for Canada if there is no improvement in the defence and security context. To this end, domestic and international insecurity is present and growing in the Americas of today.

Canada cannot solve the hemisphere's challenges, but it has shown that it is able to garner goodwill and work towards that goal. In these particularly problematic days of a growing ideological divide, Ottawa's proper role as bridge builder, as so often in the past, seems an obvious if far from easy one. In the defence and security area, its comparative advantages are real and accepted. Further emphasis by Canada on them would seem to be called for in the coming years.

In addition, Canada should consider doing a number of things now to contribute to its long-term strategic goals in the Americas. The first of these might be to place the new leftist governments in the region firmly as targeted nations (beginning with Bolivia) for our interest whatever their relative value on other scores.[53] No other nation and no other armed forces have the legitimacy to keep the door open to these countries while they go through their current difficult transitions. It would be extremely dangerous for inter-American peace if they were left cut off to do things on their own without any input from more conservative, but still understanding, countries. Their armed forces will be key to bringing internal and international change peacefully to the region. And Canada and the Canadian Forces can, like no one else, keep bridges open during these trying times.

We should also consider backing initiatives to bring Cuba and its armed forces back into the Americas in ways that will allow the U.S. to open up to that country. To wit, a senior officer's visit, and that of a naval ship, would go a long way in this regard. But a generally reinforced relationship with Havana in the defence field is the best way forward. Canada can also help in the short run by making it clear that we are available to help smaller countries which would wish to host the Conference of Defence Ministers or one of the commander's conferences of the individual armed services. The U.S. is strapped politically in this regard, but we have the experience and the funds to do so. The expansion of our MTAP assistance is also a key to a greater connection. The point is, of course, to build an independent relationship that is *mutually* beneficial and not to just be helpful to others. Nothing else will stand the test of time.

NOTES

1 For an interesting Latin American view of the economic aspects of this, see Maria Gutiérrez-Haces, 'La política internactional de comercio de Canadá,' in Athanasios Hristoulos, *Canadá: política y gobierno en el siglo XX1* (Mexico City: Porrúa, 2005), 191–230, especially 192–212.

2 This often-misunderstood evolution of North American bilateral defence is well discussed in Richard A. Preston, *The Defence of the Undefended Border: Planning for War in North America, 1867–1939* (Montreal and Kingston: McGill-Queen's University Press, 1977).

3 For a Latin American view of these years and events, see Juan A. Ortega

y Molina, *Destino manifiesto: sus razones históricas y su raíz teológica* (Mexico City: Alianza Editorial Mexicana, 1989).

4 That relationship has stood the test of time and differing values on many issues. See Seymour Martin Lipset, *Continental Divide: The Values and Institutions of the United States and Canada* (New York: Routledge, 1990).

5 For this evolution in relations see Charles P. Stacey, *Canada and the Age of Conflict, 1867–1921* (Toronto: University of Toronto Press, 1977).

6 See Nellis M. Crouse, *The French Struggle for the West Indies, 1665–1713* (New York: Octagon, 1966), and George Nestler Tricoche, *Les milices francaises et anglaises au Canada 1627–1900* (Paris: Lavauzelle, undated).

7 See James Ogelsby, *Gringos from the Far North: Canadian–Latin American Relations 1866–1968* (Toronto: Macmillan, 1976), 10–14.

8 For this see Christopher Armstrong and H.V. Nelles, *Southern Exposure: Canadian Promoters in Latin America and the Caribbean, 1896–1930* (Toronto: University of Toronto Press, 1998).

9 For the story of D'Iberville see Martin Blumenson and James Stokesbury, *Masters of the Art of Command* (Boston: Houghton Mifflin, 1975), 197–204, and Nellis M. Crouse, *Lemoyne d'Iberville: Soldier of New France* (Toronto: Ryerson Press, 1954).

10 Guillermo Calleja Leal et al., *1762 La Habana: la toma de La Habana por los ingleses* (Madrid: Ediciones de Cultura Hispánica, 1999).

11 See Eduardo Torres-Cuevas and Oscar Loyola Vega, *Historia de Cuba, 1492–1898* (Havana: Editorial Pueblo y Educación, 2002), 120–3; David Syrett (ed.), *The Siege and Capture of Havana 1762* (London: Navy Records Office, 1970).

12 For the Mexican dimension of this see the excellent Josefina Zoraida Vázquez, *México frente a Estados Unidos: un ensayo histórico, 1776–1988* (Mexico: Fondo de Cultura Económica, 1989). For an interesting overview of Anglo-American rivalry and the place of the Americas in it, see William A. Dunning, *The British Empire and the United States: A Review of Their Relations during the Century following the Treaty of Ghent* (New York: Charles Scribner, 1914).

13 For a good picture of the pan-American context see Pierre Queuille, *L'Amérique latine, la Doctrine Monroe et le panaméricanisme* (Paris: Payot, 1969). And for the British and Canadian features of some of this situation see Rory Miller, *Britain and Latin America in the 19th and 20th Centuries* (London: Longman, 1993).

14 See the early chapters of Ogelsby, *Gringos from the Far North,* and Peter McKenna, *Canada and the OAS* (Ottawa: Carleton University Press, 1995).

15 For this evolution in Canadian control of a national diplomacy see John

Hilliker, *Le Ministère des affaires extérieures du Canada, 1909–1946* (Quebec: Presss de l'Université Laval, 1990).

16 The United States had only joined the war in April 1917, after its merchant marine was repeatedly the target for German submarine attacks, and had no real deployment of troops until the end of that year. In Latin America, except for Brazil's naval cooperation with the British off Africa, only those countries physically occupied by U.S. forces or under U.S. political influence had followed Washington into the war. For Brazil see Arthur Oscar Saldanha da Gama, *A Marinha do Brasil na Segunda Guerra Mundial* (Rio de Janeiro: Capemi Editora, 1982), and Ricardo Bonalume Neto, *A nossa segunda Guerra: os brasileiros al combate 1942–1945* (Rio de Janeiro: Expressão e Cultura, 1995).

17 Canada wished, for example, for a trilateral Permanent Joint Board of Defence to replace the bilateral one worked out from 1938 to 1940 once Mexico joined the war in early 1942. This was rejected by the U.S. doubtless for reasons yet again related to Ottawa's close links with London and a possible Canadian-Mexican ganging up on the U.S.

18 The author is able to develop this further in his 'Not Even Fools Rushed in: The Canadian Military Experience in Latin America and the Caribbean,' in Bernd Horn (ed.), *Forging a Nation: Perspectives on the Canadian Military Experience*' (St Catharines, ON: Vanwell, 2002), 335–51.

19 For an interesting treatment of this subject see David Leyton-Brown, 'Managing Canada–United States Relations in the Context of Multilateral Alliances,' in Lauren McKinsey and Kim Nossal (eds.), *America's Alliances and Canada–United States Relations: North American Relations in a Changing World* (Toronto: Summerhill, 1988), 162–79.

20 This negative connection is emphasized in Peter McFarlane, *Northern Shadows: Canadians in Central America* (Toronto: Between the Lines, 1989).

21 For the wider story of this support see R.A. Humphreys, *Latin America in the Second World War*, 2 vols. (London: Institute of Latin American Studies, 1981 and 1982).

22 See Canada, *Foreign Policy for Canadians* (Ottawa: Queen's Printer, 1970), and Canada, Department of External Affairs, 'Canada and the World: A Policy Statement by the Prime Minister of Canada, the Right Honourable Pierre Elliott Trudeau, May 29, 1968,' *External Affairs* 20, no. 71.

23 For the handling of the Cuban question in the OAS see F.V. García-Amador, *La cuestión cubana en la OEA y la crisis del sistema interamericano* (Miami: University of Miami Press, 1987).

24 See Brian J.R. Stevenson, *Canada, Latin America, and the New Internationalism: A Foreign Policy Analysis, 1968–1990* (Montreal: McGill-Queen's Uni-

versity Press, 2000), 171–2. Trudeau became particularly upset with what U.S. intelligence was painting as Cuban military intervention, at Moscow's behest, in Africa. This even led Ottawa to suspend bilateral programs of development assistance. It is interesting to note that more recent scholarship has suggested that Trudeau may have been duped on the issue by secretary of state Henry Kissinger. See Piero Gleijeses, *Misiones en conflicto: Habana, Washington y Africa* (Havana: Ciencias Sociales, 2002).

25 For this political context in each of the three countries that were to join the wider NAFTA accords later, see their respective chapters in Ricardo Grinspun and Maxwell Cameron (eds.), *The Political Economy of North American Free Trade* (Montreal and Kingston: McGill-Queen's University Press, 1993).

26 For context here see B.W. Muirhead, *The Development of Postwar Canadian Trade* (Montreal and Kingston: McGill-Queen's University Press, 1992); Richard Lipsey and Patricio Meller (eds.), *Western Hemisphere Trade Integration* (London: Macmillan, 1997); and Teresa Gutiérrez-Haces, *Procesos de integración economica en Mexico y Canada* (Mexico: Porrúa, 2002). For the traditions of the Conservatives in Canada, see Charles Taylor, *Radical Tories: The Conservative Tradition in Canada* (Toronto: Anansi, 1982).

27 See Rodolfo Garrié Faget, *Organismos militares interamericanos* (Buenos Aires: Lapalma, 1968). For a Canadian view see the sections by Canadian diplomats in this author's *Canada and Latin American Security* (Montreal: Meridien Press, 1993).

28 See Jack Child, *The Central American Peace Process 1983–1991* (Boulder, CO: Lynne Rienner, 1992).

29 Interviews with Canadian Forces officers in Honduras and Ottawa, 1990.

30 For an overview of some of these issues see Jack Child, *Geopolitics and Conflict in South America: Quarrels among Neighbors* (New York: Praeger, 1985).

31 See the excellent handling of this impact in most of the country chapters of Adrian English, *The Armed Forces of Latin America* (London: Jane's, 1984).

32 See F.V. García-Amador, *La cuestion cubana en la OEA y la crisis del sistema interamericano* (Miami: University of Miami Press, 1987), 13–99.

33 John M. Kirk and Peter McKenna, *Canada-Cuba Relations: The Other Good Neighbor Policy* (Gainesville: University Press of Florida, 1997), 46–7.

34 For a solid treatment of these matters see James Rochlin, *Discovering the Americas: The Evolution of Canadian Foreign Policy towards Latin America* (Vancouver: University of British Columbia Press, 1994).

35 The author is able to develop this idea further in *What's in It for Us?* (Ottawa: FOCAL Occasional Paper No. 2, 1994).

36 For this see Peter H. Smith, *Drug Policy in the Americas* (Boulder, CO: Westview Press, 1992).

37 On the changing roles for the military in Latin America, see George With-
    ers, Lucila Santos, and Adam Isacson, 'Preach What You Practice: The
    Separation of Military and Police Roles in the Americas' (Washington,
    DC: Washington Office on Latin America, November 2010), 1–32; David
    Pion-Berlin and Harold Trinkunas, 'Democratization, Social Crisis and the
    Impact of Military Domestic Roles in Latin America,' *Journal of Political and
    Military Sociology* 33, no. 1 (Summer 2005): 5–24, and Deborah L. Norden,
    'Redefining Political-Military Relations in Latin America: Issues of the
    New Democratic Era,' *Armed Forces and Society* 22, no. 3 (Spring 1996):
    419–40.
38 See Frederick Nunn's exceptional *The Time of the Generals: Latin American
    Militarism in World Perspective* (Lincoln: University of Nebraska Press,
    1992).
39 Michael Morris and Victor Millán, *Controlling Latin American Conflicts: Ten
    Approaches* (Boulder, CO: Westview Press, 1983).
40 David Mares, 'Equilibrios estratégicos y medidas de confianza mutua en
    América Latina: la historia de una relación ambigua y compleja,' in Fan-
    cisco Rojas Aravena (ed.), *Balance estratégico y medidas de confianza mutua*
    (Santiago de Chile: FLACSO, 1996), 55–86.
41 This is not to say that conservatives and Latin American armed forces
    officers necessarily wished to be connected with a country of such progres-
    sive ideas. See the best-selling (in military circles) Dennis and Gretchen
    Small, *El complot para aniquilar a las fuerzas armadas y a las naciones de
    Iberoamérica* (Mexico City: EIR, 1993).
42 Such ideas were already gaining ground in Latin America. See Juan
    Somavía and José Miguel Insulza (eds.), *Seguridad democrática regional: una
    concepción alternativa* (Caracas: Nueva Sociedad, 1990).
43 Human security was the United Nations proposal – made its own by
    Canada and a few other nations – to put the individual human being at
    the centre of defence policy and thereby broaden the concept of defence to
    consider other areas of security such as economics, health, quality of life,
    and others. See throughout Francisco Rojas and Moufida Cgouha (eds.),
    Human Security, Conflict Prevention and Peace (Santiago: FLACSO, 2004).
44 In October 2009, the Department of Foreign Affairs and International Trade
    launched the Latin America Peacekeeping Capacity Building (LAPCB)
    project with the goal of working 'in partnership with Latin American
    Training Centres ... to enhance their ability to provide civilians, military
    and police support for United Nations (UN) operations.' Latin America
    Peacekeeping Building Project, *Newsletter*, issue 2 (May 2010): 1.
45 This may seem odd given the degree to which the U.S. has an informal but

real relationship of its own with the island's security forces, but it is a fact of U.S. domestic policy that things tend to play out in this way. See Melanie M. Ziegler, *U.S.-Cuban Cooperation: Past, Present and Future* (Gainesville: University Press of Florida, 2007).

46 See throughout G. Pope Atkins, *Latin America in the International Political System* (Boulder, CO: Westview, 1995).

47 A play on President Theodore Roosevelt's dictum that the United States should in this region 'speak softly but carry a big stick.' The author has heard this unfortunate comment from several Latin American diplomats and senior military officers from a variety of countries including Brazil, Chile, and Mexico.

48 See the extensive biography of Raúl Benítez Manaut and especially his 'Seguridad y relaciones cívico-militares en México y América Central: escenarios a inicios del siglo XXI,' in Athansios Hristoulas (ed.), *Las relaciones cívico-militares en el nuevo orden internacional* (Mexico City: Porrúa, 2002).

49 It is also worth emphasizing here that 'security' incorporates the increasingly challenging threats from organized crime and gang-related violence in the Americas. By mid-2012, the Harper government had chosen to allocate only small sums of money to combat a growing problem of crime and violence in Central America.

50 For a good overview of the history of these complications see Ismael Moreno Pino, *Orígenes y evolución del sistema interamericano* (Mexico City: Secretaría de Relaciones Exteriores, 1977).

51 See Piero Gleijeses, *Shattered Hope: The United States and the Guatemalan Revolution 1944–1954* (Princeton: Princeton University Press, 1991).

52 In mid-June 2011, the now-defunct Pearson Peacekeeping Centre in Nova Scotia organized a workshop in Paraguay on the protection of civilians in peacekeeping operations. At the same time, Diane Ablonczy, Minister of Foreign Affairs for the Americas, announced $800,000 to the Centre to assist a number of Latin American countries in training peacekeepers. Tim Harper, 'Canada's Voice Fading in the Americas,' *Toronto Star*, 21 June 2011, A7.

53 In the summer of 2011, one of the more interesting projects involving the Bolivian armed forces sought to incorporate indigenous peoples into the army academy. While the Bolivians have no history of an indigenous officer corps, Canada helped in facilitating the integration of indigenous officer cadets by providing funds for improving their Spanish, mathematical skills, and scientific knowledge. If this program were to continue into the future, it could substantially transform Bolivia's officer corps.

3 Canada's Trade Engagement with the Americas: Swimming with or against the Tide?

RICARDO GRINSPUN AND JENNIFER MILLS[1]

Two events that occurred during Brian Mulroney's government (1984–93) best frame the issues discussed in this chapter. The first was the 1 January 1989 implementation of the Canada-U.S. Free Trade Agreement (CUFTA), initiating an era in which trade agreements became a favourite tool among Canadian economic and foreign policy makers. CUFTA served as a testing platform for business-led trade agreement innovations coming out of Washington and Ottawa – for example, greater access for investors to service industries[2] and other ideas that eventually found their way into the Uruguay Round of multilateral trade negotiations. The second framing event occurred on 13 November of the same year, when Canada signed the Organization of American States (OAS) charter – an act that eventually led to full membership in the organization, a renewed sense of engagement in the hemisphere, and enhanced political relations with nations in the Latin America and Caribbean (LAC) region.[3] But it is Ottawa's consistent prioritization of trade and investment interests over the following two decades that is the focus of this chapter.

Driven by its interests in mining, finance, and other sectors, Ottawa started pressing for a Free Trade Area of the Americas (FTAA) in the 1990s, supported significant neoliberal reforms in the Americas, and promoted investor rights through bilateral treaties and other means. We will discuss our observation that tensions arose when Ottawa continued to support the neoliberal model while simultaneously promoting democratization, poverty reduction, environmental stewardship, and human rights within the OAS and throughout the (LAC) region. According to Manuel Riesco, the model has contributed to economic stagnation, human insecurity, worsening income and wealth distribution, overexploited natural resources, corrupt markets, and the abandonment of national development strategies.[4] In response, a number of so-called 'pink-tide' governments (representing the spectrum of political responses to the neoliberal crisis) are experimenting with participatory political processes and social and economic innovations, some more radical than others. Prime Minister Stephen Harper's renewed push since 2007 for strengthened ties with LAC countries is firmly linked with the trade docket: that is, by joining up with the region's most conservative governments and working as part of an effort to resist hemispheric trends.

In this chapter we will critically analyse this strategy, of which a central element was a free trade agreement with Colombia, a country that is notorious for its human rights abuses. We will argue that Canada's relevancy as a hemispheric actor will require reshuffling trade priorities toward human development, ecological sustainability, and the democratization of trade policy formation in Ottawa. After surveying Canada's efforts for hemispheric integration, we will address the failed effort to use the FTAA to implement a hemispheric regime of investor rights, as well as Canada's subsequent pursuit of these rights through sub-regional and bilateral free trade agreements (e.g., Panama, Peru, and Honduras), the expanding role of bilateral investment treaties, and its weak responses to calls for corporate social responsibility. The chapter ends with some considerations of what an alternative LAC trade approach might look like for Canada.

Hemispheric Integration

The period between Canada's OAS membership and the September 2001 terrorist attacks was marked by intense Canadian involvement with the inter-American system. Canada quickly assumed a leading role in democratic initiatives, most significantly through the creation of the OAS Unit for the Promotion of Democracy in 1991 and ongoing efforts to promote human rights, human security, and clean electoral processes (see chapter by Max Cameron and Jason Tockman). In the area of integration, Canada's reputation was bolstered by the enthusiastic support of Canadian leaders for the FTAA and their visibility during various hemispheric summits. In 1998, Prime Minister Jean Chrétien led a 'Team Canada' economic mission to Mexico, Brazil, Argentina, and Chile, a trip that included all of the country's provincial premiers and dozens of business representatives. Canada hosted several high-profile inter-American events at the end of the decade, including the Pan American Games in Winnipeg (summer 1999), the Toronto FTAA Trade Ministerial (November 1999), the OAS General Assembly in Windsor (June 2000), and most importantly, the Quebec City Summit of the Americas (April 2001).

By the beginning of the new millennium, Ottawa had become a champion of hemispheric integration, giving strong support to the four pillars (two political and two economic) of that process: (1) the presidential Summit of the Americas, held once every four years (or less), and the institutional mechanisms required to enact them; (2) the revitalization of the OAS as the hemisphere's premier political forum; (3) increased economic and financial integration in the Americas, including neoliberal convergence in economic and social policies; and (4) a process for establishing a hemispheric trade treaty and a network of bilateral and sub-regional trade arrangements based on the NAFTA model. Several 'Washington Consensus' institutions played important roles in shaping the four pillars, and in most cases Ottawa appeared to fit within the consensus. In addition to the OAS, these institutions included: the White House and government agencies such as the Office of the U.S. Trade Representative, the State Department, and the Pentagon; Congress; international financial institutions such as the World Bank, the Inter-American Development Bank, and the International Monetary Fund; business lobbies such as the U.S. Chamber of Commerce; and think tanks such as the Heritage Foundation and the American Enterprise Institute.

Although the hemispheric integration discourse of democracy, human rights, and shared prosperity coming from Ottawa and other capitals was appealing, the political will to enact anything that transcended the neoliberal prescription was limited from the start, leading to frustrations among both civil society stakeholders and a number of less influential governments. The growing gap between rhetoric and reality was very clear during the 1994 Miami Summit, and especially at the 1998 Santiago Summit, in which Canada played a leading role. Whereas the 1998 declaration focused on education, strengthening democracy, and promoting social justice, most political energy was focused on launching FTAA negotiations – a situation that sceptics perceived as largely elite-driven, characterized by an absence of meaningful participation, and lacking actual mechanisms for democratic accountability.

Plans for an FTAA were first outlined by President Bill Clinton at the 1994 summit, attended by the leaders of all countries in the hemisphere except for Cuba. Formal negotiations were launched by the leaders of those same thirty-four countries at the Santiago summit. The Canadian government described the agreement as complementary to the stated democratic, human rights, and social and economic cooperation goals of the summit process,[5] but it was generally acknowledged that the true objectives were to push for hemispheric economic integration. There was a dispute over whether economic integration would bring shared growth and sustainable development, or something else entirely. Opponents such as Public Citizen expressed their fears that the FTAA 'was intended to be the most far-reaching trade agreement in history ... [and would] create a new trade powerhouse with sweeping new authority over the Americas.'[6] At an alternative Peoples' Summit, opponents explained their opposition to the FTAA, claiming that this authority would reinforce a model that does the following:

> favors a select few, deteriorates labour conditions, accelerates migration, [and brings about] the destruction of indigenous communities, the deterioration of the environment, the privatization of social security and education, [and] the implementation of laws which protect corporations rather than citizens, as in the case of intellectual property.[7]

The clash of these two world views reached a climax during the Third Summit of the Americas, held in Quebec City in April 2001. Heads of state, business executives, and police huddled behind a four-kilometre-long and three-metre-high fence, and thousands of protesters (including those participating in a Peoples' Summit) demonstrated, marched, and were tear-gassed outside the security perimeter. Although Prime Minister Jean Chrétien tried to focus media attention on the Inter-American Democratic Charter that emerged from the meeting (meant to strengthen democratic institutions), the media instead reported on the leaders' inability to finalize the FTAA.[8] Emboldened by the successful mobilization in Quebec, national and cross-border anti-FTAA coalitions became stronger and, in several countries, politically influential.

Interest in the FTAA waned in light of the 2000 re-election of Venezuelan president Hugo Chávez, the January 2003 inauguration of Brazil's president Luiz Inácio da Silva (or Lula), and the September 2001 attacks in the United States. Under pressure from several countries (especially Brazil) and in an effort to save face, the United States and Canada agreed at the November 2003 Miami FTAA ministerial meeting (the last one to be held) to dramatically reduce the scope of the agreement (but in the end this did not help),[9] since formal FTAA negotiations have been officially suspended since February 2004 (and are largely seen as dead by most of the region). Refusing to heed the writing on the wall, the Canadian government led an effort to revive FTAA talks during the November 2005 Summit of the Americas in Mar del Plata, Argentina, but failed to achieve a consensus.[10] As late as June 2006, then minister of foreign affairs Peter MacKay still expressed a commitment to finalize the FTAA,[11] and the government's website continues to do so now.[12]

FTAA and Investor Rights

Who is behind Ottawa's strong advocacy for an FTAA? Out of the spotlight, hemispheric policy has been heavily influenced by large corporate interests, especially leaders of Canada's largest multinational corporations (many foreign-owned) who sit on the Canadian Council of Chief Executives (CCCE), a lobby that has been influential with both Liberal and Conservative governments.[13] To be sure, Canada is one of the top three investors in Latin America and the Caribbean, and therefore the stakes are high for Canadian corporations.[14] Right-leaning think tanks such as the C.D. Howe Institute in Toronto have provided analytical support, while corporate-owned media such as the *Globe and Mail* have worked to mobilize decision makers, following well-rehearsed scripts developed during CUFTA and NAFTA negotiations. Lobbyists representing these business interests are pushing for deeper corporate penetration in the hemisphere via a favourable investment regime, free trade, financial liberalization, flexible labour markets, the privatization of state enterprises, and market deregulation. However, rather than achieving these goals through discrete and reversible measures, their intent appears to be to establish an international regulatory regime that locks in place the last two decades of structural adjustment.[15] With NAFTA already in place in North America, other free trade agreements represent an ideal medium for extending this supranational constitution southward,[16] thus creating opportunities for Canadian business interests in such areas as infrastructure, electric power, water and waste management, ICT, oil and gas, and mining.[17]

A key element of Ottawa's pursuit of trade treaties is establishing a legal regime of rights for investors – with the purpose of increasing investor wealth without considering human or ecological costs. The targeting of sundry tariff and non-tariff barriers to trade, the traditional mainstay of trade negotiations, have been demoted by corporate interests in favour of using trade rules to challenge government activities that hold the potential for limiting returns on business investments. These include public ownership, social programs, industrial policies, and some forms of subsidies. NAFTA represents a new threshold in the use of trade treaties to expand and protect investor rights, both foreign and domestic.[18] An important example is NAFTA's Chapter 11, which gives private corporations important new rights and powers, including the power to sue foreign governments for actions that impinge on actual or potential profits. This 'regulatory expropriation' concept significantly expands on traditional descriptions of expropriation – the actual seizure of physical assets by a state. It also has implications for defining government regulation, since a wide range of measures and laws enacted for public policy purposes may be reinterpreted as impinging on investor rights and profitability – for example, government efforts to reduce environmental damage caused by mining.

Another major issue of concern for the emerging global investment regime is the prohibition of performance requirements – a precedent set under the NAFTA.[19] Performance requirements, then, are imposed by governments on foreign investors to support policy goals such as local purchasing and contracting. For many years, these stipulations have been used in Chile to address such issues as export performance, local content in the automotive industry, incentives for high technology industrial investment, capital control, and environmental protection.[20] Over the last decade and a half, some of these measures have been abolished, in large part due to external pressures. For example, during their FTA negotiations with Chile, Canada successfully pressured the government in Santiago to reduce its space to apply capital controls.[21]

As soon as NAFTA negotiations ended in 1992, the U.S. Chamber of Commerce in Washington, the CCCE in Ottawa, and supportive governments launched a systematic effort to globalize investment rules beyond the three NAFTA countries. The Organisation for Economic Co-operation and Development (OECD), a group representing the world's wealthiest countries, was chosen as a friendly arena for such negotiations. In 1995, a stronger set of NAFTA Chapter 11 rights was at the centre of a secretly negotiated but never finalized OECD Multilateral Agreement on Investment (MAI).[22] A vigorous public backlash in several countries occurred when Canadian activists leaked draft MAI documents in 1997; one year later, France called off all MAI negotiations. But the search for a forum to pursue new investor rights continued:

central to the proposed World Trade Organization (WTO) negotiations that failed in Seattle in 1999 was a strengthened agreement on Trade-Related Investment Measures (TRIMS). As the TRIMS option stalled, North American negotiators and lobbyists redirected their efforts toward securing strong investor rights in the FTAA and an expanded General Agreement on Trade in Services (GATS) at the WTO.

Calling the FTAA a 'dangerous NAFTA-GATS hybrid,' critics described it as a particularly serious threat because it embodied the worst features of both.[23] They were concerned about its scope and intrusiveness, which was evident in the nine negotiation topics established in 1998: market access, investment, services, government procurement, dispute settlement, agriculture, intellectual property rights, competition policy, and subsidies, anti-dumping and countervailing duties. A special group was created to address the concerns of smaller economies, and another (mostly a public relations exercise) the concerns of civil society. FTAA negotiations would be managed at the highest level, with trade ministers meeting annually to make the most important decisions, and with technical support provided by a tripartite committee consisting of the Inter-American Development Bank (IDB), the OAS, and the United Nations Economic Commission for Latin America and the Caribbean (ECLAC). According to negotiation documents, Ottawa pushed for an FTAA investment chapter that would include broad provisions for investor-state dispute settlement, expropriation and compensation, minimum standard of treatment,[24] and prohibitions on performance requirements. The FTAA was also envisioned by Ottawa as going beyond NAFTA and even GATS in terms of stronger measures protecting investments in services.[25] Taken together, these measures represent severe restrictions on the policy space required by LAC governments to strengthen their public sectors and to pursue autonomous developmental goals.[26]

Why is the inclusion of GATS-type measures in the FTAA a concern? The purpose behind GATS, which emerged from the 1994 Uruguay Round of agreements, is to force the progressive opening to international investment and the liberalization of service industries. Critics have warned that public service measures such as those proposed for FTAA inclusion hold potentially devastating effects in terms of the ability of governments to meet the needs of their poorest and most powerless citizens.[27] Rather than addressing public services as basic necessities, GATS treats them as missed commercial opportunities, unfair competition, or entry barriers for foreign services and suppliers. The measures would also curtail the regulatory and public policy-making powers of domestic governments, making it possible for transnational corporations and foreign governments to attack general, non-discriminatory public interest regulations such as health and safety standards as 'unnecessary' or 'burdensome.' There is strong concern that such rules would allow foreign investors to privatize and commercialize public services such as education and health care, and to further deregulate sectors such as telecommunications, energy, and transport. For example, water supplies in developing countries have become major targets for investment during the last decade. The protests in Cochabamba, Bolivia following the 1999 sale of the water utility to an international consortium made world headlines, leading eventually to a reversal of the privatization effort.[28]

Free Trade Agreements

In addition to the collapse of FTAA negotiations, 2003 witnessed a major setback during the WTO's Doha Round of multilateral negotiations in Cancun, Mexico. The trade and investment liberalization agenda pushed by the American and Canadian governments met with strong resistance from the economic powerhouses of Brazil, China, and India, among others. Consequently, the Canadian government, closely attuned to the needs of Washington during the post-9/11 period, shifted its focus to sub-regional and bilateral FTAs, which provided avenues for getting around failed multilateral forums. Since coming to power in 2006, the Harper government has signed agreements with the European Free Trade Association (EFTA), Peru, Panama, Colombia, Jordan, and Honduras, and is actively negotiating with several other countries and entities.[29] Trade agreements with Latin American countries are a primary component of Ottawa's renewed engagement in the LAC region, announced in July of 2007.[30]

Canada's first bilateral free trade agreement in Latin America, with Chile, came into force in 1997. As with subsequent FTAs (including Costa Rica), the agreement was based on the NAFTA model, containing schedules for removing tariffs on goods and services and eliminating import and export restrictions. The Chilean agreement (and others like it) prohibits performance requirements and ensures that investors and exporters from the partner countries operate under the same conditions as nationals, except in sectors that are explicitly excluded. Many bilateral FTAs contain sections that address investment concerns such as prohibiting expropriation without compensation. Similar to NAFTA's Chapter 11, these bilateral agreements establish investor-state dispute mechanisms through which aggrieved third parties can sue states for monetary compensation. Regarding the Canada-Chile FTA, Sebastian Herreros notes that in terms of investment, it goes well beyond WTO requirements.[31] While the financial sector was excluded in the original agreement, negotiations completed in 2007, and currently under legal review by both governments, will enhance market access in terms of cross-border financial services.[32] But it is instructive to note that a separate FTA with the European Free Trade Association has already raised problems for Chile in terms of investor-state dispute mechanisms and liberalization in public service industries. After the government attempted to decrease foreign market share in the telecommunications sector, Spanish companies threatened to retract their investments and to sue the Chilean government in accordance with that agreement.[33]

Recently signed FTAs with Peru, Colombia, and Honduras, which form the centrepiece of the Harper government's trade policy in the region, have generated considerable debate. The first two came out of stalled negotiations with the Andean Community, which proved more difficult to complete than bilateral agreements. Legislation implementing the Canada-Peru FTA was tabled in the House of Commons on 26 March 2009. On 6 June, a violent conflict broke out in Bagua in northern Peru between police and indigenous Peruvians protesting legislative changes (that were allegedly required by the U.S.-Peru FTA) and widely interpreted as violating their land rights. The conflict resulted in the resignations of top Peruvian officials and the repeal of legislative changes by the Peruvian Congress.[34] Given this crisis, Canadian advocacy groups urged Canadian senators to reject legislation for the Canada-Peru FTA.[35] Nevertheless, the Senate passed the bill within days of the protest, and the Canada-Peru FTA went into effect on 1 August 2009.

The Canada-Colombia FTA, introduced in the House of Commons on the same day as the Peruvian agreement, was set to receive royal assent before the end of 2010. Numerous human rights, labour, and citizens' organizations mobilized against the FTA, and the New Democratic and Bloc Québécois parties declared their opposition and successfully delayed passage of the bill for over a year, so the agreement entered into force only in August 2011.[36] Even though the pact includes language on human rights and labour, the strongest concern expressed by

opponents is the ongoing climate of violence in Colombia that threatens unions, indigenous peoples, and other opposition groups. The
Harper government argues that security in that country has improved
over the last decade,[37] despite strong evidence indicating an increase
in the number of trade unionists killed in 2008,[38] and the internal displacement of 3–4 million Colombians.[39] In 2008, the multi-party Standing Committee on International Trade released a report recommending
that an independent human rights impact assessment be carried out
before any FTA with Colombia is signed,[40] but the Harper government
signed the FTA just days before the report was released, and no such
assessment has been performed.

Advocacy groups take issue with the text of the Colombia FTA and
are worried the agreement could worsen the human rights situation
in that country. Three areas of particular concern are labour rights, the
environment, and corporate social responsibility. The Harper government describes the labour provisions in the Colombia and Peru FTAs
as the strongest found in any Canadian FTA[41] and claims that unlike
previous FTAs, these agreements list specific labour rights that both
parties are obligated to protect. However, the Canadian Labour Congress (CLC) notes that the agreement lacks strong provisions in terms
of human rights accountability – specifically, that complaints are to be
resolved by diplomats, and individuals cannot request the intervention of an independent review panel.[42] According to this FTA, a state
signatory may be forced to pay fines to a fund for labour initiatives, but
the limit of the maximum fine is minuscule compared to the potential
amount of money involved in investor-state disputes. Steven Shrybman expresses similar concerns regarding environmental issues, arguing that the side agreement in this area is unenforceable, and that the
agreement has no minimum standards for environmental protection –
unlike provisions for investor rights.[43] Furthermore, Shrybman argues
that since governments can be held accountable for not fulfilling stated
environmental obligations, the agreement might actually discourage
governments from making any substantial environmental commitments in this area.

A third area of concern is the combination of excessive investor rights
but an absence of any enforceable corporate social responsibility mechanism. The Harper government and the CCCE are touting the corporate
social responsibility provisions in the FTA as strong,[44] yet it only con-
tains a vague call for voluntary compliance with recognized standards.
Scott Sinclair calls this insufficient in light of the strong economic inter-

ests of investors, who may benefit at times from human rights abuses.[45] Regarding the agreement's investor-state dispute settlement mechanism, Sinclair notes that investors generally initiate more disputes than states, and the fear of drawn-out confrontations can influence states to relax or overturn regulations established in the public interest.

Still, trade negotiations continue with other Latin American countries. The Harper government completed negotiations for an FTA with Panama in August of 2009, but opposition parties in Canada have raised strong concerns about Panama's status as a tax haven; a U.S.-Panama FTA has been stalled for similar reasons.[46] The March 2010 negotiations with the Central American Four (El Salvador, Guatemala, Honduras, and Nicaragua) were the second held since 2004; in 2002 the Canadian government of Jean Chrétien signed an FTA with Costa Rica (and where both countries began talks in August 2010 to enhance the trade pact).[47] The political environments in those countries have changed greatly since leftist parties came to power in Nicaragua and El Salvador in 2007 and 2009, respectively. Additionally, the completion of the Dominican Republic–Central America–United States Free Trade Agreement (CAFTA-DR) may have dampened interest in a similar agreement with Canada, given the ongoing debate over the benefits of the U.S. agreement and the lesser role of Canada in the isthmus.

Facing stalled negotiations for a Canada–Central America Four (CA4) free trade agreement, Canada decided in late 2010 to focus its energies on crafting a bilateral deal with Honduras.[48] A keystone of Stephen Harper's August 2011 trip to four Latin American countries to bolster his Americas Strategy, which included Brazil, Colombia, Honduras and Costa Rica, was the signing of a free trade agreement with this impoverished Central American nation. Considering important Canadian mining and other interests in the country, and coinciding with the Canada-Colombia FTA coming into force during the same week, the new agreement flared up criticisms that 'Canada backs profits, not human rights'[49] in the region. Human Rights Watch reports that President Porfirio Lobo, who signed the FTA with Harper, has failed 'to hold accountable those responsible for widespread human rights violations committed by the de facto government installed after the [June 2009 military] coup.'[50] Evidence that serious human rights violations continue even under the Lobo government have not deterred Canada from deepening political and economic ties[51] or from leading the effort to steer the country back into the OAS fold in June 2011.[52]

Why Bilateralism?

This all leads to a critical question: Why is the Canadian government pursuing the bilateral option in Latin America? As mentioned, if successful with some countries, this option may help revive continent- or hemisphere-wide free trade projects or the stalled Doha Round of global trade negotiations. But these agreements have detractors all along the political spectrum – including supporters of pure multilateralism who criticize FTAs because they entail trade diversion, trigger political clashes between groups inside and outside individual agreements, and undermine the WTO.[53] However, several factors push aside these concerns, thus making bilateral agreements the preferred option in both Washington and Ottawa.

Note that the Canadian government is party to multilateral and hemispheric negotiations that have made no progress for a decade, and asymmetrical bilateral negotiations are viewed as giving Canada better leverage at the expense of economically weaker trading partners. If agreements with several countries prove successful, they can serve as starting points for future expansion, since southern governments that make commitments in the form of bilateral FTAs have less reason to oppose multilateral and regional arrangements requiring similar commitments. As Gauri Sreenivasan observes, issues generally contested by southern trading partners in multilateral negotiations are often quietly included in bilateral agreements.[54]

Another reason, of course, is protecting the assets of Canadian businesses: while actual trade in goods with Colombia and Panama, among others, is relatively minor, the stock of Canadian investments in Colombia (primarily in extractive industries) is estimated at CAD$3 billion.[55] In Honduras, Canada is the second-largest foreign investor, focused on mining, apparel, and manufacturing.[56] Still, Canadian business leaders, who 'have strongly encouraged multilateral trade liberalization as well as bilateral and regional economic agreements,' strongly support the Colombia FTA.[57] In 2007, Glen Hodgson from the Conference Board of Canada complained that Ottawa was involved in only 'three very small bilateral deals, while the rest of the world is out negotiating like crazy ... It's about time Canada really got into the game.'[58] His impatient words exemplify the 'competitive liberalization'[59] motive among the current group of Canadian policy makers – that is, the belief that 'our major competitors in international markets are furiously negotiating free trade agreements,' and that the country will suffer from passivity and inactivity.'[60] In a similar manner, the CCCE's David Stewart-Patterson raised concerns over the potential of a revived U.S.-Colombia FTA being enacted prior to passage of the Colombian bill by the Canadian Parliament, arguing then that 'implementing the Canada-Colombia agreement quickly represents an opportunity for Canada to get out in front of our international competitors.'[61]

Not surprisingly, the zeal of business advocates is designed, in part, to fortify Canada's existing investment stake in the region and to open new doors for trade expansion. By 2008, Canadian minerals and metals companies had an accumulated stock of $67 billion in direct investment abroad, mainly in the U.S. and Latin America.[62] The Mining Association of Canada is, moreover, lobbying in support of FTAs and investment treaties as a means of protecting their foreign investments. In addition to pointing out that bilateral pacts can be negotiated faster than multilateral deals, mining advocates also argue that such agreements are more likely to contain 'high octane' provisions such as investment rules that protect Canadian assets. Within the WTO's consensus decision-making regime, such terms would be impossible.[63]

The Colombian case also spotlights powerful political considerations at play. David Emerson, the former minister of international trade in the Harper government, has described the importance of the Canada-Colombia FTA as 'far more than economics. It's about lending Canada's support to social and political progress.'[64] The approval of the agreement boosts the Colombian government's legitimacy in the international community, which has eroded over the years due to scandals and ongoing internal violence. The Colombian ambassador to Canada, Jaime Duarte, acknowledged that the greatest benefit of such an agreement would be the signal that it sends to foreign investors and tourists.[65] That explains why Colombian president Álvaro Uribe visited Canada in June 2009 to defend the FTA before the International Trade Committee in the House of Commons.[66]

Similar arguments have been made in Washington – and this point has not been lost on officialdom in Ottawa. For the last two decades, the U.S. has pursued bilateral FTAs to complement and cajole progress at the ministerial level, with impetus provided by the failures in WTO and FTAA negotiations earlier in the decade.[67] In making the case for bilateral FTAs, Jeffrey Schott argues that standing on the sidelines while countries such as Canada pursue such agreements can actually support U.S. trade interests 'if they promote broad-based economic and political reforms in the partner countries and contribute to stronger and more sustainable growth in the developing countries.' On the other hand, such agreements exclude U.S. businesses from immediate economic benefits, and have the potential for establishing precedents that Washington will reject during other trade negotiations.[68] An example of this potential is found in the 1997 Chile-Canada FTA, which prohibited the use of anti-dumping laws with respect to bilateral trade – laws that are often used by U.S. administrations.[69] Schott concludes that the United States should be part of the action if it wants to influence the international trade agenda. Also, here political considerations carry weight. Note Washington's use of bilateral options to isolate Brazil over its long-standing resistance to key aspects of the FTAA – pushing the U.S. to move to establish trade accords with most Latin American countries, excluding those in Mercosur. In the case of U.S. trade arrangements with Central American nations and the Dominican Republic, the two stated motivations are controlling drug trafficking and promoting stability and democracy.[70]

Additionally, the Canadian trade/investment strategy should be analysed in the context of post-9/11 relations with the United States. The tendency in Ottawa to adopt policies and positions based on the requirements of Washington has intensified since 9/11, thus diminishing Canadian commitments to other goals.[71] Efforts aimed at advancing North American integration beyond the existing NAFTA – such as the plan to establish a Security and Prosperity Partnership in North America during the second George W. Bush administration – have framed Ottawa's engagement with LAC countries. These bilateral dynamics are arguably shaping Canada's push for FTAs in Latin America. According to Nicola Phillips, when the U.S. began negotiating more bilateral agreements, the Canadian government followed suit in order to retain some influence over American integration in the region (and to pre-empt Canadian commercial interests from being frozen out).[72] By negotiating FTAs with Washington's allies and right-wing governments, Ottawa may be able to discourage those states from making political alliances that oppose its agenda, while still supporting ongoing U.S. policies in the hemisphere.

Bilateral Investment Treaties

Bilateral investment treaties (BITs) represent a new and expanding arena of action for Canada. They are easier to negotiate because they are narrowly focused on one aspect (investment) and are more politically palatable because they are ignored by the corporate media, and therefore largely passed under the radar of the general public. The Canadian version of a BIT is called a Foreign Investment Promotion and Protection Agreement (FIPA). By mid-2012, Canada had twenty-six FIPAs in force, including nine with LAC countries: Argentina, Trinidad and Tobago, Barbados, Ecuador, Venezuela, Panama, Uruguay, Costa Rica, and Peru (in chronological order).[73] Canadian FIPAs represent a very small percentage of the 2,676 international BITs in effect at the end of 2008.[74] According to government senior policy adviser Stuart Carre, the Harper government intends to double the number of FIPAs over the next five years.[75]

For the most part, FIPAs are designed to protect the rights of investors and to secure investment liberalization.[76] The Canadian model typically includes the following provisions: profit repatriation, treatment equal to that given to local or other foreign investors, minimum protection standards, access to international arbitration, and guaranteed compensation in cases of expropriation.[77] But in terms of arbitration, FIPA provisions are open to interpretation – for example, Luke Eric Peterson describes as unclear the meaning of 'fair and equitable treatment,' as well as what constitutes a reasonable amount of information that governments must provide to investors in order to create predictable environments.[78]

Canadian and American BITs are often discussed together due to their similarities in content and adherence to current trends. The Canadian FIPA model was modified in 2003 to reflect lessons learned during previous arbitration proceedings. Both Canadian and U.S. models now contain more precise language on standards of protection and expropriation, and allow for greater transparency in dispute settlement proceedings. Many countries (including Canada) are now stating in their BITs that investment protection must not be pursued at the expense of other public concerns such as health and the environment;[79] however, similar clauses in WTO agreements have been largely ineffectual.[80] Furthermore, by including all sectors that are not explicitly excluded, North American FIPA models cover far more sectors than GATS and other multilateral agreements,[81] thus providing greater market access for foreign investors. Canada is, therefore, mimicking the U.S. practice of creating investment treaties that are increasingly restrictive in terms of public policy space.

A major component of FIPAs is access to international arbitration. Investors can petition for compensation from states based on claims that governments have not fulfilled their treaty obligations. Such disputes can arise when governments attempt to nationalize industries, change regulatory regimes, or increase taxes. According to UNCTAD, 317 known treaty-based claims had been filed internationally by the end of 2008.[82] The range of new cases filed annually (overwhelmingly by investors from developed countries) since 2002 is 28 to 48; since public disclosure is not required, the actual number of claims is unknown. The two most commonly used avenues for arbitration are the World Bank's International Centre for Settlement of Investment Disputes (ICSID) and the United Nations Commission on International Trade Law (UNCITRAL). The ICSID is the only facility specifically created to deal with investment arbitration; unlike UNCITRAL, though, it publishes a list of ongoing cases.[83] Under both scenarios, each party typically chooses one arbitrator, and a third is selected by consensus or by a supervisory body.[84] However, the absence of a system of precedence and the generally vague language of BITs suggests that arbitration outcomes are influenced by the backgrounds of the arbiters and their interpretations of the agreements themselves.[85] This lack of transparency can impair the ability of affected communities to represent their interests, and of governments to anticipate the acceptability of policy changes in terms of arbitration.

The ongoing dispute between the Canadian-owned Pacific Rim mining company and the government of El Salvador is a good illustration of the difficulties inherent to protecting both the public interest and the interests of investors. Pacific Rim initiated ICSID arbitration proceedings against El Salvador on 30 April 2009, claiming that its rights had been violated by the government's refusal to issue mining permits. The government, for its part, claimed that it had stopped issuing permits due to growing public health and environmental concerns. Responding to pressure from anti-mining activist groups, the Salvadoran opposition at that time (currently the ruling party) introduced ongoing legislation to ban precious metal mining.[86]

It is noteworthy that Pacific Rim is seeking damages through the CAFTA-DR agreement, to which Canada is not a party; the company is actually taking advantage of the fact that it has a subsidiary in Nevada.[87] As Peterson has observed, it is common and rational for companies to 'shop' around for the best treaty protection.[88] Another example is the aforementioned case of the international consortium headed by U.S.-based Bechtel Corporation that purchased Cochabamba's water utility company in Bolivia. Apparently, the consortium, which was originally registered in the Cayman Islands (which has no investment treaty with

Bolivia), moved its registration to the Netherlands (which does have one) soon after the Cochabamba contract was signed. So when the contract was cancelled, the consortium filed an ICSID complaint against the Bolivian government.[89] While the large number and decentralized nature of BITs makes shopping around a viable option for corporations, those same qualities sharply reduce the ability of governments to exert control over foreign investors. These cases raise another issue: to what extent do investment protection agreements limit the policy space of governments? Since many investment treaties involve governments with underdeveloped legal regimes capable of protecting human rights or fragile natural environments, BITs effectively create barriers for future governments wanting to raise standards that might interfere with investor rights.

Corporate Social Responsibility

Structural adjustment programs and broader neoliberal policies are being used to shape 'market-friendly' regulatory frameworks in many LAC countries. In the case of mineral extraction, this includes legislation privatizing state-owned mining, liberalizing mining and investment regulations, providing tax and capital repatriation incentives, changing water codes, militarizing protection for isolated mining sites, and loosening environmental and labour standards – all aimed at attracting foreign investment and increasing profit margins for mining corporations.[90] These changes are being locked in place via new forms of 'trade conditionality' embedded in FTAs and BITs, thereby removing democratic decision-making powers from local citizens and governments at different levels.[91] The trade agreements place investors' interests above the livelihoods and well-being of affected Chilean or Peruvian communities, and tensions can mount when companies go through with mining activities that communities resist or reject, occasionally leading to violent confrontations.[92] In November 2009, a well-known community and anti-mining activist in Chiapas, Mexico, Mariano Abarca Roblero, was murdered. A member of the Chiomuselo community, he had suffered threats, imprisonment, and violence due to his opposition to the activities of the Calgary-based Blackfire Exploration Ltd.[93] Struggles for ownership and control over natural resources are fuelling other local conflicts in parts of the Andean region and Central America, and there is mounting evidence on the negative impacts of extractive activities on local populations.[94]

In many instances, the Canadian government and corporations are responding to such evidence by creating corporate social responsibility (CSR) norms. National elected officials can thereby claim that they are responding to public pressure to rein in corporate abuses, protect public health and safety, and enforce laws and human rights commitments among Canadian corporations. Whether such responses are sufficiently forceful and indicative of real change in policy remains a question. Steps taken by the Harper government to promote CSR and to publicize industry efforts include hiring an Extractive Sector Corporate Social Responsibility Counsellor and creating a Centre of Excellence to compile information on CSR-related practices.[95] However, these efforts were condemned from the start by Canadian advocacy organizations for ignoring recommendations from government-sponsored national roundtables on extractive industries. Indeed, the National Roundtables on Corporate Social Responsibility held a meeting in 2006 to discuss issues of CSR in the mining, oil, and gas sectors and their operations in developing countries.[96] The Mining Association of Canada tried to play both sides, first signing off on the roundtable recommendations and later on expressing support for the government's CSR efforts.[97]

One recommendation of the National Roundtables was to create an independent CSR ombudsman position, but the counsellor appointed by the Harper government would not have the power to investigate cases without permission from all parties – including the corporation accused of committing human rights abuses. Other recommendations include establishing CSR standards and reporting obligations for Canadian corporations, creating human rights guidelines, and withholding government services in response to the most serious instances of non-compliance.[98] Calling the government's response 'thoroughly disappointing,' MiningWatch Canada has argued that Ottawa was heavily influenced by lobbyists from mining corporations.[99] And a Philippines-based group representing indigenous peoples sent a letter to Prime Minister Harper stating that its CSR strategy 'falls far short of upholding Canada's international commitments on human rights, indigenous peoples, and the environment,' and 'will do little to stop abuses by Canadian extractive companies from continuing unabated and unpunished.'[100] Overall, the Canadian government is taking a voluntary approach to CSR, letting corporations project images of sustainable and ethical mining without having to actually abide by enforceable standards. Communities in foreign countries that are adversely affected by Canadian corporate mining practices have no clear legal recourse. Given these circumstances, it is unlikely that serious malpractice accusations against Canadian corporations will ever be adequately addressed.

Conclusion

During the past two decades, Canada's engagement with the Americas has been marked by multiple contradictions. Positive contributions have been made in the areas of democratization, development, and human rights, but the pursuit of trade agreements that favour the rights of investors has undermined those advancements. With few exceptions,[101] Ottawa has marched in lockstep with Washington and supported North American corporate interests – a trend that intensified after the 9/11 attacks. The Harper government's subtle support for a military-installed government in Honduras,[102] its discontinuation of funding for established human rights organizations,[103] and its tacit support for a Colombian regime tainted by human rights abuses all suggest that its stated priorities of 'strengthen[ing] democratic institutions' and 'promoting human rights'[104] in the LAC region are more rhetoric than reality. It appears that the May 2011 federal election victory securing a majority Conservative government has served to reinforce these policies, as signalled by Harper's August 2011 trip to Latin America, which included bolstering Canadian business interests in Brazil, marking the entry into force of the Canada-Colombia FTA with a Bogota visit, and an announcement of the Canada-Honduras FTA in San Pedro Sula.

Several new LAC governments are currently responding to failed neoliberal policies and their attendant problems – including growing economic disparities, increasing social tensions, worsening human security, and environmental deterioration. In addition, emerging social movements campaigning for social participation and economic accountability, and new forms of economic relations are being considered and enacted via the Bolivarian Alternative for the Americas (ALBA) – an incipient effort toward regional integration based on 'a new vision of social welfare and equity'[105] rather than trade liberalization and foreign investment protection. Proposed by Venezuelan president Hugo Chávez in 2001 as an alternative to the U.S. and Canadian-promoted FTAA, ALBA member states now include Cuba, Bolivia, Nicaragua, Dominica, Honduras,[106] Ecuador, St Vincent and the Grenadines, Antigua, and Barbuda.[107] It is too early to assess ALBA's prospects and potential impacts, especially given its reliance on Venezuela and the effects of the current economic crisis on that country's oil-backed finances. Nevertheless, ALBA's guiding principle is worthy of note: subordinating trade and investment rules in favour of a state-centred development strategy that supports the efforts of participating governments to meet the needs of their respective populations.[108] On the political front, the Latin American desire for autonomy from its northern neighbours was strikingly clear when the Latin American and Caribbean Community of States was established in February 2010 – where no invitations were extended to either the United States or Canada. It is no surprise that the Canadian government is doing its best to ignore these developments. But it may wish to rethink that position as 2012 comes to a close.

Would it not be better for Ottawa to participate in a different set of hemispheric relationships, based on trade and investment rules that advance a people-centred agenda? The answer must be strongly affirmative if we take Canada's neighbourly responsibilities seriously, acknowledge its formal international commitments to advancing human rights, and push for it to become a meaningful and credible player in the Americas. This would require seeking mutual benefits for the peoples of Canada and the countries of Latin America, rather than exploiting an already challenging socio-economic situation in order to impose an investor's bill of rights via trade and investment agreements.

Envisioning a new agenda is not difficult to contemplate, but mustering the political will to implement it often is. Canadian officials in Ottawa should no longer pursue trade agreements modelled after NAFTA, investment agreements replicating NAFTA's Chapter 11, or FTAA-type continental accords. An alternative economic cooperation agreement would have clearly worded protections for human rights, as well as for the policy space national governments require to pursue human development, corporate accountability, ecological sustainability, and democratic governance goals. Performance requirement prohibitions and regulatory expropriation clauses that prevent governments from regulating foreign investments would be eliminated. Investor-state lawsuit mechanisms and other rules that prioritize investor rights over labour, health, environmental, and community rights would also be removed, as would intellectual property protections that unfairly favour northern patents over indigenous knowledge.

Official Ottawa should also remember that health, safety, and environmental standards would no longer be categorized as trade barriers, but as government policies enacted to protect their citizens from social and physical harm. Market access provisions must be adjusted so as to fit local development needs, such as those of impoverished rural economies, rather than serving agricultural and other corporate interests. Furthermore, service industry provisions would acknowledge that education, health care, clean water, electricity, and pensions are essential services rather than profit-making opportunities. Finally, by making dispute settlement mechanisms transparent and participatory, and by democratizing its trade policies, Ottawa can send a message that hemispheric prosperity and fairness are the responsibility of all Canadians, and not just business elites.

NOTES

1 The authors would like to acknowledge editorial support from Jon Lindemann. This chapter draws in part on earlier work by one of the authors in Yasmine Shamsie and Ricardo Grinspun, 'Missed Opportunity: Canada's Re-engagement with Latin America and the Caribbean,' *Canadian Journal of Latin American and Caribbean Studies* 35, no. 69 (2010): 171–99.
2 Jeffrey J Schott, 'Implications for the Uruguay Round,' in Jeffrey J. Schott and Murray G. Smith (eds.), *The Canada–United States Free Trade Agreement: The Global Impact* (Washington, DC, and Halifax: Institute for International Economics and Institute for Research on Public Policy, 1988), 173–7.
3 C. Sheck et al., *Canada in the Americas: New Opportunities and Challenges*, DFAIT Policy Staff Paper no. 94/06 (Ottawa: Department of Foreign Affairs and International Trade, 1994).
4 Manuel Riesco, 'Rise and Decline of Neoliberalism in Chile,' paper presented at the Seminar on "Latin America in Crisis," Center for Social Theory and Comparative History, UCLA, Los Angeles, June 2003. Also see Harry E. Vanden and Gary Prevost, *Politics of Latin America: The Power Game*, 3rd ed. (New York: Oxford University Press, 2009): 164–78; Emir Sader, 'The Weakest Link? Neoliberalism in Latin America,' *New Left Review* 52 (July/August 2008): 5–31; and Arthur MacEwan, 'The Neoliberal Disorder: The Inconsistencies of Trade Policy,' *NACLA: Report on the Americas* 35, no. 3 (March 1995): 27–33.
5 DFAIT, *Free Trade Area of the Americas (FTAA) – About the FTAA* (Ottawa: Foreign Affairs and International Trade Canada, last updated 14 January 2008), http://www.international.gc.ca.
6 Public Citizen, *Free Trade Area of the Americas* (2010), http://www.citizen.org/trade/ftaa/.

7 Public Citizen, *Final Declaration from the III Summit of the Peoples in Argentina* (Washington, DC: Global Trade Watch, Public Citizen, 2005).
8 Maude Barlow, *Summing Up the Summit* (Ottawa: The Council of Canadians, 2001); Jen Chang et al., *Resist!* (Halifax, NS: Fernwood, 2001).
9 Public Citizen, *The Beginning of the End of the FTAA: Crisis Leads to Scaling Back, Punting Hard Decisions with No Instructions to Overcome Differences* (Washington, DC: Global Trade Watch, Public Citizen, 2003), 1.
10 DFAIT, *Free Trade Area of the Americas (FTAA) – About the FTAA.*
11 Peter MacKay, 'Notes for an Address by the Honourable Peter MacKay, Minister of Foreign Affairs and Minister of the Atlantic Canada Opportunities Agency, 36th General Assembly Meeting, Organization of American States' (Ottawa: Foreign Affairs Canada, 2006).
12 DFAIT, *Free Trade Area of the Americas (FTAA): Key Questions and Answers on the FTAA Process*, http://www.international.gc.ca/trade-agreements-accords-commerciaux/agr-acc/ftaa-zlea/faq.aspx (accessed 24 August 2011).
13 For a discussion of Ottawa's embrace of the FTAA negotiations, see Stephen J. Randall, 'In Search of a Hemispheric Role: Canada and the Americas,' in Norman Hillmer and Maureen Appel Molot (eds.), *Canada among Nations 2002: A Fading Power* (Toronto: Oxford University Press, 2002): 238–43.
14 Stephen Harper, 'Prime Minister Harper Signals Canada's Renewed Engagement in the Americas,' (Ottawa: Office of the Prime Minister, 17 July 2007). This speech, in Santiago, Chile, set the stage for the government's enhanced role in hemispheric affairs.
15 The official government language states that in 'recent years, economic and legal reforms have helped create a *more predictable environment* for commercial engagement' (emphasis added). DFAIT, *Seizing Global Advantage – Latin America and the Caribbean: A Global Commerce Strategy Priority Market* (Ottawa: Foreign Affairs and International Trade Canada, 2011).
16 On this point, see Stephen Clarkson, *Uncle Sam and Us: Globalization, Neoconservatism, and the Canadian State* (Toronto: University of Toronto Press, 2002).
17 DFAIT, *Seizing Global Advantage.*
18 Steven Shrybman, *World Trade Organization*, 2nd ed. (Toronto: Lorimer, 2001).
19 Ibid.
20 UNCTAD, *Foreign Direct Investment and Performance Requirements: New Evidence from Selected Countries* (New York: United Nations Conference on Trade and Development, United Nations, 2003).
21 Raúl E. Sáez, 'Trade in Financial Services: The Case of Chile,' in *Free Trade*

Agreements and Financial Services in Latin America and the Caribbean – LCR Study (Background Paper) (Washington: Finance, Private Sector and Infrastructure Department, Latin America and the Caribbean Region, World Bank, 2006).

22 Andrew Jackson and Matthew Sanger, *Dismantling Democracy: The Multilateral Agreement on Investment (MAI) and Its Impact* (Halifax, NS: James Lorimer and Canadian Centre for Policy Alternatives, 1998).

23 Scott Sinclair, *FTAA: A Dangerous NAFTA-GATS Hybrid* (Ottawa: Canadian Centre for Policy Alternatives, 2003).

24 'Minimum standard of treatment' means that the host country will accord treatment to investments of foreign investors in accordance with the international norms encompassed by the customary international law minimum standard. See SICE, *Dictionary of Trade Terms* (SICE – Foreign Trade Information System, Organization of American States), http://www.sice.oas.org/dictionary/IN_e.asp.

25 Sinclair, 'FTAA: A Dangerous NAFTA-GATS Hybrid.'

26 Kevin P. Gallagher, 'Trading Away the Ladder? Trade Politics and Economic Development in the Americas,' *New Political Economy* 13, no. 1 (2008): 37–59.

27 Ellen Gould and Clare Joy, *General Agreement on Trade in Services: In Whose Service?* (London: World Development Movement, 2000); Scott Sinclair, *Gats: How the World Trade Organization's New 'Services' Negotiations Threaten Democracy* (Ottawa: Canadian Centre for Policy Alternatives, 2000); Scott Sinclair, *The GATS and Canadian Postal Services* (Ottawa: Canadian Centre for Policy Alternatives, 2001).

28 William Finnegan, 'Leasing the Rain,' *The New Yorker*, April 2002, 43–52.

29 It is also worth noting that Canada's official development assistance budget has been reoriented toward the Americas and away from impoverished Africa. See Campbell Clark, 'Canada Seeks Strategic Ties by Focusing Aid on Americas,' *Globe and Mail*, 24 February 2009, A9.

30 David Emerson, 'Notes for an Address by the Honourable David Emerson, Minister of International Trade, Delivered at the Canadian Council for the Americas, British Columbia, "Re-Engaging the Americas through Trade and Investment" – February 22' (Ottawa: Foreign Affairs and International Trade Canada, 2008).

31 Sebastian Herreros, 'The Chile-Canada Free Trade Agreement,' in Gary P. Sampson and Stephen Woolcock (eds.), *Regionalism, Multilateralism, and Economic Integration: The Recent Experience* (Tokyo and New York: United Nations University Press, 2003), 167–201.

32 PMO, 'Backgrounder – Developing Partnerships, Trade and Investment

Initiatives in Chile,'(Ottawa: Office of the Prime Minister, 17 July 2007); DFAIT, *Canada-Chile Free Trade Commission – Seventh Meeting of the Canada-Chile Free Trade Commission: Joint Minutes* (Ottawa: Foreign Affairs and International Trade Canada, 2009).

33 M. Manger, 'International Investment Agreements and Services Markets: Locking in Market Failure?' *World Development* 36, no. 11 (2008): 2456–69.

34 Laura Carlsen, 'Victory in the Amazon,' *Americas Program Report* (22 June 2009), http://americas.irc-online.org/am/6206.

35 CF, CoC, and MW, 'Letter to Senator Marjory LeBreton and Senator James Cowan. June 30' (Ottawa: MiningWatch Canada, Council of Canadians, and Common Frontiers 2009).

36 House of Commons, '40th Parliament, 2nd Session, edited Hansard, number 060, Monday, May 25' (Ottawa: Parliament of Canada, 2009); Kady O'Malley, 'Updated – Order of the Day – Can't You Just Feel the Recalibration?' Inside Politics Blog, CBC.ca, 12 March 2010. The original Bill C-23 'died in the order paper' when Parliament was prorogued in late December 2009. The bill was eventually reintroduced as C-2 immediately with the reopening of Parliament in March 2010.

37 PMO, 'Canada Signs Free Trade Agreement with Colombia,' news release (Ottawa: Office of the Prime Minister, 21 November 2008).

38 Amnesty International, *2009 Amnesty International Report: State of the World's Human Rights* (London: Amnesty International, 2009).

39 Amnesty International, *Everything Left Behind: Internal Displacement in Colombia* (London: Amnesty International, 2009).

40 CIIT, *Human Rights, the Environment and Free Trade with Colombia* (Ottawa: Standing Committee on International Trade, House of Commons, 2008).

41 Government of Canada, 'Canada Concludes Negotiations for Free Trade, Labour Cooperation and Environment Agreements with Colombia,' news release (Ottawa: Government of Canada, 7 June 2008).

42 CLC, *Submission to the House of Commons Standing Committee on International Trade Concerning the Free Trade Agreement between Canada and the Republic of Colombia. September 14* (Ottawa: Canadian Labour Congress, 2009).

43 CCIC, *Making a Bad Situation Worse: An Analysis of the Text of the Canada-Colombia Free Trade Agreement* (Ottawa: Canadian Council for International Cooperation, 2009), 31.

44 CCCE, *Canada's Role in the World: The Global Economic Crisis and the Canada-Colombia Free Trade Agreement* (Ottawa: Canadian Council of Chief Executives, 2009).

45 CCIC, *Making a Bad Situation Worse.*

46 Alexandre Deslongchamps and Eric Sabo, 'Opposition Lawmakers May Stall Canada-Panama Free Trade Accord,' Bloomberg.com, 14 August 2009.

47 DFAIT, *Canada – Central America Four (CA4) Free Trade Agreement Negotiations* (Ottawa: Foreign Affairs and International Trade Canada), http://www.international.gc.ca, 2009.

48 But as a statement from DFAIT noted: 'Canada remains open to re-engaging in negotiations with Guatemala, El Salvador and Nicaragua, once negotiations with Honduras are complete.' See Government of Canada, *Canada-Central America Four Free Trade Agreement Negotiations* (Ottawa: Department of Foreign Affairs and International Trade, June 2011).

49 Todd Gordon, 'Canada Backs Profits, Not Human Rights, in Honduras,' *Toronto Star*, 16 August 2011.

50 HRW, *World Report 2011: Honduras* (New York: Human Rights Watch, 2011).

51 Gordon, 'Canada Backs Profits, Not Human Rights, in Honduras.'

52 DFAIT, 'Canada Welcomes Lifting of Suspension of Honduras from Organization of American States,' news release (Ottawa: Foreign Affairs and International Trade Canada, 1 June 2011).

53 C. Fred Bergsten, 'A Competitive Approach to Free Trade,' *Financial Times*, 4 December 2002. Also see Matthew B. Adler, *Stumbling Forward on Trade: The Doha Round, Free Trade Agreements, and Canada* (Toronto: C.D. Howe Institute, 2008); Danielle Goldfarb, 'U.S. Bilateral Free Trade Accords: Why Canada Should Be Cautious about Going the Same Route,' in *The Border Papers* (Toronto: C.D. Howe Institute, 2005).

54 Gauri Sreenivasan, 'Canadian Trade and Investment Policy, 2006–08,' in Teresa Healy (ed.), *The Harper Record* (Ottawa: Canadian Centre for Policy Alternatives, 2008).

55 Government of Canada, *An FTA with the Andean Community Countries of Colombia and Peru: Qualitative Economic Analysis – June 2007* (Ottawa: Foreign Affairs and International Trade Canada, 2007), 9.

56 Carl Meyer, 'Harper to Help Honduras Put Up "Open for Business" Sign,' *Embassy Magazine*, 10 August 2011; CCIC, *Honduras: Democracy Denied* (Ottawa: Canadian Council for International Co-operation, 2010).

57 CCCE, *Canada's Role in the World: The Global Economic Crisis and the Canada-Colombia Free Trade Agreement.*

58 CIIT, *Ten Steps to a Better Trade Policy: Report by the Standing Committee on International Trade* (Ottawa: Standing Committee on International Trade, Parliament of Canada, 2007), 10.

59 Bergsten, 'A Competitive Approach to Free Trade.'

60 CIIT, *Ten Steps to a Better Trade Policy.*

61 CCCE, *Canada's Role in the World*.

62 MAC, *2009 Facts and Figures – A Report on the State of the Canadian Mining Industry* (Ottawa: The Mining Association of Canada, 2009), 49.

63 Barrie McKenna, 'Regional, Bilateral Deals Seen as Impeding Trade,' *Globe and Mail*, 18 January 2005, B13.

64 David Emerson, 'Notes for an Address by the Honourable David Emerson, Minister of International Trade, Delivered at the Canadian Council for the Americas, British Columbia, Re-Engaging the Americas through Trade and Investment' (February 2007).

65 Lee Berthiaume, 'Colombia Trade Deal A Post-Prorogation Government Priority,' *Embassy Magazine*, 13 January 2010.

66 Michelle Collins, 'Liberals Welcome Colombian Visit,' *Embassy Magazine*, 17 June 2009.

67 Jeffrey J. Schott, 'Assessing U.S. FTA Policy,' in Jeffrey J. Schott (ed.), *Free Trade Agreements: U.S. Strategies and Priorities* (Washington: Institute for International Economics, 2004), 359–81.

68 Jeffrey J. Schott, 'Free Trade Agreements: The Cost of U.S. Nonparticipation. Testimony before the Subcommittee on Trade Committee on Ways and Means, United States House of Representatives, March 29' (Washington: Peterson Institute for International Economics, 2001).

69 Ibid.

70 See José M. Salazar-Xirinachs and Jaime Granados, 'The U.S.-Central America Free Trade Agreement: Opportunities and Challenges,' in Jeffrey J. Schott (ed.), *Free Trade Agreements: U.S. Strategies and Priorities* (Washington: Institute for International Economics, 2004), 225–75, and Goldfarb, 'U.S. Bilateral Free Trade Accords.'

71 Ricardo Grinspun and Yasmine Shamsie (eds.), *Whose Canada? Continental Integration, Fortress North America and the Corporate Agenda* (Montreal and Kingston: McGill-Queen's University Press, 2007).

72 N. Phillips, 'US Power and the Politics of Economic Governance in the Americas,' *Latin American Politics and Society* 47, no. 4 (2005): 1–25.

73 DFAIT, *Listing of Canada's Existing FIPAS* (Ottawa: Foreign Affairs and International Trade Canada, 2011), http://www.international.gc.ca.

74 UNCTAD, *IIA Monitor No. 3: Recent Developments in International Investment Agreements* (New York: United Nations Conference on Trade and Development, 2009).

75 CCIC, *Investment Treaties and Extractive Industries: Implications for Human Rights and Sustainable Development* (Ottawa: Canadian Council for International Cooperation, 2009).

76 DFAIT, *Canada's FIPA Program: Its Purpose, Objective and Content* (Ottawa:

Foreign Affairs and International Trade Canada, 2009), http://www.inter-national.gc.ca.

77 Ibid.

78 Luke Eric Peterson, *Human Rights and Bilateral Investment Treaties: Mapping the Role of Human Rights Law within Investor-State Arbitration* (Montreal: Rights and Democracy, 2009).

79 UNCTAD, *Bilateral Investment Treaties 1995–2006: Trends in Investment Rulemaking* (New York: United Nations Conference on Trade and Development, 2007).

80 Lori Wallach and Patrick Woodall, *Whose Trade Organization? The Comprehensive Guide to the WTO*, rev. ed. (New York: New Press, 2004).

81 R. Adlung and M. Molinuevo, 'Bilateralism in Services Trade: Is There Fire behind the (Bit-) Smoke,' *Journal of International Economic Law* 11, no. 2 (2008): 365–409.

82 UNCTAD, *IIA Monitor No. 1: Latest Developments in Investor-State Dispute Settlement* (New York: United Nations Conference on Trade and Development, 2009).

83 OECD, *Transparency and Third Party Participation in Investor-State Dispute Settlement Procedures* (Paris: Organisation for Economic Co-operation and Development, 2005).

84 ICSID, *ICSID Additional Facility Rules* (Washington: World Bank Group, 2006).

85 K. Tienhaara, 'What You Don't Know Can Hurt You: Investor-State Disputes and the Protection of the Environment in Developing Countries,' *Global Environmental Politics* 6, no. 4 (2006): 73–100.

86 Michael Busch, 'El Salvador's Gold Fight,' *Foreign Policy in Focus*, 16 July 2009.

87 Ibid.

88 Peterson, *Human Rights and Bilateral Investment Treaties*.

89 Finnegan, 'Leasing the Rain.'

90 MiningWatch, *On the Ground Research: A Research Agenda for Communities Affected by Large-Scale Mining Activity* (Ottawa: MiningWatch Canada, 2000); Timothy David Clark and Liisa North, 'Mining and Oil in Latin America: Lessons from the Past, Issues for the Future,' in Liisa North, Timothy Clark, and Viviana Patroni (eds.), *Community Rights and Corporate Responsibility: Canadian Mining and Oil Companies in Latin America* (Toronto: Between the Lines Press, 2006), 1–16.

91 Ricardo Grinspun and Robert Kreklewich, 'Consolidating Neoliberal Reform: "Free Trade" as a Conditioning Framework,' *Studies in Political Economy* 43 (Spring 1994): 33–61; Nagesh Kumar and Kevin P. Gallagher,

'Relevance of "Policy Space" for Development: Implications for Multilateral Trade Negotiations,' in *RIS Discussion Paper #120* (GDAE's Globalization and Sustainable Development Program, 2007).

92 After Peruvian protesters in Santa Ana objected to the negative environmental impacts of mining projects in the summer of 2011, the outgoing government of Alan Garcia stated that the Canadian mining firm Bear Creek Mining Corp's project was no longer in the 'best interest' of the public. William Lloyd George, 'Peru Halts Canadian Mining Project after Deadly Clashes,' *Globe and Mail*, 27 June 2011, A1; and Brenda Bouw, 'Bear Creek Takes Legal Action against Peru after Cancelled Project Spurs Selloff,' *Globe and Mail*, 28 June 2011, B4.

93 MiningWatch, *Mexican Activist Murdered for Opposing Canadian Mining Company – Killing Sparks Protest at Canadian Embassy in Mexico City* (Ottawa: MiningWatch Canada, 2009).

94 See cases from Rights Action (www.rightsaction.org), KAIROS, and Amnesty International Canada.

95 DFAIT, 'Canada launches CSR strategy – April 8' (Ottawa: Foreign Affairs and International Trade Canada, 2009), http://www.international.gc.ca.

96 DFAIT, *The National Roundtables on Corporate Social Responsibility* (Ottawa: Department of Foreign Affairs and International Trade, 2008).

97 MAC, *2009 Facts and Figures*, 56.

98 CNCA, 'An Important Step Forward: The Final Report of the National Roundtables on Corporate Social Responsibility and the Canadian Extractive Industry in Developing Countries,' press release (Montreal: Canadian Network on Corporate Accountability, 2007).

99 Lee Berthiaume, 'CSR Counsellor Met with Anger, Allegations,' *Embassy Magazine*, 14 October 2009; and MiningWatch, *The Government's New 'CSR Counsellor' for the Extractive Sector* (Ottawa: MiningWatch Canada, 2010).

100 Expert Group, 'Letter to the Canadian Government' (Manila, Philippines: Expert Group Meeting on Extractive Industries, Indigenous Peoples' Rights and Corporate Social Responsibility,' 29 March 2010).

101 One example was Lloyd Axworthy's tenure as foreign minister during the late 1990s, when there was a focused effort to advance human security. See Joseph Jockel and Joel Sokolsky, 'Lloyd Axworthy's Legacy: Human Security and the Rescue of Canadian Defence Policy,' *International Journal* 56, no. 1 (Winter 2000–1): 1–18.

102 For example, the Canadian government refused to suspend development aid or to condemn human rights abuses at the hands of the Honduran military. Unlike most Latin American governments, Canada immediately joined with the U.S. to recognize the November presidential elections. For

further analysis, see Yves Engler, 'Canada and the Coup,' *The Mark*, 23 July 2009; and Ben Wood, 'Barrick's Gold,' *Canadian Dimension*, 29 October 2009).

103 Juliet O'Neill, 'Government Cuts Funding to KAIROS Human-Rights Group,' *Montreal Gazette*, 7 December 2009.

104 DFAIT, *Canada's Engagement in the Americas* (Ottawa: Foreign Affairs and International Trade Canada, 2009).

105 David Harris and Diego Azzi, *ALBA – Venezuela's Answer to 'Free Trade': The Bolivarian Alternative for the Americas*, Occasional Paper 3 (Bangkok: Focus on the Global South, 2006), 3.

106 The Honduran Parliament withdrew from ALBA in January 2010 in the wake of the June 2009 military coup. See 'Honduras Announces Withdrawal from ALBA,' *El Universal*, 13 January 2010.

107 Martin Hart-Landsberg, 'Learning from ALBA and the Bank of the South: Challenges and Possibilities,' *Monthly Review* 61, no. 4 (September 2009): 1–20.

108 Ibid.

4 Canada and the Democratic Charter: Lessons from the Coup in Honduras

MAXWELL A. CAMERON AND JASON TOCKMAN

'Not the most glorious moment for the OAS.' That was the response of a senior Canadian official when asked what the June 2009 coup in Honduras meant for the Organization of American States (OAS) and the Inter-American Democratic Charter (IADC), the multilateral document signed in 2001 by OAS member states pledging to respect and uphold representative democracy. 'It started beautifully,' he added, 'and then gradually fell apart.'[1]

The fight over the coup in Honduras occurred at a peculiar moment in the history of hemispheric affairs. As many Latin American governments began to shift to the left,[2] and in the face of the failure of the project of Western Hemispheric integration symbolized by the fate of the Free Trade Agreement of the Americas (FTAA), which was to have been negotiated by 2005, and is now in a vegetative state, the underlying consensus that supported the Democratic Charter at the time of its negotiation in 2001 seemed to have evaporated.[3] Not only did the Charter seem to lose relevance, but the OAS itself was challenged by the rise of the twelve-nation Union of South American Nations (UNASUR) and other diplomatic fora. The OAS, always seen as a club dominated by the United States, was mostly sidelined as Latin American countries moved increasingly to achieve greater independence from U.S. influence – in part because of Washington's distraction with events in the Middle East, Afghanistan, and its own economic malaise, and partly due to the region's gradual disenchantment with policies advocated by Washington (especially the so-called 'Washington Consensus').[4]

So why did the entire Western hemisphere, indeed the entire world, come together to condemn the coup in Honduras, and then unravel in the face of the stubborn refusal of the de facto Honduran regime to allow the reinstatement of ousted president José Manuel Zelaya? What does this dramatic (at times melodramatic) story – in which a president was flown into exile in his pyjamas, blocked from landing his plane when he attempted to fly back, and then smuggled himself back into the country to take refuge in the Brazilian embassy in Tegucigalpa – tell us about hemispheric efforts to promote democracy in Latin America and Canada's role in particular? Did the international community over-react, and thereby reinforce the cohesion of the coup-regime, or was it not firm enough at the outset, and thus allowed the interim government to become entrenched too quickly? Is the Democratic Charter – which was not used in advance of the crisis but which was invoked for the first time ever to expel a nation from the OAS – an 'imperfect instrument,' as one official put it, or was the instrument too hastily used and then prematurely discarded in the face of the November 2009 Honduran presidential elections?

Canada, the Coup, and Its Aftermath

Suddenly, with the coup in Honduras, the OAS and the Democracy Charter appeared to take centrestage. After years of bickering between Washington and Caracas, after all the hand wringing about the spread of anti-Americanism in the South, there was an immediate and spectacular unanimity in the response of every country (including the Harper government) in the Western hemisphere: the coup in Honduras was unacceptable. For the first time ever, a country was expelled from the organization based on non-compliance with the Democratic Charter. Cuba had been expelled from the OAS in 1962 (when Canada was not a member), but that was long before the Charter. In fact, an OAS meeting had just been held months before the Honduran coup – not entirely ironically, as it happens, in San Pedro Sula – to find ways of re-integrating Cuba into the Western hemisphere.[5] Cuba has long been a member in full standing with most countries of the hemisphere outside the U.S., so the initiative was more about updating the posture of the OAS than anything else.

Yet the moment's unanimity papered over fundamental disagreements that would re-emerge very quickly as the coup government in Tegucigalpa hunkered down and prepared to ride out the storm. In fact, the dispute between Zelaya and the Honduran Congress, the military, and the Supreme Court mirrored wider divisions within the region. Zelaya was seen by his adversaries as an emerging Bolivarian leader who would take Honduras down the path blazed by Venezuela's Hugo Chávez into a process of political change that would threaten their core interests and values, just as similar political changes had occurred in Bolivia, Ecuador, and on the Central American isthmus, in Nicaragua. In power, Zelaya had grown increasingly impatient with the unwillingness of local elites to tolerate even modest reforms. The flashpoint for disagreement emerged, not surprisingly, around the topic of constitutional reform. A cabinet official in the Zelaya government had gone so far as to call the constitution an 'eyesore' (the untranslatable Spanish term used was *adefecio*).[6] The idea that Honduras needed a new constitution was neither novel nor surprising. The appeal to constituent power – the principle that the people have the right to choose their own form of rule, including by means of periodic constitutional reform – has become part of the repertoire of left-wing political strategy since Chávez successfully used a constituent assembly in 1999 to rewrite Venezuela's constitution and, in the process, consolidate his power.

And so the international response began to fray as leaders who were neither part of nor sympathized with Latin America's left turns (notably countries like the U.S., Canada, Costa Rica, Peru) began to feel the domestic heat as a result of their advocacy of the restitution of a 'Bolivarian' leader. Within the OAS, the consensus tended to favour the countries of the Bolivarian Alternative for the Americas (or ALBA), which is yet another indication of the decline of U.S. influence in the region. The secretary general of the OAS, who had never been the favoured candidate of the United States,[7] José Miguel Insulza of Chile, aligned himself with the ALBA countries knowing that his own re-election depended on cultivating their support. (By this point, Insulza's hopes of running for president in Chile had been long forgotten, freeing him up to be both more energetic and more controversial as a leader of the OAS.) Canada was thus forced to walk a tightrope between wanting to support multilateralism (which is the nation's underlying posture in international affairs, given that as a small country with few power resources to wield in international affairs Canada has historically sought to foster rule-based processes), and not wanting to alienate the United States.

To understand the complexities of the Canadian position, a little history is in order. The next section describes the evolution of Canada's foreign and trade policies and democracy promotion in the Americas since 1990. It reviews Canada's entry into the OAS and its role in the development of the Democratic Charter. It also discusses Canadian trade policy in the Americas, from the North American Free Trade

Agreement (NAFTA) to the Canada-Chile Free Trade Agreement to the
FTAA to the current trade agenda, including bilateral trade agreements
with Peru and Colombia, as well as the government of Stephen Harper
and its policy of 'engagement with the Americas.' We then discuss the
coup in Honduras, briefly recounting the forces precipitating the crisis,
the overthrow of Zelaya, and the specific actions taken by the branches
of the Canadian government after the coup. In this context, we discuss
the idiosyncrasies of the Honduran constitution. We also assess the
claims of coup leaders and refute the contention that Zelaya's removal
followed a constitutional order. This is followed by an overview of the
response of the international community and the actions taken by the
OAS and United Nations, and the Oscar Arias-moderated negotiations.
We conclude with a discussion of Honduras's reintegration into the
OAS in 2011.

Canada's Initial Hemispheric Engagement

In the 1990s, Canadian foreign policy began to shift toward a greater focus on Latin America. With the transitions of the 1980s and the
end of the Cold War, Latin America was becoming more democratic.
Moreover, following the debt crisis and the 'lost decade' of the 1980s,
the region began to embrace market reforms with greater enthusiasm.
Together, these changes, both political and economic in nature, seemed
to promise an era of greater harmony and cooperation between Latin
America and the United States. This, in turn, eliminated the biggest
historical barrier to Canadian engagement with the region: the fear of
being caught in the often fraught relations between Canada's largest
trading partner and the other countries in Washington's so-called 'backyard.' However, the new pattern of cooperation (or 'community') was
largely based on a 'consensus,' the so-called 'Washington Consensus'
based on the goals of trade and investment liberalization, deregulation,
privatization, and fiscal austerity. At first, the neoliberal shift resulted
in spectacular changes. Canada joined the OAS in January 1990, participated in the NAFTA negotiations with Mexico and the United States,
and pushed for the creation of the Unit for the Promotion of Democracy
within the hemispheric body.[8]

Canada supported the development of Resolution 1080 and the
Washington Protocol, which essentially made democracy a condition
of membership in the OAS and made the forcible removal of a democratic government cause for exclusion. (Indeed, Ottawa responded

aggressively to the 1991 military coup in Haiti, which saw the country's first democratically elected president, Jean Bertrand Aristide, forcibly removed from power.) However, no sooner was Resolution 1080 put into effect than an event occurred which demonstrated that the threats to democracy in the region were about to take a more subtle form: President Alberto Fujimori closed the Peruvian Congress, suspended the constitution, removed top Supreme Court judges, and began to rule by decree in April 1992, an event that was described as an *autogolpe*, or presidential self-coup. It was very hard to respond to this measure because the sitting president retained electoral legitimacy, and indeed was widely applauded domestically for his actions. Despite public support, the *autogolpe* lay the foundations for an increasingly authoritarian government in Peru, and Canada found itself unexpectedly in the eye of the maelstrom as the host of the 2000 OAS General Assembly in Windsor, Ontario, when Fujimori was re-elected in an electoral process that the OAS found did not meet accepted international standards. A High Level Mission was sent to Peru, led by Canadian foreign minister Lloyd Axworthy and OAS secretary general César Gaviria, and under their auspices, the OAS created dialogue roundtables to bring together the government and the opposition after Fujimori's resignation and flight to Japan.[9]

Canada and Peru then led the effort to create an Inter-American Democratic Charter,[10] an idea that was proposed by Peru in the 2001 Summit of the Americas in Quebec City. The Charter, which was, ironically, signed on 11 September 2001 in Lima, Peru, not only defined democracy broadly, but also spelled out the enforcement provisions that would come into play with the coup in Honduras eight years later. There was one major dissenter in Quebec City: Hugo Chávez. The newly elected (or, indeed, 're-elected,' for Chávez had submitted himself to a 're-legitimation' process following the adoption of the 1999 Bolivarian Constitution) president of Venezuela disliked the emphasis of the Charter on 'representative' democracy, preferring instead the language of 'participatory' democracy. This was a harbinger of the future, for after Chávez, a succession of left-leaning governments would be elected in the region, many of which shared Chávez's suspicions about representation and a preference for popular participation.

As the cooperative tone of hemispheric affairs of the early 1990s gave way to new tensions and conflicts by the early 2000s, a pro-sovereignty mood eclipsed the earlier emphasis on building stronger Western-style democracies. At issue is whether the trends in the region are moving away from democratic pluralism, or toward a different understanding of democracy. By 2007, policy makers in Ottawa started to express a fear of the former:

> Since Canada first developed policies in support of democratic development, the international environment has changed. Over the last decade, the growth in the number of democracies has levelled out. Evidence shows that many countries are sliding back to non-democratic forms of government. While progress is being made in some countries, in others democracy is up against very significant obstacles and its fragility is increasingly apparent.[11]

Though still concentrating on advancing democratic principles, the Harper government, more explicitly than previous governments, framed Canada's 're-engagement' with the region in more ideological terms. Government officials lamented the level of polarization and ideological discord in the region, yet tended to attribute this to the spread of influence of Bolivarian thought or twenty-first-century socialism.[12] The Canadian government seemed to want to position itself in the middle ground between ideological extremes, but this meant defining Canadian policy in ideological terms more explicitly than previous governments in Ottawa had done. In a July 2007 speech in Santiago, Chile, Harper indicated that Canada would focus on: (1) strengthening and promoting freedom, democracy, human rights, and the rule of law; (2) building strong, sustainable economies through trade and investment; and (3) meeting security challenges, including environmental and health crises.[13] Yet, in so doing, he suggested that Canada was advancing a 'third way' between two perceived models of development. In an interview he said:

> There is a perception in the region that there exist only two models for development, one that is focused on social justice, the other on economic liberalization. Canada offers a different model, and illustrates that these are not mutually exclusive. We are an open society based on the values of freedom, democracy, human rights, and the rule of law. We have a strong economy that benefits from our close relationships with our trading partners. We are a proud and independent country with a unique and evolving cultural diversity.[14]

In another context, he remarked that the choice for Latin America and the Caribbean 'is not simply between unfettered capitalism and cold

war socialism. The Canadian model of democratic freedom and economic openness, combined with effective regional and social support,
offers a middle course for countries seeking democratic institutions,
free markets and social equality.'[15] Although the phraseology of a 'third
way' suggested that Canada would occupy a moderate middle ground,
in fact the Harper government was one of the most conservative in the
hemisphere, especially after the election of Barack Obama in the United
States. In its enthusiasm for bilateral trade negotiations, the Harper
government found allies among the more conservative governments in
the region, like Colombia under President Álvaro Uribe and Peru under
presidents Alejandro Toledo and Alan García. The notion of a 'middle
course' was at best a conceit and, at worst, a meaningless phrase.

In short, there are three key points to keep in mind as we review
Canada's role in responding to the June 2009 coup in Honduras. First,
Canadian engagement with the Americas – though heavily infused by a
preference for democratic pluralism from the early 1990s onward – has
always been predicated on the idea that Canada can reconcile its special
relationship with the United States with the potential to play its typical
role of good multilateral citizen in the Americas. Second, this particular
tightrope act has become more difficult as the region as a whole shifts
away from the Washington Consensus and begins to experiment with
more participatory forms of democracy. Third, in Canada's current 're-
engagement,' which is partly designed to ensure its policy is helpful to
the United States, it is difficult to separate democracy promotion (and
hemispheric security issues) from a rigid ideological policy lens.[16] In
light of Zelaya's shift toward the ALBA countries, this tension would
become particularly evident in efforts to resolve the democratic crisis
in Honduras.

Anatomy of a Coup

The events that precipitated the coup that overthrew Manuel Zelaya
are now well known. Elected in 2005 with the centre-right Liberal Party,
Zelaya subsequently moved increasingly to the left and aligned himself with the Venezuela-led Bolivarian Alternative for the Americas
(ALBA), upsetting Honduras's political establishment and powerful
business community.[17] Part of Zelaya's program involved a popular
referendum on whether the country would elect a constituent assembly
to draft a new constitution, which might have included removing the
long-standing restriction on only one four-year term for the presidency. The Honduran right quickly seized on that precise issue, claiming

Zelaya's principal interest was enabling himself to run for re-election, which the Honduran constitution had heretofore expressly prohibited. Indeed, the controversial article 239 of the constitution goes so far as to exclude the sitting president from even *proposing* to change this provision, on penalty of immediate dissolution of his or her term.[18] Nonetheless, Zelaya's plebiscite was non-binding, constituting little more than a public opinion poll, did not specifically deal with the question of term limits, and would only come into force after his term had ended.

On 27 May 2009, members of the Honduran Supreme Court ruled that the referendum was illegal, and the Congress affirmed the court action with a resolution against the public consultation. Zelaya sought the support of the head of the armed forces, General Romeo Vásquez Velásquez, who declined, prompting his firing by an increasingly cornered Zelaya on 24 June. The High Court immediately ruled the firing illegal, nullifying Vásquez's termination. Three days before the scheduled poll, the president amassed a large group of supporters and staged an action at the air force barracks where the ballots were being held, seizing them to ensure that the referendum actually went forward. Tensions continued to escalate and rumours of a coup began to circulate. On 25 June, Honduran Attorney General Luis Alberto Rubi filed a legal brief with the Supreme Court, charging Zelaya with abuse of authority, acting against the 'form of government,' usurpation of powers, and being a traitor to the country. The following day, Honduran Supreme Court documents supposedly indicated that the court ordered the military to arrest Zelaya, although, critically, the court papers show no ruling on the question of removing the president from office.[19]

At around 5:30 on the morning of 28 June, the day on which the consultation was to take place, heavily armed and hooded soldiers stormed Zelaya's residence – without the support, as some coup supporters claimed at the time, of any Congressional fiat. The president was roused from his sleep with guns pointed at his head and, still clad in his pyjamas, was put on a plane bound for Costa Rica. No trial was held to determine if Zelaya was guilty of the charges laid against him; and the forged letter of resignation – oddly dated 25 June– was quite evidently a fraud. Later that day, the Honduran Congress swore in congressional president Roberto Micheletti as the country's interim president. The Supreme Court legitimated the coup with a retroactive memorandum informing Hondurans and the international community that the deposed Zelaya had not possessed the character worthy of high office.[20] Thus, while it was the military's removal of Zelaya from the country that formally interrupted Honduras's constitutional order, the coup d'état was made complete by the actions of the Congress and the Supreme Court ex post facto.

Certain features of the Honduran constitution contributed to the crisis. Costa Rican president and Nobel Peace Prize winner Oscar Arias went so far as to characterize the Honduran constitution as 'the worst in the entire world.'[21] His reasons are not hard to fathom. On the one hand, the constitution includes various questionable provisions, one being the aforementioned article 239, which not only prohibits presidential re-election, but also 'makes it a crime to talk about re-election.'[22] This was the charge publicly laid against Zelaya by those that opposed him, although the provision was not invoked in the Supreme Court's order to arrest the president. On the other hand, the constitution lacks key components, such as a provision for impeachment of the executive, that are present in most constitutions. It should not be surprising that political actors will occasionally turn to extra-constitutional measures where the magna carta provides no mechanism to confront chronic excesses by the executive. At the same time, the difficulty of reforming the constitution makes the political regime more rigid. Title VII provides that the constitution can only be amended by a two-thirds vote by two consecutive sessions of the Congress; moreover, provisions related to the presidential re-election or term of office may not, under any condition, be amended.

Those who defend Zelaya's ouster claim that in pushing forward with the referendum, he disregarded rulings by the Honduran Supreme Court and legislature; he inappropriately sacked the head of the armed forces; violated the constitution by speaking about changing presidential term limits, and thereby triggered the self-executing termination of his presidency; and that he led a 'mob' against an air force barracks to recover referendum ballots printed by his Venezuelan ally, Chávez, with whom Zelaya shares socialist ambitions. There is perhaps both a kernel of truth and a dose of polemic in each of these claims. However, none of these arguments undermines the fundamental issue at hand: namely, that the forced removal of President Zelaya constituted a breach of Honduras's constitutional order. Democracy was unquestionably interrupted, setting a dangerous precedent in a region hoping to leave behind a painful era of military coups, dictatorships, and 'dirty' wars.

The argument made in some quarters is that what transpired in Honduras was essentially a 'constitutional coup,' that the military was merely responding to a decision by the Supreme Court, and that the interim president would only be seated until pending presidential elections (the latter did come to pass, although, as will be discussed below, the legitimacy of the election is highly questionable, and it lacked any real external observation). But the concept of a constitutional coup has no place in law or scholarship; it is at best a trope to designate a Machiavellian ruse whereby a constitution is changed by what appears to be legal means when, in fact, it is weakened to perpetuate incumbents in power. A coup is, by definition, a change in the constitutional order by non-constitutional means. This is precisely what took place in Honduras.[23]

Moreover, the question of writing a new constitution well exceeded the issue of term limits – which was the firing offence branded by Zelaya's opponents. It reflects today the aspirations of a large segment of the Honduran population – including rural residents, indigenous groups, labour unions, and the urban poor – to alter what they perceive to be an exclusionary political system that has failed to deliver economic gains in one of the hemisphere's most impoverished countries. The existing constitution's built-in mechanisms that militate against reform are viewed by many Hondurans as an impediment to necessary social and economic changes. In this context, the battle over constitutional reform and the subsequent coup d'état should be viewed not as a contest over who occupies the executive post, but over the future direction of the country – a contest that the entrenched political elite appears to have won, at least for now. In addition, the sustained street demonstrations against the coup reflected not so much an allegiance to Zelaya as a political figure, nor principally a commitment to democratic principles, but as the belief held by many Hondurans that Zelaya was the leader most likely to deliver some of the reforms for which they still hope to see implemented.

International Reaction and Canada's Response

The coup was repudiated by the international community with remarkable unanimity. The OAS promptly and 'vehemently' condemned the 'unconstitutional alteration of the democratic order.'[24] At one level, the OAS was primed to respond quickly to the unfolding events. Zelaya had just requested that the secretary general travel to Tegucigalpa, explicitly invoking the Democratic Charter, perhaps because he intuited that Insulza faced a serious threat to his incumbency. The trip by

Insulza was scheduled to be on the Monday following the coup, but it was derailed by the dramatic events that seemingly caught everyone by surprise. The OAS had, just a few months earlier, held its General Assembly in San Pedro Sula and yet, embarrassingly, neither OAS officials nor other foreign leaders had connected the dots.

Upon hearing the news, the secretary general called Canada's ambassador to the OAS, Graeme Clark, who was, at the time, the Chair of the Permanent Council, and asked him to convene the member states.[25] There was outrage and indignation as leaders heard the news, and the Permanent Council quickly agreed to suspend the session so that a working group could draft a proper resolution. Not surprisingly, the negotiations over the language to be used in the declaration were difficult. Canada's role in this context was essentially that of the facilitator: to find consensus among the member states rather than enter the partisan fray. The Canadian government quickly came to the position that the coup was to be condemned, in spite of its concerns about Zelaya's behaviour. Some countries, like Argentina and the ALBA nations, wanted much stronger language. The United States, for its part, was wary of being caught in a situation like the crisis in April 2002 when Chávez was illegally overthrown. At that time, the U.S. quickly acquiesced to the coup, which subsequently fizzled and Chávez was restored, to the mortification of Roger Noriega, the U.S. ambassador to the OAS. This event did much to sour relations between Washington and a number of Latin American nations. The initial resolution of the OAS at that moment was – with all the wisdom of hindsight – unrealistic, calling for the return of Zelaya within seventy-two hours. Although laudable as a goal, this clearly reflected the miscalculation of many members of the OAS with respect to the cohesion and strength of the unconstitutional government in Tegucigalpa.

Outside the OAS, condemnation was echoed by many countries, with not a single utterance of official support for the de facto regime being voiced from any corner of the world. Indeed, not a single country recognized the Roberto Micheletti regime.[26] While many called for Zelaya's immediate restoration – including the OAS, most of Latin America, and Spain – others (like Canada) used more nuanced language, stopping short of specifically affirming Zelaya as the only legitimate president. On the day of the coup, U.S. president Barack Obama said that he was 'deeply concerned' and called on 'all political and social actors in Honduras to respect democratic norms'; the following day, Secretary of State Hillary Clinton added that the situation had 'evolved into a coup.'[27] Canada's minister of state of foreign affairs for the Americas, Peter Kent, released a statement that read: 'Canada condemns the coup d'état that took place over the weekend in Honduras, and calls on all parties to show restraint and to seek a peaceful resolution to the present political crisis.'[28] At the other end of the spectrum, Bolivia, Venezuela, Ecuador, El Salvador, and Nicaragua all withdrew their ambassadors to Honduras.

Irrespective of preliminary stances, the wider international community quickly coalesced around the position that any acceptable resolution of the coup must include the restoration of Zelaya to the presidency. On 30 June, with Zelaya in attendance, the UN General Assembly approved by acclamation a resolution to condemn the coup, demand the immediate reinstatement of President Zelaya, and call on all states to recognize no other president of Honduras except Zelaya. Among the long list of co-sponsors were the United States and Canada.[29] On 4 July, the OAS unanimously voted to suspend Honduras's membership by a vote of 33 to 0, making it the first country to be treated as such since Cuba had been 'excluded' in 1962.[30] To the extent that the OAS's suspension of Honduras aimed to send the harshest possible rebuke to the democratic interruption, it accomplished its aim. The coup leaders quickly understood that they would have few if any external allies in the ensuing months to come. In the end, this would prove to be the high-water mark in support for Zelaya.

Ironically, however, by promptly expelling the new regime, the OAS may have played its strongest card too fast. If there was one event that symbolized this impetuousness, it was Zelaya's questionable attempt to fly back to Honduras – supported by Insulza and other leaders who flew on a separate plane. This episode was seen as a disaster in the OAS, one that showed that emotions were running too high and this was burning bridges with the de facto authorities. Some heavy back-pedaling began, and eyes shifted to the United States, where on 7 July, Zelaya met with Secretary of State Clinton, who secured commitments from both Zelaya and Micheletti to submit to negotiations overseen by Costa Rica's Arias. This initiated what was to become a drawn-out and agonizing process (no doubt a key aim of the Micheletti camp) that sought to pick up the impasse reached by the OAS under the auspices of a seven-point San José Accord, as proposed by President Arias.[31]

Canada played a supporting role in the negotiations sponsored by Arias. The role fell largely on the shoulders of minister of state for the Americas Peter Kent. A former journalist, Kent was a relative newcomer to politics, having been elected to Parliament in a Toronto riding in October 2008. His knowledge and experience with Latin America was limited, although in the 1980s he had reported on Nicaragua while working for NBC News in Miami. Kent's website provides some insight into the work he was doing during that time: 'His beat spanned an era when many countries of the region struggled to survive communism and narco-terrorism.' Kent represented Canada, instead of foreign affairs minister Lawrence Cannon, as part of an OAS delegation that travelled to Honduras in late August to urge approval of the San José Accord. In this instance, there was never any question of Canadian involvement in the Honduras crisis, in part because Kent cultivated a cordial and, by the standards of Canadian involvement in the OAS, close working relationship with Secretary General Insulza. He was taken seriously by both Zelaya and Micheletti. Although Kent does not speak Spanish, which meant he had to be accompanied by a translator, he was active in most of the key meetings and spent a lot of time (above all considering the fact that in the Canadian system a member of Parliament is expected to be present in the House) on the telephone working for a resolution of the crisis.

As weeks turned to months, it became increasingly apparent that Zelaya's restoration was unlikely. Canada quietly (though arguably not enthusiastically) maintained its support for the restoration of Zelaya behind closed doors, what with the ALBA countries parsing every word that came out of Canadian officials' mouths. The carefully crafted message was always: 'We have the San Jose accord and the San Jose-Tegucigalpa accord, let's implement it.' But as the months rolled by and November's scheduled presidential election drew nearer, it became increasingly unlikely that Zelaya would be restored to public office.

Many countries began to impose limited punitive measures against Honduras to try to increase pressure on the regime. For instance, the United States revoked the visas of numerous Hondurans associated with the coup and suspended $16.5 million in military aid;[32] the European Union suspended around $90 million in aid;[33] and Honduras's neighbours Nicaragua, El Salvador, and Guatemala announce a temporary cessation of cross-border trade. International institutions similarly began to withhold funds, with the World Bank announcing a 'pause' on the release of some $270 million.[34] Canada, however, chose not to suspend any visas or aid, continuing to provide even military financing to Honduras. In the words of Kent: 'This isn't the time to talk about suspending, cutting aid or imposing sanctions.'[35]

Amid the near-unanimous international position that the November elections would not be recognized if Zelaya was not restored to power, a breakthrough finally seemed to occur on 30 October, when both the Zelaya and Micheletti camps agreed to the Tegucigalpa-San Jose Accord. The principal components of the accord were that the Honduran Congress would vote on the restoration of President Zelaya, a government of national reconciliation would be formed within a week, and a truth and reconciliation commission would be established. But hardly had the ink dried when the U.S. announced a major about-face in its position on the coming elections. On 3 November 2009, in an interview with CNN en Español, assistant secretary of state for western hemisphere affairs Thomas Shannon stated that the U.S. would recognize the November elections irrespective of whether Zelaya was returned to power.[36] U.S. ambassador to Honduras, Hugo Llorens, declared, 'The elections will be part of the reality and will return Honduras to the path of democracy.'[37] And parting with diplomatic norms, U.S. Ambassador to the OAS Lewis Anselem asserted that other countries' refusal to recognize the elections was tantamount to 'magic realism.'[38] This new U.S. position was a response, at least in part, to the congressional hold placed on two Obama nominees – Shannon to the post of ambassador to Brazil and Arturo Valenzuela to fill Shannon's vacancy (which Valenzuela subsequently left in July of 2011) – by Republican Senator Jim DeMint. DeMint, who had travelled to Honduras the previous month to meet with leaders of the coup regime, issued a press release on 5 November that read:

> Today, U.S. Senator Jim DeMint (R-South Carolina), a member of the Senate Foreign Relations Committee, announced he has secured a commitment from the Obama administration to recognize the Honduran elections on November 29th, regardless of whether former President Manuel Zelaya is returned to office and regardless of whether the vote on reinstatement takes place before or after November 29th. Given this commitment, which Senator DeMint has requested for months, he will lift objections on the nominations of Arturo Valenzuela to be Assistant Secretary of Western Hemisphere Affairs and Thomas Shannon to be U.S. Ambassador to Brazil.[39]

The U.S.'s reversal provided a sufficient opening for Micheletti and the Honduran Congress to interpret the accord in line with their political goals, and it quickly became clear that the de facto regime would hold onto power until the election. What is certain is that Zelaya's miscalculation that the other parties (Micheletti and the U.S. administration) were acting in good faith would cost him any shot at returning to the presidency. What is subject to debate is whether the Obama administration was also snookered, or whether they predicted, or in some sense choreographed, the drama that eventually unfolded.

The events that transpired in relation to the Honduran coup draw attention to some of the challenges facing Canada's focus on democracy promotion, the continued relevance and shortcomings of the OAS, and the Democratic Charter itself. Before 28 June, the organization appeared to be declining in regional significance. It faced an ascendant competitor: UNASUR took the lead in resolving Bolivia's September 2008 crisis between President Evo Morales and the eastern departments, during which twenty peasants were massacred by anti-governmental paramilitaries in Pando. The Summit of the Americas seems to have lost focus ever since the rising Latin American 'pink tide' torpedoed the proposed FTAA. At the fifth summit, in Trinidad and Tobago in April 2009, the most significant decisions made were to allow the re-entry of an uninterested Cuba into the inter-American system, and to schedule subsequent meetings.[40] It is thus fair to say that the Honduran coup did breathe some new life into the OAS and the Democratic Charter.

More important, albeit on a limited basis, the crisis in Honduras shed light on several inadequacies of the Charter, triggering debates over how to improve it so as to better prevent and respond to future democratic interruptions. One obvious step, which Canada may wish to take up at some point, is to clarify what constitutes an 'unconstitutional alteration of the constitutional democratic order' in articles 19 and 20. This elucidation could prevent democratic interruptions such as that which occurred in Honduras, inasmuch as clear guidelines would outline for political actors those actions that would be perceived as a coup by the inter-American system. A related reform, which Insulza has proposed, would be to widen the institutional actors that are permitted to make claims before the OAS under the Democratic Charter.[41] In addition to the executive, the OAS could conceivably send diplomatic missions or consider resolutions in response to requests made by other chambers of government, regionally elected officials and political parties, as well as indigenous nations and civil society organizations. Together, these reforms could conspire and throw up early warning signs that a democratic interruption is imminent.

Canada's Democracy-Promotion Role

While it is true that Canada has aggressively pursued democracy promotion since joining the OAS in 1990, this often has to be reconciled with other foreign policy objectives. For example, Canadian foreign-policy makers are sometimes torn between the competing imperatives of multilateralism and the need to cultivate a 'special relationship' with the United States. This was highlighted in Canada's response to the Honduran constitutional crisis. As a relatively small country, Canada seeks to support multilateralism and a rules-based international order, yet relations with the United States are the single most important driver of Canada's external policy.

The most awkward moments for Canadian foreign policy arise when the United States abandons multilateral institutions. Such moments may force Canadian policy makers to choose between their prefer-ence for multilateralism and their desire to protect relations with the United States. This is a choice the United States does not face in the same way. A major difference between Canada and the United States is that Canadian foreign-policy makers are more attuned to the think-ing in Washington than vice versa, because of the massive asymmetries of power between the two nations. Foreign policy in Washington is far more likely to be driven by the need to balance and accommodate the interests and preferences of domestic forces than to accommodate partners or allies. The combination of the greater power of domestic constituents relative to the influence of other countries in shaping U.S. policy, coupled with the greater power that the United States exercises in the world, especially in regions like Latin America, ensures that U.S. policy is far more likely to be unilateral. It takes a willingness to risk potentially costly conflict and retaliation for Canada to oppose U.S. unilateralism. This can be done if the domestic rewards are sufficient, which means there must be a major domestic current of public opinion in opposition to U.S. policy, as there was, for example, at the time of the March 2003 invasion of Iraq. Of course, willingness to risk conflict is lowest among those whose interests (mostly economic) are most con-sistently served by close ties to the United States. Conservative govern-ments have tended to be close to the business community, which means that their domestic base is risk averse when it comes to managing rela-tions with the United States.

All of these considerations came into play in the coup in Honduras. Canadian officials quickly and consistently denounced the coup; they worked assiduously within the OAS to seek a resolution of the crisis; and the government dedicated high-level personnel to ensure Canadian involvement in seeking a resolution to the crisis. Officially, Canada did everything possible to uphold the principles of multilateralism, including, in this instance, the enforcement of the Democratic Charter. A more nuanced examination suggests that Canada's actions represented the minimum required in terms of upholding the Democratic Charter and the Harper government's commitment to engagement with and support for democracies in the region. By working behind the scenes and saying little in public about their role, Canadian officials sought to preserve a margin of manoeuvre that would allow Canada to support actions by the United States even where such actions went outside and (we would argue) undermined the position of the OAS and the Democratic Charter – actions, by the way, that Canada never criticized. Canada was one of a few countries that sided with the U.S. in opposing resolutions that refused to recognize Honduras's November 2009 elections *without the prior reinstatement of Zelaya*. Moreover, the actions and statements by Canadian policy makers reflected their evident distaste for President Zelaya and his government and an eagerness to distance Canada from the position of those countries that backed Zelaya before and after the coup – that is, the members of ALBA. These points will be considered in turn.

Kent's involvement in the crisis might be read as a signal of the importance assigned by the Harper government to hemispheric issues. Whereas Canada has been at the margins of similar issues in the past, here was a top official engaged with the file like no previous cabinet official since foreign minister Lloyd Axworthy led the OAS high-level mission to Peru in 2000. Critics, on the other hand, argued that Kent lacked experience. John M. Kirk and Peter McKenna observed: 'Even when an OAS delegation of Latin American foreign ministers first visited Honduras in August, Canada sent Peter Kent, a junior minister of state for the Americas, instead. It was extremely poor form, and sent out the wrong message to the rest of our hemispheric partners.'[42] One Canadian official disputed this view, saying it was unclear which hemispheric partners were bothered by the fact that Kent was a rookie; he appeared to get along well with his counterparts in Chile, Mexico, and elsewhere. Perhaps Brazilian diplomats would have liked someone of a higher rank; they were, after all, more deeply engaged in the crisis, especially after Zelaya took refuge in their embassy.[43] Certainly, Kent did not pretend to be an expert on the region, nor did this stop him from playing an aggressive role.

Even if the prime minister had tapped someone with more stature, such as then-foreign affairs minister Lawrence Cannon, it is important to recognize that the Harper government is one of the most centralized in recent Canadian history, and few cabinet officials have any latitude to operate at the margins of instructions from the Prime Minister's Office (PMO). Whether Kent was the official in charge, or someone else, the tone and direction of Canadian policy would come from the PMO and would not have varied significantly from the position that Kent consistently articulated. Moreover, the Conservative government regarded the Department of Foreign Affairs as hostile territory, and devoted considerable effort in ensuring its activities were 'aligned' with government priorities. This too contributed to the tight-lipped quality of the diplomatic effort. Very little could be said or done without permission from Ottawa, and what appeared on the public record was a consistent, terse, and disciplined message.

Critics noted that Canada's statements about the coup and actions taken against the de facto regime were often among the most circumscribed in the hemisphere. Meanwhile, Canada offered more than veiled criticisms of Zelaya. At one point, for example, Kent chastised Zelaya for contributing to the crisis that resulted in his overthrow, saying 'there has to be an appreciation of the events that led up to the coup.'[44] Asked to clarify this, Kent said the coup was 'unquestionably illegal and must be reversed' but that Canada 'recognizes the context which preceded the coup' and that the 'supreme court and congress had acted within the constitutional framework up to the moment that the armed forces arrested and expelled Zelaya.'[45] This implies a judgment that the assessment of Zelaya's behaviour as unconstitutional was well founded, even if his removal and exile were not. As well, an aid to the ousted Honduran president explained that Canada's disposition to Zelaya was regularly conveyed by Kent in his telephone diplomacy, during which the minister allegedly, 'blatantly attacked [Zelaya] or made direct complaints.'[46]

By coming close to publicly blaming Zelaya for the crisis,[47] Canadian officials were able to deflect pressure for stronger sanctions against the de facto regime. Some officials lamented the lack of leverage over Honduras, noting that aid for 2009 had already been disbursed and military assistance amounted to little more than language training. Yet it is hard to accept the claim that more could not have been done to bring pressure to bear on the regime. Honduras is the second-largest recipient of Canadian Official Development Assistance (ODA) in the Americas, and Canada is one of the largest foreign investors in Honduras.[48] A more likely reason why this leverage was not used is that the Harper government was not about to take any steps that might be perceived as prejudicial to Canadian business interests in Honduras. Interviewed on CBC's *The Current*, Kent responded to the accusation that Canadian policy is shaped by an interest in protecting commercial and mining interests by saying 'Canadians should be proud of' apparel manufacturer Gildan Activewear and mining firm Goldcorp.[49] He went on to give the precise dollar amount of Nicaragua-Honduran cross-border trade that was affected by President Zelaya's attempts to return to his country at one of the border crossings.

More disturbingly, the Canadian government did not condemn the extensive human rights abuses carried out by the armed forces and police under the coup government,[50] which, according to the human rights group Committee of Relatives of the Detained-Disappeared in Honduras (COFADEH) involved at least 708 documented cases of human rights violations, including the right to physical integrity, free association, peaceable protest, free movement, and life.[51] This is consistent with the findings of a December 2009 report by the Inter-American Commission on Human Rights:

> Along with the loss of institutional legitimacy brought about by the *coup d'état*, during its visit the Commission confirmed that serious human rights violations had been committed, including killings, an arbitrary declaration of a state of emergency, disproportionate use of force against public demonstrations, criminalization of public protest, arbitrary detention of thousands of persons, cruel, inhuman and degrading treatment, poor detention conditions, militarization of Honduran territory, an increase in incidents of racial discrimination, violations of women's rights, severe and arbitrary restrictions on the right to freedom of expression, and serious violations of political rights. The Commission also established that judicial remedies were ineffective in protecting human rights.[52]

Canada's silence on human rights in Honduras can be juxtaposed against Kent's willingness to decry Venezuela's interventions into the private media: 'Canada is concerned over the Venezuelan government's recent suspension of broadcasting of six television stations ... These events are further evidence of a shrinking democratic space in Venezuela. Freedom of expression and access to information from a wide range of sources are fundamental elements of a healthy democracy.'[53] In Honduras, however, where democratic space was much narrower, independent information was prohibited, and the media were muzzled, there was neither a word of criticism from Canada, nor did this affect the snap judgment that the elections held on 29 November were free and fair. Such a discrepancy suggests that a never publicly articulated anti-Chávez ideological bias had an influence on Canadian foreign policy, since diplomats privately acknowledged that Canadian policy was more ideologically driven than was the position of most other countries.[54]

Indeed, the Harper government's anti-Chávez sentiment appears to afflict Canadian foreign policy to a greater degree than it does the U.S. – especially on matters of democratic pluralism. This flows from the framing of Canada's position as representing a balance between ideological extremes, a framing that is more likely to encourage polarization than encourage engagement with democracies in the region. Not surprisingly, the Chávez government lashed back at the Canadian government after an official visit by Minister Kent to Venezuela in January 2010 during which he met with several members of the opposition, but the highest-ranking official he was able to meet was the chair of the Foreign Relations Committee. Venezuela's ambassador to the OAS, Roy Chaderton, belittled Kent by labelling him an 'ultraright' journalist and suggested that Venezuela would take no advice from a Prime Minister (Harper) who had prorogued Parliament to avoid debate on the torture of Afghan detainees.[55]

In one key respect, Canadian officials failed to use the Democratic Charter in a principled way: that is, Canada should have withheld recognition of the Honduran elections of 29 November 2009. The presidential elections were held under conditions that raise at the very least prima facie questions about whether they can be considered free and fair; and, perhaps more to the point, the absence of properly accredited international observation makes assertions about the outcome just that – assertions. Anyone can read the news headlines and say 'that there was a strong turnout for the elections, that they appear to have been run freely and fairly, and that there was no major violence.'[56] The Democratic Charter falls short of requiring all countries to invite international observers but it creates a strong presumption that this should be the norm. In Honduras, the OAS (and the European Union) took the position that it could not observe the elections unless invited by both Zelaya and the coup government. In other words, the election could only be observed and given the OAS seal of approval as long as its legitimacy was not contested, which the organization was obviously loath to do. Since the deal with Zelaya fell through, the election was not properly monitored.[57]

Whereas most Latin American nations refused to recognize the elections as valid, Canada joined the U.S. in recognizing Porfirio Lobo as the new president on the grounds that he received the vote of 57 per cent of those who went to the polls. For some commentators, this signifies a stamp of approval of the coup, a position captured by Bolivian ambassador to the OAS, José Pinelo, at a 4 December 2009 meeting of the OAS: 'Recognizing Mr. Lobo is the same as recognizing Micheletti. It means ... trusting that those who took power with guns on June 28th, suddenly turned into democrats on November 29th, administering or allowing free elections.'[58] As Laura Carlsen, director of the Americas Program for the Center for International Policy, reported from Tegucigalpa:

The coup's dictatorial decrees restricting freedom of assembly, freedom of speech and freedom of movement held the nation in a virtual state of siege in the weeks prior to the elections. Over forty registered candidates resigned in protest. Members of the resistance movement were harassed, beaten and detained. In San Pedro Sula, an election-day march was brutally repressed.[59]

On the night of the election, Honduras's Supreme Electoral Tribunal (TSE) released the election results, claiming that 62 per cent of the electorate had gone to the polls, in what many observers have argued was a deliberate inflation of the election figures to give the process, as well as the coup itself, legitimacy. It was within this window that many countries, including Canada on 1 December, endorsed the election results.[60] Several days later, the TSE revised the number of those who voted down to 49 per cent, which, after subtracting the 153,730 ballots that were either left blank or spoiled – 6.7 per cent of the ballots cast – represents about 45 per cent of the total electorate.[61] Having secured 57 per cent of the votes, and assuming zero fraud, *Lobo's support signifies 26 per cent of the electorate* (approximately 1.2 million out of 4.6 million registered voters), in an election in which the majority did not participate, and held under conditions that cannot be certified as meeting international standards of democratic fairness and freedom.

Denouement: The Truth Commission, Zelaya, and Reintegration into the OAS

The most important element of the Tegucigalpa-San José accord – the restitution of Zelaya – was never implemented. Subsequent to the election of the government of President Lobo, implementation came to be understood in terms of two goals: first, the return of Zelaya from exile to Honduras with protection from prosecution for himself and his followers; and, second, a Truth and Reconciliation Commission (TRC, hereafter CVR in its Spanish acronym) would be created to clarify the events surrounding the removal of Zelaya. On 1 June 2011, shortly after Zelaya returned home on 28 May, Honduras was re-admitted to the OAS by a vote of 32 to 1 (with only Ecuador in opposition). A joint effort by Colombia and Venezuela, normally diplomatic foes, paved the way.

Canadian policy makers did not wait to normalize relations with Honduras. When Prime Minister Harper travelled to Tegucigalpa as part of an official tour of the region in August 2011, he not only lavished warm praise on President Lobo; he announced the successful conclusion of the trade talks that were begun before Honduras rejoined the OAS in June. A tougher line with Honduras would have required progress in the implementation of the recommendations of the truth commission prior to the negotiation of a trade agreement, especially improvements in the human rights situation. In contrast, Harper called human rights advocates who were critical of the trade deal with Honduras 'protectionists' who did not care about the people on whose behalf they claimed to advocate.[62]

Nevertheless, Canada should be lauded for providing support to the CVR. The Department of Foreign Affairs assigned senior Canadian diplomat Michael F. Kergin to participate as a commissioner, and he worked under the direction of Eduardo Stein, who was well versed in the democracy-promotion jurisprudence in the Americas, having led the OAS mission to Peru in 2000. That mission resulted in a report that sent the OAS on a collision course with the Fujimori regime. Given Stein's stature and integrity, it was not surprising that the report, which was released in July 2011, and entitled *Para que los hechos no se repitan*, provided a thorough and balanced review of the events surrounding the coup and made detailed recommendations for political reform. It did not mince words when describing the events of 28 June 2009 a *golpe de Estado*,[63] even as it asserted egregious violations of the constitution perpetrated by Zelaya.

The report noted that the OAS response came too late, in part because of the Democratic Charter's 'executive bias.' Only executive branches of government are represented in the OAS and can call for the application of the Charter, but problems often arise from tensions between the executive and legislature and judiciary. The report also called for more and better monitoring; preventive diplomacy to avoid similar crises; and the need to develop strategies and instruments to deal with crises arising from tensions between state powers, as well as the lack of mechanisms for conflict prevention and resolution.[64] Finally, the report made wide-ranging recommendations for extensive and profound political reforms in Honduras, including the need to recognize the right of the people to exercise their constituent power to change the constitution. It highlighted the poor quality of the written constitution, the fact that it did not have an impeachment clause, and the extraordinary rigidity created by the inclusion of articles that are supposedly non-amendable.[65]

Conclusion

The coup in Honduras did not provide a shining example of Canada's successful defence of democracy in the Americas. Overall, it set a poor precedent to allow an officially unobserved election to erase the stain of illegitimacy created by a military coup. *Borron y cuenta nueva* (wipe the slate clean and start again) is a poor excuse for good policy. And yet, future historians may find that the coup, and the response it provoked, initiated a process that culminated in change. At the very least, the episode exposed the fact that Honduras has a defective constitution, and there will be pressure to change it. The CVR found that the removal of Zelaya was illegal, yet the de facto government used the claim that it had a constitutional basis to hang onto power and stymie the international community. The international community has to get a lot smarter about dismissing tendentious claims about the constitutionality of coups.

First, Canada played a big role in the creation of the Democratic Charter, and the Harper government (with a majority after the May 2011 federal election) should continue to work to ensure that it is used more effectively and more consistently. Secretary Insulza and other OAS officials have acknowledged that the coup in Honduras has exposed important problems with the Charter. From the standpoint of officials in Ottawa, three are particularly noteworthy. First, as noted by the CVR, the Charter has a bias in favour of the executive branch of government. Through their diplomats, presidents, and prime ministers, member states have a say in the OAS – but not via their legislatures or courts. There are no formal mechanisms for other branches of governments to appeal directly to the OAS when crises are brewing. Needless to say, institutional participation should be expanded in the future.

Second, the Charter does not spell out explicitly enough what counts as an unconstitutional interruption of the democratic order; nor does it have the means to deal with 'eyesore' constitutions – that is, constitutions that are fatally flawed in ways that invite constitutional crises. By seeking to engage other branches of government in dealing with constitutional crises before they become ruptures of the constitutional order, Canada should strongly urge the empowerment of the OAS to be more preventive and proactive in its diplomatic efforts.

Finally, it is important for Canada to push to close the loophole that the coup in Honduras clearly exposed – namely, the use of caretaker coups that remove an elected leader and then run out the clock until new elections have been held. The key to closing this loophole is precisely to refuse to automatically recognize the newly elected authorities (under any circumstances) and to insist upon a negotiated process of reintegration into the OAS in which the Democratic Charter provides the framework. After more than twenty years of championing the issue of democracy promotion within the OAS, Canada should use this experience and record to argue forcefully for these kinds of changes.

NOTES

1 Telephone interview with senior Canadian official conducted on a not-for-attribution basis, 15 January 2010. By mid-2010, Canada was actively involved in seeking to end Honduras's isolation within the OAS.

2 See Benjamin Arditi, 'Arguments about the Left Turns in Latin America: A Post-Liberal Politics?' *Latin American Research Review* 43, no. 3 (2008): 59–81; Patrick Barratt, Daniel Chavez, and César Rodríguez-Garavito (eds.), *The New Latin American Left: Utopia Reborn* (London: Pluto Press, 2008); Maxwell A. Cameron, 'Latin America's Left Turns: Beyond Good and Bad,' *Third World Quarterly* 30, no. 2 (2009): 331–48; Maxwell A. Cameron and Eric Hershberg (eds.), *Latin America's Many Lefts: Political Parties, Insurgent Movements, and Alternative Policies* (Boulder, CO: Lynn Rienner, 2010).

3 For a discussion of the origins of the Inter-American Democratic Charter, and Canada's role, see Andrew Cooper and Thomas Legler, *Intervention without Intervening? The OAS Defense and Promotion of Democracy in the Americas* (New York: Palgrave Macmillan, 2006). A more sceptical view is presented by Mikulas Fabri, 'The Inter-American Democratic Charter and

Governmental Legitimacy in the International Relations of the Western Hemisphere,' *Diplomacy and Statecraft* 20, no. 1 (2009): 107–35.

4 See Eric Hershberg and Fred Rosen (eds.), *Latin America after Neoliberalism: Turning the Tide in the 21st Century?* (New York: NACLA and the New Press, 2006).

5 At this 2009 OAS General Assembly meeting, member states unanimously resolved to revoke its 1962 resolution which excluded Cuba from the body – in the face of significant U.S. opposition. The Cubans (who have expressed little interest in rejoining the organization), however, would have to meet certain conditions before they could be admitted. First, the Cuban government would have to initiate a dialogue with the hemispheric forum and express an interest in rejoining the body. Havana would then have to participate in the organization 'in conformity with the practices, purposes, and principles of the OAS.' Still, this should be seen as an overall success for the OAS. See Mary Beth Sheridan, 'OAS Lifts Cuba's Suspension, with Provisos,' *Washington Post*, 4 June 2009, A8.

6 'Patricia Rodas Dice que Constitución Es un Adefesio,' *El Heraldo*, 24 June 2009, http://www.elheraldo.hn/Ediciones/2009/06/25/Noticias/Patricia-Rodas-dice-que-Constitucion-es-un-adefesio (accessed 2 March 2010). The term was used by senior OAS officials in discussing the crisis in Honduras; statements made on a not-for-attribution basis, Washington, DC, 15 October 2009.

7 The United States had preferred former Mexican foreign minister Luis Ernesto Derbez for the position of secretary-general.

8 Peter McKenna, *Canada and the OAS* (Ottawa: Carleton University Press, 1995).

9 See chapter 4 of Cooper and Legler, *Intervention without Intervening?*

10 Inter-American Democratic Charter, Organization of American States General Assembly, Lima, Peru, 11 September 2001.

11 Foreign Affairs and International Trade Canada, *A New Focus on Democracy Support. Government Response to the Eighth Report of the Standing Committee on Foreign Affairs and International Development: Advancing Canada's Role in International Support for Democratic Development*, Ottawa, 2 November 2007, 5. http://www.international.gc.ca/democracy_support.aspx (accessed 17 January 2008). Original report by the House of Commons Standing Committee, *Advancing Canada's Role in International Support for Democratic Development: Report of the Standing Committee on Foreign Affairs and International Development*, 39th Parliament, 1st Session, Ottawa, July 2007, http://cmte.parl.gc.ca/Content/HOC/committee/391/faae/reports/rp3066139/391_FAAE_Rpt08_PDF/391_FAAE_Rpt08-e.pdf.

12 Senior Canadian official, personal communication, Department of Foreign
    Affairs, Ottawa, 7 October 2008. Statement made on a not-for-attribution
    basis.
13 Office of the Prime Minister of Canada, Stephen Harper, *Prime Minister
    Harper Signals Canada's Renewed Engagement in the Americas*, Santiago,
    Chile, 17 July 2007, http://pm.gc.ca/eng/media.asp?id=1759 (accessed 17
    January 2008).
14 Stephen Harper, interview, *Americas Quarterly* (Fall 2007): 8–10.
15 Government of Canada, *Prime Minister Stephen Harper Addresses the House
    of Commons in a Reply to the Speech from the Throne*, 17 October 2007, http://
    www.sft-ddt.gc.ca/eng/media.asp?id=1373 (accessed 22 August 2008).
16 As Shamsie and Grinspun put it, 'Ottawa's relations with the region are
    governed by, and regularly subverted to, powerful economic and security
    interests – strategic alignment with U.S. hemispheric priorities would fall
    in this category – which undermine its efforts to address social and demo-
    cratic development goals in the region.' Yasmine Shamsie and Ricardo
    Grinspun, 'Missed Opportunity: Canada's Re-engagement with Latin
    America and the Caribbean,' *Canadian Journal of Latin American and Carib-
    bean Studies* 35, no. 69 (2010): 171–99.
17 For a discussion of ALBA, see Martin Hart-Landsberg, 'Learning from
    ALBA and the Bank of the South: Challenges and Possibilities,' *New Left
    Review* 61, no. 4 (2009): 1–18.
18 See Constitution of Honduras, 1982.
19 The authenticity of these court documents remains in question, and OAS
    Secretary-General José Miguel Insulza has suggested that the Honduran
    Supreme Court had 'no idea what was going on' at the time of the coup.
    See José Miguel Insulza, Canadian Foundation for the Americas Roundta-
    ble, Ottawa, September 14, 2009, and Supreme Court of Honduras, 'Comu-
    nicado Especial,' 29 June 2009.
20 Supreme Court of Honduras, 'Comunicado Especial,' 29 June 2009.
21 See 'Costa Rica's President Warns South Florida Conference about Hondu-
    ran Elections,' *South Florida Sun-Sentinel*, 30 September 2009.
22 José Miguel Insulza, Canadian Foundation for the Americas Roundtable,
    Ottawa, 14 September 2009.
23 See Maxwell A.Cameron, 'A Coup Is a Coup Is a Coup,' *The Mark*, 13
    October 2009, http://www.themarknews.com/articles/568-a-coup-is-a-
    coup-is-a-coup, and Maxwell A. Cameron and Jason Tockman, 'A Diplo-
    matic Theater of the Absurd: Canada, the OAS and the Honduran Coup,'
    NACLA Report on the Americas 43, no. 3 (May/June 2010): 18–22.
24 Organization of American States, 'Suspension of the Right of Honduras

to Participate in the Organization of American States,' General Assembly Resolution XXXVII-E/09, 4 July 2009.

25 Interview with Peter Kent on CBC radio, *The Current*, 29 July 2009, http://www.cbc.ca/thecurrent/2009/200907/20090729.html.

26 José Miguel Insulza, Canadian Foundation for the Americas Roundtable, Ottawa, 14 September 2009.

27 Hillary Clinton, United States Department of State daily press briefing, 29 June 2009.

28 Foreign Affairs and International Trade Canada, 'Statement by Minister of State Kent on the Situation in Honduras,' news release, 28 June 2009.

29 United Nations General Assembly, 'Situation in Honduras: Democracy Breakdown,' Resolution A63/L74, June 30, 2009.

30 In early June 2011, the Honduran government, at a special session of the OAS General Assembly, was reinstated as a full-fledged member of the hemispheric body.

31 By the time an 'agreement' was seemingly reached between Zelaya and Micheletti in late October 2009, the number of points in the San José Accord had reached 12.

32 From a news release by the U.S. Embassy in Honduras, 8 July 2009, http://honduras.usembassy.gov/pr-07-08-09-eng.html. At that time, the U.S. government additionally warned of the possible cutoff of $180 million in other forms of aid. In September, the amount of funds suspended by the U.S. government was scaled up to $30 million; see http://www.state.gov/r/pa/prs/ps/2009/sept/128653.htm.

33 See website of European Commission External Relations Commissioner Benita Ferrero-Waldner: http://ec.europa.eu/commission_barroso/ferrero-waldner/speeches/index_en.htm.

34 See World Bank news release: http://go.worldbank.org/P02ECB42H0.

35 Laura Payton, 'No Plans for Sanctions Against Honduras: Kent,' *Embassy*, 25 August 2009.

36 See interview at http://www.youtube.com/watch?v=asbYkOMvbj8.

37 'Embajador de EE.UU. Dice que los Comicios Devolverán la Democracia a Honduras,' *EFE*, 8 November 2009, http://mx.news.yahoo.com/s/08112009/38/n-latam-embajador-ee-uu-dice-comicios.html (accessed 31 January 2010).

38 Ginger Thompson, 'U.S. Tries to Salvage Honduras Accord,' *New York Times*, 10 November 2009. http://www.nytimes.com/2009/11/11/world/americas/11honduras.html?_r=2 (accessed 31 January 2010).

39 See 'DeMint: Administration Commits to Recognize Honduran Elections,' news release, http://demint.senate.gov/public/index.

cfm?FuseAction=PressReleases.Detail&PressRelease_id=c6542515-c3af-d65a-085d-537015ff8a97.

40 While the declaration does include a few new social commitments, such as efforts to expand tertiary education and combat mother-to-child transmission of HIV, most of the text consists of statements that 'reaffirm,' 'renew,' 'redouble,' and 'reiterate' pledges made at previous summits, and in other fora. The text also 'encourages' signatories to adopt various provisions, such as renewable energy and sustainable development of bio-fuels, 'as appropriate'; see Declaration of Commitment of Port of Spain, 'Securing Our Citizens' Future by Promoting Human Prosperity, Energy Security, and Environmental Sustainability,' Fifth Summit of the Americas, Port of Spain, Trinidad and Tobago, 19 April 2009. At the VI Summit of the Americas in Cartagena, Colombia, in April 2012, both Canada and the U.S. found themselves at odds with most of the other countries on turning the hemispheric page on Cuba. See Frank Bajak and Vivian Sequera, 'U.S., Canada Alone at Summit in Cuba Stance,' *Miami Herald*, 13 April 2012.

41 José Miguel Insulza, Canadian Foundation for the Americas Roundtable, Ottawa, 14 September 2009.

42 John M. Kirk and Peter McKenna, 'Canada Falters over Crisis in Honduras,' *The Guardian*, 31 December 2009.

43 Telephone interview with senior Canadian official conducted on a not-for-attribution basis, 15 January 2010.

44 Marc Lacey and Ginger Thompson, 'Envoy Prepares to Visit Honduras,' *New York Times*, 3 July 2009, A10. http://www.nytimes.com/2009/07/03/world/americas/03honduras.html.

45 Kent interview, CBC, *The Current*, 29 July 2009.

46 Personal electronic communication on a not-for-attribution basis, 15 November 2009.

47 According to one aid to the ousted Honduran president during his telephone calls with Zelaya, Kent sometimes, 'blatantly attacked [President Zelaya] or made direct complaints.' Personal electronic communication on a not-for-attribution basis, November 15, 2009.

48 See Kent interview, and Kirk and McKenna, 'Canada Falters over Crisis in Honduras.' According to the Canadian International Development Agency, 'CIDA's 2007–2008 disbursements for projects and initiatives in Honduras: $17.09 million,' http://www.acdi-cida.gc.ca/acdi-cida/ACDI-CIDA.nsf/Eng/JUD-129123554-NN3 (accessed 30 January 2010).

49 Kent interview.

50 John M. Kirk, 'Harper's Many Missteps in the Americas,' *Embassy*, 22 July 2009, 9.

51 Dina Meza, 'COFADEH Documentó 708 Casos de Violaciones a los Derechos Humanos de Junio a Diciembre,' 19 January 2010, http://www.defensoresenlinea.com/cms/index.php?option=com_content&view=article&id=591:cofadeh-documento-708-casos-de-violaciones-a-los-derechos-humanos-de-junio-a-diciembre-&catid=54:den&Itemid=171 (accessed 31 January 2010).

52 Inter-American Commission on Human Rights, *Honduras: Human Rights and the Coup d'État* (Washington: Inter-American Commission on Human Rights, 30 December 2009), 2.

53 From Peter Kent's official website, 'Canada Concerned over Free Speech Rights in Venezuela,' http://www.peterkent.ca/EN/8128/105449 (accessed 30 January 2010).

54 Comment by official in the Department of Foreign Affairs and International Trade, made on a not-for-attribution basis, Ottawa, 8 October 2009.

55 Chaderton mistakenly characterized the scandal as involving the torture of detainees rather than their transfer to Afghan authorities at a time when Canadian officials knew that prisoners were being tortured. Nevertheless, the criticism of Harper's penchant for proroguing Parliament has a solid foundation: constitutional experts have argued that the prorogation of Parliament to avoid a vote of non-confidence, which occurred in late 2008, was 'of questionable constitutionality'; see Andrew Heard, 'The Governor General's Decision to Prorogue Parliament: Parliamentary Democracy Defended or Endangered?' Centre for Constitutional Studies, Discussion Paper No. 7 (2009).

56 Foreign Affairs and International Trade Canada, 'Canada Congratulates Honduran People on Elections,' news release, 1 December 2009.

57 The U.S-based National Democratic Institute (NDI) did help to deploy and provide training for a Honduran non-governmental organization to monitor the elections. In addition, the Inter-American Dialogue in Washington did take the position that the presidential elections were legitimate and thus should be recognized by governments around the world. See Daphne Morrison, 'A Discussion on the Honduran Elections,' (Washington, DC: Inter-American Dialogue, 9 December 2009).

58 Quoted in Jesse Freeston, 'Transcript: Honduran Elections Exposed' (Tegucigalpa: The Real News Network, 15 December 2009).

59 Laura Carlsen, 'The Sham Elections in Honduras,' *The Nation,* 14 December 2009.

60 In mid-February 2010, Canada's Peter Kent visited Honduras to hold talks with President Lobo. If there was ever any doubt about Ottawa's endorsement of the new government, one should read Government of Canada,

'Statement by Minister of State Kent on Inauguration of Honduran President,' press release (Ottawa: Department of Foreign Affairs and International Trade, 28 January 2010).
61 Supreme Electoral Tribunal of Honduras, 'Elecciones Generales 2009,' http://200.30.166.30/escrutinio/pais.php (accessed 30 January 2010).
62 Mark Kennedy, 'Protesters Denounce Canada-Honduras Free Trade Deal,' *Montreal Gazette*, 20 August 2011. By early 2012, the human rights situation in Honduras still remained precarious, especially for journalists, opponents of the regime, and poor landowners. See Frances Robles, 'Honduras Becomes Murder Capital of the World,' *Miami Herald*, 23 January 2012, and Elisabeth Malkin, 'In Honduras, Land Struggles Highlight Post-Coup Polarization,' *New York Times*, 15 September 2011.
63 Informe de la Comision de la Verdad y Reconciliacion, *Para que los hechos no se repitan* (Honduras, 2011), 202.
64 Comision de la Verdad y Reconciliacion, 416.
65 Comision de la Verdad y Reconciliacion, 398–9.

5 Canada-Mexico Relations: Moving beyond 65 Years of Stunted Growth

DUNCAN WOOD

Though the Canadian government does not always admit it, it would be fair to say that Canada's relations with the world of the Americas begin with Mexico. Not only is Mexico far and away Canada's most important Latin American economic partner, but the two countries share an increasing number of perspectives in foreign policy and are partners in the North American Free Trade Agreement (NAFTA). The common ground, of course, does not end there; thanks to their common membership in the NAFTA, and due to the realities of geography, both nations must deal extensively with the United States on a daily basis.

The year 2009 marked the sixty-fifth anniversary of formal diplomatic relations between Canada and Mexico. The two countries celebrated the history of their relations and the potential for the future with a series of official events, academic conferences, and ministerial visits. Unfortunately, 2009 will also be remembered not for the celebrations that took place, but rather for the Canadian imposition of a visitor's visa on Mexican nationals seeking to travel to Canada.[1] The fallout from this event has left deep scars in the short term (and still continues to raise the ire of Mexicans in late 2012) and has forced actors on both sides to re-evaluate the direction the overall relationship is taking.

This chapter looks at the history and current state of Canada-Mexico relations, and argues that it is the context of the North American economic and political region that has both driven the bilateral relationship but also prevented it from fully developing over the last twenty years. Canada-Mexico relations, then, remain stunted largely because Canada fears losing its privileged and special relationship with the United States, and key actors in the country have viewed Mexico's participation in the process of North American integration as a threat to that relationship.

Furthermore, I argue that Mexico is an important partner for Canada both regionally and globally, and that the relationship should be encouraged to develop beyond what is currently envisioned in either Ottawa or Canada's major business centres. In order to do so, the chapter suggests a series of actions to be taken by both the Canadian and Mexican governments to increase mutual understanding, heighten interaction, and deepen the overall relationship. Most importantly, politicians and officials in Ottawa need to begin to see its relationship with Mexico in a multifaceted way, both within the North American context and beyond, and to delink positive developments in the bilateral relationship from progress or stagnation in Canada-U.S. relations.[2]

A Brief History of a Conflicted Relationship

Canada's reluctance to see Mexico as a full and equal partner in North America can be traced back to the origins of the NAFTA. Having just signed a free trade agreement with the U.S., Canada immediately saw its preferential access to U.S. markets threatened by Carlos Salinas de Gortari's ambitions to sign the world's first free trade agreement (FTA) between a developed and developing nation. Canada's mostly defensive reaction, of course, was to propose a three-way deal, preserving its special status by forming part of a regional trade group that would challenge the European Union (EU) bloc.[3]

This proposal, however, was not without controversy. A number of groups within Canada believed that Mexico was a distant neighbour that would not make a reliable partner for Canada. In the end, however, the realization that the U.S.-Mexico deal would proceed and that staying outside of the agreement would risk not only losing Canada's preferential position in the U.S. market but also creating 'hub and spoke' style free trade agreements between the U.S. and a string of other countries, effectively forced Canada to the negotiating table.

In September 1990, the then Business Council on National Issues (BCNI) submitted a report on the prospective North American free trade deal which outlined the Canadian business perspective.[4] Based on work by Michael Hart, the report stressed the fundamental changes that were underway in the Mexican economy and in Mexican economic policy, noting the dramatic shift toward a free market posture. Although Canada-Mexico trade was still relatively small, as the report clearly noted, future economic growth in Mexico needed to be taken into consideration. Quoting a Royal Bank of Canada report from the same month,[5] the Business Council emphasized the 'substantial investment opportunities' in Mexico that would arise in the coming years.

Most importantly, the report stressed that, regardless of Canada's decision to engage more closely with it, Mexico would integrate more and more closely with the United States through a free trade agreement and productive interdependence. If it opted to stay outside of the U.S.-Mexico FTA, Canada would see an erosion of its 'present preferential access to the American market with no offsetting access (to) the Mexican market, and probably divert trade and investment as a result of increased competition from Mexico in attracting United States as well as offshore trade and investment.'[6] Furthermore, rejecting participation in the FTA would likely encourage a U.S. preference for the 'hub and spoke' system of bilateral trade pacts, which would maximize both U.S. benefits and U.S. negotiating power.

Based on views such as this, the Canadian Parliament decided to opt in favour of Canadian participation in the NAFTA and a more active engagement with Mexico. A process of 'discovery' began that evolved into a slowly deepening relationship between the two countries. As Canada and Mexico began to discover each other, through diplomatic channels, business ties, cultural exchanges, and, of course, tourism, the economic weight of the relationship increased. Between 1993 and 2008, total trade between the two countries rose from $3.5 billion to more than $22 billion (although it experienced a significant contraction in 2009 during the economic crisis) – and with Canadian direct investment reaching almost $4 billion.[7] (The Canadian International Development Agency also disbursed some $7.5 million in aid initiatives and programs in Mexico for 2008–9.)[8] By the end of the 1990s, more than a million Canadians were visiting Mexico every year, and many were repeat visitors. As a result, Mexico began to look like a country that was less far off, less strange, and, though still considered exotic, more 'normal' than before.

Explaining Canada-Mexico Relations

Over the years, a number of different individuals and analytical perspectives have attempted to explain the Canada-Mexico axis. A variety of terms have been used to describe how each nation views each other, or how exactly one should view the other. A prime example of this is Teresa Gutierrez-Haces. As one of the most respected Mexican Canadianists, she has argued that both Canada and Mexico always see the other in the context of the United States, that is, as '*el vecino del vecino*' (the neighbour of the neighbour).[9] In the book *Canadá: Un estado posmoderno*, she argued that the distance between the two countries was less important than the enormous influence of the United States in their respective daily existences, something that created an almost insurmountable obstacle to better understanding and rapprochement. The powerlessness of the two nations to escape the gravity of the U.S. pull is a common theme in studies of Canada-Mexico relations, just as it colours so many of the policy debates centred in both countries. It is a useful and commonly employed tool for teaching Mexican students about Canada, too.[10]

Nonetheless, over the years a number of scholars have sought to go beyond the weight of geography and history to try to understand both the heart of the bilateral relationship and its true potential. Another long-standing analyst of the relationship, Isabel Studer,[11] argued in the 1990s that Canada and Mexico should see each other as more than just 'distant neighbors' and should engage more fully and deeply. MacLean and Wood,[12] in their 2000 assessment of the relationship, argued that the two countries should adopt a relationship based on the principles of partnership in both North America and in Latin America. This work used the term 'new partnership' to describe the two countries' potential relationship in the hemisphere, and indeed various writers have suggested that Canada and Mexico should view each other as strategic partners.

Accordingly, there have been a number of academic attempts to reconceptualize and redefine the bilateral relationship over the years. In 2005, in the wake of the announcement of the Security and Prosperity Partnership (SPP), the C.D. Howe Institute convened a seminar on the 'Canada-Mexico Conundrum,' with support from the Instituto Tecnológico Autónomo de México (ITAM) and the University of Alberta Business School. The goal of the seminar was to find common ground between the two countries, and what emerged was a series of suggestions (discussed later in this chapter) to help increase understanding. However, the seminar concluded that Canada and Mexico had markedly divergent priorities in North America, and that the development gap between the two countries made it difficult to overcome this fact.[13]

In November of the same year, at York University, another conference looked to identify 'big picture realities' in the relationship and called on participants to 'think outside the box.' In this case a more optimistic perspective emerged, suggesting that Canada and Mexico had a number of avenues open to them to deepen their interdependence. First, the increasing common ground between the two nations on matters of foreign policy was seen as a reason to strengthen bilateral ties, with meaningful diplomatic networking put forward as a vital component. Secondly, building on the framework of Canada-Mexico Partnership (see below), sub-state actors were seen as a valuable driver for deepening and moving the relationship forward.[14]

Also in 2005, surely the most active year in terms of academic interest in the bilateral relationship, the Canadian Foundation for the Americas (FOCAL) organized a meeting in Ottawa titled 'Where Are We Going? Canada and Mexico Looking beyond 2006,' in which analysts and government representatives discussed the future of the bilateral relationship, describing it as 'a dynamic, mature and very strong relationship, to the point that for Canada it is only second to the relationship with the United States in the context of the Americas.'[15] Furthermore, the strategic relationship between the two countries was explained by reference to the 'multiple linkages structured around the principles of convergence, coincidence and complementarity.'[16]

More recently, the Mexican Council of Foreign Affairs (COMEXI) and FOCAL began a project named the Canada-Mexico Initiative (CMI). Bringing together senior representatives from academia, the private sector, and government, the CMI aims 'to create an independent working group that will bring forward ideas to add dynamism, deepen and broaden the relationship between Mexico and Canada.'[17] The CMI also promises to play a key role in helping to form the policy agenda that will emerge in the Canada-Mexico Partnership.

The Mexican Seasonal Agricultural Workers Program

The main highlight of the burgeoning bilateral relationship in the early years of the NAFTA, however, was not the level of imports, exports, or FDI but rather a small program allowing Mexican agricultural workers to come to Canada on a seasonal, temporary basis. The Seasonal Agricultural Workers Program (SAWP) was created over forty years ago to bring in seasonal workers from the Caribbean to provide much-needed low-skilled agricultural labour to Canada. The program added Mexico to its list of eligible countries in 1974, creating the Mexican Seasonal Agricultural Workers Program (M/SAWP), which had by the late 1990s become a symbol of the growing interdependence between Canada and Mexico, with rising numbers of Mexican workers participating. Furthermore, Mexican commentators have always made a comparison, perhaps unfairly, with the treatment of migrant workers in the United States, highlighting the comparatively generous wages and benefits of the Canadian program. This has meant that the M/SAWP has become a flagship for the bilateral relationship, despite the emergence of minor but troublesome problems in recent years.

The benefits of the SAWP in general and the M/SAWP in particular for Canada are quite clear. Seasonal demand for low-skilled agricultural workers in key sectors (fruit, vegetable, horticultural, or FVH) is met at a reasonable cost at peak times when there is a shortage of such labour available in Canada. This increases the competitiveness of the Canadian agricultural sector and is a beneficial addition to the value chain in Canadian rural communities, as it frees up local labour for other tasks.

A 2003 North-South Institute report on the M/SAWP noted that it provided 'a formal program of "managed" circular migration.'[18] By facilitating the temporary migration of Caribbean and Mexican agricultural workers into Canada to meet demand for labour, providing them with fair and just compensation, and securing their safe return to Mexico at the end of the season, the program provides a mutually beneficial quid pro quo for Mexican workers and Canadian farmers. The M/SAWP is widely known in Mexico as an example of Canada's 'fairer' immigration culture.

In its first year, the M/SAWP brought 203 workers to Canada, but this number steadily grew to 10,000 by the end of the 1990s and currently stands at around 17,000 per year. The net impact of this employment on families and communities has not been adequately measured, although it is estimated that M/SAWP workers send home around $80 million a year in remittances.[19] But another 2003 study from the North-South Institute noted that the long-term impact on sending communities was minimal, as most of the income earned by workers from the program was spent on daily consumption and supporting their families rather than investing in business opportunities in their home towns.[20] The same report also found that, although Mexican workers were in general very happy with the program, there was still ample room for improvement, especially with regards to an absence of training opportunities, a lack of understanding of the Canadian system of taxation and benefits, and, an issue that would become important in later years, the fact that around 20 per cent of the workers felt they had received treatment that was 'regular or bad,' suggesting that some mistreatment of workers was occurring in Canada.

The Late 1990s: The Dangers of Intimacy

It has often been remarked that, as interdependence increases, so do the opportunities for serious conflict. In the case of Canada-Mexico relations, the distance between the two countries in terms of geography, culture, and the low level of commercial and financial exchange had made it easy to idealize the relationship and talk of the potential for future collaboration and of creating a strategic partnership. Academic papers called for a closer coordination of foreign policies and more Canadian involvement in Mexico, based on the principle that the two had shared interests and would benefit from more integration. However, the differences between the business and government cultures of Canada and Mexico were brought into stark relief when the Canadian firm Bombardier (in conjunction with GEC Alsthom, a French firm) bid on a $500 million contract to build subway cars for the Mexico City transport system in July 1997. Having seen the only rival bid rejected for technical reasons, Bombardier assumed that it had thus legitimately won the bidding round. The decision had been suspiciously postponed earlier that year from May to July, just before the elections for a new Mexico City government. The rival company, a Spanish firm named CAF – which was working with Mitsubishi (Japan) and ICA, a Mexican firm – then filed an objection to the process, and Bombardier saw its contract cancelled and had little choice but to wait until the new city government of Cuauhtemoc Cardenas took office for a final resolution.

The controversy was further deepened when the Canadian ambassador to Mexico, Marc Perron, made inflammatory comments about the state of Mexican corruption with direct reference to the Bombardier case in an interview with a Mexican magazine, calling the case 'a very sordid tale' and claiming that Mexican corruption exceeded what he had witnessed in the Middle East.[21] Mexican ambassador to Canada, Sandra Fuentes-Berain, retorted that 'Canadians are participating in every tender offer in Mexico' and 'when they win, they never complain.' The scandal that erupted after the ambassador's comments resulted in his removal from the post, but it served to highlight to the Canadian business and policy sectors the continued complications of doing business with, and in, Mexico. Nonetheless, Canadian trade and investment in Mexico continued to grow, and Bombardier itself has since won a number of contracts for subway cars, and it has also invested heavily in the Mexican aerospace sector (see below).

Diplomatic relations after the Bombardier incident were naturally strained but entered a rebuilding phase with the appointment of Stanley Gooch as Canadian ambassador in 1997, an appointment which succeeded in stabilizing relations at the local level and smoothing over the rancour that had emerged after the Bombardier affair. Talk emerged from Canada of the need to adopt a trilateral approach to North American relations, and Canada intensified contact between civil society groups in the two countries.

The Bush Presidency and New Strains in the North American Triangle

At the same time as Canada and Mexico were attempting to rebuild their relations, Mexico and the United States were rapidly building their own bilateral relationship. As the numbers of Mexican immigrants to the U.S., both documented and undocumented, increased in the latter part of the decade, and as Mexican economic and inward FDI growth spurred U.S. interest, the two countries became more deeply integrated than ever before. This reached a climax with the 2000 election of George W. Bush, who made it a priority of his administration to negotiate a new deal for Mexican migrants (which never materialized) and made his first official trip abroad as U.S. president in 2001 to Mexico, visiting President Vicente Fox on his ranch in San Cristobal. The meeting of these two 'cowboy' presidents, including the presentation of boots from Fox to Bush, was seen as heralding a new era of increasingly close relations. This was in stark contrast to the state of U.S. bilateral relations with Canada, to which President Bush did not make an official visit until December 2004. Indeed, the choice of Mexico as the destination for Bush's first foreign visit was greeted with hand wringing in Canada, as commentators interpreted it as a deliberate snub for Canada after Prime Minister Jean Chrétien's not-so-implicit support for Bush's opponent, Al Gore, in the presidential race in 2000. Of course, worse was to come, as U.S.-Canada relations became ever more strained after the 9/11 attacks and the lead-up to the 2003 war in Iraq.[22]

That the events of 11 September 2001 irrevocably and fundamentally changed the nature of North American relations should not come as a surprise. The tensions and competitive pressures unleashed on Mexico and Canada as a result, however, were unexpected. First of all, the terror attacks revealed the differences between the two countries in their handling of the bilateral relationship with the U.S. Whereas Canada announced immediate and unequivocal support of the United States after the attacks in New York and Washington, the Mexican executive branch hesitated, unsure of how to respond to the U.S. in such a way as to show support without alienating Mexican public opinion. This hesitancy raised hackles in the corridors of power in Washington and did not go unnoticed in Ottawa.

The Canadian government's policy response to 9/11 was, of course, to anticipate U.S. concerns over its border, bringing to the negotiating table the Smart Border Declaration in December 2001 (and now the 'perimeter security' arrangement of 2011–12).[23] Encompassing the secure flow of people and goods, the security of border infrastructure, and the exchange of information, the Smart Border Accord addressed not only U.S. security concerns, but also a future vision of the border in which goods and people could move in a more efficient way.

That Canada went ahead with a bilateral deal with the U.S. over border controls without seriously considering a trilateral approach to the issue brought a chilly response from Mexico City. To be sure, Mexican officials questioned the Canadian government's commitment to the principle of trilateral cooperation and were dismayed when they received the unofficial explanation that Canada was trying to avoid the 'Mexicanization' of the U.S.-Canada border. While the Canadian decision to do all it could to keep the U.S. border open cannot be faulted, the rather insensitive treatment of its NAFTA partner was met with hostility in Mexico. Seeking to minimize the damage, Mexico began negotiations with the U.S. over its own version of a 'Smart Border' deal. Closely mimicking the Canadian declaration, the Mexican deal also addressed issues of secure flows, infrastructure, and information exchange.

The gap between the two countries on the future of relations with the U.S. and the direction of North American integration was made worse in 2002 when Mexican president Vicente Fox called for a new deal for the NAFTA partners. Fox's idea of a 'NAFTA-plus' agreement, including an immigration deal nicknamed 'the whole enchilada' by his foreign minister Jorge Castaneda, called for a social fund within NAFTA to redistribute funds from richer to poorer regions in North America, and for a common currency.

The reaction to the NAFTA-plus proposal in Ottawa was noticeably frosty. The insistence of the Fox administration to reform U.S. immigra-

tion law heightened the fears over the 'Mexicanization' of border relations in North America. And as far as a common currency went, Ottawa
responded that a common currency would inevitably be the U.S. dollar and this would mean a loss of control over inflation and monetary
policy in Canada. This fear of losing economic sovereignty meant that
Canada was reluctant to seriously consider the rest of Vicente Fox's proposals. In fact, the suggestion for a NAFTA social fund received even
shorter shrift, with Canadian officials challenging Mexico to account
for the billions of dollars in annual trade surpluses between the two
nations before requesting additional funds. The overall direction of the
bilateral relationship in the context of North America seemed stalled,
even in reverse, requiring embarrassed explanations from Canadian
diplomatic staff to perplexed Mexican officials.

Intriguingly, as Canadian officials found themselves defending their
position on North American integration to their Mexican counterparts,
the intensification of contact between the two sides seemed to propel
a better understanding and to make possible the discovery of common ground and perspectives. This was a process that would intensify
over the next few years as the two countries became ever closer, mostly
through diplomatic channels.

Both Canada and Mexico then faced similar challenges in their bilateral relationships with the U.S. as the Bush administration sought
UN approval for an invasion of Iraq in 2002–3. Canada's support was
requested in the form of committing of troops to the exercise; Mexico's
in the form of diplomatic support through the UN Security Council
resolution authorizing the invasion. Having been elected as a non-permanent member of the Security Council for the period 2002–3, Mexico
faced a particularly problematical decision: by voting 'no' to the U.S.-
sponsored resolution, it would alienate its closest ally and trading partner; by voting 'yes' it would violate several key principles of its own
foreign policy tradition of non-intervention and alienate public opinion at home; by abstaining it would negate the Mexican government's
arguments about the importance of participation in the Security Council. Canada's decision not to provide troops to the invasion needed to
be explained and softened by the fact that Canada was already heavily
committed to the ongoing NATO military campaign in Afghanistan.
Interestingly, this common dilemma actually helped Canadian and
Mexican diplomats find a new area of mutual concern. As the UN debacle continued, both countries joined in calls for a reform of the UN.

Although the two countries did not see exactly eye to eye on what shape the reform should take, it highlighted a growing rapprochement between the two at the diplomatic level. A prime example is to be found in the security realm. As Mexico's democratic transition process continued, and as political attitudes changed, a new, 'multi-dimensional' understanding of security emerged, one that was much more in tune with Canadian ideas of Human Security than the interpretations that had historically emerged from Mexico. This is not to say that Mexican and Canadian understandings of security were now entirely in sync; rather they were no longer mutually exclusive, and this made a more constructive dialogue much easier to sustain.

In 2004 and 2005, the fruits of this increased diplomatic interaction were seen in two major developments that promised to redefine the bilateral relationship. In 2004, the two countries celebrated the sixtieth anniversary of their diplomatic relations and in October signed the Canada-Mexico Partnership (CMP) agreement, a multidimensional mechanism to shape the future of bilateral relations. Including government, business, academic, and other private sector actors, the CMP attempted to build a deeper relationship between the two countries that went beyond mere government-to-government links. In 2006, the provincial and state governments were also invited to participate, signalling a new era in bilateral relations and further facilitating the interaction between sub-state actors.

Heralded as 'an avenue to advance our economic cooperation in sectors such as trade, investment, science and technology, education, capacity building, labour mobility, institutional reforms and citizen-focused government,'[24] the CMP is an intriguing development in the relationship between the two countries. In a truly innovative way, the CMP attempts to give private sector actors equal standing with governments in the talks, so that there is a wider public invested in the relationship. Accordingly, the CMP is organized around issue areas: in its first five years of existence, working groups have addressed Trade, Investment, Science and Technology, Housing, Human Capital (research collaboration, student mobility, and academic partnerships), Agribusiness, Energy, Labour Mobility, Environment and Forestry, and Urban Sustainability.

This impressive list of topics, however, belies the fact that there has been little meaningful impact in terms of policy that has emerged from the CMP. Although meetings have been dynamic, and there has been significant interest from a wide range of actors, it is difficult to find concrete examples of where the partnership has significantly changed the course of the relationship. The government of Canada claims that the CMP 'encourages partnering between the public and private sectors to develop realistic and results-oriented action plans that matter to real people,' yet the meetings do not appear to have produced very much in the form of tangible action. One of the problems here is that the CMP meets only once a year; in order to generate more interest, and to flesh out recommendations and action plans, it would make sense to hold more frequent meetings and to provide the necessary support from both public and private funds. Nonetheless, the CMP is one of the areas of the relationship that offers the most optimism; if the two federal governments are willing to support the partnership in a more meaningful way, and to provide better follow-through in the policy agenda, the CMP will create a more dynamic relationship that engages ever more stakeholders.

The second development worth noting in this period was the release in 2005 of Canada's International Policy Statement (IPS), titled *A Role of Pride and Influence in the World*. The IPS was an attempt to redefine Canadian foreign policy in the light of the changing structure of global relations, the rise of new, emerging markets, and the emergence of new threats such as global terrorism. An impressive document, the IPS was the product of long and intense negotiations between various branches of government connected to Canada's international activities (including DFAIT, Defence, and CIDA). The statement was significant for relations with Mexico in two key ways. First, Mexico was specifically referenced as a 'North American partner' and, second, the region itself was defined repeatedly in the document as 'including Mexico.'

This acceptance of Mexico, then, as a key partner in the region and in the world came at a crucial juncture. It coincided with the rapprochement that was taking place after the conflicts of the immediate post-9/11 environment, and it went hand in hand with a new evaluation of Mexico by Canada's business elite. Whereas business interests had previously been the driving force behind the rejection of Mexico as an integral part of the North American economic and political space, by 2005 there emerged a growing consensus that North America extended from the Arctic to the Suchiate River on the border between Mexico and Guatemala. This change in attitude, propelled by opinion leaders such as Wendy Dobson of the University of Toronto and combined with efforts by pro-Mexico officials in the bureaucracy in DFAIT, helped to drive the growing interest in understanding Mexico and seeking new ways to define the future of the relationship.

At the trilateral level, the signing of the Security and Prosperity Partnership (SPP) in Waco, Texas in 2005 highlighted a new phase in North American relations. The heavy focus of the SPP on security issues, and a prosperity agenda that emphasized business competitiveness rather than development, says much about the weakened position of the Mexican government going into the Waco Summit. President Vicente Fox's calls for progress on migration issues and for a more broadly defined integration dialogue fell on deaf ears – therefore, the SPP largely represented a U.S.- and Canadian-driven agenda. The Canada-U.S. dominance of the SPP seemed to appease voices in Canada that feared for the relationship with the U.S., implicitly welcoming the fact that Mexico had been left out in the diplomatic cold.

This led to the outbreak of Canadian academic and policy conferences focused on Mexico that were seen in 2005 and 2006 in the run-up to the controversial 2006 Mexican presidential election. The major seminars and conferences organized by FOCAL, York University, and the C.D. Howe Institute respectively (mentioned at the beginning of this chapter) signalled a renewed interest in both Mexican politics and the country's role in North America. With a new administration in Ottawa and the upcoming presidential election in Mexico, a new institutional framework under the CMP, a growing track record in foreign policy cooperation, and with Canada feeling secure in its relationship with the U.S., it seemed as though Canada-Mexico relations were about to embark on a new, more positive course.

This, however, proved to be a false dawn. With the election of the Stephen Harper government in Canada in January of 2006, the emphasis in Ottawa switched firmly to strengthening the bilateral relationship with the United States and amicably resolving long-running disputes such as the thorny softwood lumber controversy. As Mexican officials hurried to establish contact with the new government, in place of long-standing contacts they had cultivated with the previous Liberal government representatives, the chaos of the 2006 Mexican election brought a sense of uncertainty and instability to the bilateral relationship.

A perceptible stagnation entered the relationship at this point, punctuated by the emergence of intermittent problems. One of these concerned the rising number of complaints being lodged against the Canada-Mexico SWP. Growing reports of abuses by employers and of workers not receiving fair pay and benefits culminated in a case put to the Quebec court system concerning the right of temporary workers to unionize.[25]

At the same time as this once shining example of bilateral cooperation was coming under increasing scrutiny, pressure was building in
Parliament to address the growing problem of Mexican asylum seekers
in Canada. Mexico was at the time the only Latin American country
whose citizens did not require a visitor's visa to travel to Canada, and
this fact had not gone unnoticed by Mexican citizens looking to start
a new life outside of Mexico. This was especially so since the United
States had tightened its immigration and border controls. Indeed,
Mexicans increasingly saw Canada, with its generous asylum laws and
the absence of a visa requirement, as a viable alternative. In the 2000s,
a growing number of Mexicans moved to Canada to satisfy demand
for labour across the country in general, but particularly in Alberta.
This legal migration, often temporary, was viewed favourably by most
Canadian elites, but the rising number of Mexican refugee claimants in
Canada raised some eyebrows.

By 2008, Mexicans had become the single largest group of refugee
claimants in Canada, totalling 9,400, up 15 per cent from the year before,
and representing 25 per cent of all refugee claims nationally. Though
only a small number (11 per cent) of their claims were accepted by the
review board, the costs imposed on the system were becoming unacceptable.[26] As pressure mounted on the Harper government to address
the problem, Mexican officials declined to talk about the issue, and a
mutually acceptable bilateral solution did not emerge, and the issue
still remains unresolved in late 2012.

The beginning of the sixty-fifth anniversary year of the bilateral relationship coincided with the beginning of the Barack Obama administration in January 2009. This brought with it fears of a reassessment
of NAFTA, of a closing of markets, and of a reduced interest in North
America. The effective dismissal of the SPP seemed to confirm concerns
that relations with Canada and Mexico would be a second-tier issue for
the administration, and the U.S. government's response to the financial crisis, in particular the 'Buy American' provisions of the American Recovery and Reinvestment Act of 2009, nearly brought Canadian
authorities to the point of panic. Once again, Canada focused its atten-
tions on securing its special relationship with the U.S., and more and
more voices were heard in Ottawa calling for a vision of North America
that ended at the Rio Grande. Mexico, too, was focused on the U.S.,
working closely with the new administration to structure the huge payments being made available from the Merida Initiative (a bilateral program to assist Mexico in the worsening conflict with drug cartels).

Figure 5.1. Mexican Refugee Claimants in Canada

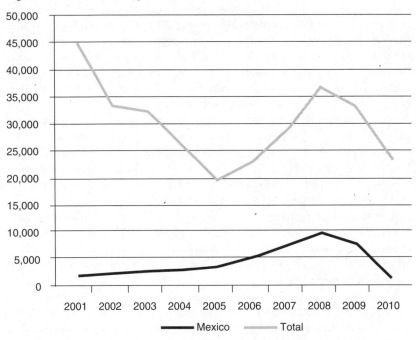

Source: http://www.cic.gc.ca/english/resources/statistics/facts2010/temporary/25.asp

This was hardly an auspicious start to the anniversary year. It was made much worse in the summer of 2009 when the Canadian government announced that it would be imposing a visa on Mexicans wishing to visit Canada. The impact of this development was profound. Although Mexican government officials had been aware that the imposition of a visa was likely, no one had expected it to be introduced so abruptly. The following announcement was made on 13 July:

> Beginning 12:01 a.m. EDT on July 14, 2009, Mexican nationals will require a visa to travel to Canada, Citizenship, Immigration and Multiculturalism Minister Jason Kenney announced today. For the first 48 hours, Mexican citizens may apply for entry on arrival in Canada. After 11:59 p.m. EDT July 15, 2009, a visa will be required.[27]

In less than three days, then, Mexican travellers, most of whom had booked their travel weeks or months in advance, were supposed to gather all required personal information and supporting documentation (including bank records and a criminal background check), go to their nearest consular facility, pay the processing fee of $150 dollars (1810 pesos), and hope that the visa would be approved before the time of travel. There emerged many stories of people who had booked their children into summer camp facilities in Canada and then had to back out, receiving no compensation for their cancellations.

Not surprisingly, Canada's stringent visa process received a lot of bad press, even earning a mention in a well-known Mexican soap opera.[28] A high-profile case involving a well-known Mexican chef who had been invited to guest chef at a dinner in Montreal without financial compensation, and was then refused a visa, highlighted many of the problems of the nascent process. The impact on tourism figures was dramatic. Whereas in January 2009, 22,396 Mexicans travelled to Canada, by February of 2010, that number had fallen to 9,407.[29] Granted, the influence of the economic recession in Mexico should be taken into consideration when we view this figure, but it is fair to say that the visa requirement has had a major impact.

Mexico's diplomatic response to the incident was to immediately impose a visa requirement on visiting Canadian government officials, and then to require a passport for Canadian travellers beginning in March 2010 (previously any official ID was sufficient).[30] Cleverly designed not to have a major impact on the tourism industry, the Mexican response embarrassed the Canadian government.[31] However, although the effects of the visa debacle were acute, and have been significant in terms of Mexican public opinion, it is unlikely that it will have a long-lasting and drastic impact on the overall bilateral relationship. By the spring of 2010, the annual meeting of the CMP had taken place in Niagara-on-the-Lake in Ontario, with a 'business as usual' approach.

Furthermore, 2009 was important for the bilateral relationship in a more favourable sense. Despite the growing problems at the diplomatic level, the constructive and highly encouraging cooperation between all three NAFTA countries on the issue of the H1N1 influenza virus suggested that the region's institutional cooperation was more resilient than many had first thought. The support received by Mexico from both Canada and the U.S., particularly with regard to allowing flight routes to remain open, created a lot of positive goodwill in Mexico City.

Figure 5.2. Canada-Mexico Trade, 1993–2010 ($millions)

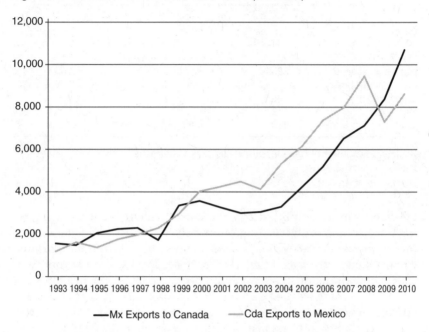

— Mx Exports to Canada   — Cda Exports to Mexico

Trade and Investment

The economic relationship is one that suffered heavily in 2009, as the recession in Mexico and in the U.S. impacted on the North American economy in general. Mexico's deep recession, in particular, had a profound effect on two-way trade figures. Within the NAFTA region as a whole, trade fell by an astonishing 25.9 per cent, dropping to the same point as in 2004. Bilateral trade between Canada and Mexico fell by 16.4 per cent, reaching a total of US$21.9 billion. Within this total, Mexican exports to Canada accounted for US$14.6 billion (a decrease of 12.9 per cent from the previous year), with Canadian exports to Mexico amounting to US$7.3 billion (a decrease of 22.7 per cent).

Despite this sharp downturn in trade figures, the overall picture of trade relations between the two countries is highly encouraging. Since the beginning of the NAFTA, bilateral trade has increased four-fold, achieving an average annual growth rate of 11.1 per cent between 1993 and 2009. The strength of this trading relationship rests in large part

Table 5.1. Main Canadian exports to and imports from Mexico, 2008

Export	Value (CAD$millions)	Import	Value (CAD$millions)
Motor vehicles	877.4	Electrical machinery &	
Grain and oil seeds	825.4	equipment	5,700
Electrical machinery &		Motor vehicles	4,000
equipment	798.6	Machinery	2,400
Machinery	512.1	Mineral fuels & oils	994.3
Articles of iron & steel	389.9	Furniture & bedding	656.9

Source: Government of Canada, DFAIT, http://www.international.gc.ca/commerce/
strategy-strategie/r2.aspx.

on the continued importance of the North American automobile sector, but also demonstrates a significant diversification of bilateral trade into areas such as televisions, vegetable oils, beef, cellphones, printed circuits, beer, and basic foodstuffs. A closer look at the raw numbers shows how dramatic this growth has been (see table 5.1). In 1988, Canada-Mexico trade totalled $2.4 billion, with Mexican exports twice the size of Canada's. By 1994, it had risen to $6.5 billion. By 2002, the two-way trade between Canada and Mexico more than doubled from $6.5 billion to $15.1 billion. In 2008, before the economic recession, bilateral trade had reached $23.8 billion, with Mexican exports to Canada ($17.9 billion) exceeding imports from Canada ($5.8 billion) to the tune of more than $12 billion.[32]

Mexico is now Canada's third-largest supplier of merchandise goods, which in 2009 reached 4.5 per cent of all Canadian imports, and was exceeded only by the United States and China. More importantly, in 2009 Mexico surpassed Japan to become Canada's fourth-largest export market, with 2.3 per cent of all Canadian exports, topped only by the U.S., UK, and China. In short, this meant that Mexico had become Canada's third most important trading partner overall.[33]

In terms of investment, the Canadian business presence in Mexico is radically different from what it was twenty years ago. In 1990, Canada was only a minor investor in Mexico, with Canadian foreign direct investment (FDI) standing at $245 million. By 1997, that figure had gone up to $1.09 billion, and the total accumulated value of Canadian direct investment in the country stood at $2.1 billion. By the end of that year Canada had become the fourth-largest investor in Mexico, up from

Figure 5.3. Canadian FDI in Mexico (US$bn)

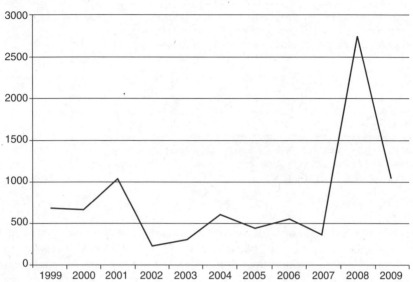

ninth in 1993, and some 842 Mexican companies had received direct Canadian investment.[34] The growth in trade and, more importantly, the Chapter Eleven provisions of the NAFTA guaranteeing the security of investments by citizens of fellow NAFTA countries clearly encouraged this dramatic growth.

There are now over 2,800 Canadian companies active in the Mexican market, and Canada has become Mexico's fifth-largest foreign investor. By 2008, Canadian direct investment in Mexico totalled almost $3.8 billion, and is important in banking, mining, energy, urban and rail transit equipment, aerospace, automotive, and agri-food. The list of Canadian firms in the country includes many of Canada's foremost corporations such as Scotiabank, Bombardier, Goldcorp, Canadian Pacific, Magna, Fairmont, and Four Seasons Hotels. Despite the security problems that have racked Mexico in recent years, the number of Canadian companies interested in the Mexican market continues to grow.

The purchase of Inverlat bank by the Bank of Nova Scotia in 1997 (completing the purchase in 2003) was one of the most significant acquisitions of a Mexican firm by a Canadian investor in that it gave a strong Canadian presence in what had once been a stronghold of Mexi-

Table 5.2. Foreign mining companies in Mexico

Country of origin	Companies	% of total
Canada	198	75.3
USA	39	14.8
UK	7	2.7
Australia	5	1.9
Japan	3	1.1
China	2	0.8
South Korea	2	0.8

Source: Government of Mexico, Anuario Estadístico de la Minería Mexicana Ampliada, 2008, Secretaria de Economía, http://www. economia.gob.mx/?P=1032.

can nationalism.[35] The banking sector had only begun to be opened up to foreign ownership in 1997, and since that date Spanish banks such as BBVA and Santander have dominated the market. Scotiabank Inverlat, however, has been a highly successful venture and is now Mexico's seventh-largest bank.

Mining is another sector where Canadian firms dominate (see table 5.2).[36] By 2008, 198 Canadian mining companies were operating in Mexico (over 75 per cent of all foreign businesses in the sector). Further, according to a 2004 article by Cecilia Costero, Mexico imports 75 per cent of its machinery used for mining from Canada.[37] After the manufacturing industry, mining is the second-largest Canadian capital interest in Mexico. In 2000, this investment stake totalled more than US$150 million.

A third area where Canadian firms have taken the lead in recent years is the aerospace sector. Bombardier, despite its negative experiences in the late 1990s, has stayed in Mexico and has increased its investment stake. A major development for the company occurred in 2006 when Bombardier began operations at its new aerospace plant in Queretaro, in central Mexico. In 2008, the company inaugurated a second plant, this time within the newly opened Queretaro Aerospace Park. In addition to its public transport equipment operations, Bombardier chose Queretaro because of the emerging cluster of aerospace-sector firms in the area, and due to the presence of the National Aeronautic University of Queretaro (UNAQ), which opened in March 2009. Employing over 1,000 people in Queretaro alone, Bombardier has become a major source of local economic growth and technical and technological progress, working closely with the UNAQ in curriculum development and providing funding for its programs.[38]

The Future and Policy Recommendations

Despite the impressive progress that has been made in the bilateral relationship since the early 1990s, unlike the U.S.-Canada and U.S.-Mexico axes of North America, Canada's relations with Mexico are seen as being of secondary importance by many elite groups across the country. And despite the dynamic nature of trade and investment ties, the Canada-Mexico economic relationship lacks the same intense inter-dependence, and it ranks down the list in terms of vital national inter-est considerations – unlike economic relations between Canada and the U.S., or even those between the U.S. and Mexico.

At the level of the Canadian executive branch, Mexico is all too often a second thought in terms of foreign relations. The cultural hangover of empire, and the novelty of Asia's rise, means that Europe, Japan, and China continue to receive higher-profile treatment from Ottawa. This is despite the fact that Mexico is Canada's third-largest trading partner and a major destination for Canadian FDI.[39] A large part of this is a func-tion of the prevailing predominance of the U.S. in the minds of senior policy makers in Canada. To be sure, the first priority of Canadian for-eign policy still remains to 'keep the U.S. border open' and to maintain the flow of goods south, which impacts directly on elite perceptions of Mexico in the context of North America. Furthermore, Mexico is not yet an 'assumption' in Canadian politics – or in the public mindset – in the same way that the U.S. is for both Canadians and Mexicans.

One reason for this continues to be the low level of cultural and societal understanding that could otherwise facilitate stable long-term cooperation. Despite rising immigration levels from Mexico, Canada's multicultural society lacks a strong Mexican influence. Even among Canadians of Latin American origin, Chileans and Central Americans have been more vocal and better organized within Canadian society. This stands in stark contrast to the U.S., where American citizens of Mexican origin are emerging as the single largest minority group in the country. Although conflicts have inevitably arisen from this, the large number of Mexicans in the U.S. has facilitated an acceptance and understanding of Mexico – however grudgingly – within the United States.

In this final section of the chapter, I outline a number of policy proposals designed both to deepen the overall relationship and to explore
new avenues for mutual benefit at the bilateral, regional, and international levels. In many of these areas, I argue that it makes sense to adopt,
intensify, and enhance the approach begun under the CMP to bring in
civil society, the private sector, and state/provincial governments.

Foreign Policy

It would be foolish and short-sighted for the two federal governments
to ignore the numerous areas of interest and potential cooperation in
the coming years. Three central items stand out on the foreign policy
agenda as areas for productive collaboration between the two countries.

First, we should recognize that Mexico and Canada have complementary interests in the region of Central America. Given Canada's historical connection to the region, and Mexico's status as a major regional
power (particularly in the economic and diplomatic fields), and, most
importantly, Mexico's interest in a stable and prosperous Central America, it makes perfect sense for the two countries to work together to
develop programs to aid both government and civil society there. An
intriguing possibility exists in working on a trilateral basis with Colombia: Mexico has already collaborated with Colombia on a number of
issues relating to regional development, including energy. Canada, of
course, maintains excellent relations with Colombia since the coming
to power of Álvaro Uribe and Juan Manuel Santos; if this cooperation
continues post-Uribe, then trilateral programs in the region could be
greatly facilitated.

The second area that may hold potential is that of peacekeeping and
peacebuilding. At present, the Mexican constitution limits the capacity
of the armed forces to operate outside of Mexico – but there is a qualitative change underway in the interpretation of this. Partly this has been
helped by Canadian engagement with Mexican authorities and with
the military on the issue, including a 2008 conference bringing together
Mexican military and government representatives with speakers from
other Latin American military organizations that have participated in
international peacekeeping missions. The Mexican federal electoral
institute (IFE) has already been active internationally in Afghanistan
and Iraq in promoting free and fair elections, and there is a need to
think beyond just military participation in peacekeeping operations
(PKOs) as a way for Mexico to play a broader role in UN peace mis-

sions. Canada has enormous experience in the issue area and can provide valuable training to those agencies of the Mexican military (such as the navy) that are ready to engage beyond the country's borders.

The third priority for foreign policy collaboration concerns the growing entente that has emerged between the two countries since 2002 in the United Nations itself. Both Mexico and Canada have a distinguished history of membership and active participation in multilateral forums, a classic component of middle-power behaviour.[40] Since 2002, Mexico has once again been a temporary member of the UNSC (2009–10). In the meantime, of course, the UN has lost even more relevance as the G20 has become a more important and active grouping of countries (with the participation of both Canada and Mexico) and as Mexico regularly participates at G8 summits as part of the invited G5 group (China, India, Brazil, Mexico, South Africa). It is important for both countries that the UN remain a viable global forum, both to protect their interests from great-power domination and to advance their policy preferences at the global level. What's more, the increased understanding between Canada and Mexico in the UN should be seized upon as a foundation for cooperation in other multilateral forums (especially in the OAS) and as a source of extra pressure to bring the United States to the bargaining table. Given the plight of the World Trade Organization (WTO), and the global regime for climate change, a unified front from Canada and Mexico would be useful in trying to formulate a united North American approach.

Security Cooperation

Since the beginning of 2007, the Felipe Calderón administration has been involved in a war on the drug cartels, which are effectively controlling many areas of Mexico. According to the *Los Angeles Times*, by May of 2010 more than 22,000 people had died in the conflict and the surrounding violence.[41] Having deployed 45,000 troops and 5,000 federal police officers to 18 of Mexico's 31 states, the Mexican government is still struggling to maintain law and order in the country. In October 2007, the Calderón and Bush administrations announced the Merida Initiative (MI), a bilateral program (which also includes some funds for Central American countries) to increase security cooperation against the drug cartels. Costing more than US$1.6 billion over three years, the Merida Initiative involves a substantial transfer of hardware, enhances Mexican intelligence capacities, and provides training for its security personnel. Most importantly, the MI involves the development of institutionalized cooperation between U.S. and Mexican security and intelligence forces at hitherto unforeseen levels.[42]

Merida also provides an opening for constructive cooperation on security between Mexican and Canadian authorities. Rather than merely duplicating the MI on a smaller scale, it would make sense for the authorities to examine how Canadian capabilities in police and army training and intelligence gathering can complement Mexican resources and what is already going on through Merida. Canada has already begun engaging with CISEN, the Mexican intelligence service, but Canada's police forces hold valuable experience in building databases and sharing information across jurisdictions. Closely related to this is the judicial reform process taking place in Mexico. Canada could provide much-needed expertise and support for Mexican judges as they transition to a system more akin to the Anglo-Saxon model.

Education

Human capital has been identified in the CMP as a central element in the drive for international competitiveness, and the collaboration of university associations from both countries, along with government agencies, has shown the potential for meaningful cooperation. The provinces of Canada should be key players in this dialogue, and an improvement of educational standards in Mexico would clearly benefit regional labour markets and competitiveness.

A harmonization of educational standards may be too ambitious a goal in the short term, but preliminary steps could be taken that focus on the university level. Identifying universities that meet common standards would be of great assistance in encouraging partnerships and also entrance into graduate school. Mexico's university system has developed a highly entrepreneurial nature, one that has produced centres of excellence that can be fruitfully engaged by its Canadian counterparts.

Health

Mexico and Canada both have public health care systems that are underfunded and are sure to face resource crises in the future. In provinces such as Ontario, for example, we hear of shortages of doctors and health care professionals in rural areas. In Mexico, however, there is no shortage of well-trained medical professionals who need well-paid jobs and the opportunity to practise. Two simple ideas present them-selves. First, we could contemplate training programs in Canada to furnish Mexican doctors and nurses with the necessary knowledge to allow them to practise in the Canadian context. To make this happen, though, federal and provincial authorities, universities, and hospitals in both countries need to engage with Mexican health care profession-als and organizations. The exchange of medical know-how and exper-tise would benefit both scientific communities as well as health care recipients.

A more daring plan would allow Canadian patients to seek health care in vetted hospitals and clinics in Mexico and have that care cov-ered by provincial health insurance plans. Mexico has a large number of excellent hospitals that provide care at lower cost than Canadian public facilities. Private insurance companies have for a few years been encouraging clients to seek health care in India, at a fraction of the cost. Why not look at Mexico as a low-cost, regional alternative for Canadian patients? Senior citizen care could easily be included in such an agree-ment, with ready access to long-term-care facilities.

Energy and Climate Change

Mexico's looming oil crisis means that, with a continued drop in pro-duction numbers, the country will become a net oil importer some time between 2015 and 2020. Though there is little that Canada can do to change that situation, there are a number of areas of cooperation that can aid Mexico's energy sector.

First, despite Mexico's tradition as an oil nation, it has underinvested in educational and training programs for geologists and petroleum engineers. More dynamic exchange programs between Canadian and Mexican universities that focus specifically on these academic areas will help to bolster Mexican human capital for the future of the oil industry. Canada can also assist Mexico in terms of regulation, as the country's new National Hydrocarbons Commission (Comisión Nacional de Hid-rocarburos or CNH) tries to streamline Mexico's regulatory process. The Alberta Energy Resources Conservation Board (ERCB) provides an extremely successful model that would be of great use in approving Exploration and Production (E&P) projects in areas such as Mexico's Chicontepec field, where PEMEX is currently drilling over 1,000 wells a year. Another area of cooperation worth investigating is that of carbon capture and storage (CCS). PEMEX has already begun experimenting with the reinjection of CO^2 into tapped-out oil wells, but the research and development work being undertaken in Alberta through the $2 billion CCS Fund there could be of great benefit to Mexico.

It is worth considering areas of potential collaboration in renewable energies as well. The CMP has already identified interest on the part of Mexico in collaborating with Canadian firms in mini-hydroelectric and wind power generation. Both of these areas are undergoing a period of growth in Mexico at present. Mexico's expertise in wind energy, particularly the challenges of designing wind turbines for extreme weather conditions, should be of interest to Canadian authorities as well. The technology being developed by Canadian firm IOGEN, specializing in cellulosic ethanol production, would be of enormous interest to the Mexican agricultural sector, and to PEMEX, although considerations of intellectual property will likely prove to be an important obstacle. Lastly, Canadian expertise, particularly from the province of Ontario, in the area of smart grids and smart metering, could provide much-needed technical assistance for Mexico's Comisión Federal de Electricidad (CFE) as it attempts to upgrade its own national grid.

One last area for cooperation is directed toward the future of carbon markets and carbon regulation in North America. Though the United States has yet to pass any kind of national carbon regulation legislation, the Waxman-Markey and the Kerry-Lieberman bills in Congress give us an idea of what the future holds. Canada and Mexico need to enter into a dialogue (perhaps coordination) about how each will respond to such legislative initiatives, particularly as to how it impacts on trade with the U.S. Under a new carbon regime in the U.S. there is the very real possibility that imports into the United States from countries that do not have a comparable carbon regulatory framework may well have to pay a stiff import tariff. This would prove hugely disruptive to North American trading relations. Mexico and Canada must be prepared to meet this challenge when and if it should arise – preferably by working in concert.

Indigenous Affairs

Indigenous peoples or First Nations are hugely important in both the history and present-day reality of both Canada and Mexico. Of course, the histories of the two countries in their dealings with indigenous populations are vastly different. Whereas land treaties, separation, confrontation, and eventual cohabitation with the prospect of political and economic development mark the history of government relations with First Nations in Canada, in Mexico relations have been defined by the culture of *mestizaje*, a cruel reality of marginalization that was ultimately exemplified by the deadly Chiapas rebellion in 1994.

Given the recent successes attained by Canadian First Nations in their dealings with federal and provincial governments, it is worth considering engagement between Canadian tribes and their counterparts in Mexico, a form of 'indigenous diplomacy,' to help Mexican indigenous peoples in their struggle. They are seeking a constructive dialogue with the Mexican federal government that will lead to significant advances in their standard of living. Canadian First Nations may be able to play an 'honest broker' role here. A sense of community and brotherhood in the hemisphere could result from such interaction, as well as heightened prestige and recognition on the international stage.

Final Thoughts

Mexican president Felipe Calderón's visit to Canada in late May of 2010 came at a crucial juncture for Mexico's bilateral relationship with Canada.[43] Among other things, Calderón sought recognition of his efforts to modernize Mexico and to take on the drug cartels in his country, a thankless task that has garnered him little domestic support and has resulted in a worsening of drug violence throughout Mexico.[44] Of course, Calderón faced the very real prospect that the remainder of his mandate would be as a lame duck president, lacking a majority in Congress, and losing the 2012 presidential elections to the Institutional Revolutionary Party's (PRI) Enrique Pena Nieto. For the bilateral relationship, though, his visit was a chance to jump-start the relationship after the visa debacle of 2009 and to seek renewed interest from the Canadian private sector after the drastic declines in trade and investment the previous year.

The potential of the Canada-Mexico relationship, however, cannot be fully realized unless Canada acknowledges that Mexico is a crucial partner in North America, that strong relations with Mexico are not mutually exclusive to a 'special relationship' with the U.S., and that Canadian competitiveness depends in large part on Mexico's continued economic development.[45] As Jean Séguin, the vice-president of Engineering and Supply Chain with Bombardier Aerospace has noted: 'Mexico is key to the development of a highly competitive aerospace industry in Central and South America, as well as to Bombardier's increased competitiveness in the international marketplace.'[46] Put simply, Canada's federal government needs to think along these same lines.

Having endured the problems of 2009, the bilateral relationship is now in urgent need of a retooling and revitalization, beginning with both countries encouraging greater political and economic investments in the coming years. The way to do this is to bring more participants into the dialogue between the two countries and move beyond the mere rhetoric of partnership. Projects such as the CMP and the CMI will help in that, but much more is needed. Assisting the incoming Pena Nieto administration with its ongoing struggle to change Mexico would be a valuable start and would greatly enhance Canada's standing in a country that will be a key global player as the twenty-first century advances.

NOTES

1 See Staff, 'Canadá impone visa a Mexicanos,' El Economista Online, 13 July 2009.
2 For more on this point, see Colin Robertson, 'Embracing the Americas, Starting with Mexico,' *Policy Options* (May 2011): 40–4; Alex Bugailiskis and Andrés Rozental (eds.), *Canada among Nations 2011–2012: Canada and Mexico's Unfinished Agenda* (Montreal and Kingston: McGill-Queen's University Press, 2012).
3 See Donald Barry, Mark O. Dickerson, and James D. Gaisford (eds.), *Toward a North American Community?* (Boulder, CO: Westview Press, 1995).
4 Business Council on National Issues (BCNI), 'Canada-Mexico-United States Free Trade: A Canadian Business Perspective,' Ottawa, 27 September 1990, 1–11, http://www.ceocouncil.ca/publications/pdf/test_71f952b980aa cfb4707830010ff0a922/SEPT_27_90_ENG_Canada_Mexico_United_States_ Free_Trade_A_Canadian_Business_Perspective.pdf.
5 Royal Bank of Canada, 'Mexico-U.S. Free Trade Talks: Why Canada Should Get Involved,' *Econoscope* (Special Edition) (September 1990): 10.
6 BCNI, 'Canada-Mexico-United States FreeTrade,' 7.
7 Government of Canada, *Mexico: Fact Sheet* (Ottawa: Department of Foreign Affairs and International Trade, April 2010), 1.
8 Government of Canada, *Mexico: Fact Sheet* (Hull, Quebec: Canadian International Development Agency, May 2010), 1. CIDA disbursements in Mexico did drop to $2.6 million for the 2009–10 period. See Government of Canada, *Country Profile: Mexico*, (Gatineau: Canadian International Development Agency, 2011).

9 Teresa Gutiérrez-Haces, *Canadá un Estado posmoderno* (Mexico: Plaza y Valdes, Editores, 2000).
10 Duncan Wood, 'Overcoming the Butterfly Effect: Teaching Canadian Studies in Mexico' *Canadian Foreign Policy* 14, no. 1 (Fall 2007): 93–100.
11 Ma. Isabel Studer Noguez, 'Las relaciones México-Canadá: al encuentro del otro vecino distante,' *Este País* 65 (agosto 1996): 1–6.
12 George MacLean and Duncan Wood, 'A New Partnership for the Millennium? The Evolution of Canadian-Mexican Relations,' *Canadian Foreign Policy* 7 (Winter 2000): 35–55.
13 Danielle Goldfarb, *The Canada-Mexico Conundrum: Finding Common Ground*, Backgrounder no. 91 (Montreal: C.D. Howe Institute, July 2005): 1–10.
14 Andrew Cooper, 'Thinking Outside the Box in Canada-Mexico Relations: The Long Road from Convenience to Commitment,' and Duncan Wood, 'The Future of Mexico-Canada Relations: Bilateral and Trilateral solutions in North America,' in Daniel Drache (ed.), *Big Picture Realities: Canada and Mexico at the Crossroads* (Waterloo, ON: Wilfrid Laurier University Press, 2008): 237–50 and 251–68.
15 Canadian Foundation for the Americas, *Where Are We Going? Canada and Mexico Looking beyond 2006*,' conference report, p. 1, http://focal.ca/pdf/Mexico_conference.pdf.
16 Ibid., 2.
17 Canadian Foundation for the Americas, 'Research Forum on North America – Canada-Mexico Initiative,' http://www.focal.ca/projects/rf-northamerica/index_e.asp.
18 Veena Verma, 'The Mexican and Caribbean Seasonal Agricultural Workers Program: Regulatory and Policy Framework, Farm Industry Level Employment Practices, and the Future of the Program Under Unionization,' *Executive Summary* (Ottawa: North-South Institute, December 2003): 1–162, http://www.nsi-ins.ca/english/pdf/exec_sum_verma.pdf.
19 Government of Canada, 'Seasonal Agricultural Workers Program,' http://www.canadainternational.gc.ca/mexico-mexique/work-travail/sawp-ptag.aspx?lang=en.
20 G. Verduzco and M. I. Lozano, 'Mexican Farm Workers' Participation in Canada's Seasonal Agricultural Labour Market and Development Consequences in Their Rural Home Communities' (Ottawa: North-South Institute, 2003), 1–14, http://www.nsi-ins.ca/english/pdf/exec_sum_verduzco.pdf.
21 Anthony DePalma 'Canadians' Charge of Graft in Mexico Causes Tempest,' New York Times Online, 8 October 1997, http://www.nytimes.com/1997/10/08/world/canadians-charge-of-graft-in-mexico-causes-tempest.html?pagewanted=all.

22 On these points, see Paul Cellucci, *Unquiet Diplomacy* (Toronto: Key Porter Books, 2007).

23 Department of Foreign Affairs and International Trade Canada, 'The Canada-U.S. Smart Border Declaration,' http://www.dfait-maeci.gc.ca/anti-terrorism/declaration-en.asp.

24 Government of Canada, DFAIT, 'The Canada-Mexico Partnership,' http://www.canadainternational.gc.ca/mexico-mexique/cmp-pcm.aspx?lang=en.

25 Jessica Murphy, 'Quebec Decision Advances the Rights of Migrant Workers,' *Globe and Mail*, 3 May 2010, A6.

26 Tom Marshall, 'Thousands of Mexicans Walk Canada's Asylum Tightrope,' *Guadalajara Reporter*, 3 July 2009, http://guadalajarareporter.com/news-mainmenu-82/international-mainmenu-105/24996-thousands-of-mexicans-walk-canadas-asylum-tightrope.html.

27 DFAIT, 'Canada Imposes a Visa on Mexico,' http://www.cic.gc.ca/english/department/media/releases/2009/2009-07-13.asp.

28 Anca Gurzu, 'Mexicans Declare "Surprise, Anger" at Visa Application Process,' *Embassy Magazine*, 28 April 2010, 1, http://embassymag.ca/page/printpage/visa-04-28-2010.

29 Ibid.

30 AFP, 'Mexico Imposes New Visa Rule on Canadian Officials,' 16 July 2009, http://www.google.com/hostednews/afp/article/ALeqM5iY-GHs6209MqF9xT1qO_ZI7eyJsUw.

31 Canadian tourists, who numbered over 1.5 million in 2011, are obviously important to Mexico's key tourism sector.

32 Two-way trade between Canada and Mexico reached over $27 billion for 2009–10, marking a sizeable increase over the previous year. Total direct Canadian investment in Mexico also increased to $4.6 billion for the same time period. These figures are drawn from Government of Canada, *Fact Sheet: Canada-Mexico Relations* (Ottawa: Department of Foreign Affairs and International Trade, May 2011).

33 Government of Mexico, Secretaria de Economia, 'Mexico-Canada Trade and Investment from Mexico in Canada,' http://www.nafta-mexico.org/ls23al.php?s=54&p=3&l=2#.

34 Angel Gurria, 'México y Canadá: una genuina alianza bilateral,' *Revista Mexicana de Política Exterior* 51 (1997): 265–96.

35 Business News Americas, 'IN BRIEF: Scotiabank Buys Inverlat Stake for US$322mn,' 30 April 2003, http://www.bnamericas.com/news/banking/Scotiabank_buys_Inverlat_stake_for_US*322mn.

36 As mentioned by Ricardo Grinspun and Jennifer Mills, anti-mining activist Mariano Abarca Roblero was murdered in Chaipas, Mexico in November

2009. After vigorously opposing the mining activities of Calgary-based Blackfire Exploration Ltd, he had been threatened with violence and imprisonment. But it was not a major story in Mexico – probably overshadowed by other bad-news stories on drug wars, economic crisis, and H1N1. In late August 2011, the RCMP opened an investigation into Blackfire's alleged funnelling of bribes into the personal bank account of Julio Cesar Velazquez Calderon – the Mayor of Chicomuselo, the town where Blackfire's mine is located in the state of Chiapas – 'to keep the peace and prevent local members of the community from taking up arms against the mine.' But the Mounties were not investigating anything to do with the brutal murder of Mr Abarca. Greg McArthur, 'Miner Raided over Bribery Allegations,' *Globe and Mail*, 29 August 2011, A3. Still, there have been a number of issues involving mining operations (both foreign and domestic) in Mexico in recent years, and it is likely that the behaviour of mining firms will come under increasing government scrutiny in the coming years.

37 Cecilia Costero, 'Relaciones Actuales México-Canadá en el sector minero,' *Revista Mexicana de Estudios Canadienses* (nueva época), numero 007 (Asociación Mexicana de Estudios sobre Canada, June 2004): 13–27.

38 Bombardier corporation, press release, 'Bombardier Learjet 85 Aircraft Composite Structure Manufacturing to Take Place at Querétaro Facility,' Mexico City, 29 May 2008, http://www2.bombardier.com/en/3_0/pressrelease.jsp?group=3_0&lan=en&action=view&id=10224&sCateg=3_0.

39 According to Jennifer Jeffs, the president of the Canadian International Council, the annual per capita income of Mexico's 110 million people has recently surpassed the US$10,000 mark, a significant plateau for purposes of development status. Jennifer Jeffs, 'A Stronger Mexico Is Good for Canada,' *Globe and Mail*, 25 May 2010, A15.

40 Interestingly, Canada joined with a number of Latin American countries to back the Mexican candidate, Central Bank Governor Agustin Carstens, in a failed bid for the top job at the IMF in June 2011. Kevin Carmichael, 'Why the Middle Powers Won't Back Lagarde,' *Globe and Mail*, 27 June 2011, B3.

41 Richard A. Serrano, 'Mexico under Siege,' *Los Angeles Times*, 11 May 2010, A7, http://projects.latimes.com/mexico-drug-war/#/its-a-war. By mid-2012, drug-related violence in Mexico had claimed almost 50,000 Mexican lives since 2006. See Andres Oppenheimer, 'Mexico's Violence Is Up, and So Is Tourism,' *Miami Herald*, 17 March 2012.

42 In late March 2012, the first trilateral meeting of defence ministers was held in Ottawa, where discussions focused on achieving greater military cooperation, combating the drug trade, and working together on disaster

response efforts. See Bruce Cheadle, 'North American Defence Ministers to Tackle Drug Trade in Ottawa Meeting,' *Winnipeg Free Press*, 27 March 2012.

43 Continued bilateral interaction at the ceremonial and ministerial level has continued since Calderón's May 2010 visit to Canada, including the September 2010 visits of Canada's governor general and minister of labour to Mexico City. In mid-June 2011, Mexico's secretary of the economy Bruno Ferrari also met with his Canadian counterpart, Ed Fast, and foreign minister John Baird in Ottawa to seek ways of strengthening trade and economic linkages between the two countries. Government of Canada, 'Canada and Mexico Continue to Strengthen Economic Ties,' news release (Ottawa: Department of Foreign Affairs and International Trade, 13 June 2011) and Barrie McKenna, 'Putting Canada-Mexico Trade in High Gear,' *Globe and Mail*, 16 June 2011, B12.

44 On his visit to Canada, Calderón held private discussions with Prime Minister Harper, the governor general, and federal party leaders, spoke before Canada's House of Commons, and met with provincial and business leaders. Besides the controversial visa flap, which dominated the talks, the visit focused on trade and investment, climate change, and Canadian assistance for battling the drug cartels in Mexico. Bruce Campion-Smith, 'Ottawa's Visa Rule Is Costing Canada Visitors, Mexican President Says,' *Toronto Star*, 28 May 2010, A14; Campbell Clark, 'Mexico Pushes Ottawa to Act on Climate Change,' *Globe and Mail*, 28 May 2010, A5; and Mike Blanchfield, 'Mexican President Pleads for Visa Changes,' *Chronicle Herald*, 28 May 2010, B2. In a meeting with the *Globe and Mail*'s editorial board, Calderón had this to say: 'The relationship between Mexico and Canada is much more than the visa problem. I am not coming only to talk about that. I believe that Canada and Mexico are natural partners and friends.' Marina Jimenez, 'Profile on Felipe Calderon: 22,700 dead, $8billion, zero regrets,' *Globe and Mail*, 29 May 2010, A1.

45 Canada's credibility in the Americas will also be enhanced by strengthening bilateral relations with Mexico. See Marina Jimenez, 'Why We Should Deepen Ties with Mexico,' *Globe and Mail*, 25 May 2011, A3.

46 Bombardier Corporation, 'Bombardier Learjet 85 Aircraft Composite Structure Manufacturing to Take Place at Querétaro Facility,' press release, Mexico City, 29 May 2008, http://www2.bombardier.com/en/3_0/pressrelease.jsp?group=3_0&lan=en&action=view&id=10224&sCateg=3_0.

6 Through Sun and Ice: Canada, Cuba, and Fifty Years of 'Normal' Relations

PETER MCKENNA AND JOHN M. KIRK

It is not always easy to encapsulate in a few words the essence or defining characteristics of Canadian-Cuban relations. In many ways, it is a fascinating, confounding, and unique bilateral relationship.[1] It has experienced periods of intense engagement, not-so-subtle patches of tough sledding, and times where it seemed to be ostensibly drifting on autopilot. Since 1959, it has been a typically normal relationship in every sense of the term, with both countries maintaining uninterrupted diplomatic, political, commercial, and people-to-people contacts for over fifty years. Irrespective of the political party in power in Ottawa or the tenor of the overall relationship, they have always agreed to talk to each other – as opposed to not talking at all or talking over each other's head. Accordingly, one of the key questions to consider here is: Why has it been a normal relationship – particularly given the huge contextual significance of the United States for both Canada and Cuba? This chapter also explores the strengths and weaknesses of Canada's decades-long approach (with a specific focus on the Jean Chrétien years) of constructively (or not so constructively) engaging the Cubans.

To begin, it is fair to say that Canada has not always had particularly good relations with Cuba. Nor has it always had particularly poor relations with Havana either.[2] (Still, relations under the Conservative government of Stephen Harper, elected in January 2006, are probably as low as they have ever been.) But to understand this seemingly 'on-again, off-again' Canadian-Cuban relationship, one has to factor into the bilateral equation the fundamental geopolitical and economic reality of the U.S. 'hyperpower.' To be sure, the 'U.S. factor' plays a fundamental role – domestically and externally in both Ottawa and Havana – in shaping Canada-Cuba relations.[3]

Outlining Canada-Cuba Engagement

The five decades of the Cuban revolutionary process have proven to be a fascinating backcloth for these two countries to attempt to develop solid bilateral relations, relations which have survived periods of great stress and tension. Indeed, there have been both notable successes and failures, as one would expect from proponents of two such radically differing systems. But the relationship has been historically underscored by an unwavering commitment to engage with each other – across a wide range of policy and issue areas – no matter what the current state of bilateral relations. Both countries realize that they get more benefits and advantages from engaging and talking to each other than from not doing so. Put simply, a policy of engagement – although not always smoothly executed – works in the interests of both countries.

Notwithstanding the occasional diplomatic flare-up and sharp disagreement, relations for the past fifty years have been cordial or 'normal.' It is worth mentioning that the label of the ruling political party in Canada has mattered little, as illustrated by John Diefenbaker's Progressive Conservative government (1957–63).[4] Clearly, the initial honeymoon came under Diefenbaker, a lawyer and avowed nationalist from a poor German immigrant background on the prairies who was resentful of the U.S. superiority complex. He maintained a profound loathing of President John F. Kennedy (a shared sentiment), was willing to give Cuba's revolutionary government a chance to prove itself, and was keen to fill the commercial vacuum left after U.S. trade linkages were abruptly terminated. He also sought to resist stiff U.S. pressure to break relations with Cuba, refused to endorse Washington's economic embargo against Cuba, and was less than a willing ally during the nerve-wracking Cuban missile crisis of 1962.

Yet, the Liberal government of Lester Pearson (1963–8) deliberately put the relationship in a political deep freeze – ostensibly out of deference to both the Kennedy and Johnson administrations in the U.S. One event in particular speaks volumes about the sometimes confounding nature of Canada-Cuba relations. At one point, the Pearson government was panic-stricken over the prospect of having to invite Fidel Castro to attend Canada's 1967 Expo celebrations in Montreal. The Canadians did everything they could to politely dissuade the Cuban leader from attending, bizarrely arguing that the RCMP could not ensure his safety. Correctly reading the diplomatic tea leaves, Havana sent notification that Fidel Castro would not be able to attend the international celebrations after all.[5]

Arguably, the apex of bilateral relations came under Pierre Trudeau's tenure (especially during the 1968–76 years). Trudeau had a strong interest in developing a more independent foreign policy path for Canada, along with a deep awareness of the Third World's aspirations.[6] He spoke Spanish, had a particular interest in Latin America, and was committed to diversifying Canada's foreign policy posture. He also shared similarities with Fidel Castro: both were lawyers, were educated by Jesuits, had social justice interests, were widely travelled, and had a profound understanding of underdevelopment and social marginalization.

As a demonstration of the extremely cordial nature of bilateral relations at the time, one incident stands out. When Cuba's ambassador to Canada, Pepe Fernández de Cossío, met with Trudeau in 1968, their entire conversation took place in Spanish. And it was obvious from the beginning that both men were committed to injecting some new vitality into the bilateral relationship. In fact, Cossio even offered to send to Canada's then Department of External Affairs (DEA) – which had often recoiled at the thought of closer Canada-Cuba relations – his summary report of the meeting (which he would also be sending to his superiors in Havana). It was a sign that the Canadian-Cuban relationship had indeed reached a new and groundbreaking level of engagement.

There is little dispute that the highwater mark of Trudeau's Cuba policy came during his controversial visit in early 1976 (the first by a NATO head of government). In his speech to some 25,000 screaming Cubans, Trudeau concluded with a dramatic flourish: 'Viva Cuba y el pueblo cubano … Viva el Primer Ministro Fidel Castro. Viva la amistad cubano-candiense.'[7] At the same time, differences over the Angola War led to a cooling off after 1976; yet relations remained friendly, and the strong personal relationship between the two endured for years later. Castro's presence as an honorary pallbearer at Trudeau's funeral in October 2000 illustrated the close family ties that had been cemented earlier.

No such friendly connections characterized the Canada-Cuba relationship during the subsequent reign of Brian Mulroney's Progressive Conservative government (1984–93). Under Mulroney, there was a conspicuous shift in bilateral interchange and dialogue. Much of that change can be explained by Mulroney's obsession with refurbishing and recasting the Canada-U.S. relationship in a more favourable light.

As Mulroney himself once declared, 'Good relations, superb relations with the United States of America will be the cornerstone of our foreign policy.'[8] Diplomatic inertia became the order of the day; there were scant ministerial exchanges and precious little in the way of new foreign policy initiatives toward Havana.

As far as the right-leaning Mulroney government was concerned, the Cubans were essentially on their own. Indeed, when the March 1993 'storm of the century,' with its hurricane-like winds, hit Cuba with a devastating thud, complicated even further by the hardship imposed by the demise of the Soviet Union, Canada did virtually nothing. The only time that the Mulroney government sought to engage the Cubans was when Cuba sat as a non-permanent member of the UN Security Council during the first Gulf War in 1990–1. At that time, Canada was seeking resolutions from the world body to back the expulsion, by force if necessary, of Iraq from Kuwaiti territory. But the Cubans were unmoved by the Canadian overtures and subsequently voted against such UN resolutions.

In seeking to differentiate himself from Mulroney's 'cosy' relationship with Washington, Prime Minister Jean Chrétien (1993–2003) sought to cultivate warmer relations with Havana.[9] His new approach, though, was based on the same old dictum: that engaging the Cubans was the best way to secure meaningful and enduring political and economic reforms in Cuba. He also wanted to show U.S. president Bill Clinton that Canada's policy of 'constructive engagement' could be more successful than four decades of U.S. hostility and isolation. As Chrétien himself once opined, 'Isolation leads nowhere. But if we are engaging them, discussing with them, offering help … the people of Cuba and the President of Cuba will certainly be happy to have a dialogue.'[10]

The early years of Chrétien's government were especially productive, largely under the tutelage of foreign affairs minister Lloyd Axworthy (who would make two visits to the country). Canada led the charge to have Cuba readmitted to the OAS, reopened a modest development assistance program under the Canadian International Development Agency (CIDA), encouraged connections with NGOs and universities, and promoted business ties.[11] (Significantly, two-way trade jumped dramatically from $250 million in 1994 to roughly $1 billion in 2003–4.) Canada became one of the island's most important foreign investors, was a major source of Canadian tourists, and signed a 14-Point Joint Declaration with the Cubans in 1997 – the only such agreement where the Cuban government agreed to discuss the thorny issue of human rights. In addition, the Chrétien government consistently opposed the U.S. economic embargo (though regularly criticizing Cuba's human rights record at the Geneva meetings of the UN Human Rights Commission), urged Washington to read just its Cuba policy, and steadfastly rejected the anti-Cuba Helms-Burton law.

But there would be lows as well. Chrétien's April 1998 visit to Cuba was largely a disaster.[12] He sought to lecture Fidel Castro about human rights and democratic freedoms. In a very testy meeting between the two leaders, Chrétien brandished a list of prisoners whom he wanted released from Cuban prisons (the so-called Group of Four). Castro was not amused. In the months that followed, Canada strengthened its criticism of Cuba, reduced development assistance, discouraged Canadian investment in Cuba, and supported several anti-Cuban U.S. initiatives at the UN Human Rights Commission in Geneva; in late 1999 the prime minister referred to the need to inject some 'northern ice' into the relationship.

After an internal policy review within the Department of Foreign Affairs, efforts to reintegrate Cuba into the OAS were halted. A proposed joint public health project in Haiti was stopped, Cuban phone calls were not promptly returned, and ministerial visits were abruptly cancelled. (Tellingly, Cuba was not invited to the Third Summit of the Americas in Quebec City in 2001 – although at earlier ones in Miami and Santiago, Canada had expressed support for Cuba to be included.) The arrest of seventy-five opponents of the Cuban government in March 2003 made bilateral matters even worse. It would be mostly downhill from there.

The frostiness in the bilateral relationship had been building for several years. First, the Pan-American Games took place in Winnipeg in the summer of 1999. The *Winnipeg Sun* ran a competition on who could guess the correct number of Cuban athletes who would defect. To entice participants, the newspaper offered a prize of an all-inclusive paid holiday to Varadero, Cuba. Security was poor; Cuban athletes were harassed; and Fidel Castro unwisely dubbed Canada 'territorio enemigo.' To compound the injury, Castro also criticized Chrétien on national television after the April 2001 Summit of the Americas in Quebec City, comparing him in a negative light to Pierre Trudeau. (In the following May Day parade, a huge papier maché head of Chrétien was paraded and mocked in the streets of Havana.) It was clear that Canada-Cuba relations had sunk to their lowest point in almost ten years. While they would recover somewhat toward the end of Chrétien's tenure, and it is worth emphasizing they were never in jeopardy of being severed completely at any time, the coolness in bilateral relations has not yet thawed fully.

Relations with Cuba have cooled even more under the Conservative government of Stephen Harper (from 2006 onwards). For its first two years in office, there was nary a word about Cuba from the Harper government. (When contacted in Ottawa and Washington, Canadian officials were at a loss to explain the finer details of the Harper government's Cuba policy.) For a variety of reasons, including the lack of foreign policy expertise within the Harper team, deeply ideological convictions, and a preference to curry favour with the anti-Cuba Bush administration in the U.S., it was thought best to say as little as possible about Cuba. Stephen Harper's obsessively controlling style of governance and his own right-leaning ideology also cast a dark shadow over Canada-Cuba relations. Not surprisingly, then, the bilateral relationship has been effectively placed in a holding pattern – even more so given Harper's sweeping majority election victory in May 2011 – with few prospects for improvement going forward.

To underscore the tension in bilateral relations under Harper, both the Canadian and U.S. governments released similarly worded communiqués on 21 May 2008 (a day late as it turned out) celebrating the anniversary of Cuba's independence (20 May) and the election of Tomás Estrada Palma in 1902. Referring to a 'Day of Solidarity with the Cuban People,' the Canadian government press release went on to note: 'Canada continues to monitor developments in Cuba closely, and we are concerned about the plight of political prisoners, especially those suffering from poor health' and called for 'a process of political and economic reform.'[13] What is important to note here is that official Ottawa had never issued such a statement in the past. While the day in question is regularly celebrated as a holiday in Miami, it is definitely not in Havana, where that date is seen as one of shame. It was no wonder that the Cubans began to wonder whether the bilateral relationship had fallen to a new low, and whether this was an ominous sign of the future for Canada-Cuba relations under Harper.

Canada's meagre response to the devastating hurricanes of Gustav and Ike in September 2008 (which caused roughly $10 billion in damages on the island) was also particularly telling. Ottawa initially earmarked only $100,000 in disaster relief – to be distributed among Cuba, Haiti, and the Dominican Republic! (In comparison, developing countries like Algeria, Namibia and Trinidad and Tobago gave more than $1 million each.) While it was later raised to $1 million, it was a miserly sum given Canada's standing as a wealthy G8 country. That paltry amount spoke loudly about the priority being accorded to Canada's relations with Cuba.

In a January 2009 newspaper interview, Peter Kent, then Canada's outspoken minister of state for the Americas, had this to say about Cuba: 'Some [people] are too willing to accept a candy-coated vision of what life in Cuba really is. It's still a good place to go and have a great vacation in an artificial bubble. But Canadians should be realistic … It is still a dictatorship, any way you package it.'[14] And in another interview three months later, Kent spoke critically about reintegrating Cuba into the hemispheric fold:

> I would say the majority of countries in the Organization of American States feel that Cuba, while it is welcome to return, should return after embracing the democratic practices and principles set out in the OAS charter. And our concern would be that if, in their enthusiasm to welcome Cuba back into the OAS, it was accepted as it is today, that would be a negative in the sense that some of the wobbling democracies, or less-democratic democracies, might be tempted to go toward the Cuban status quo rather than continue on the road to real democracy.[15]

A casual meeting with Kent by one of the authors in Ottawa in May 2008 revealed the surprising news that he was unaware of Cuba's total disinterest in rejoining the OAS and had a superficial grasp of the Cuba file.

Furthermore, at the fourth Summit of the Americas in Trinidad and Tobago in mid-April 2009, Prime Minister Harper once again confirmed the frosty tone of Canada-Cuba relations. While singling out the U.S. economic embargo against Cuba for criticism in an interview with the right-wing Fox News, he also slighted the Cubans by referring to himself as 'an anti-Communist Conservative.' (In one of his newspaper op-eds or 'Reflexions,' Fidel Castro subsequently described Harper as 'an openly rightist man and the only one to have been ill-mannered toward Cuba.') Additionally, Harper went on to say the following during the Summit's proceedings: 'President Obama has indicated a new openness to Cuba … we would hope the Cuban government would reciprocate and look at some of the changes it needs to make.'[16] Of course, demanding that the Cubans *needed* to make certain changes was a surefire way to close off any interest in Havana's wanting to do so.

Another sign of the deterioration in Canada-Cuba relations came with the abrupt cancellation of Kent's May 2009 visit to Havana, which was to be the first by a Canadian cabinet minister in almost ten years.[17] No public reason was given for the cancellation and no alternative date was offered by the Cubans, who were annoyed at some of the unwelcome and insensitive comments emanating from the Harper government. Indeed, in the week prior to his scheduled visit, Kent declared: 'I want to reinforce the message that the PM delivered to the Summit of the Americas, to encourage productive, constructive responses to the U.S. gesture. Also to stress again our encouragement of the release of political prisoners and the opening of institutions to democratic practices.'[18] In an apparent diplomatic tit-for-tat response, Ottawa was late in approving the proper visitor's visa for Cuba's minister for trade and investment Rodrigo Malmierca, who was slated to attend the annual shareholders' meeting of Sherritt International – the single largest foreign investor in Cuba – in Toronto. Evidently, the visa request was not denied; it just failed to be processed in time to allow Malmierca to make his flight to Canada in late May. Obviously, the childish nature of Ottawa's conduct suggests that any thaw in relations with Cuba during the Harper period is not likely to materialize any time soon.

On a more positive note, Kent's replacement as junior minister for foreign affairs (Latin America and consular affairs), Diane Ablonczy, has sought to improve the tenor of bilateral relations. She visited Havana in early January 2012 and held productive meetings with her Cuban counterparts. And in March she met with Cuba experts in Canada to discuss possible opportunities for improving bilateral relations with the island. But these positive moves have to be juxtaposed with Harper's persistent coolness toward Havana, as demonstrated by his unwillingness to agree to have Cuba participate in the April 2012 VI Summit of the Americas in Colombia and any forthcoming summits. 'We do believe that the Summit of the Americas should be restricted to democratic countries and that Cuba should be encouraged to come as a democratic country in the future,' he said.[19] This approach to Cuba, however, left Canada (along with the U.S.) badly isolated on the issue of summit participation, tied us too closely to Washington's stance, and did little to improve Ottawa's standing in the wider hemisphere.[20]

But even in the face of a rigid ideological approach, bilateral relations, although strained, still continue to be cordial. There is, for example, a parliamentary association of Canadian MPs and senators from all parties with interests in Cuba. Its former leader, Senator Marcel

Prud'homme, was awarded the prestigious Medal of Friendship by the Cuban government in April 2009; Canadians still make up the largest contingent of tourists (over 900,000 in 2010 or the equivalent of 8 million Americans); Sherritt International (with interests in nickel and cobalt, energy generation, and oil exploration and development) is still the principal investor in Cuba; Canadian NGOs such as OXFAM and the World Wildlife Federation are still active in Cuba; and some two dozen Canadian universities still have exchange agreements with their Cuban counterparts. So, even when bilateral relations hit pockets of obvious turbulence, they still continue to muddle through in a normalized fashion.

Untangling the Canada-Cuba Dynamic

All of this leads to the critical question: How do we explain why both countries seek to maintain 'normal' relations – especially since there have been such strains on bilateral ties over the years? Do the two countries actually need each other for their own foreign policy reasons? What are the core motivating forces for both Canada and Cuba? Crudely put, what is in it for Ottawa and Havana? A multitude of factors – political, symbolic, commercial, electoral, international, and historical in nature –help to shed some explanatory light on this intriguing bilateral relationship.

Historical connections – from the days when sailing ships from Nova Scotia once plied the waters of the Caribbean trading cod, potatoes, and lumber for sugar, molasses, and rum – make it almost impossible to sever the relationship entirely. Even in the face of intense U.S. pressure, Canada has not wavered once in its commitment to maintain full diplomatic relations with Havana.[21] The historical record also shows that Canada was quick to recognize the revolutionary government in Cuba, has consistently voted against the U.S. economic embargo at the UN every fall, and has rarely allowed rigid ideological convictions to jeopardize its overall relationship with Cuba. Indeed, Canada's decision in 1962 not to break official relations with Cuba (one of only two countries in the Americas not to do so) is often cited by both countries as a singularly defining moment.

In addition to this storied history, trade and investment opportunities have also been important policy drivers for Canadian policy makers. Significantly, trade between the two countries has grown steadily over the years – from $375,000 in 1985 to just over $1.4 billion in 2010.[22]

To be sure, the business community in Canada has been a strong advocate of dialogue and exchange with the Cuban government and people.
They have always recognized that closer political relations hold the key
to opening up Cuba's commercial doors (and, to a lesser extent, those
of the wider Americas), and the U.S. embargo gives Canadian corporations competitive advantages and a niche market for their goods and
services.

One should not discount the influence and impact of the so-called
'Cuba card' in shaping Canada's engagement policy toward the island.
Recognizing the crucial electoral, symbolic, and nationalistic value of
Canada's relations with Cuba, Canadian political leaders have never
missed an opportunity to showcase Canada's distinct and different
Cuba policy in contrast with the isolationist and hostile tendencies of
successive U.S. administrations. They know that for reasons of domestic political consumption it is in their best interests to demonstrate foreign policy independence – real and imagined – from U.S. influence.
Not only is it politically popular in Canada, but highlighting a 'Made-
in-Canada' Cuba policy, especially when the 'mouse' can occasionally
tweak the nose of the 'elephant,' also reassures Canadians about their
sense of pride and national identity. Put simply, a Cuba policy that
clearly differentiates Canadians from their American cousins is good
policy and even better politics.

In addition, the durability of bilateral relations can be explained, in
part, by Canada's fairly recent 'discovery' of the Americas as a key foreign policy focus. From Pierre Trudeau to Stephen Harper, successive
Canadian governments have come to realize that Canada's future very
much rests in this hemisphere – as evidenced by our joining the Organization of American States in 1990, negotiating a North American Free
Trade Agreement (NAFTA) in 1994, and undertaking high-profile roles
in the Summit of the Americas processes. But if Ottawa is to preside
over a credible and successful Americas policy, it will need to cultivate
stronger relations with revolutionary Cuba. There are some in Ottawa
who recognize that Cuba is highly regarded in the region and that it
punches well above its weight class internationally. But they are in the
minority among powerful government functionaries, most of whom
grew up during the Cold War era. Likewise many in DFAIT have yet to
recognize fully the significance of the Pink Tide – the dozen or so left-of-
centre governments elected in the region since the first Chávez election
in 1998. By courting and engaging the Cubans, Canada not only sends a
potent message to a host of other Latin American and Caribbean coun-

tries (which serves to bolster Canada's legitimacy, image, and influence throughout the region), but it also delivers a pointed message to officialdom in Washington. Stated differently, Ottawa's Americas strategy cannot possibly reach its full potential if relations with Cuba are totally dysfunctional or barely breathing. It is not clear whether, because of ideological reasons, the current prime minister understands this.

As for Cuban motivations, the explanatory reasons have been similar in many respects to Canada's, though there are some key differences.[23] For instance, cordial relations with Canada offer the Cuban political leadership a certain degree of international respectability and credibility that can be repackaged for both domestic as well as external consumption. When Cuba is able to showcase its relationship with a respected member of the G8 industrialized countries, it sends out the right message to the international community of states: if Canada has no qualms about dealing with Havana, then why should the rest of the world (especially Canada's closest neighbour, the United States)? The April 1998 official visit of Prime Minister Chrétien was a major propaganda coup for Havana, since it underscored friendly bilateral relations and highlighted the anachronistic nature of U.S. policy towards Cuba.

In many ways, the bilateral relationship is an obvious win-win situation for the Cubans, with very few risks involved.[24] In a challenging global economic marketplace (and especially after the demise of the Soviet Union in the early 1990s), Cuba has been aggressively searching for reliable and strategic trading partners, which makes an advanced, Western country like Canada particularly valuable. While today's Cuba has still not completely turned the corner economically (and is particularly hurting from the 2009–10 downturn in the global economy and the devastating 2008 hurricane season), two-way trade with Canada has become acutely important for the Cubans. In fact, Canada has become a key supplier of high-tech goods, basic consumer durables, management service expertise, and crucial spare parts for U.S.-made equipment. Similarly important for the economy is the strong Canadian tourist presence in Cuba, who make up approximately 40 per cent of all foreign tourists.

Clearly, the Cuban government is interested in strengthening political and economic relations with Canada for a number of pragmatic reasons: the Canadian government is a key supplier of financing and credit; approximately seventy Canadian companies comprise the largest source of badly needed foreign investment; and some 900,000 Canadians travel to Cuba annually, generating important revenue and employment on the island. Canada also provides valuable develop-ment assistance funds, including CIDA's outstanding programs and technical expertise. Additionally, Canadian officials are now (or rather have been in the past) involved in improving Cuba's banking system, tax structure, tourism sector, and its economic planning procedures and institutions.

In sum, constructive relations with Canada provide a host of benefits to Cuba, and without any onerous preconditions. Cuban officials know that, for the most part, the Canadian government does not do Washing-ton's bidding and is not seeking to destabilize the Cuban government or punish the Cuban people.[25] Cuban authorities also recognize that a cordial and constructive relationship with Canada could prove valu-able to Havana some time down the road. Indeed, Canada has often been touted as an important intermediary in any future Cuba-U.S. rapprochement.

Assessing Canada's 'Constructive Engagement' Approach

From the early days of the Chrétien Liberals in 1993, Canada's Cuba policy has embraced commercial exchange, mutual respect, and dip-lomatic dialogue. It has rejected the time-honoured U.S. strategy of economic embargo, the view of Cuba as a 'rogue state,' and the interna-tional political ostracism of Cuba. As secretary of state for Latin Amer-ica and Africa Christine Stewart explained in 1995: 'Canada's policy toward Cuba has been one of constructive engagement – we believe that political and economic advances can be encouraged by maintain-ing a dialogue with the Cuban people and government.'[26] During the April 1998 Santiago Summit of the Americas, Chrétien reiterated this view when he noted: 'The policy of positive engagement is one I've practised for a long time.'[27] And just prior to his departure for Havana in late April, he explained once again: 'Isolation leads nowhere. But if we are engaging them, discussing with them, offering help … the peo-ple of Cuba and the president of Cuba will certainly be happy to have a dialogue.'[28] Not unexpectedly, then, Canadian officials have indicated on numerous occasions their endorsement of constructive engagement and 'business-as-usual' relations – especially at a time of apparent tran-sition in Cuba – over isolation and high-pitched rhetoric.

This approach was given more emphasis, however, when Lloyd Axworthy was appointed foreign affairs minister in early 1996. At that time, the official government line crystallized around the idea that engagement was far more likely to achieve positive results and change in Cuba than the U.S. policy of sanctions and confrontation, which has failed to bring about a regime change and fundamental reform after almost fifty years. Upon returning from his January 1997 visit to Cuba, Axworthy was fairly blunt in stating: 'The reality is that I think we've gone further than anything they [the Americans] have been able to accomplish, by building those bridges' and more successful than 'holding a megaphone in a Senate committee room.'[29] During a press briefing after attending an OAS conference in Washington in early March of 1998, Axworthy once again stated boldly: 'The whole embargo and the Helms-Burton bill is totally counterproductive. It just doesn't work.'[30] And just prior to Chrétien's April 1998 visit to Cuba, Axworthy remarked: 'To criticize the U.S. economic embargo against Cuba, and the Helms-Burton legislation, is not to argue for the status quo in Cuba. Rather, it is to react to an approach that runs contrary to our own. It is to criticize a policy that has proven unsuccessful in achieving its own stated goals, and that is the source today of much suffering among the Cuban people.'[31]

Particularly since the early 1990s, there has been no shortage of opinions – from government officials, academics, NGOs, the media, and the general public – on the effectiveness of Canada's Cuba policy of 'constructive engagement' or 'principled pragmatism.' The term 'constructive engagement' actually originated during the waning years of the Carter administration when a frustrated President Carter came to the realization that it was complicated and difficult to make human rights considerations the centrepiece of U.S. foreign policy. The concept was subsequently picked up by the Reagan administration in the mid-1980s and became the guiding principle for its policy toward apartheid South Africa (and Saddam Hussein's Iraq). The idea was to engage the South African government in dialogue, commerce, and support for civil society and, in doing so, to foster meaningful change and the eventual dismantling of the pillars of apartheid. In the case of South Africa, though, the strategy was heavily criticized and, as events in the country would prove, was largely seen as ineffective and, worse, a lifeline to the apartheid regime.

Like the U.S. approach toward South Africa in the 1980s, Canada's policy of constructive engagement with Cuba maintains the same overriding assumptions and thinking with regard to means and goals. First, it begins from the premise that engaging the targeted state is the most effective means or strategy for altering the behaviour of that same government, and it does so through the maximization of a variety of linkages. Second, it accepts as a given the fact that the government in question is not only rational and pragmatic, but that it is also interested in introducing structural reforms of a more open and liberal-democratic nature. Third, it operates on the basis of an inevitable choice – rightly or wrongly – between engagement or isolation, and the use of a 'carrot' versus a big 'stick.' Fourth, it is underscored by a belief that 'quiet diplomacy' rather than the 'megaphone' approach (and its attendant threats of punitive measures) is a more suitable means of moving a repressive or 'illiberal' regime along the path of creating more political and economic space. Last, it assumes that meaningful change and reform instituted by the engaged country will not be immediate or necessarily recognizable over the short term but will eventually and inevitably take place over a longer period of time, as part of a more gradual process of transitioning.

In terms of the relationship between means and goals, the proponents of engagement profess to offer a more realistic and effective strategy for promoting positive change. Constructive engagement is a more pragmatic, non-ideological, and ultimately more realistic approach to fostering political and economic reform in a country such as Cuba. Accordingly, it avoids catering to a knee-jerk, politically expedient approach of punishing a country for what you view as 'wrongdoing' and 'misconduct.' Indeed, the argument is that the process of change can best be initiated only when a country is engaged with (rather than estranged from) the targeted country and can express its concerns about, for example, the lack of political freedom, systematic torture, or poor prison conditions face to face with the government in question. Isolation, so the argument goes, accomplishes very little, and limits the ability to convince a country to initiate reforms. Through engagement a country can acquire more leverage and access to influence the behaviour of the rights-abusing state. Dialogue, political interaction, and commercial exchange thus create a strong incentive for the offending regime to initiate reforms so as not to jeopardize the benefits and advantages accruing from that very engagement and interchange.

In theory at least, engaging a country such as Cuba is supposed to foster change through the very act of engagement. At the core of this argument is the contention that engagement will invariably lead to an infusion of liberal ideas and values (at the elite and mass level) in the targeted societies. From dialogue at the political level, then, world leaders can educate or sensitize a leader of an authoritarian state on the finer points and advantages of democratic pluralism, respect for human rights, and greater political freedom. And when representatives from a foreign country meet and speak with university professors, lawyers, spokespeople for NGOs, and students – or provide support to other groups within civil society – they help to encourage positive change from within. When resources are offered to grass-roots organizations and reform-minded people on the ground – the critical forces for social change – it is expected that these same groups and individuals will press the government for more political space and accountability or that these ideas will filter upwards from the grass roots to the political leadership.

With greater economic or commercial exchange, it is hoped that the Cuban government will eventually introduce additional positive reforms. This argument is underscored by the idea that economic liberalization and free markets in the targeted country will necessarily contribute to a political 'apertura' (or opening). As human rights scholar Jack Donnelly explains: 'Economic support that appears to help stabilize repression actually undermines it.'[32] The opening of markets and the introduction of free enterprise will, over a period of time, have a salutary effect in terms of improving the human rights climate in revolutionary Cuba. And sustained economic growth in Cuba will set in motion a host of powerful economic and political forces – including a reduced role for the state (as both an employer and benefactor), the dismantling of the existing order, the sharing of authority, and the growth of a liberal-minded middle class. An expanding middle class, with its accompanying stake in the existing system, will eventually press for change and a voice in the polity, for governmental accountability, and for greater political space. Lastly, expanded commercial contact, especially with Western commercial enterprises, can infuse not only its Cuban workforce, but also the political leadership in Cuba, with ideas about greater personal freedom.

However, this theory is not wholly applicable to the Cuban scenario, for a variety of reasons. In the first place, the revolutionary government in Havana is fearful of how the United States – just ninety miles away – would seek to exploit any attendant political and economic space that might result from greater liberalization in Cuba. It is understandably concerned given the fact that successive U.S. administrations have sought to destroy the Cuban revolution, to assassinate Fidel Castro, to turn a blind eye to (illegal and terrorist) activities of armed Cuban exiles, and to pressure numerous governments to break relations with

Cuba. Indeed, the so-called Trading with the Enemy Act stands as a potent reminder to Cubans of the enmity which the United States still feels toward Cuba, fifty years after it broke diplomatic relations with Havana. This is something which proponents of constructive engagement in Cuba need to bear in mind at all times.

Since the beginning of the 'Special Period in Time of Peace' (precipitated by the termination of preferential economic and financial arrangements with the USSR and the Eastern Bloc) in the 1990s, Cuba has initiated a series of necessary or forced economic liberalization measures of particular significance, including the legalization of hard currency in 1993. This was shortly followed by the reopening of the farmers' markets; the transformation of state farms into co-operatives; permission for some 200,000 Cubans to work for themselves; the opening of small restaurants; the establishment of chains of hard currency stores; and an open invitation to foreign investors to establish business operations in Cuba. Since assuming the presidency in early 2008, Raúl Castro has instituted his own set of symbolic and significant reforms.[33] Other changes have included: the lifting of prohibitions on buying a number of consumer durables (including cellphones, DVD players, and kitchen appliances); the decision to allow Cubans to stay at hotels on the island; the removal of salary limits; permission for Cubans to hire others to work for them; and the distribution by June 2011 of 1.7 million acres of arable land in long-term leases to 128,000 private farmers. Additionally, a further set of reforms has been debated and may well be introduced in the medium term: the elimination of travel restrictions within the country; the deregulation of the rental and sale of property and cars; and a determination to reduce the differential between the 'convertible peso' (or CUCs) and the Cuba peso (currently 24 to 1) and ultimately to put in place a single monetary currency.[34]

On the political front, however, the changes have been noticeably limited. It is undoubtedly true that the visit of Pope John Paul II in early 1998 (and Pope Benedict's March 2012 visit) allowed Cuba to become the focus of international media attention and has had a salutary effect on church-state relations. It is also true that the number of political prisoners has decreased dramatically in recent years, as a study of the 2011 Amnesty International report will indicate. Cuba has also moved to sign two major international human rights covenants. These are not insignificant changes in Cuba and should be recognized and encouraged by foreign governments like Canada. It is highly unlikely, however, that the revolutionary government will undertake dramatic changes in

Cuba's political structures, allow opposition media to function freely, or radically alter Cuba's socialist constitution. But as Canada's Cuba policy suggests, engagement is a work in progress, and not something that is expected to deliver results overnight.

Has Constructive Engagement Worked?

If Canadian governments have long believed that the U.S. approach has been unsuccessful and even counterproductive, then this raises an important question for Canada's own policy of constructive engagement: Has it successfully achieved its stated objectives in Cuba during the Chrétien years? Those objectives were succinctly outlined by minister Christine Stewart while attending a 1994 conference in Havana organized by *The Economist* magazine: 'First, we are here to promote several concrete Canadian interests, especially in terms of commercial activities. Second, we wish to support positive, peaceful change in Cuba, both political and economic.'[35] She then went on to say that Canada wanted 'to encourage Cuba's full, constructive participation in international affairs.' Stewart concluded by declaring: 'Finally, we want the Canadian government not to be an impediment, standing in the way of Canadian organizations and individuals pursuing their own activities and dialogues with Cubans because of historic restrictions on official development assistance.'[36] Axworthy himself once summarized Canada's policy by explaining: 'Our engagement is designed to provide Cuba with the assistance and support that will be needed if a peaceful transition is to occur with full respect for human rights, genuinely representative government institutions and an open economy.'[37]

Still, how do we evaluate what worked in terms of Canada-Cuba relations – particularly during the Chrétien years – and what did not? Stated differently, what exactly were the various strengths and weaknesses of the Chrétien approach? While evaluating the efficacy of constructive engagement or principled pragmatism is a worthy pursuit, we should not forget that altering the behaviour of other states – especially by a middling power – is an extremely difficult undertaking. As Mark Entwistle, Canada's former ambassador to Cuba for the years 1993–7, has written: 'It is simply not in the power of Canadian "constructive engagement" to affect political reform, improve human rights, or open the economy in Cuba.'[38] Indeed, the simple maintenance of uninterrupted bilateral relations with revolutionary Cuba did not invest Ottawa policy makers with special powers to extract fundamental societal concessions from their Cuban counterparts. As Entwistle went on to explain: 'Political change will take place only when the Cuban political leadership, in its calculation of its own domestic politics, deems it to be in its interest.'[39]

We argue that engagement in general was more productive than isolating and punishing the Cuban government. In the end, the principal policy objective was to foster and encourage meaningful political and economic reforms in Cuba. (One should not forget that Canada derived certain benefits from its engagement policy, including trade and investment opportunities, electoral advantages, and the enhancement of Canada's reputation and image throughout the entire region.) Therefore, the governmental measures and initiatives that 'worked' were those that helped to realize this overarching policy aim.[40]

Clearly, there were aspects of the Chrétien government's 'constructive engagement' approach that worked reasonably well – such as dialogue, ministerial exchanges, and high-level visits. Most of these undertakings were well received by the Cubans, came without any diplomatic strings attached, and set the stage for bilateral discussions on the sensitive issue of human rights. Canada's opposition to mainly U.S. efforts to ostracize and sanction Cuba in various multilateral fora – especially on the U.S. embargo and Helms-Burton – was viewed most favourably by Havana. Often, though, the major flaw in this modus operandi came in the actual execution, particularly the specific details of the exchanges and the heavy-handed tact that was adopted periodically by the Canadian side. There was a serious failure on the part of Canadian officials to recognize that the Cubans – however wrong-headed and frustrating – march to the beat of their own drum.

This was particularly noticeable at the time of Prime Minister Chrétien's high-profile visit to Cuba in April 1998. James Bartleman, Chrétien's principal foreign policy adviser, maintained that the visit itself should not have taken place until the Castro government was first prepared to pay a price for the international credibility that such a meeting would confer upon Havana.[41] Three months before the visit, Bartleman met with President Castro to see whether he might be willing to make more concessions – especially on the human rights front. 'I emphasized that human rights issues were of great importance to the Canadian people and to the prime minister personally, and that continued progress would lead to even closer Canada-Cuba relations,' he wrote.[42] Fidel Castro, though, reacted angrily to Bartleman's remarks and refused to accept any concessions or conditions being attached to a Chrétien visit.

'Don't ask Cuba to do anything which would damage it,' groused Castro, 'and Cuba will not ask Canada to do anything that would embarrass it.'[43] It was an important lesson how *not* to engage the Cubans on bilateral matters.

From the very beginning, the aggressive tone of Chrétien's demands did not go down well with his host, President Castro. For whatever reason, Chrétien decided to set aside diplomatic niceties and any low-hanging diplomatic fruit and cut immediately to the more intractable human rights issues.[44] Evidently, Castro had been prepared – as a gesture of Canada-Cuba amity – to release three low-level political dissidents during Chrétien's visit. But he was taken aback when Chrétien abruptly raised the stakes and called for the immediate release of the prominent 'Group of Four' critics, whom the Cubans were adamantly opposed to releasing at that time. As Bartleman explained: 'It was at this point that Castro probably decided that the policy of constructive engagement with Canada had reached the limits of its usefulness.'[45]

The heavy-handed Chrétien approach of pressing the Cubans aggressively, making unreasonable demands, and seeking to attach preconditions was a sure recipe for diplomatic failure. It did not work for a variety of reasons, not the least of which was the fact that human rights are viewed in Cuba as a key plank of the one-dimensional U.S. approach. Cubans also believe that, as a developing country, social human rights such as the right to education, health care, employment and housing – are far more important than civil and political rights. It is one thing to raise the question of human rights in the context of a series of other bilateral matters, but to focus on this sensitive issue only, as Chrétien insisted, reeked of U.S.-style diplomacy and was essentially a non-starter for the Cubans. What Chrétien and his officials forgot was that the Cuban government would not be pushed around (having survived all manner of U.S. efforts to undermine the revolution), told what to do, or have to answer for themselves to another country. (For the Cubans, this pressure from abroad is seen as meddling in domestic affairs; by the same token they refrain from criticizing Canada's appalling human rights record in terms of First Nations socio-economic conditions.) By failing to understand and appreciate deeply felt Cuban pride, a potent and long-standing nationalistic sentiment, and an implacable sense of Cuban independence and sovereignty, Chrétien's ill-considered strategy was doomed from the very beginning.

Moreover, adopting a hard line toward Havana and resorting to undiplomatic language is similarly unproductive. When Chrétien broached the topic of Castro's intransigence at the 2001 Summit of the Americas in Quebec City, talked about putting some 'diplomatic ice' on the bilateral relationship, and criticized the Cuban government for the March 2003 crackdown on dissidents, the totality of these slights only angered Havana. Pointing fingers at the Cubans, lecturing them about the importance of human rights issues, and mimicking an ideologically laced U.S. disposition will only get their backs up. As former Canadian ambassador to Cuba Keith Christie once remarked: 'The question is, how do you affect the system? You can shout at people, but this government doesn't take it very well. Or you can sit down with them and have an impact over time.'[46]

Ambassador Christie's view within the foreign policy bureaucracy at 'Fort Pearson,' however, tended to be in the minority. Instead, the prevailing conservative viewpoint and tough line toward Havana among officials within the Department of Foreign Affairs and International Trade (DFAIT) often dominated during the Chrétien years (and continues to this day). There seemed to be a near-obsession with the (civil and political) human rights angle to the exclusion of the bigger picture in bilateral relations. And the often harsh exchanges with Cuban diplomats (especially during John Manley's tenure as foreign affairs minister), the use of the UN Human Rights Commission meetings in Geneva to gang up on Cuba (often in concert with the United States), and officialdom's scepticism about the prospects for change in Cuba were not helpful in terms of cultivating a constructive Canada-Cuba relationship. This negative view was aptly summed up when one Canadian official, who was asked to comment on the results of the Canada-Cuba 14-point Joint Declaration, deadpanned: 'Sweet fuck all.'[47]

What *did* work effectively for the Chrétien government, though, was its willingness to eschew the long-standing U.S. strategy of economic embargo, to discard the mentality of viewing Cuba as a 'rogue state' or an 'outpost of tyranny' (to use the unfortunate Bush reference), and to dismiss any notion of ostracizing Cuba hemispherically. As secretary of state for Latin America and Africa Christine Stewart explained in 1995: 'Canada's policy toward Cuba has been one of constructive engagement – we believe that political and economic advances can be encouraged by maintaining a dialogue with the Cuban people and government.'[48] And during the April 1998 Santiago Summit of the Americas, Chrétien reinforced this view when he noted: 'The policy of positive engagement is one I've practised for a long time.'[49] And just prior to his departure for Havana in late April, one senior Canadian government official stated:

'Clearly, isolation has not achieved its end and I don't think the proponents of isolation can claim they've had a positive impact on Cuba. It's
our view that the best way to impose your values on another country is
through engagement.'[50]

It also helped that Canada's engagement policy was bolstered by the
quiet and purposeful diplomatic efforts of Lloyd Axworthy. His tact
and disposition worked because he approached the relationship with
professionalism, in a positive tone, and in a respectful manner. (After
a direct and discreet appeal by Axworthy, he was able to secure the
release of Cuban dissident writer Ismael Sambra in May 1997.) The
Cubans also appreciated his and Chrétien's repeated comments about
the ineffectiveness of the decades-old U.S. economic embargo. 'The
whole embargo and the Helms-Burton bill is totally counterproductive.
It just doesn't work,' declared Axworthy during a press briefing after
attending an OAS conference in Washington in early March of 1998.[51]

When Canada has worked quietly behind the scenes, adopted a more
respectful tone, and dialled back the harsh rhetoric, it has achieved
greater diplomatic success. Because it avoided focusing exclusively on
human rights concerns, for instance, the relationship with Cuba was
able to move forward. Indeed, it was within a posture of diplomatic
dialogue, commercial exchange, people-to-people contacts, and a targeted development assistance program that the Chrétien government
was able to build up much-needed trust and credibility. Additionally, it
did not go unnoticed that Canadian embassy officials in Havana deftly
avoided meeting with any domestic dissident groups in Cuba – unlike
various European countries that would routinely invite dissidents to
their respective national day celebrations in the capital. And it was
on the basis of this trust and non-ideological discourse that Canada
was able to raise difficult issues like human rights, democratization,
and the release of political prisoners. By putting in place a series of
confidence-building measures – such as fostering university-level
exchanges, commercial joint ventures, positive statements at the OAS,
and tough talk about Helms-Burton – Ottawa's engagement policy was
more productive.

The model vehicle for this type of successful approach was the January 1997 Joint Declaration of the Ministers of Foreign Affairs of Canada
and Cuba, which created the Canada-Cuba Joint Committee on Human
Rights (whose members included Canada's ambassador to Cuba and
the director of North American affairs in the Cuban foreign ministry).
The value of this effort came not only from codifying it in a written doc-

ument, but also from situating the human rights issue among a host of other bilateral considerations. Moreover, the Joint Declaration was the only agreement that Cuba had signed with another country that specifically mentioned human rights. As then Canadian ambassador to Cuba, Keith Christie, noted at the time: 'They are now committed to talking to us on issues they won't talk about very openly with anyone else.'[52] The key point here is that the Chrétien government's delicate and respectful method – which envisaged results that would materialize over the long term – struck the correct diplomatic note in dealing with the Cubans.

Indicative of his more constructive approach to Cuba, Prime Minister Chrétien suggested that Canada's policy of engagement, in the wake of his own trip to Cuba in 1998, had helped to create a rapprochement between Washington and Havana.[53] Speaking to reporters after a private meeting with U.S. president Bill Clinton, Chrétien remarked: 'What I can say, is that my trip to Cuba didn't create as much controversy as some had expected that we'd have ... The reaction of the president and his spokesman were very moderate under the circumstances.'[54] He also took the opportunity to add: 'I explained to him that I saw progress, like the fact that my speech has been broadcast and that my speech was in the newspaper and they let me meet with the NGOs (nongovernmental organizations) that I wanted and the (Roman Catholic) cardinal and so on.'[55] When pressed by reporters a little further on his contention, he pointed out that the U.S. Chamber of Commerce was calling for openness with Cuba, along the lines of the Canadian position. He then went on to quip: 'I guess they understood my argument when I said: "Don't rush, you guys, one day you will recognize Cuba, but don't rush because by the time you are there, you'll be welcomed in Canadian hotels."'[56]

To briefly summarize the central lessons of Chrétien's approach to Cuba one would need to begin with the tone and tact of the bilateral conversation. The prime minister's April 1998 visit to Havana is an obvious case in point. It revealed a critical point: You cannot browbeat the Cubans into doing something that they clearly do not want to do.[57] As Castro pointed out upon Chrétien's departure: 'The only way to obtain nothing from Cuba is to put on the pressure.'[58] And raising the decibel level in bilateral discussions is equally fraught with difficulties. But where Canada proved most successful – especially in the area of human rights and democratic pluralism – was by broaching these topics with discretion and respect, and in a non-ideological fashion.

Accompanying this quiet but purposeful diplomatic strategy was a scrupulous effort not to emulate the obviously flawed U.S. approach. If the Chrétien government had adopted an inflexible and hard-line posture, Canada would have made no progress with the Cuban government. It was important that Canada sought to differentiate itself from the U.S. perspective – even taking Washington to task for its outdated embargo and discredited policy of isolation and confrontation. By agreeing to disagree strongly with the Americans over Cuba, the Chrétien government was able to build up some diplomatic trust and credit in Havana. Indeed, it was critical that the Cubans know that Ottawa decision makers were not doing Washington's bidding or acting as its stalking horse in multilateral forums like the OAS.

A simple lesson derived from the Chrétien period was that engagement worked best when there were no strings attached. In other words, insisting upon preconditions in order to move the bilateral relationship forward would only set relations back several steps. Again, this lesson was brought home to Canadians after Chrétien's face-to-face demands fell flat with his Cuban hosts. The Cuban government, as we learned, works on its own agenda and timeline. It also bears repeating that Chrétien's policy of engagement was never conceived of as a quick fix or an overnight success, but as a continuous work in progress.[59]

An integral part of this Cuba policy was to broaden and deepen relations across a wide swath of policy issues, such as trade enhancement, people-to-people contacts, ministerial visits, technical assistance, and foreign aid. It was important to send out the message to the Cubans that Canada's Cuba policy was not simply one-dimensional or, worse yet, held hostage by human rights considerations. And it was through these varied and layered points of contact that the Chrétien government was able to build the necessary rapport, trust, and credibility with the Cuban side. This, in turn, was the entrance fee that enabled Canadian officials to visit the thorny issue of human rights, among others, with their Cuban counterparts.

Lastly, we learned that during the Chrétien years, the Canada-Cuba relationship functioned best when those at the top were fully engaged in the bilateral file. Not only was Prime Minister Chrétien seized with the finer points of Canada's Cuba policy, but so, too, was foreign affairs minister Lloyd Axworthy. (One could easily notice a cooling of relations between the two countries when John Manley took over the Foreign Affairs portfolio.) As was also illustrated during the Chrétien period, it required the sustained attention of other cabinet members, senior officials in both DFAIT and the Prime Minister's Office (PMO), and, most important, Canada's ambassador in Havana. It is another crucial lesson for Canadian policy makers: without this high-level engagement, the bilateral relationship will not be able to move forward in a positive and productive manner.

Conclusion

How do we make sense of Canada's long-standing engagement with revolutionary Cuba? First, we need to realize that bilateral relations have always been intriguing, occasionally complicated, and unusually fluid. It is also important to bear in mind that the 'U.S. factor' (and the overt and covert pressures of the last eleven U.S. presidents) has been a major factor in determining Ottawa's principled and pragmatic Cuba policy. Still, the bottom line remains the same: it gets more from Cuba (and places itself in a better position to influence events on the island) by talking and interacting with them. Not surprisingly, the evolving policy of U.S. president Barack Obama, which promised to embark on a 'new beginning' with Cuba, has fallen short of resuming full diplomatic and economic relations with Havana and still remains unfocused.[60] Nevertheless, it does pose significant policy challenges for Canada.

To date, Stephen Harper's policy toward Cuba appears to be more reminiscent of the failed and stagnant posture of George W. Bush, and this at a time when events are changing quickly in Cuba (in the wake of recent congresses of the Cuban Communist Party in 2011 and 2012) and in the region as a whole (for example, the so-called 'Pink Tide' of approximately a dozen left-leaning governments in Central and South America). The natural advantages developed and cultivated by Ottawa for almost five decades are now being gradually flushed away by a prime minister who has a strong ideological edge and who does not understand the nature and workings of Canada-Cuba relations or indeed political currents in the region. As a result, Canadian linkages in Cuba – politically and economically – are in relative decline. Given Harper's repeated claims that the Americas are a key focus of his foreign policy, this deliberate ignoring of Cuba would seem to be a huge mistake (not least in terms of Canadian commercial interests). Indeed, his inability to grasp the nuances and finer points of Canada's relationship with Havana will likely damage our reputation and profile in the wider Americas. For this reason, it is time for Ottawa to replace ideology with pragmatism.

Officials in Ottawa also need to realize that Canada is becoming less significant for Cuba – particularly given the Canadian government's diplomatic cold shoulder of the past ten years. Conversely, Cuba's linkages with Latin America and the Caribbean have grown significantly, as witnessed by the April 2009 Summit of the Americas in Trinidad and Tobago and the May OAS General Assembly meeting in Tegucigalpa, Honduras. Rapidly increasing trade with China and Russia, ongoing support from Venezuela, income from medical internationalism (an estimated $6–8 billion last year, compared with $2.3 billion for gross tourism income), and growing political ties with the Rio Group and the ALBA countries will all contribute to Cuba's important standing in the South. Canadian policy makers should not forget that Havana has other options – including increased trade, investment, and people-to-people contacts with its long-time nemesis, the United States.[61] One should not ignore the fact that, despite the Trading with the Enemy policy, the United States was actually the largest exporter of agricultural products to Cuba in 2008 – totalling some US$711 million.[62] While this has been reduced since then (as a result of a policy of import-substitution introduced by Havana as a cost-cutting measure), the United States remains one of the largest exporters of food products to Cuba and is a clear competitor for Canadian exporters.

On a more positive note, the body politic of Canada is manifestly ahead of the Harper government's ill-considered Cuba position. The 900,000-plus Canadian tourists who regularly travel to Cuba, the important work of the NGOs, the academic and professional links, the traditional business connections, will all probably outlast Harper's short-sighted and excessively ideological understanding of the country. With a Conservative majority government, there is unlikely to be any dramatic improvement in the near term. But if there is to be any change in tone and substance in bilateral relations, it will have to come from a Canadian initiative. In the end, Canada will most likely 'muddle through' in various permutations of engagement and dialogue (more or less constructively), as it has done for the last fifty years. But in doing so, it will once again spurn the tremendous potential that would result from closer ties with Havana.

NOTES

1 Take, for example, the tacit agreement between Canada and Cuba that Cuban defectors, while on the tarmac in Gander, Newfoundland, would

be permitted to leave their aircraft and join waiting Canadian immigration
authorities. During the 1980s and early 1990s, Aeroflot and Air Cubana
would make regular refuelling stops there. There was no ill will on either
side over the defections, and perfectly understood diplomatically by both
countries. On one particular stop at the Gander International Airport in
1972, President Fidel Castro actually decided to try his hand at tobog-
ganing. During a rather rough ride down a local snow hill, Castro was
suddenly ejected from the sled – all to the shock and horror of his personal
security detail, who quickly scurried over to assist him. Confidential interview with a CBC Radio producer in St John's, Newfoundland and Labrador, 6 July 2009.

2 See, for example, Peter McKenna and John M. Kirk, 'Canada-Cuba Rela-
tions: Old Wine in New Bottles?' in Michele Zebich-Knos and Heather N.
Nicol (eds.), *Foreign Policy toward Cuba: Isolation or Engagement?* (Boulder,
CO: Lexington Books, 2005), 67–86.

3 It is worth bearing in mind that successive Canadian governments –
irrespective of their political stripe – have argued that their general policy
goals vis-à-vis Cuba have basically been the same as those of the United
States. The critical difference has been in the actual means utilized by their
respective governments to secure a more democratic, market-oriented,
and open Cuba. See Peter McKenna and John M. Kirk, '"Sleeping with an
Elephant": The Impact of the United States on Canada-Cuba Relations,'
in Morris Morley and Chris McGillion (eds.), *Cuba, the United States, and
the Post-Cold War World* (Gainesville: University Press of Florida, 2005),
148–79.

4 For a recent treatment of Diefenbaker's nuanced Cuba policy, see Dennis
Molinaro, '"Calculated Diplomacy": John Diefenbaker and the Origins of
Canada's Cuba Policy,' in Robert Wright and Lana Wylie (eds.), *Our Place
in the Sun: Canada and Cuba in the Castro Era* (Toronto: University of Toronto
Press, 2009), 75–95.

5 Government of Cuba, 'Correspondence from Américo Cruz to Raúl Roa –
June 1, 1967' (Havana: Ministry of External Relations Archives).

6 See also Greg Donaghy and Mary Halloran, '*Viva el pueblo cubano*: Pierre
Trudeau's Distant Cuba, 1968–78,' in Wright and Wylie (eds.), *Our Place in
the Sun*, 143–62.

7 Quoted in John M. Kirk and Peter McKenna, *Canada-Cuba Relations: The
Other Good Neighbor Policy* (Gainesville: University Press of Florida, 1997),
110.

8 Quoted in Lawrence Martin, *Pledge of Allegiance: The Americanization of
Canada in the Mulroney Years* (Toronto: McClelland and Stewart, 1993), 57.

9 Chrétien also recognized that there were political points to score from adopting a Cuba policy that was noticeably different from Washington's. Confidential interview with a former Chrétien-era cabinet minister, 9 July 2009.

10 Quoted in Canadian Press, 'PM Calls Cuba Visit "Positive Engagement,"' *Globe and Mail*, 22 April 1998, A2.

11 As of May 2010, Canada's ODA to Cuba for 2008–9 reached $9.45 million. Email correspondence with a Canadian foreign service officer, 25 June 2010. That figure declined slightly for 2009–10, coming in at roughly $8 million.

12 For a critical treatment of this visit (and constructive engagement in general), see Robert Wright, '"Northern Ice": Jean Chrétien and the Failure of Constructive Engagement in Cuba,' in Wright and Wylie (eds.), *Our Place in the Sun*, 195–222.

13 See Foreign Affairs and International Trade Canada, 'Minister Bernier Issues Statement in Recognition of Day of Solidarity with the Cuban People,' news release, 21 May 2008, 1.

14 See Mike Blanchfield, 'Canada Can Play a Role in Emerging Cuba,' *National Post*, 6 January 2009, A6.

15 Quoted in Michelle Collins, 'Implementing Harper's Americas Vision,' *Embassy Magazine*, 29 April 2009, 12.

16 See Mike Blanchfield, 'Harper Hails Americas Success Story,' *National Post*, 20 April 2009, A2. Also see John M. Kirk and Peter McKenna, 'Our Disappearing Cuba Advantage,' *Embassy Magazine*, 25 March 2009, 4.

17 The ministerial visit eventually took place 12–14 November in Havana, where Kent discussed trade issues as well as other bilateral matters with his Cuban counterparts. In addition to meeting with several Cuban ministers and senior government officials, he spoke with the Archbishop of Havana, representatives of civil society, and members of the Jewish community. According to both Canadian and Cuban sources, it was a highly successful government-to-government encounter and extended well beyond the scheduled forty-five minutes. See Government of Canada, 'Minister of State Kent Concludes Successful Visit to Cuba,' news release (Ottawa: Department of Foreign Affairs and International Trade, 17 November 2009), 1, and 'Cuba y Canadá quieren impulsar sus relaciones económicas,' El Nuevo Herald Online, 13 November 2009, http://www.elnuevoherald.com/2009/11/13/586983/cuba-y-canada-quiren-impulsar.html.

18 Significantly, Kent did make a successful visit to Cuba in November 2009, but only after a frank exchange of views between both foreign ministries

laying out the ground rules. Quoted in Michelle Collins, 'Cuba Cancels Kent Visit as Conservatives Stick to Guns,' *Embassy Magazine*, 13 May 2009, 1. According to a December 2010 WikiLeaks release of U.S. diplomatic cables, it is worth noting that the U.S. head of mission in Havana, Jonathan Farrar, was critical of Kent's visit for not raising issues about human rights. The cable indicated that Canada 'failed to meet with independent civil society or make public pronouncements [on human rights] after the visit of Minister Kent.' Quoted in Colin Freeze, 'U.S. Diplomats Damned Ottawa for Being Soft on Cuban Abuses,' *Globe and Mail*, 18 December 2010, A20.

19 Quoted in Mark Kennedy, 'Division on Cuba Ends Summit of Americas on Frosty Note,' *Ottawa Citizen*, 16 April 2012, A1.

20 See Peter McKenna, 'Canada Needs a New Approach to Cuba,' *Ottawa Citizen*, 18 April 2012, A12.

21 During the George Bush-Jean Chrétien era, the U.S. government repeatedly raised the issue of Cuba. Invariably, cabinet-level U.S. officials would express their dissatisfaction to their Canadian counterparts about Canada's position. Canadian ministers stood their ground and pointed out that the U.S approach to Cuba was not working effectively. Confidential interview with a former Chrétien-era cabinet minister, 9 July 2009.

22 Given the global downturn of 2008–10, two-way trade has slumped noticeably, with import and export figures dropping by some 50 per cent. See 'Imports to Cuba and Exports from Cuba Decline Sharply in 2008,' HavanaJournal.com, 20 October 2009, http://havanajournal.com/business/print/8829/. According to a DFAIT official, two-way trade for 2009 dipped considerably to $818 million (email communication with a Canadian foreign service officer, 25 June 2010). The 2010 trade figure is drawn from Government of Canada, *Canada-Cuba Fact Sheet* (Ottawa: Department of Foreign Affairs and International Trade, May 2011).

23 See Peter McKenna and John M. Kirk, 'Canada-Cuba Relations: "Northern Ice" or Nada Nuevo?' in Sahadeo Basdeo and Heather N. Nicol (eds.), *Canada, the United States, and Cuba* (Miami: North-South Center Press, 2002), 63–6.

24 Cubans in general have always looked fondly upon Canada's decision, along with Mexico, not to sever diplomatic relations with Cuba and cede to U.S. pressure in the early 1960s.

25 Canada's vigorous condemnation of the extraterritorial aspects of the 1992 Torricelli Act and the 1996 Helms-Burton law were obviously well-received in Havana.

26 Department of Foreign Affairs and International Trade, 'Notes for an Address by the Honourable Christine Stewart, Secretary of State (Latin

America and Africa) to the 25th General Assembly of the Organisation of American States,' 6 June 1995, 3.

27 Cited in Janice Tibbits, 'Chretien to Visit Cuba,' *Halifax Chronicle Herald*, 19 April 1998, A19.

28 Quoted in Jim Brown, 'Chretien Leaves on "In Your Face" Cuba Trip,' *Halifax Daily News*, 26 April 1998, 10.

29 Cited in 'Cuba Likened to Appeasing Hitler,' *Globe and Mail*, 24 January 1997, A8, and Douglas Farah, 'Cuba Signs Broad Pact with Canada,' *Guardian Weekly*, 2 February 1997, 15.

30 Quoted in Paul Koring, 'Axworthy, Helms Aide Slug It Out on Cuba,' *Globe and Mail*, 7 March 1998, A1.

31 Lloyd Axworthy, 'Why Canada Is Involved So Closely with Cuba,' *Globe and Mail*, 19 March 1998, A23.

32 Jack Donnelly, *International Human Rights*, 3rd ed. (Boulder, CO: Westview Press, 2006), 129.

33 These reforms were accelerated and expanded in the wake of Cuba's April 2011 Party Congress, where a series of measures were introduced to reduce government spending (including layoffs of public sector workers), to cut state subsidies, to give more autonomy to state enterprises, to encourage more foreign investment, and to allow more market mechanisms to operate within the country. See Jeff Franks, 'Cuban Communists Opt for Old Guard to Lead Reforms,' *Montreal Gazette*, 20 April 2011, A17, and Sonia Verma, 'Cuba's Challenge: Open Up Economy, But Stay Communist,' *Globe and Mail*, 21 April 2011, A13. Those reforms are still continuing in mid-2012, as Raúl Castro moves to lift many of the travel restrictions on Cubans. See Paul Haven, 'After 50 Years, Cubans Hope to Travel Freely,' Miami Herald Online, 1 May 2012, http://www.miamiherald.com/2012/05/01/v-print/2777920/after-50-years-cubans-hope-to.html.

34 See Peter McKenna and John M. Kirk, 'The Revolution Continues – But It's Adapting,' *Ottawa Citizen*, 10 January 2009, B7. Under Raúl's tenure, thousands of Cubans have set up private businesses – ranging from cutting hair to plumbing and electrical repair – to relieve some of the stress on the public sector, which is moving to lay off over 1 million Cuban workers. This current embrace of market capitalism and entrepreneurship is also intended to bring in much-needed tax revenue to the Cuban state. See Kevin G. Hall, 'Private Economy Grows Slowly,' *Miami Herald*, 19 April 2012, 10B.

35 Government of Canada, 'Notes for an Address by the Honourable Christine Stewart, Secretary of State (Latin America and Africa) to the Economist

Conference's Second Round Table with the Government of Cuba,' 14 July 1994, 4.

36 Ibid.

37 Axworthy, 'Why Canada Is Involved So Closely with Cuba.'

38 See Mark Entwistle, 'Canada-Cuba Relations: A Multiple-Personality Foreign Policy,' in Wright and Wylie (eds.), *Our Place in the Sun*, 292.

39 Ibid.

40 Havana deserves its fair share of criticism for periods when Canada-Cuba relations were not working as smoothly as they could have. For more critical evaluations of Chrétien's engagement approach, see Cristina Warren, *Canada's Policy of Constructive Engagement with Cuba: Past, Present and Future*, background briefing (Ottawa: Canadian Foundation for the Americas, 2003), 1–12, and Michael Bell, Eugene Rothman, Marvin Schiff, and Christopher Walker, *Back to the Future? Canada's Experience with Constructive Engagement in Cuba*, Occasional Paper (Miami: Institute for Cuban and Cuban-American Studies, 2002), 1–31.

41 James Bartleman, *Rollercoaster: My Hectic Years as Jean Chretien's Diplomatic Advisor, 1994–1998* (Toronto: McClelland and Stewart, 2005), 280.

42 Ibid., 294.

43 Ibid., 294.

44 Jean Chrétien, *My Years as Prime Minister* (Toronto: Alfred A. Knopf, 2007), 345.

45 Bartleman, *Rollercoaster*, 299. By contrast, Cuba released dozens of human rights activists in 2010 and 2011, doing so on its own initiative, and without international pressure.

46 Quoted in Andrew Philips, 'Looking for Progress,' *Maclean's*, 19 January 1998, 43.

47 Ibid.

48 Government of Canada, 'Notes for an Address by the Honourable Christine Stewart, Secretary of State (Latin America and Africa) to the 25th General Assembly of the Organisation of American States,' 6 June 1995, 3.

49 Cited in Janice Tibbits, 'Chretien to Visit Cuba,' *Halifax Chronicle Herald*, 19 April 1998, A19.

50 Quoted in Janice Tibbits, 'Chretien Plans to Visit Castro,' *Halifax Daily News*, 19 April 1998, 12.

51 Quoted in Koring, 'Axworthy, Helms Aide Slug It Out on Cuba,' A1.

52 Cited in Paul Knox, 'Canadian Officials Laud Growing Cuban Connection,' *Globe and Mail*, 20 January 1998, A8.

53 Pope John Paul also asked Chrétien to use his good offices with Cuba to gain visas for 181 Catholic missionaries who wanted to gain entry to Cuba.

See Alan Freeman, 'Pope Asks for Chrétien Aid on Cuba,' *Globe and Mail*, 20 May 1998, A1.

54 Quoted in Helen Branswell, 'Chretien Gives Clinton Cuba Briefing,' *Halifax Chronicle Herald*, 17 May 1998, A9.

55 Cited in Tim Harper, 'US-Cuba Gap Closing, Chretien Says,' *Toronto Star*, 17 May 1998, A11, and Eileen McCabe, 'US and Cuba Edging Closer, Chretien Says,' *Montreal Gazette*, 17 May 1998, A10.

56 Harper, 'US-Cuba Gap Closing,' A11.

57 For a fuller explanation of this point, see Wright, '"Northern Ice."'

58 Quoted in Paul Knox, 'Castro Defines "Change" Differently,' *Globe and Mail*, 29 April 1998, A10.

59 Additionally, there was a stark realization among Canadian officials that the only real alternative to engagement was a discredited U.S.-style approach of ostracism and provocation.

60 As is often the case with the U.S.-Cuban dynamic, the path to any normalization of bilateral relations is typically strewn with many obstacles. See Esteban Israel, 'Contractor Arrest May Ruffle Obama's Cuba Overture,' *Washington Post*, 15 December 2009, A9, and Will Weissert, 'Castro Says U.S. on Offensive in Latin America despite Obama,' *Miami Herald*, 14 December 2009, A11. While the Cuban government has conveyed its interest in improving bilateral relations throughout 2011–12, official Washington continues to raise serious concerns about the lack of progress on civil and political rights and the imprisonment of U.S. subcontractor Alan Gross. See Mimi Whitefield, 'U.S. and Cuba Say They'd Like to See a Changed Relationship,' Miami Herald Online, 11 May 2012, http://miami-herald.com/2012/05/11/v-print/2795508/us-and-cuba-say-they'd-like-to.html.

61 On this point, see Peter McKenna, 'Will Canada and Barack Obama Collide in the Americas?' *FocalPoint* 7, no. 8 (November 2008): 7–8.

62 Figure cited in Martha Brannigan, 'From Truffles to Fox Furs, U.S. Ships More Than Food to Cuba,' *Miami Herald*, 5 September 2009, A1.

7 Canadian Assistance to Haiti: Some Sobering Snags in a Fragile-State Approach

YASMINE SHAMSIE

Canada's relationship with Haiti has been an enduring one. Canadian politicians, diplomats, aid bureaucrats, and non-governmental organizations have been actively engaged in the country since the 1960s and more intensely since the dramatic elections that brought Jean-Bertrand Aristide to power in 1990. The appointment of Haitian-born Michaëlle Jean (a daughter of Haitian exiles) as Canada's governor general in 2005 further symbolized the significant links between Port-au-Prince and Ottawa. Although Canadian engagement with Haiti stems largely from relations with Quebec and the related issue of Canadian unity, humanitarian considerations have also driven our support to the country. Most recently, Canada launched a rapid full-scale response to the catastrophic, magnitude 7.0 earthquake that levelled the country's capital, Port-au-Prince, on 12 January 2010 (and the October outbreak of cholera).[1] This is sure to be followed by a continued commitment to the country's recovery efforts over the coming months, years, and onward.

While our commitment to the country has been steadfast, the policy lens that directs our efforts has changed. Prior to the 1990s, aid had been more humanitarian in nature, aimed at material sufficiency and basic needs (food, education, shelter, health, etc.). Since the mid-1990s, the more expansive goal of building peace has framed our interventions. Still, more recently, since 2004, the task of reducing Haiti's so-called 'fragility' has underpinned our aid allocations. While a forceful discourse about poverty reduction, democracy building, and development remains, it is now intertwined with more explicit security and stability considerations. This chapter suggests that Canada's focus on state fragility, in conjunction with a broader peacebuilding approach, deserves careful consideration because it influences the selection and de-selection of Canadian policy priorities in Haiti. Given space considerations, I focus on one Canadian objective to make my case: the goal of achieving poverty-reducing economic development.

Although the government of Haiti has designed its economic development plan around two strategic pillars, thus far Canada has chosen to support one – the export-processing zone pillar – with far more vigour than the other – the agriculture and rural development (A&RD) pillar. There are a number of reasons for this, but one which has been largely unexplored, and which I take up here, is the fragile-state policy framework of analysis. I argue that by adopting a fragile-state lens, Canada's overriding objective has been to make Haiti less conflict-vulnerable, rather than less poor. To be sure, addressing the country's vulnerablilty to conflict entails a commitment to poverty reduction; however, it is no longer the overarching objective. Moreover, the distinction between poverty reduction for humanitarian reasons versus poverty reduction to allay instability or prevent conflict is critical. As I will argue below, despite our avowed commitment to reducing poverty, if we are endeavouring to reduce it because it contributes to conflict, rather than for strictly humanitarian reasons, our aid is more likely to flow to localities and social groups that we view as predisposed to conflict, rather than to the poorest. While the two groups may often overlap, this is not always the case. Indeed, in Haiti's case, the poorest are not necessarily the most conflict vulnerable. I conclude that while a fragile-state lens still accommodates an ethical responsibility to others, it also places Canadian and international security considerations at the forefront of our interventions. Labelling Haiti a fragile state may accord it strategic relevance but it also leads to targeted aid that may very well overlook the most vulnerable and marginalized – that is, the rural poor.

I begin by summarizing Haiti's recent history and outlining the main reasons for Canada's sustained engagement with the small nation. In the two sections that follow, I show that Canada has adopted a peacebuilding approach complemented by a focus on fragile-state programming. This is followed by an analysis that highlights the potential tensions associated with an approach that seeks to reduce poverty while being acutely mindful of stability concerns. The final section explores how an analysis that starts by identifying the root causes of conflict and instability in Haiti can ultimately contribute to the historical marginalization of the rural poor.

Canadian Aid: What Kind of Aid and Why the Sustained Engagement?

The catastrophic events of January 2010 once again highlighted the well-known fact that Haiti is the poorest country in the Western hemisphere. It has an annual estimated gross domestic product per capita of $390, and 78 per cent of Haitians live on less than $2 per day. Another 54 per cent live on less than $1 per day (UNDP 2009). The World Bank (2006b, iii) notes that the country also 'suffers from substantial inequality, with nearly half of the national income going to those in the richest 10 percent of the population.' Haiti's rural areas and its peasant farmers are without doubt the most destitute. The rural poor account for three-quarters of the country's poor, with only one-quarter of these having access to safe water and one in six to adequate sanitation (Erikson 2004, 4). The country's adult literacy rate is 51.9 per cent, and health expenditure per capita is US$83 (UNDP 2005). Given these statistics, it is not surprising that the country is extremely vulnerable to external shocks such as soaring world prices for food and fuel and natural disasters, both of which it experienced in 2008, 2009, and early 2010.

Although Haiti has never been at war, it has experienced many of the negative effects associated with violent conflict: human rights abuses, population displacements, a shattered economy, and prolonged stretches of international intervention. In just the last twenty years, the country suffered a military coup in 1991 (President Jean-Bertrand Aristide's first ouster), a period of brutal military rule (October 1991 to September 1994), and a U.S.-led multinational intervention in 1994 aimed at restoring the president to power. This was followed by a period of vigorous international engagement (1994–8) with Canada and other donors focusing on democracy building, sustainable development, and improving governance. This first international peacebuilding effort essentially ended in 2000, when many key donors withdrew their aid in response to political instability, poor governance, corruption, and election irregularities (Muggah 2007).

Regrettably, political discord and worsening social conditions simmered over the next two years, leading to increasingly frequent bouts of criminal and politically motivated violence in 2003. The prolonged instability culminated in a series of attacks on police posts by armed groups, who eventually threatened to march on the capital. The decision by key actors (the United States, Canada, and France) to allow the constitutional government to fall, forced President Aristide to flee into exile for a second time, on 29 February 2004. A U.S.-led Multilateral Interim Force (MIF), with Canadian, Chilean, and French participation landed in Haiti immediately after the president's forced departure but was swiftly replaced, in June 2004, by a United Nations Stabilization Mission, known by its French acronym, MINUSTAH, which is made up of a large Brazilian contingent.

The election of President René Préval, in February 2006, and of a new parliament soon after, signalled the beginning of a fresh wave of peacebuilding efforts, including a reinvigorated Canadian effort. Since 2006, the road to recovery has been difficult, however. In 2008, the country experienced a food crisis, devastation from a series of hurricanes and tropical storms, and the ripple effects of a global financial crisis. The following year was a bit better, but political tensions surfaced in the fall of 2009, leading to the removal of the prime minister and the dissolving of cabinet. Early in 2010, the country was dealt its most severe blow when it experienced a devastating earthquake that ravaged the capital and surrounding communities. Once again, the government of Haiti and outside actors (Canada and other donors) are dealing with a humanitarian emergency that will require a colossal relief effort. It is too soon to know when Canadian engagement will revert to pre-earthquake priorities such as peacebuilding and economic development. But based on statements by Canadian officials thus far, the powerful momentum springing from humanitarian efforts is likely to drive Ottawa straight into longer-term development activities once the relief effort is complete.

Canadian official development assistance to Haiti began in 1968. Presently, support to Haiti is significant. Prior to the January 2010 earthquake, Canada had allocated more than $555 million to promoting representative democracy, reducing poverty, and strengthening security and public safety for the period 2006–11. Often exceeding $100 million a year in disbursements, Ottawa is second only to the United States in terms of bilateral aid provision.[2] If we take a regional snapshot, since 2004, Haiti has been Canada's most important recipient of development assistance in the Americas.

Historically, Canadian assistance to Haiti has sought to promote sustainable development and human security, which has included an emphasis on poverty reduction, safety and security, democratic development, and good governance (CIDA 2004, 5; Muggah 2007; Shamsie 2006; Baranyi 2007). For instance, during the 1980s, aid focused on livelihood improvement, basic needs, and economic progress. In the early to mid-1990s, Canada adopted a peacebulding framework aimed at achieving sustainable peace and security. This peacebuilding approach has persisted with the arrival of the UN Stabilization Mission (MINUS-TAH) in 2004.

The MINUSTAH has a multidimensional mandate which includes establishing an appropriate security structure (police, justice and penitentiary system, border management, etc.) and tackling development and humanitarian objectives. The dual objectives of stabilization and development embodied in the mandate remind us that notions of order, stability, and containment have never been far from international development policy. As Mark Duffield has astutely noted: 'The benevolence with which development cloaks itself, its constant evocation of rights, freedom and the people – conceals a stubborn will to manage and contain disorder rather than resolve it' (Duffield 2007, viii). Hence, the fact that Canada's assistance to Haiti since the mid-1990s has been marked by an increasingly pronounced emphasis on stability and security needs to be in the forefront of our analysis.

There are several reasons for Canada's long-standing engagement in Haiti. The most often-cited explanation relates to a core Canadian interest: national unity (or issues about separation). Quebec considers Haiti a foreign policy priority because of language ties[3] and the fact that a large Haitian diaspora has made the province its home. Haiti is a priority country for Quebec and therefore a country of interest at the national level. Indeed, it is worth noting that Quebec pursues its own relations with Haiti through its provincial ministries and from its position as an independent member of la Francophonie. Haiti is the top beneficiary of Quebec's Direction de l'aide internationale (DAI) (Quebec 2009), and the majority of Canadian non-governmental organizations (NGOs) working in Haiti are based in the province. Haiti is also the top beneficiary of assistance provided by the Direction du développement international (DDI), part of the province's Ministère des relations internationales. Since the 1960s, Quebec has sent missionaries, physicians, and individuals with various kinds of expertise to the Caribbean nation. For instance, during the 1990s, the province established a number of collaborative efforts in education, health, economic cooperation, police, and energy. Since 1997, it has funded almost sixty projects at a cost of CAD$3.86 million. Trade between Haiti and Quebec totaled approximately CAD$23 million in 2002 (CAD$21 million in Quebec exports), representing close to 60 per cent of all Canadian exports to Haiti that year (Ministère des relations internationals du Québec 2006).[4]

In addition, the approximately 100,000-strong expatriate community, one of the largest in North America (Patriquin 2006), is a significant political force in its own right. The Haitian diaspora's substantial political weight comes from its size and the fact that it is well-coordinated and has become a vital part of Quebec's society with important contributions to the province's cultural, economic, and social development. Finally, the fact that it is geographically concentrated in Montreal gives it added political weight and disproportionate electoral import in certain ridings.[5] Indeed, CIDA notes that the diaspora 'has been a significant driver behind Canadian support to Haiti' (CIDA 2004, 11). For instance, Canada's military intervention in 1994 was influenced by 'concerns emanating from the Haitian community in Montreal and the perceived need to address these "francophone" interests in the government's foreign policy' (Keating 2001, 220). In sum, Haiti is a Quebec foreign policy priority, making it difficult to ignore. The province's political weight at the national level (it holds seventy-five parliamentary seats) makes it a crucial electoral battleground. Any political party that wants to form a cabinet representing all regions of the country needs to build support in Quebec.[6]

While the Quebec factor stands out, Canadian concern for Haiti springs from a number of other sources as well. Most recently, Ottawa announced a renewed interest in Latin America. In fact, engagement with Haiti fits nicely with the Harper government's strengthened focus on the region. If we look beyond the hemisphere, Ottawa's long-standing commitment to, and participation in, the intergovernmental organization la Francophonie also accommodates a Haiti foreign policy focus.

Furthermore, foreign policy developments since 2001 have served to reinforce Canadian engagement in the small nation. Canada's 2005 *International Policy Statement: A Role of Pride and Influence in the World* (IPS) accorded priority to 'countries in or emerging from crisis and of overriding strategic importance' (Canada 2005, 24). Haiti fits neatly into this category of assistance. In addition, one should not overlook the fact that taking a leadership role on Haiti contributes positively to the so-called 'main game of Canadian foreign policy' (Cooper and Rowlands 2005, 4), our relations with Washington. There is little doubt that assisting Haiti fits well with U.S. strategic interests in the region, given Washington's concerns about uncontrolled migration and other cross-border threats such as drug trafficking. Moreover, our willingness to significantly boost our aid to Haiti from 2004 onward could be viewed as a conciliatory move vis-à-vis Washington following Canada's refusal to send troops to Iraq in 2003.

Finally, it is worth noting that, as the most populous nation in the Caribbean with 8.3 million people, the movement of Haiti's people has caused concern for Canada's regional partners – the Dominican Republic and CARICOM countries. The Bahamas, Cuba, Dominica, and other Caribbean islands have regularly received Haitian migrants (Maguire 2006; Treco 2002). Of equal importance is the country's geographic position, which has also made it a conduit for drug trafficking, with repercussions for its Caribbean neighbours as well as Washington. In sum, our involvement in Haiti is likely to persist because it does triple duty, fulfilling humane internationalist objectives (Pratt 2000) by assisting the poorest country in the hemisphere, supporting our strategic partnerships with Washington and the Caribbean, and advancing global security interests more broadly.

A Peacebuilding Agenda with an Added Fragile-State Dimension

Canadian assistance to Haiti is characterized by two interrelated features: it is firmly embedded within a peacebuilding framework and informed by the concept of 'state fragility.' Peacebuilding is most often described as a set of measures and actions that 'identify and support structures which will tend to strengthen and solidify peace in order to avoid a relapse into conflict.'[7] It aims to rebuild the institutions and infrastructures of nations which have experienced conflict, and to address the underlying economic, social, and cultural causes of those conflicts to ensure they do not recur. Managing violent conflict, which includes creating political space for dialogue, building and supporting state and local capacity for sustaining peace, and contributing to the elimination of the root causes of conflict, entails a wide range of responsibilities and activities, including but not limited to: judicial reform, police training, civil society building, and the advancement of economic development.

The fact that Canada and other donors have adopted a peacebuilding approach in Haiti is not unexpected. The presence of the MINUSTAH signals a de facto conflict management focus, and the descriptor of the Mission as a 'stabilization' operation is self-explanatory. Initially, MINUSTAH was tasked with maintaining a secure and stable environment and supporting the development of a peaceful political process. Although it became more involved in coordinating development efforts after the 2006 elections, the security part of its mandate has remained a priority. Indeed, a few months prior to the earthquake, the Security Council had noted in its resolution authorizing the Mission's extension that the situation in Haiti remained 'a threat to international peace and security in the region, despite the progress achieved thus far.' This judgment will likely be markedly reinforced in the post-earthquake recovery period.

It is worth noting that Canada is a strong backer of the MINUSTAH. According to the Department of Foreign Affairs and International Trade (DFAIT) website, there are five military staff officers in the Mission, close to one hundred police officers from the various police services of Canada, and approximately forty civilians in various units in the Mission. In sum, Canada regards its engagement as an ongoing peace-building process and is utilizing concepts and deploying strategies that are firmly linked to enhancing stability as well as human and global security.

The second distinguishing feature of Canada's approach is its classification of Haiti as a vulnerable 'fragile state.' It is a designation that reflects the concerns of outsiders about the Haitian state's ineffectiveness and the harmful ripple effects that Haiti's poor governance can produce. International donors and global governance institutions have slightly different understandings of state fragility (see Hannan and Basada 2007),[8] but Canada has adopted the Organisation for Economic Co-operation and Development's (OECD) definition, which characterizes fragile states as 'lacking in the capacity and or will to deliver security, stability, basic needs, social and economic development and human rights to their citizens' (OECD-DAC 2001; OECD Development Cooperation Directorate 2007; CIDA 2005). The point at issue here is that fragile states fail in the provision of both security and basic needs. They are often referred to as 'poor performers,' and the notion of 'difficult partnerships' has emerged to describe the relationship between their governments and international donors.

Although the fragile-state concept emerged in the 1990s, it gained increased currency after the terrorist attacks of 11 September 2001 (9/11). One important component of Washington's response to 9/11 was the Pentagon's 2002 National Defense Strategy, which identified fragile and failed states as a major threat to U.S. and international security (Eizenstat, Porter, and Weinstein 2005). Although initially employed by the U.S. foreign policy establishment, the fragile-state concept is now firmly embedded within Western donor policy. And the unparalleled acknowledgment of the need to prevent and manage state fragility stems from the belief that many of the world's most dangerous problems – terrorism, drug trafficking, ethnic conflict, organized crime, infectious diseases, etc. – originate in fragile or failed states and that terrorists could take advantage of the vacuum left by poor or absent governance to harm the West (MacLean, Black, and Shaw 2006).

The fragile-state focus has also been associated with a renewed emphasis on combating poverty and a heightened concern about instability. As noted earlier, the fragile-state policy discourse focuses on the fact that these countries, due to a lack of capacity and/or political will, regularly overlook or threaten the human security of their citizens. The discourse also emphasizes the inability of these countries to achieve economic prosperity and social progress while simultaneously preserving a satisfactory degree of order (Duffield 2007, 163). Thus, state fragility, or the likelihood of partial or complete state failure, has become both a strategic development policy and a sustainable peace issue for the West. The OECD's development arm, the Development Assistance Committee (OECD-DAC), neatly summarizes the security rationale that dominates assistance to these states:

> Before the September 11, 2001 attacks, fragile states were mainly seen as countries facing serious developmental challenges, often lacking a functional government. As such, most fragile states had little broader strategic significance for OECD countries. Consequently, their problems were perceived primarily through a development and humanitarian lens. This perception changed following 9/11, however, and fragile and failing states have increasingly become a preoccupation of the international community. (OECD-DAC 2006, 17)

This quotation is also instructive because it draws attention to the tight link posited between poverty and conflict. Indeed, the strategic interest in fragile states emerged in conjunction with an international policy and scholarly consensus that views poverty and underdevelopment as associated with conflict and instability (Collier et al. 2003; Stewart 2003; Goodhand 2003). This statement by the U.S. Permanent Representative to the UN, Susan Rice, immediately following the UN Security Council's renewal of Haiti's peacekeeping mission in 2009, reflects this perspective:

> Haiti reminds us yet again that we should not view security and develop-

ment as separate spheres. Indeed, they are inextricably linked. The absence of one will undermine the other. During our trip, my colleagues and I saw compelling evidence firsthand how poverty and unemployment, especially among Haiti's young people, have created an environment conducive to potential civil unrest – one that could undo many of Haiti's hard-won gains. The Secretary-General has correctly underscored the relationship between progress on security and progress in socioeconomic and development efforts. The United States could not agree more. (Rice 2009)

Although a U.S. policy statement, it captures the tenor of Canada's approach to Haiti as well and illustrates the degree of importance donors assign to containing and controlling the negative effects associated with Haiti's underdevelopment (Duffield 2007).

In line with this outlook, a significant portion of development assistance to fragile states is directed at areas of state weakness. Strengthening governmental institutions (or boosting state capacity) is increasingly viewed as a precondition for progress on all other peacebuilding fronts. Particular attention is given to the security apparatus, specifically building functioning law enforcement and judicial systems. Support is also directed at coast guard services, border policing, and efforts to track migration flows. Donors also focus on capacity building in the civil service, banking system, and social service ministries.

While the fragile-state concept has been widely endorsed by officialdom, its value has been queried both conceptually and practically. For instance, Susan Woodward argues that it assumes and attempts to build a very particular 'normative model of state – a liberal democratic state that is market-friendly, transparent, and accountable, with very specific institutional requirements' (Woodward 2008b). She also notes that much of the capacity building is aimed at fulfilling 'the tasks that outsiders consider necessary for their own national interests and for international order,' leading her to label the end product an 'internationally responsible state' or a 'reliable partner' for outsiders (Woodward 2008b, 25). In a similar vein, Mark Duffield, who has examined fragile states as 'a relation of international governance rather than a concrete thing,' has suggested that what donors are really seeking to convert fragile states into are 'governance states' or states that no longer require the imposition of reforms through conditionality. Successful governance states, according to Duffield, are led by elites who have effectively internalized neoliberal doctrine (Duffield 2008, 10).

Other scholars and practitioners, particularly those from the global

South, have reflected on the excessive analytical emphasis placed upon the internal characteristics and dynamics of fragile states. The point here is that international factors leading to increased fragility are given insufficient attention, leading to one-sided policy prescriptions. The Canadian Council for International Co-operation has also made this same point: 'Donor analysis and understanding of state failure must include explicit links between state failure and other donor policy areas, including the arms trade, trade in conflict resources, and the impacts of foreign investors' (CCIC 2005, 5). Finally, some of the fiercest critics of the fragile-state concept argue that it flows from a notion of peacebuilding that is imperialist in intent or nature, as well as providing a convenient justification for increasingly interventionist policies, including the use of military force (Châtaigner and Ouarzazi 2007; Bendaña 2008; Chandler 2006).

Canada's Fragile-State Approach in Haiti

Soon after 9/11, Canada acknowledged the security problems associated with fragile states by modifying its international development agency's (CIDA) mandate in 2002 to include the phrase, 'to support international efforts to reduce threats to international and Canadian security' (Simpson and Tomlinson 2006). Not long after, Ottawa echoed Washington's concerns about fragile and failing states in its 2005 *International Policy Statement* (IPS).

> Failed and failing states pose a dual challenge for Canada. In the first instance, the suffering that these situations create is an affront to Canadian values. Beyond this, they also plant the seeds of threats to regional and global security ... More ominously, the impotence of their governing structures makes them potential breeding grounds or safe heavens for terrorism and organized crime. (Canada 2005)

Ian Smillie (2007, 63) has astutely noted that the topic of weak or fragile states receives more attention in the sections of the 2005 International Policy Statement (IPS) related to defence than to the sections related to development, attesting to the significant national and global security considerations informing this policy current. Although Canada's motives for giving aid have never been divorced from self-interest (Pratt 2001a, 2001b, 1999; Brown 2008; Tomlinson 2001), the concept's more explicit linkage with national and global security considerations is noteworthy. It has influenced Canada's choice of aid recipients, favouring strategically important partners (Afghanistan, Iraq) and the size and make-up of aid disbursements (Afghanistan receives far more assistance than Haiti).[9]

Haiti has been designated 'fragile' because of its poor governance, weak economy, the presence of armed groups that occupied parts of the country in 2004, episodes of public insecurity due to gang violence and kidnappings, and concern that uncontrolled migration and other cross-border threats such as drug trafficking could affect its neighbours. In 2005, Canada's ambassador to Haiti described the country as 'a perpetual nest of instability in our hemisphere' and expressed concern about 'Haiti's precarious situation and its ability to destabilize neighbouring countries of the Caribbean' (Boucher 2005, 2). In sum, although Ottawa does not view Haiti as a likely host to international terrorists, it considers the country's poor governance and development malaise as threats to its citizens, neighbouring countries, and the broader international community. Arguably, this view still prevails today in late 2012.

In this context, Canada has piloted the OECD-Development Assistance Committee's (DAC) Principles for Engagement in Fragile States and Situations[10] in Haiti since 2005 (CIDA 2008, 37). In so doing, it has adopted a number of OECD-DAC-recommended aid strategies aimed at lessening fragility. For instance, CIDA has abandoned conventional development instruments in favour of a context-specific approach tailored to Haiti's particular needs; made a commitment to long-term engagement; and reconsidered the practice and usefulness of conditionality (CIDA 2004). Canada is also addressing fragility through a blended approach to peacebuilding. The OECD-DAC's Fragile States Group (FSG) argues that 'successful development in a fragile environment depends, at least in part, on well sequenced and coherent progress across the political, security, economic and administrative domains' (OECD-DAC 2006, 56). Following from this, Canada has adopted a 'whole-of-government' or '3D' (development, diplomacy, and defence) approach that strives for coherence, collaboration, and coordination among government agencies and departments. This approach was employed to support Haiti's 2006 presidential and legislative elections: Elections Canada led an international mission to monitor the Haitian elections; CIDA provided funding for the establishment of 9,209 voting centres and the registration of 3.5 million voters (CIDA 2008); and DFAIT, through its Stabilization and Reconstruction Taskforce (START), provided twenty-five police advisers to assist with local security at polling stations, funded local electoral guards, and provided communications equipment (OECD-DAC 2006, 69).

While post-2004 Canadian aid has supported a number of goals, there is little doubt that security has been a core objective. According to Robert Muggah (2007, 186), immediately following President Aristide's second ouster in 2004, 'Canada adopted a "security first" perspective.' In response to the governance vacuum, Canadian aid was aimed at fostering a secure and stable environment and assisting the vestiges of Haitian National Police and the country's coast guard in re-establishing law and order. Muggah adds that by March 2005, CIDA had dispensed CAD$500,000 to disarmament, demobilization, and reintegration programs, perhaps the first time the aid agency had contributed to such security-related activities (Muggah 2007, 186). Still, according to Stephen Baranyi, between 2004 and 2006, 'Canadian ODA seems to have been fairly evenly spread' over the key areas of intervention 'with the traditional areas of CIDA support receiving the greatest funding' (Baranyi 2010 pre-publication draft, 7).

Since the election of the Préval government in 2006, the focus on stabilization has persisted; in fact, it has received added attention. In his analysis of 2006–8 aid disbursements, Baranyi suggests that 'while Canada has maintained a balance of investments in the main areas of development cooperation, it seems to be spending more in the area of security and less in the area of democratic governance.' He attributes this trend to 'the winding down of electoral assistance after 2006 and the ramping up of DFAIT/START and RCMP programming on security' (Baranyi 2010 pre-publication draft, 13). The Department of Foreign Affairs and International Trade Canada, through its Stabilization and Reconstruction Task Force (START) and the Global Peace and Security Fund has indeed expanded its security-related activities in Haiti, focusing on three priorities areas: increasing security by reducing violence, enhancing the rule of law, and improving regional stability by addressing factors of instability in Haiti. Projects include: improving the capacity of the police, strengthening security along the border with the Dominican Republic, and improving the conditions in Haitian prisons (Canada 2009; Canada-DFAIT n.d). As noted earlier, the effects of the devastating 2010 earthquake are likely to reinforce the prominence of a security focus.

Poverty Reduction and Sustainable Development Blunted by a Security-Driven Approach

Haiti's poorest have traditionally resided in the country's rural hinterland and the shantytowns of the capital. In this final section, I highlight how intellectual and practical efforts to better integrate security and development policy, coupled with the adoption of a fragile-state lens, have led Canada to prefer economic development strategies that favour Haiti's urban poor. Which economic development sectors international donors ultimately choose to support is determined by a variety of factors, including ideological, bureaucratic, national interest, and so forth.[11] However, the impact of the fragile-state policy current has been largely unexplored. I suggest that a peacebuilding framework, complemented by this policy current, is boosting the appeal of the export-processing zone model, while serving to entrench the historical neglect of rural development and agriculture in Haiti.

Canada supports a private sector–led approach to economic development, which capitalizes on Haiti's economic comparative advantages (such as abundant cheap labour). Rejuvenating the country's export-processing zones (EPZs) is, therefore, considered a major priority. During the 1980s, Haiti was second only to Mexico among U.S.-centred subcontracting territories in the Western hemisphere, with 240 multinational corporations employing 60,000 Haitian workers (Thomas 1988, 95). In 1985, one year before Jean-Claude Duvalier was forced into exile, Haiti was ranked ninth in the world in the assembly of goods for U.S. consumption. The sector generated more than half of the country's industrial exports and earned one-quarter of its foreign exchange (McGowan 1997, 5). Inspired by this record, the president of CIDA declared in a 2007 speech his optimism and confidence regarding the positive effects that would flow from the reactivation of Haiti's EPZs.[12] More recently, Canada's former minister of international cooperation, Bev Oda, also expressed her confidence in this trade-driven, neoliberal approach to development noting that export-processing zones hold great promise (Payton 2009, 5). Facilitating foreign direct investment, partnering with the private sector, and establishing a desirable legislative and fiscal environment are viewed by the Canadian government as the way forward for Haiti.

At the same time, because poverty and inequality are recognized as chief sources of instability, we have seen a steady push for 'pro-poor' growth in fragile states including Haiti. Canada has made poverty reduction a central objective of its development assistance and naturally supports pro-poor growth. In contrast to conventional economic growth, pro-poor growth leads to significant reductions in poverty by benefiting the poor and giving them more access to economic opportunities. It can be pursued through a range of economic strategies: export manufacturing, private capital investment, the revitalization of agriculture, tourism, infrastructure development, micro-enterprise development, and so on. Keeping this in mind, the government of Haiti crafted an economic development plan in 2009 entitled *Haiti: A New Paradigm* (Government of Haiti 2009). A more streamlined version of the country's 2007 Poverty Reduction Strategy, it emphasized two objectives: raising productivity in agriculture and taking advantage of U.S. trade legislation – HOPE II – to build up light manufacturing through the revival of export-processing zones (EPZs).[13] Together, the two strategies are expected to create much-needed employment and address the problem of food security. As noted above, Canada has strongly supported the former but has been slow to show an interest in A&RD.

EPZs are viewed as 'pro-poor' because of their job-creating potential. A&RD also has compelling poverty-reducing merits. A survey of the extensive literature on pro-poor growth is not possible here,[14] but the evidence in support of addressing rural development and agricultural needs in poor countries is powerful. A crucial research finding is that countries which successfully generated poverty-reducing growth explicitly targeted rural areas; developed policies aimed at improving incomes in the agricultural sector; and actively promoted labour-intensive economic development activities (Agence Française de Développement et al. 2005). Moreover, the World Bank has estimated that 'GDP growth originating in agriculture is at least twice as effective in reducing poverty as GDP growth originating outside agriculture' (World Bank 2007, 6). Recent scholarship has also shown that investments in agriculture generally favour the poor more than similar investments in manufacturing (Dorosh and Haggblade 2003). Finally, if we look at the countries that have managed to achieve poverty-reducing growth, we find that they all focused on boosting productivity and incomes in agricultural and non-farm rural sectors (Lipton and Ravallion 1995).

Given that the largest proportion of Haiti's poor live in rural areas, that the majority of Haitians depend directly or indirectly on agriculture for their livelihoods, that donors want to discourage migration from rural to urban centres, and that non-farm rural economic activities are highly labour-intensive, a focus on agriculture and rural development appears compelling.

Moreover, a favourable set of circumstances has emerged in the last few years that would seem to support a higher profile for A&RD. Since 2001, there has been a generalized call for increased aid and investment to A&RD. Major aid agencies and donor governments (the European Union, the World Bank, and the UN Food and Agriculture Organization, among others) have begun to reconsider their interventions in this sector and to develop a policy set to battle rural poverty and food insecurity (Maxwell 2003). As for Canada, there are indications that the A&RD could receive increased attention. Then CIDA minister Bev Oda announced in December 2009 that Canada's aid agency would be prioritizing food security, stating the following: 'The strategy is to increase the productivity of the farmers, the agricultural sector in the developing countries. The first order of business is to try to make sure that they can feed themselves, number one' (Berthiaume 2009). Yet, in spite of fresh thinking on A&RD, Haiti's donors (including Canada) have been reluctant to accord this sector a primary place in their development plans thus far.[15] Prior to outlining how the fragile-state policy set favours urban interventions, it is worth quickly considering three commonly cited reasons for the feeble support to A&RD: the severity of problems in Haiti's agricultural sector, bureaucratic or institutional factors, and a general dismissal of the sector's economic promise.

Regarding the first rationale, Canada and other donors argue that productivity in the sector is abysmal and that the environmental conditions pose serious constraints on rural development. They also point to the fact that land tenure problems limit potential development in rural areas (Fukuda-Parr 2009, 11; Damais 2008). The structural constraints are indeed formidable in Haiti's case: average land holdings are small, deforestation has led to soil erosion, there is a lack of irrigation, access to credit is extremely poor, and access to markets is difficult due to decaying or non-existent infrastructure (McGuigan 2006; United Nations Security Council 2009, 9). Still, these are the constraints faced by the majority of the poorest farmers, who are also among the most vulnerable people in the world today. According to the UN Millennium Project's Hunger Taskforce (2005), '80 percent of food-insecure people live in rural areas,' with fully half being smallholder farmers battling these very conditions (Cohen 2007, 2–3). The truth is that Haiti's circumstances are no more daunting than those in many other rural areas of the developing world. Finally, I would argue that a private sector–led approach to development (which Canada and others support) also faces harsh conditions in Haiti. According to the World Bank, these include: 'weakness of national savings, political instability, poor infrastructure, the almost complete absence of foreign investment, difficult access to credit, the concentration of businesses in Port-au-Prince, and the unprecedented liberalization of the economy in 1986' (Government of Haiti 2004, 24).

The second reason Canada has not supported A&RD relates to bureaucratic imperatives, as is often the case with aid allocation. CIDA has gained much expertise and experience in certain areas – namely, education, health, gender programming, police training, and justice reform. It perceives itself as having a comparative advantage with respect to these portfolios and is therefore keen to support them. Agriculture and rural development, on the other hand, has not been a significant component of Canada's development assistance since the 1970s, and, as Ian Smillie has noted, the agency's rush to embrace the 'integrated rural development' fad at that time resulted in poor returns (Smillie 2009).[16]

Finally, it is important to acknowledge that Canada's neglect of A&RD is not extraordinary but simply indicative of a more general pattern. Both public spending and aid to A&RD have been stagnant or in decline in the majority of developing countries for almost three decades, which, parenthetically, would mean that few national aid agencies are likely to house expertise in this sector, making the bureaucratic impediment even more difficult to overcome. According to the United Nations Conference on Trade and Development (UNCTAD), between 1980 and 2000 both multilateral and bilateral donors reduced their aid to the sector. Multilaterals cut their funding by 85 per cent over the period 1980–2002 – from US$3.4 billion to US$.5 billion – while bilateral donors reduced their aid by 39 per cent (Panitchpakdi 2009). According to The Reality of Aid's 2008 Report, since total aid actually increased by '250% in real terms over the same period, this means *agriculture's share of total ODA* has dropped even more sharply, from 17% in 1982 to a meagre 3% in 2005' (Reality of Aid Network 2008; emphasis added). To be clear, I acknowledge that a confluence of factors help explain why A&RD, a sector with strong poverty-reducing merits, has been overlooked. But my contention is that the peacebuilding and fragile-state orientation also predisposes donors towards urban interventions and away from the rural arena.

First, as one might expect, a policy paradigm that seeks to dampen conflict and instability will automatically focus on where 'instability' is manifested. In Haiti's case, the conflict and political disturbances that emerged post-2004 have taken place primarily in the capital, Port-au-Prince, along with some urban centres. For instance, in 2006, the influential NGO International Crisis Group identified the most pressing tasks as: dealing with illegal armed gangs, breaking the international crime/

political power at ports and borders, and coping with rising drug trafficking and kidnapping (International Crisis Group 2006). Aside from
the problem of makeshift airstrips employed by narco traffickers landing in the countryside, the wellsprings of these problems are urban.
More recently, the UN Security Council, following its 2009 visit to the
country, emphasized that 'persistent poverty and youth unemployment
in urban areas have created an environment that is vulnerable to civil
unrest and, possibly, renewed gang activity.' It also added: 'Instances
of civil unrest involving violence have increased since December 2008,
with 64 demonstrations reported in February 2009, two-thirds of which
were motivated by socio-economic concerns (UN-Security Council
2009, 3). Once again, this account of instability and disorder is an urban
one. Finally, it is worth noting that in November 2009, Colonel Bernard
Ouellette, the MINUSTAH's Chief of Staff and a Canadian, noted the
following: 'The biggest military challenge is Port-Au-Prince. There are
more than two million people in Port-au-Prince and there are different areas in Port-au-Prince that are still riskier than other places in the
country' (Department of Defence – Canada 2009). The spotlight here,
once again, is on urban-based gang violence and civil unrest that manifests itself in the capital or cities.

Given the emphasis placed on the dangers associated with societal
breakdown in Port-au-Prince, it is not surprising that Canada and other
donors are seeking to promote productive investment and employment generation in urban spaces. Because the rural world is not a site
of instability, or a strategic part of the country that is affected by violence, donors, including Canada and the UN Mission (MINUSTAH),
have been more inclined toward an urban-based economic recovery
and development strategy (UN-Security Council 2009; Payton 2009). In
short, export-processing zones, at least in their view, will reduce poverty and create jobs in conflict-prone areas, thereby helping to consolidate hard-won stability gains.

Second, the whole-of-government approach employed in fragile
states, as well as OECD guidelines for working in fragile states, are
two more security-related factors that direct Canada and other donors
towards a focus on urban development efforts. These policy directives
recommend that economic development strategies 'be designed to complement the security assistance to "consolidate" the peace' (François
and Sud 2006, 149). This prescription cements the links, discussed earlier, between development and security. In Haiti's case, this once again
has the effect of directing economic development interventions to

where 'there is no peace' or where they can 'help build the peace' – that is, urban spaces.

Further, it is worth noting that a security lens approach tends to high-light problems associated with high population densities. For instance, DFAIT initiated an online discussion on fragile states in 2005 in which it included a section devoted to 'failed and fragile cities.' Behind this urban focus is the assumption that social exclusion in cities is a source of urban violence and that urban spaces facilitate the rapid spread of infectious diseases. That there is no category relating to 'fragile rural spaces' suggests that the circumstances of the rural poor are less urgent, in part because they are perceived as less dangerous. This seems to once again have the effect of prioritizing urban rather than rural develop-ment interventions.

Another issue to be considered is the MINUSTAH's influence on overall development efforts. Although the Mission is not tasked with addressing economic development, as the coordinator of all UN engagement in Haiti, it is engaged in these debates and has a position on economic recovery efforts. For MINUSTAH, signs of success, or at least of progress, have been critical. This is, in part, because of the Mis-sion's temporary nature; it needs to make a difference in a bounded time span. Additionally, it is because of the sizeable economic and personnel resources involved in these operations. Stated differently, it becomes essential for the Mission to demonstrate its presence is help-ing, that there is a positive impact in a short period of time, and that its interventions are indeed leading to stability and peace. The prob-lem for those advocating in favour of rural interventions is that rural development is a long slog. While the UN Security Council's March 2009 Report noted that food insecurity was a driver of instability (food riots) in 2008, it did not highlight an urgent need for a rural-based development strategy. This could be because the need for quick and visible results overrides other considerations. One part of the solution to food riots is increased local production, but that requires long-term interventions in a difficult setting. Conversely, the export-processing zone model, which the Mission has endorsed, is perceived as a rapid job creator – even if experience has shown these jobs to be fleeting. Moreover, it is worth signalling that populations are widely dispersed in rural settings, making aid interventions more challenging, whereas assistance to city dwellers is facilitated by the density of populations allowing for a faster and broader reach and therefore better chances of speedy success.[17]

Another key point relates to the fact that interventions in fragile states are based on an analysis of the 'root causes' of fragility or instability. In Haiti's case, this type of analysis has thus far also tended to support urban-based development interventions. Haiti's bouts of instability have not been attributed to issues of land reform, land seizures, or conflicts in the countryside related to land tenure. To be sure, peasant organizations have participated in social mobilizations and demonstrations over the last 25 years, leading them to march on the capital; but the roots of conflict in Haiti have not been ascribed to rural-based issues.[18] Because both peacebuilding interventions and the fragile-state policy discourse aim to prevent renewed violence or instability, donors tend to prioritize aid that addresses the conditions for basic stability and the causes of instability. Haiti's rural world is obscured in this analysis because of the lack of unrest in the countryside and the perceived absence of a rural-based 'root cause' of conflict.

Furthermore, the root causes of fragility in Haiti direct aid to areas that have no association with the rural world. Donor documents cite poor governance, corruption, and predatory elites as well as unspeakable poverty as the root causes of fragility and instability. This has led donors to pursue a two-pronged approach. As noted earlier, capacity building or institutional strengthening in key areas is advanced to deal with governance issues, while attention to poverty as a contributing factor to fragility is addressed through support to social sectors such as health and education (rather than to productive activities such as agriculture). What we have then is the crowding out of traditional policy demands by new demands springing from the fragile-state policy framework.

The recognition by both scholars (Fukuyama 2004; Chesterman 2004; Fearon and Laitin 2004; Krasner 2004; Paris 2004) and practioners (OECD 2007) that more attention needs to be devoted to institution building is shifting aid dollars away from productive investment, ensuring a sector like agriculture remains marginalized. Fukuda-Parr (2009, 9) uses OECD data to show that, in 2007, 'only 2% of Haiti's project aid went to productive sectors (which include Agriculture, Forestry and Fishing; Industry, Mining and Construction; Trade policies and Regulations, and Tourism). The bulk of assistance was aimed at social infrastructure and services (82% of project aid or 72% of total aid)' (Fukuda-Parr 2009, 11). In 2007, the sector received US$9.8 million or 1.5 per cent of official development assistance (Fukuda-Parr 2009, 18). In sum, the sidelining of the rural world (food security, rural development, agriculture) is reinforced by a renewed focus on state building and institutional strengthening.[19] It is worth re-emphasizing here that aid directed to state building in fragile states tends to prioritize state functions associated with the negative effects of fragility. For instance, the ministry of agriculture forms part of the state and definitely could do with some strengthening but is not typically considered an area of strategic intervention under the fragile-state policy set. On the other hand, border security, as noted earlier, would receive assistance; indeed, Canada is contributing to the refurbishment of border police stations along Haiti's border with the Dominican Republic. But a preoccupation with stability and order – largely at the expense of rural communities – misses a critical element in any attempts to develop Haiti in a sustainable fashion.

Conclusion

Since 1994, Canada's assistance to Haiti has been aimed at the broad goal of securing sustainable peace; hence the adoption of a peacebuilding framework. Ten year's later, Canadian interventions have also been informed by the 'fragile-state' policy current. This chapter has explored some of the implications associated with the fragile-state concept that now guides Canada's overall strategy, programmatic focus, and tools of intervention in Haiti (CIDA 2004).

There are two main themes running through this chapter. First, as Duffield has astutely observed, the fragile state 'is used as a generic expression of concern' – concern for the citizens of fragile states, but also for outsiders (Duffield 2007, 159). In line with the risks these states pose to their neighbours and to global security, the fragile-state policy set privileges state building aimed at certain state functions, in particular those that help contain the harmful effects of fragility: security, law and order, budgetary maintenance, and social services. As a policy lens, it tells us a lot about Canadian fears – specifically, our alarm about countries like Haiti that seem perpetually on the threshold of emergency. Canada's decision to view Haiti through the fragile-state policy lens, moreover, signifies that its own national strategic interests – advancing Canadian, regional, and global security – have become more prominent. More ethically inspired motives are still present in 2012 but are now intermingled with apprehension or concern about the potential ripple effects of Haiti's ineffective state and its vulnerable peoples.

The second point is that implicit in the notion of state fragility is the assumption that poverty and underdevelopment are associated with conflict. Following from this, Canada believes: 1) that by addressing poverty it is reducing the likelihood of conflict and 2) that by targeting its aid at the root causes of conflict, it is laying the foundations for effective poverty reduction. The proposition, although elegant, is not so straightforward. There are challenges and tensions associated with translating the conceptual linkage between poverty and security into specific policy and political initiatives. Briefly put, not all policy responses or aid interventions can be mutually supportive of security and poverty reduction. And, where resources are limited, there is a palpable danger of security and stability considerations overriding poverty-reduction goals.

This, I have argued, is happening in the area of economic development, where the exhausted, demoralized, and indeed starving people that live in rural Haiti have been accorded less attention than their counterparts in the urban arena. Canada and other donors committed to pro-poor growth have devoted more attention and resources to urban-based development strategies (export-processing zones) than A&RD.[20] While there are a number of reasons for this, this chapter highlights the fragile-state policy set, a factor that has barely been explored let alone directly acknowledged. This policy current and the peacebuilding framework for our interventions tend to direct attention and resources toward spaces where poverty is more likely to invite unpredictability. To put it bluntly, under this policy lens, Haiti's rural world becomes of limited strategic importance given the dearth of strikes, protests, and general instability. This, I have tried to show, poses a significant challenge to Canada's commitment to helping the largest segment of Haiti's poor.

If I were to extract an overarching policy recommendation from this analysis in 2012, I would say that our goal in Haiti should be to reduce poverty by helping Haiti's poorest – that is, those most in need of our assistance. By making our objective to reduce poverty as well as to contribute to a more secure Caribbean neighbourhood and a less strife-riven world, we are muddying the policy waters. When dealing with the poorest country in the hemisphere, Canada needs to employ a policy lens that focuses squarely on the security of Haitians, not on strictly global, regional, or national security considerations. Simply put, our interventions are unlikely to yield long-term benefits for Haitians if our own well-being and security – let alone that of the world – forms a key part of the equation. The competing rationales will inevitably collide. No doubt, this recommendation is likely to be viewed as idealistic and impractical. Then again, perhaps we should take note of the prescient words of the late Mitchell Sharp, who was a quintessential policy maker in Ottawa, minister of foreign affairs, and someone with a realistic mindset about what was politically possible. He once warned that 'if the purpose of aid is to help ourselves rather than to help others, we shall probably receive in return what we deserve and a good deal less than we expect' (Carty and Smith 1981, 38–9).

NOTES

1 Some media coverage has referred to Canada's response to quake-ravaged Haiti as unprecedented. Along with some $135 million in additional funds for the relief effort (and a pledge to match contributions from ordinary Canadians), the Harper government deployed several air and naval assets, agreed to hold an emergency summit in Montreal in March 2010 of major donor countries, and dispatched the 200-plus members of Canada's Disaster Assistance Response Team (DART). All in all, some 2,000 Canadian soldiers, air crew, and sailors were on the ground in and around the Haitian capital and neighbouring Jacmel. See Campbell Clark and Rhéal Séguin, 'Canada to Take Charge at Quake's Core,' *Globe and Mail*, 19 January 2010, A1; Gloria Galloway and John Ibbitson, 'Ottawa Prepares to Send Hundreds of Troops, Gear to Haiti for Historic Effort,' *Globe and Mail*, 16 January 2010, A1; and Campbell Clark and Gloria Galloway, 'Once Slammed for Sluggish Response, Canada Swiftly Sends in the Troops,' *Globe and Mail*, 14 January 2010, A1.
2 It is worth emphasizing that Haiti is the largest recipient of Canadian development assistance in the Americas – totalling some $256 million for 2009–10. Government of Canada, *Haiti: CIDA Report* (Gatineau: Canadian International Development Agency, 2011), 1.
3 It is important to note that approximately 15 per cent of Haitians speak French while all Haitians speak Haitian Creole. Due to Haiti's status as a French colony, French is regularly used by the government and Haiti's elites in their dealings with the international community.
4 Two-way trade between Canada and Haiti is comparatively small, reaching only $74 million for 2009–10. See Government of Canada, *Fact Sheet: Canada-Haiti Relations* (Ottawa: Department of Foreign Affairs and International Trade, May 2011). Only a handful of Canadian companies actually operate in country, including Air Canada, Scotiabank, Gildan Activewear,

and Laprise Group. Tavia Grant, 'A Year of Setbacks and Success for Canadian Companies in Haiti,' *Globe and Mail*, 12 January 2011, B4.

5 According to Canada's 2001 census, there are approximately 54,000 Haitian-born immigrants in Canada, about 46,000 in the city of Montreal (Simmons, Plaza, and Piche 2005, 4–6). A more impressive statistic that groups together Haitians born in Haiti and Canada is 130,000 (International Crisis Group 2007, 5).

6 In 2006, Stephen Harper's Conservatives tripled their popular support in Quebec to 24.6 per cent. That breakthrough in Quebec meant that, for the first time since 1993, Canada now had two federal parties with MPs from all regions of the country.

7 *An Agenda for Peace's Preventive Diplomacy, Peacemaking, and Peace-Keeping*. A/47/277-S/24111, June 17, 1992. Report of the Secretary-General pursuant to the statement adopted by the Summit Meeting of the Security Council on January 31, 1992. Of course, peacebuilding was just one tool in the peace and security kit; other tools included preventive diplomacy, peacemaking, and peacekeeping.

8 There is an extensive literature on state fragility; see for instance: Browne 2007; Lockhart 2006; World Bank 2006; Department of International Development UK 2005; Châtaigner and Gaulem 2005; François and Sud 2006; Carment 2003; Rotberg 2003; Bendaña 2008; Woodward 2008a; USAID 2005.

9 For an excellent discussion of these themes, see Brown 2008.

10 Guidelines for engaging with Haiti include: take the context as a starting point; do no harm; make state building a central objective; prioritize prevention; recognize the links among political, security, and development objectives; promote non-discrimination as a basis for inclusive and stable societies; align with local priorities according to context; agree on practical coordination mechanisms among international actors; act fast; and avoid pockets of exclusion (OECD – DAC 2007, 65).

11 For instance, I have argued elsewhere that the export-processing zone (EPZ) model is attractive because of the ideological assumptions about economic development that donors hold. The model conforms to their strongly held assumptions that integration into global markets is essential to economic advancement and that trade and foreign direct investment (FDI) lead to economic development (Shamsie 2009).

12 Robert Greenhill, speech given at the 2007 Annual Convention of the Canadian Institute for International Affairs, Montreal, 23 March.

13 In 2006, the U.S. Haitian Hemispheric Opportunity through Partnership and Encouragement Act (HOPE II) was passed. This trade legislation is

204 Canada Looks South

expected to allow Haiti to break into the U.S. garment market, potentially creating 100,000 jobs.

14 The scholarly and policy related literature on the links between inequality, economic growth, and poverty is voluminous. This chapter does not attempt to summarize the important research that has been carried out in this area; others have done this very well. For those interested in exploring the notion of pro-poor growth as a route to sustainable poverty reduction, see: Ravallion and Datt 2002; Cornia and Court 2001. For those interested in the more general links between public spending, agriculture, and poverty reduction see: Fan, Zhang, and Zhang 2000; Fan, Hazell, and Thorat 2000.

15 The Inter-American Development Bank (IADB) stands out here. It has a history of working in the A&RD sector, although the levels of investment have fluctuated over the years.

16 More recently, Susan Whelan's tenure as head of CIDA (January 2002– December 2003) stands out since she did make agriculture a thematic focus of CIDA's work. The focus was, however, abandoned when Aileen Carroll took over in December 2003.

17 One of the key impediments to development and even reconstruction in Haiti is the problem of land ownership and the legal constraints surrounding this issue. Who owns most of the land in Haiti is contested because a number of people lay claim to it, thus preventing the building of schools, waterworks, and roads. As David Morley, the CEO of Save the Children Canada remarked: 'How do we do that when nobody knows who owns the land half the time?' Quoted in Campbell Clark, 'Land Dispute and Heaps of Rubble Have Stalled the Job of Rebuilding a Country,' *Globe and Mail*, 13 January 2011, A10.

18 I am indebted to Lisa Kowalchuk for leading me to this observation.

19 A focus on food security and tapping into the country's tremendous agricultural potential has also been advocated by the Canadian international development organization Development and Peace. 'Haiti: One Year Later,' *Globe and Mail*, 12 January 2011, L7.

20 Some outside observers have suggested that the focus should be less on aid and more on trade; on creating a middle class via the establishment of small and medium-sized enterprises (in the tourism and energy sectors); and by enhancing job creation through trade, joint ventures with Haitian firms, and sufficient financial credit. See Sonia Verma, 'Forging a New Haitian Strategy: Trade, Not Aid,' *Globe and Mail*, 26 May 2011, A12. As of mid-2012, the situation on the ground – notwithstanding over $10 billion in foreign aid – is grim, with unemployment sitting at 70 per cent, 600,000 Haitians still living in squalor, and rubble remaining in earthquake-ravaged villages.

See Trenton Daniel, 'Modest Gains Mark Haitian Leader's First Year,' Miami Herald Online, 12 May 2012, http://www.miamiherald.com/2012/05/12/v-print/2796344/modest-gains-mark-haitian-leaders.html.

REFERENCES

Agence Française de Développement, German Development Policy, UK Department for International Development (DFID), and World Bank. 2005. *Pro-Poor Growth in the 1990s. Lessons and Insights from 14 Countries.* Washington: World Bank.

Baranyi, Stephen. 2007. *Le Canada, Haïti et les dilemmes de l'intervention dans les 'États Fragiles.'* Paper presented at the Latin American Studies Association Congress in Montreal, 5–8 September 2007.

– 2010 pre-publication draft. 'Canada and the Travail of Partnership in Haiti.' In *Haiti's Governance Challenges and the International Community,* edited by J. Heine and A. Thompson, 1–20. Waterloo, ON: Centre for International Governance Innovation (CIGI).

Bendaña, Alejandro. 2008. 'Fragile Premises and Failed States: A Perspective from Latin America.' In *Fragile States or Failing Development? Canadian Development Report 2008,* edited by North South Institute, 71–88. Ottawa: North South Institute.

Berthiaume, Lee. 2009. 'CIDA's Food Strategy Aimed at Willing Partners.' *Embassy Magazine.* 2 December.

Boucher, Claude. 2005. 'What Are the Elements of a Successful Exit Strategy? Cautionary Tales from Haiti.' Notes for a speech by Mr Claude Boucher, Canadian Ambassador to Haiti. Paper read at 'Fragile, Dangerous and Failed States: Implementing Canada's International Policy Statement,' 25–7 November at Victoria.

Brown, Stephen. 2007. *Aid to Fragile States. Do Donors Help or Hinder?* United Nations University – World Institute for Development Economics Research.

– 2008. 'CIDA under the Gun.' In *What Room for Manoeuvre? Canada among Nations 2007,* edited by J. Daudelin and D. Schwanen, 91–107. Montreal: McGill University Press.

Canada. 2005. *Canada's International Policy Statement: A Role of Pride and Influence in the World.* Ottawa: Government of Canada.

– 2009. 'Minister Cannon Welcomes Haitian Prime Minister to Canada 2009.' News release. Ottawa: Department of Foreign Affairs and International Trade.

Carment, David. 2003. 'Assessing State Failure: Implications for Theory and Policy.' *Third World Quarterly* 24, no. 3: 407–27.

Carty, Robert, and Virginia Smith. 1981. *Perpetuating Poverty: The Political Economy of Canadian Foreign Aid*. Toronto: Between the Lines.

CCIC. 2005. *The Post-911 Security Agenda and Canadian Foreign Policy: Implications for the Global South*. Ottawa: Canadian Council for International Cooperation.

Chandler, David. 2006. *Empire in Denial: The Politics of Statebuilding*. London: Pluto Press.

Châtaigner, J.M., and F. Gaulem. 2005. *Agir en faveur des acteurs et des sociétés fragiles: pour une vision renouvelée des enjeux de l'aide au développement dans la prévention et la gestion des conflits*. Paris: Agence Française de Développement.

Châtaigner, Jean-Marc, and Leslie Ouarzazi. 2007. 'Fragile States and the New International Order.' In *Comment*. Madrid: FRIDE.

Chesterman, Simon. 2004. *You, the People: The United Nations, Transitional Administration, and Statebuilding*. New York: Oxford University Press.

CIDA. 2004. *Canadian Cooperation with Haiti: Reflecting on a Decade of 'Difficult Partnership.'* Ottawa: Canadian International Development Agency.

– 2005. *On the Road to Recovery: Breaking the Cycle of Poverty and Fragility, Guidelines for Effective Development in Fragile States*. Ottawa: CIDA.

– 2008. *Report on Plans and Priorities Estimates 2007–2008*. Canadian International Development Agency. http://www.tbs-sct.gc.ca/dpr-rmr/2006-2007/inst/ida/ida01-eng.asp.

Cohen, Marc J. 2007. *Food Security: Vulnerability Despite Abundance*. Washington, DC: International Peace Academy.

Collier, Paul, L. Elliott, H. Hegre, A. Hoeffler, M. Reynal-Querol, and N. Sambanis. 2003. *Breaking the Conflict Trap: Civil War and Development Policy*. Oxford: Oxford University Press.

Cooper, Andrew, and Dane Rowlands. 2005. 'A State of Disconnect – The Fracturing of Canadian Foreign Policy.' In *Canada among Nations 2005: Split Images*, edited by Andrew Cooper and Dane Rowlands, 3–20. Montreal: McGill-Queen's University Press.

Cornia, Giovanni Andrea, and Julius Court, eds. 2001. *Inequality, Growth, and Poverty in an Era of Liberalization and Globalization*. Helsinki: UNU/ WIDER.

Damais, Gilles. 2008. Interview by author, Inter-American Development Bank, Port-au-Prince, 24 May.

Department of Defence – Canada. 2009. Transcript of video United Nations Stabilisation Mission in Haiti (MINUSTAH), 20 November 2009 [cited 20 December 2009]. http://www.comfec-cefcom.forces.gc.ca/pa-ap/ops/hamlet/MINUSTA-eng.asp. DFAIT. 2009. Summative Evaluation of START's *Global Peace and Security Fund – Haiti*.

Department of International Development UK. 2005. *Why We Need to Work More Effectively in Fragile States*. London: DFID.

Dorosh, Paul, and Steven Haggblade. 2003. 'Growth Linkages, Price Effect, and Income Distribution in Sub-Saharan Africa.' *Journal of African Economies* 12, no. 2: 207–35.

Duffield, Mark. 2007. *Development, Security and Unending War*. Malden: Polity Press.

– 2008. *Ineffective States and the Sovereign Frontier. An Overview and Agenda for Research*. http://www.ces.uc.pt/publicacoes/oficina/256/256.pdf.

Eizenstat, Stuart, John Edwards Porter, and Jeremy Weinstein. 2005. 'Rebuilding Weak States.' *Foreign Affairs* 84, no. 1: 134–46.

Erikson, Daniel. 2004. *Haiti: Challenges in Poverty Reduction*. Conference report. Washington: Inter-American Dialogue.

Fan, S., P. Hazell, and S. Thorat. 2000. 'Government Spending, Agricultural Growth and Poverty in Rural India.' *American Journal of Agricultural Economics* 82, no. 4: 1038–51.

Fan, S., L. Zhang, and X. Zhang. 2000. *Growth and Poverty in Rural China: The Role of Public Investment*. Washington, DC: International Food and Policy Research Institute.

Fearon, James, and David Laitin. 2004. 'Neotrusteeship and the Problem of Weak States.' *International Security* 28, no. 4: 5–43.

François, Monika, and Inder Sud. 2006. 'Promoting Stability and Development in Fragile and Failed States.' *Development Policy Review* 24, no. 2: 141–60.

Fukuda-Parr, Sakiko. 2009. *Empowering People: Human Rights Review of Haiti's Poverty Reduction and Growth Strategies*. New York: The New School.

Fukuyama, Francis. 2004. *State-Building: Governance and World Order in the 21st Century*. Ithaca, NY: Cornell University Press.

Goodhand, Jonathan. 2003. 'Enduring Disorder and Persistent Poverty: A Review of the Linkages between War and Chronic Poverty.' *World Development* 31, no. 3: 629–46.

Government of Haiti. 2004. *Interim Cooperation Framework, 2004–2006*. Summary report. Port-au-Prince.

– 2009. 'Toward a New Paradigm of Cooperation.' Presented at Conference on the Economic and Social Development of Haiti III, Port-au-Prince.

Hannan, Usman, and Hany Basada. 2007. *Dimensions of State Fragility: A Review of the Social Science Literature*. Waterloo: Centre for International Governance Innovation.

Hodgson, Jim. 2006. 'Dissonant Voices: Northern NGO and Haitian Partner Perspectives on the Future of Haiti.' In *Haiti: Hope for a Fragile State*, edited by Y. Shamsie and A.S. Thompson, 99–110. Waterloo, ON: Wilfrid Laurier University Press/The Centre for International Governance Innovation.

International Crisis Group. 2006. *Haiti: Security and the Reintegration of the State*. Port-au-Prince/Brussels: ICG.

– 2007. *Peacebuilding in Haiti: Including Haitians from Abroad*. Washington: ICG.

Keating, Tom. 2001. 'Promoting Democracy in Haiti: Assessing the Practical and Ethical Implications.' In *Ethics and Security in Canadian Foreign Policy*, edited by R. Irwin, 208–27. Vancouver: UBC Press.

Krasner, Stephen. 2004. 'Sharing Sovereignty: New Institutions for Collapsed and Failing States.' *International Security* 29, no. 2: 85–120.

Lipton, M., and M. Ravallion. 1995. 'Poverty and Policy.' In *Handbook of Development Economics*, edited by J. Behrman and T.N. Srinivasan, 2551–657. Amsterdam: North Holland.

Lockhart, Clare. 2006. 'From Aid Effectiveness to Development Effectiveness: Strategy and Policy Coherence in Fragile States.' Unpublished paper.

MacLean, Sandra, David Black, and Timothy Shaw. 2006. Introduction. In *A Decade of Human Security*, edited by S. MacLean, D. Black, and T. Shaw, 3–18. Aldershot: Ashgate.

Maguire, Robert. 2006. 'Assisting a Neighbour: Haiti's Challenge to North American Policy-Makers.' In *Haiti: Hope for a Fragile State*, edited by Y. Shamsie and A. Thompson, 25–35. Waterloo, ON: Wilfrid Laurier University Press.

Maxwell, Simon. 2003. 'Six Characters (and a Few More) in Search of an Author: How to Rescue Rural Development before It's Too Late.' Paper prepared for the 25th International Conference of Agricultural Economists held in Durban, South Africa, 18–22 August. Overseas Development Institute.

McGowan, Lisa. 1997. *Democracy Undermined Economic Justice Denied: Structural Adjustment and the Aid Juggernaut in Haiti*. Washington, DC: The Development Gap.

McGuigan, Claire. 2006. *Agricultural Liberalisation in Haiti*. London: Christian Aid.

Ministère des relations internationales du Québec. 2006. *Haiti: Relations with Quebec*. http://www.mri.gouv.qc.ca/en/action_internationale/pays_regions/amerique_du_sud/haiti/relations.asp.

Muggah, Robert. 2007. 'The Perils of Changing Donor Priorities: The Case of Haiti.' In *Exporting Good Governance: Temptations and Challenges in Canada's Foreign Aid Program*, edited by J. Welsh and N. Woods, 169–202. Waterloo, ON: The Centre for International Governance Innovation/Wilfrid Laurier University Press.

OECD. 2007. *Principles for Good International Engagement in Fragile States*.

OECD-DAC Draft Paper. Development Cooperation Directorate and Development Assistance Committee. 8/Rev2 2007. http://www.oecd.org/dataoecd/59/55/34700989.pdf.

OECD–DAC. 2001. *Poor Performers: Basic Approaches for Supporting Development in Difficult Partnerships*. Paris: OECD.

– 2006. *Whole of Government Approaches to Fragile States*. Paris: OECD.

– 2008. *DAC Peer Review of Canada*. OECD-DAC. http://www.oecd.org/dataoecd/48/61/39515510.pdf.

OECD Development Cooperation Directorate. 2006. *Piloting the Principles for Good International Engagement in Fragile States*. Concept Note. http://www.oecd.org/dataoecd/4/25/35238282.pdf.

Panitchpakdi, Supachai. 2009. *Statements by Supachai Panitchpakdi, Secretary-General of UNCTAD (2008–2009). High-Level Meeting on Food Security for All* (26 January 2009). http://www.unctad.org/Templates/webflyer.asp?docid=11033&intItemID=3549&lang=1.

Paris, Roland. 2004. *At War's End: Building Peace after Conflict*. Cambridge: Cambridge University Press.

Patriquin, Martin. 2006. 'Accusing Canada of Corruption.' *Maclean's*, 6 March, 19.

Payton, Laura. 2009. 'Haiti: Canada's Second-Biggest Aid Recipient Still Needs "Everything."' *National Post*, 15 September.

Pratt, Cranford. 1999. 'Competing Rationales for Canadian Develoment Assistance.' *International Journal* 54, no. 2: 306–23.

– 2000. 'Alleviating Global Poverty or Enhancing Security: Competing Rationales for Canadian Development Assistance.' In *Transforming Development: Foreign Aid in a Changing World*, edited by J. Freedman, 37–59. Toronto: University of Toronto Press.

– 2001a. 'The Impact of Ethical Values on Canadian Foreign Aid Policy.' *Canadian Foreign Policy* 9, no. 1: 43–53.

– 2001b. 'Moral Vision and Foreign Policy: The Case of Canadian Development Assistance.' In *Ethics and Security in Canadian Foreign Policy*, edited by R. Irwin, 59–76. Vancouver-Toronto: University of British Columbia Press.

Quebec, Relations Internationales. 2009. *Relations Internationales Québec – Haiti*. http://www.mri.gouv.qc.ca/en/relations_quebec/ameriques/amerique_du_sud/haiti/relations.asp.

Ravallion, M., and G. Datt. 2002. 'Why Has Economic Growth Been More Pro-Poor in Some States of India Than Others?' *Journal of Development Economics* 68: 381–400.

Reality of Aid Network. 2008. *The New Aid Agenda for Agriculture*. http://www.realityofaid.org/rchecknews.php?table=rc_jan08&id=1.

Rice, Susan. 2009. *Statement by Ambassador Susan E. Rice, U.S. Permanent Representative to the United Nations, on Haiti, in the Security Council Chamber.* http://usun.state.gov/briefing/statements/2009/april/126516.htm.

Rotberg, Robert. 2003. 'Failed States, Collapsed States, Weak States: Causes and Indicators.' In *State Failure and State Weakness in a Time of Terror*, edited by R. Rotberg, 1–25. Washington: Brookings Institution Press.

Shamsie, Yasmine. 2006. 'It's Not Just Afghanistan or Darfur: Canada's Peacebuilding Efforts in Haiti.' In *Canada among Nations 2006: Minorities and Priorities*, edited by A.F. Cooper and D. Rowlands, 209–31. Montreal and Kingston: McGill-Queen's University Press.

– 2009. 'Export Processing Zones: The Purported Glimmer in Haiti's Development Murk.' *Review of International Political Economy* 16, no. 4: 649–72.

Simmons, Allan, Dwaine Plaza, and Voctor Piche. 2005. *The Remittance Sending Practices of Haitians and Jamaicans in Canada.* Toronto: CERLAC.

Simpson, E., and Brian Tomlinson. 2006. 'Canada: Is Anyone Listening?' In *Reality of Aid 2006: Focus on Conflict, Security and Development*, 256–61. New York: Zed Books.

Smillie, Ian. 2007. 'Boy Scouts and Fearful Angels: Canada's Agenda.' In *Exporting Good Governance: Temptations and Challenges in Canada's Aid Program*, edited by J. Welsh and N. Woods, 41–74. Waterloo, ON: Wilfrid Laurier University Press and The Centre for International Governance Innovation.

– 2009. 'Foreign Aid and Canadian Purpose: Influence and Policy in Canada's International Development Assistance.' In *Canada among Nations: 100 Years of Canadian Foreign Policy*, edited by R. Bothwell and J. Daudelin, 183–208. Montreal and Kingston: McGill-Queen's University Press.

Stewart, Frances. 2003. 'Conflict and the Millennium Development Goals.' *Journal of Human Development* 4, no. 3: 325–51.

Thomas, Clive Y. 1988. *The Poor and the Powerless: Economic Policy and Change in the Caribbean.* New York: Monthly Review Press.

Tomlinson, Brian. 2001. 'Tracking Change in Canadian ODA: New Directions for Poverty Reduction.' *International Journal* 56, no. 1: 54–72.

Treco, Ria N.M. 2002. *The Haitian Diaspora in the Bahamas.* Miami: Florida International University.

UN–Security Council. 2009. *Report of the Secretary-General on the United Nations Stabilization Mission in Haiti.* New York: UN.

UNDP. 2005. *2005 Human Development Reports.* http://hdr.undp.org/statistics/data/countries.cfm.

– 2009. *Focus on Haiti. United Nations Development Programme, Crisis Prevention and Recovery.* http://www.undp.org/cpr/we_work/Haiti08.shtml.

United Nations Security Council. 2009. *Report of the Security Council Mission to Haiti* (11 to 14 March 2009). New York: United Nations.

USAID. 2005. *Fragile States Strategy*. Washington, DC: USAID.

Woodward, Susan. 2008a. *Peacebuilding and 'Failed States': Some Initial Considerations*. http://www.ces.uc.pt/publicacoes/oficina/256/256.pdf.

– 2008b. *Fragile States: Exploring the Concept*. FRIDE 2004. http://www.fride.org.

World Bank. 2006a. *Engaging with Fragile States: An IEG Review of World Bank Support to Low Income Countries under Stress (LICUS)*. http://www.world-bank.org/ieg/licus/docs/licus_ce.pdf.

– 2006b. *Haiti. Options and Opportunities for Inclusive Growth*. Country Economic Memorandum. Washington, DC: World Bank.

– 2007. *World Development Report 2008: Agriculture for Development*. Washington, DC: World Bank.

8 Canada-CARICOM Relations: Beyond the Trade Agenda?

RAMESH CHAITOO

Recent articles on Canada's re-engagement with the Americas seem to focus on supporting democracy or raising democratic issues in certain states in Latin America. But this is not new; Canada's perceived interests in the Americas have long been more political than economic, apart from the well-known story of Canadian banks in the region and the forays of Canadian mining companies in several countries. But what about Canada's interests and relations in the Caribbean, which has traditionally not had the turmoil and instability of many of its neighbours on the continent?

For the Commonwealth Caribbean, which is relatively stable, there was not much to be said or to do, given their small populations and size. Foreign relations really meant some programming by the Canadian International Development Agency (CIDA) on basic needs and infrastructure in countries like Jamaica, Guyana, and the Eastern Caribbean States, and some regional programs to support education and disaster preparedness, among a few other areas.[1] More recently, funding has been provided for implementation of the CARICOM Single Market. For the Spanish Caribbean, the attention was focused on treading a sensitive but supporting third path by not denouncing Cuba, like the Americans have done for decades. And with regard to Central America, the concerns were conflict and security issues along with human rights and democratic development. Until recently, Canada did not pay much attention to the Dominican Republic. For the French Caribbean, which really means Haiti – which has suffered grievously under the yoke of dictatorship – it was a question of providing basic needs development assistance, good governance, and peacekeeping, and working tentatively with a series of weak governments that often perished like mayflies. In the meantime, thousands of citizens from the Caribbean either emigrated to or sought refuge in Canada for a variety of reasons.

This chapter will not revisit the structures for management of bilateral relations between Canada and the Caribbean Community (CARICOM) group.[2] Several authors have done that over the years – including Sahadeo Basdeo and Jerry Haar and Anthony Bryan.[3] Instead, it will examine the overall relationship in terms of historical cooperation and bilateral linkages and try to consider what needs to change in order to stimulate a more dynamic trade and investment pattern and foster greater economic development in the region. It poses the question: if there is really a special relationship and affinity between Canada and the Caribbean, why is the economic and political relationship so anemic on the CARICOM side? It will also examine some social issues such as increasing crime and insecurity and the role that Canada can play in mitigating these challenges. From a policy standpoint, it argues that the current bilateral, trade-related negotiations between Canada and CARICOM should also solve the long-standing market access issues for rum, adjust the restrictive rules of origin for CARICOM products, and provide member countries with effective new market access for services in Canada. Lastly, whatever new legal framework for economic interaction emerges must also provide for helping economic agents in the Caribbean take advantage of opportunities in the Canadian marketplace.

Whither the Bilateral Relationship?

The Caribbean Community (CARICOM) consists of twelve island states and three continental countries, with a combined population of about 15.2 million. Haiti accounts for over half (8.5 million) of this amount; and the smallest state, St Kitts and Nevis, has a population of only 55,000. The combined gross national income (GNI) of the fifteen member states of CARICOM is roughly $US36 billion. But there are significant differences in the size of their respective economies and their levels of development. About half are lower middle-income countries, while the rest are upper middle-income countries; and Haiti is the poorest country in the hemisphere. All are considered members of the Small Island Developing States grouping that share similar sustainable development challenges. These include: small populations; human resource constraints; susceptibility to natural disasters; poor diversification that results in dependence on a few traded commodities and tourism; weak regional, national, and local institutions; and vulnerability to external shocks. Another common characteristic shared by CARICOM countries is a high debt level – fourteen of the fifteen CARICOM states are ranked among the top thirty of the world's highly indebted emerging market economies in terms of debt as a percentage of their gross domestic product (GDP).

The so-called 'special relationship' between Canada and the Caribbean has so often been written and spoken about that it is almost cliché. But it is true that Canada has been widely perceived as a 'player' in the region – oftentimes speaking for the region within international fora like the G8. For too long, though, the CARICOM group of countries have seen Canada as mainly a donor (a nice and friendly one at that, and a country that makes few impositions on the region) to provide development support or technical assistance, but they have not seen it worthwhile to seek greater inroads in the Canadian market or to participate in value chains in Canada in order to enhance their own growth. And similarly, for many years Canada has not done much to energize the cosy but somewhat staid relationship. Indeed, the last major initiative by Canada for CARICOM was in 1990 at the summit in which Prime Minister Brian Mulroney announced increases in aid to the region, improvement of the product coverage under CARIB-CAN, enhanced access for rum, and debt forgiveness of $182 million for eleven countries.[4] In April 2007, when Prime Minister Harper met with CARICOM leaders in Barbados, it was long overdue for Ottawa to start taking the region more seriously. Among other things, Harper promised an aid package of CAD$600 million over ten years, and, more important, trade negotiations were officially launched (and they continue rather timidly and slowly as of late 2012).

It is worth noting here that in the late 1970s a noticeable economic decline in the Caribbean and a sharp reduction in Canada-Caribbean trade led to a comprehensive review in 1980 of Canadian policy toward the Commonwealth Caribbean. It resulted in the establishment of a Joint Trade and Economic Committee (JTEC), which became the key mechanism for regular dialogue and monitoring of Canada-CARICOM economic relations. But the JTEC seems to have faded into obscurity in recent years, and there is obviously inadequate interaction between policy makers on both sides. Furthermore, Canada-CARICOM prime ministerial summits alone – every five years or so – cannot serve to cultivate a deep and vibrant bilateral relationship.

In retrospect, the 2007 Canada-CARICOM summit, though highly publicized, was not particularly successful – since precious little has happened since. Interestingly, Prime Minister Jean Chrétien had also met with CARICOM leaders in 2001; and he, too, promised to engender something significant on the bilateral trade front (which never actually materialized). In fact, since that earlier interaction, it was expected that a new trade agreement between Canada and CARICOM would have been negotiated by now. But those negotiations only commenced in December 2009 – some eight years later and two years after Prime Minister Harper's summit with CARICOM leaders. And it was generally expected that these negotiations would probably end just before the expiry of the waiver in the World Trade Organization (WTO) for the unilateral CARIBCAN preferences (in December 2011); but it is more likely that the negotiations will drag on into 2013 and require some kind of temporary solution by Canada in terms of its WTO obligations.[5] Moreover, there appears to be very little enthusiasm among CARICOM members for securing a new trade agreement – as will be touched upon later.

Part of the reason for the lack of creativity in terms of bilateral initiatives is due to conventional thinking in CARICOM, or perhaps inadequate attention to how best to manage the relationship with Canada. Successive generations of Caribbean politicians and senior officials have been content with simply seeking development support from Canada. But little strategic thought has actually gone into how to improve or revitalize the bilateral economic and cultural relationship. Indeed, shortly after Harper announced the $600 million aid envelope in April 2007, some senior officials in the Caribbean argued that it should be increased because CARICOM was about to negotiate a trade agreement with Canada. They felt that Canada should provide additional trade-related resources to 'compensate' for CARICOM's agreement to provide market access to Canadian companies – even though the region already has great difficulty spending the aid funds from donors in a timely manner (and projects are routinely extended beyond their initial completion dates).

As a result, Canada's attention has focused on addressing the problems of the Caribbean, and not on its strengths or positive attributes; and no attempt has been made to identify or enhance the complementarities between Canada and CARICOM. For instance, a Canada-driven initiative intended to get perspectives from outside the traditional official circles, referred to as the Canada-Caribbean Ideas Forum, was launched in 2007 and repeated in 2008.[6] But there are no similar policy-oriented or scholarly discussions in CARICOM about how to strengthen the relationship with Canada. Clearly, much work needs to be done to deepen and widen the Canada-Commonwealth Caribbean relationship.

Canadian Aid to the Caribbean

A large part of Canada's historical foreign policy emphasis on the Caribbean consists of development assistance or aid. This has not changed in recent years. In March 2009, Canada rationalized its aid to the developing world but kept the Caribbean in its list of preferred beneficiaries. In fact, Canadian development assistance to the Caribbean is one of its oldest programs. According to CIDA, the anglophone Caribbean has received approximately $2 billion since 1963. Recent aid spending in the region has totalled about $30–$35 million per year, and a new ten-year programming framework for CARICOM was approved in June 2007.[7] This is expected to amount to at least $600 million or an average of $60 million per year.

In the early days, CIDA funded major infrastructure projects, earmarked funds to the University of the West Indies, and also provided stand-alone scholarships. As the program evolved, though, the main focus moved to other priority areas. For example, under the Canadian Regional Development Programming Framework of 1993, CIDA invested in human resource development, private sector development, HIV/AIDS research, the environment, trade policy development, social infrastructure, educational and leadership development, public sector economic management, gender equality, and institutional strengthening of the CARICOM and Organization of Eastern Caribbean States Secretariats.[8] More recently, Canada has provided regional support for disaster management, crime prevention, leadership programs, trade competitiveness, and information technology training, among others.

Table 8.1 shows total aid to CARICOM states from all Canadian sources. It reveals an obvious shift in emphasis from funding of national programs to regional initiatives in recent years. Compared to other much larger and poorer countries in Africa and Asia, the CARICOM group seems quite privileged in terms of Canada's aid disbursement.[9] (This is, of course, apart from the generous assistance to Haiti.) In July 2007, Canada increased its commitment to $555 million over five years (2006–11) for rebuilding and developing Haiti, based on four key priorities: encouraging good governance; establishing open and accountable government; combating corruption; and fortifying the rule of law. Canada is now Haiti's second-largest bilateral donor, and the aid pro-

Table 8.1. Total Canadian development assistance to CARICOM* (CAD$millions)

	2001	2002	2003	2004	2005	2006	2007	2008
National	60.65	54.09	42.60	73.16	32.13	42.83	26.17	41.77
Regional	12.22	18.46	17.42	44.55	24.85	42.04	36.22	44.51
Total	72.87	72.56	60.02	117.71	56.98	84.86	62.39	86.28

* Excludes Haiti.
Source: Data supplied by CIDA.

gram for Haiti is CIDA's second-largest. Nevertheless, the devastating earthquake of 2010 has added to the Herculean development tasks and challenges in Haiti.

Caribbean Influences in Canada

Official Canadian statistics from the 2006 census revealed that almost 350,000 persons in Canada originated in the Caribbean (and Bermuda). In a population of 33 million, that figure is not statistically significant. Nevertheless, this number compares well with the total of Chinese (466,940) and Indians (443,690) in Canada from countries with populations of more than a billion.[10] What is even more interesting is the fact that over the years several politicians, some famous athletes (including Olympians Donovan Bailey and Bruny Surin), authors, poets, playwrights, musicians, and a few significant businesspeople in Canada have come from the Caribbean.[11] Even the former governor general, Michaëlle Jean, has Haitian roots. The influence of West Indians, in particular, on the cultural scene in Canada is demonstrated by the fact that the single biggest cultural event in any major Canadian city is the Caribana festival, which brings thousands of visitors and significant economic benefits to the city of Toronto each summer.

At a more functional level, Canada is well served by professionals of Caribbean heritage in almost every field of endeavour. As Mary Anne Chambers, former Ontario minister of children and youth services and senior vice-president of Scotiabank (1998–2002) pointed out in 2008:

I served on the Board of two Ontario hospitals, where the Chiefs of Surgery, Pediatrics and Psychiatry, were all University of the West Indies medical graduates. The immediate past president of the Registered Nurses Association of Ontario is a daughter of the island of St. Lucia. Two weeks ago, I attended the retirement celebration for Dr. Avis Glaze, a daughter of

Jamaica, whose most recent contributions to education in Canada include the creation of Ontario's character education curriculum and the leadership of the province's literacy secretariat. She has shared her expertise with educators in Australia and Singapore. A scientist in Toronto, who is leading a team of researchers in developing alternative energy sources, and the project's funders, are graduates of Caribbean schools. Ontario's Deputy Minister of Emergency Management is a son of Barbados, as is a Deputy Chief of Canada's largest municipal police service. The head of the regional council for Canada's largest carpenters' union is a son of Jamaica, and Ontario's first Fairness Commissioner, who is tasked with the oversight of access to professions and trades by internationally trained individuals, is a daughter of Grenada.[12]

Over the years, thousands of Caribbean-trained university graduates have settled in Canada, and many professionals still migrate to the country on an annual basis. Table 8.2 reveals that, on average, about 3,300 Caribbean persons became landed immigrants in Canada over the period 1999–2008. While this pales in comparison to the average number of total immigrants per year of 235,000 for the same period, it is significant for the CARICOM region. The loss of skilled, tertiary-trained people as they move to North America to seek better economic opportunities remains a major issue for Caribbean economies. According to the World Bank (WB), the seven countries with the highest emigration rates for college graduates in the world are in the Caribbean. Indeed, Guyana is the world leader, with 89 per cent of its college graduates having left the country between 1965 and 2000. Emigration rates are also high in Jamaica (85 per cent of university graduates) and Trinidad and Tobago (79 per cent).[13] Guyana, according to the International Organization for Migration, still has the highest migration rate for tertiary-trained persons in the entire world.

University and college students from CARICOM also are a small but important component on Canadian campuses. Table 8.3 shows the number of students from CARICOM states who have studied in Canada in the past ten years. It is, therefore, not surprising that at a special forum in Bridgetown in January 2008 to celebrate one hundred years of the Canadian Trade Commissioner Service in Barbados, the president of Durham College in Ontario was part of the delegation of Canadian businesswomen. Canadian tertiary institutions actively recruit students from the Caribbean and will undoubtedly continue to do so. It is also highly likely that the change in Canadian immigration rules in 2008

Table 8.2. New permanent residents in Canada by CARICOM country of origin

	1999	2000	2001	2002	2003	2004	2005	2006	2007	2008
Jamaica	2.346	2.463	2.775	2.457	1.983	2.130	1.880	1.686	2.113	2.312
Haiti	1.429	1.653	2.484	2.218	1.945	1.657	1.719	1.651	1.614	2.509
Guyana	1.323	1.274	1.665	1.432	1.394	1.321	1.176	1.263	1.248	1.089
Trinidad & Tobago	1.164	896	917	937	693	724	844	804	990	1.018
St Lucia	83	103	116	83	94	113	188	189	269	289
St Vincent & Grenadines	204	267	283	240	193	291	340	374	566	428
Grenada	287	370	345	248	219	288	288	357	357	288
Barbados	120	128	157	132	79	89	124	100	140	144
The Bahamas	21	17	22	20	22	24	34	42	31	70
Dominica	53	71	74	66	58	46	49	73	74	54
Belize	34	26	23	33	15	26	36	29	30	53
Antigua & Barbuda	17	13	35	16	27	15	30	37	20	43
St Kitts & Nevis	11	14	11	11	13	10	7	7	11	28
Suriname	13	15	20	19	15	22	12	10	25	10
Total	7.105	7.310	8.927	7.912	6.750	6.756	6.727	6.622	7.488	8.335

Source: www.cic.gc.ca/english/resources/statistics/facts2008/permanent/10.asp.

Table 8.3. Caribbean students in Canada by source country

	1999	2000	2001	2002	2003	2004	2005	2006	2007	2008
Jamaica	247	301	375	265	212	236	234	235	303	345
Trinidad & Tobago	218	220	227	220	234	274	267	319	340	283
Barbados	110	123	129	112	133	123	108	96	117	112
The Bahamas	130	91	152	184	209	159	198	171	82	91
Guyana	43	48	38	54	54	54	58	62	72	77
St Lucia	64	85	64	54	64	54	55	49	56	44
Antigua & Barbuda	32	46	33	30	34	38	34	31	24	30
St Vincent & the Grenadines	34	45	38	34	30	24	19	22	17	20
St Kitts & Nevis	16	10	17	17	19	15	17	19	13	14
Grenada	47	38	31	30	20	18	23	22	12	10
Dominica	26	35	18	14	15	14	9	8	9	8
Total	967	1,042	1,122	1,014	1,024	1,009	1,022	1,034	1,045	1,034

Source: http://www.cic.gc.ca/english/resources/statistics/facts2008/temporary/09.asp.

that now allow foreign graduates of Canadian universities to work in Canada will lead to more Caribbean students staying permanently in the country.

Temporary Workers in Canada

Of all CARICOM states, only citizens of Antigua and Barbuda, the Bahamas, Barbados, St Kitts and Nevis, St Lucia and St Vincent, and the Grenadines do not need visas to enter Canada. To be sure, the visa requirement for Jamaica and Trinidad and Tobago remains an issue for businessmen and tourists, but it is unlikely to change in the near future given security and other concerns discussed below. Nevertheless, Canada still provides some economic opportunities for temporary workers from CARICOM states. Table 8.4 shows the number of temporary Caribbean workers in Canada in recent years. Though the numbers are relatively low, if we consider the small size of the population of several of these countries, it is still significant. The average number of temporary workers in Canada for the period was about 8,300 per year out of a total annual average of 129,000 foreign workers.

The vast majority of these temporary workers consist of agricultural labourers, who come under the Seasonal Agricultural Workers Program. For various reasons, there were few CARICOM professionals working temporarily in Canada from 1999 to 2008. The main impediments are certification and qualification requirements at the provincial level, which also make interprovincial movement of Canadian professionals very difficult. Nevertheless, the contribution of seasonal agricultural work is quite significant to some communities in Jamaica, Trinidad and Tobago and the Eastern Caribbean. Estimates suggest that these workers earn more than $58 million a year – a portion of which is sent back in the form of remittances.

Canadian-Caribbean Commercial Linkages

Historically speaking, Canada-CARICOM trade relations have deep and extensive roots. The most recent trade figures indicate that two-way trade had reached some $1.8 billion in 2007 – with imports from the region totalling $1.13 billion.[14] In March 2009, *The Economist* pointed out that 'Canadian firms make chemicals in Trinidad and drill for natural gas offshore, mine nickel in Cuba and gold in Suriname, seek oil off Guyana and run cable television in the Bahamas and Jamaica.'[15]

Table 8.4. Caribbean temporary workers in Canada by source country

	1999	2000	2001	2002	2003	2004	2005	2006	2007	2008
Jamaica	5,608	5,508	5,959	5,637	5,981	6,008	6,223	6,531	6,745	7,320
Trinidad & Tobago	1,714	1,873	1,875	1,733	1,684	1,719	1,664	1,580	1,407	1,356
Barbados	629	669	702	645	548	582	535	497	473	389
St Vincent & Grenadines	220	258	244	215	208	206	246	285	273	299
St Lucia	115	115	135	99	133	135	179	193	268	295
Dominica	96	116	125	102	111	130	176	102	104	109
Grenada	123	118	93	83	70	77	90	79	98	89
Guyana	114	143	145	67	45	64	49	29	60	78
Haiti	89	101	102	105	64	98	103	80	78	49
St Kitts & Nevis	29	24	31	28	20	19	33	27	31	29
The Bahamas	10	14	9	6	7	7	5	9	10	22
Total	8,747	8,939	9,420	8,720	8,871	9,045	9,303	9,412	9,547	10,035

Source: www.cic.gc.ca/english/resources/statistics/facts2008/temporary/03.asp.

Canada's banks have historically had a dominant role in the Caribbean commercial banking industry; they own the three largest banks in the English-speaking Caribbean. (It is a well-known story in the region that the Bank of Nova Scotia or Scotiabank opened its first international branch outside the U.S. in 1889, in Kingston, Jamaica.)[16] Additionally, several Canadian energy companies have significant investment stakes in Caribbean-based providers of electricity in Barbados, Belize, and St Lucia. Canadian investors are also very active in the tourism industry throughout much of the Caribbean.

Canada is also a significant source of foreign direct investment (FDI) for CARICOM, but this is mainly in the financial services sector. Canadian investment in Caribbean economies increased dramatically from US$28 billion (stock) in 2000 to US$53 billion in 2006, the bulk of which is portfolio investment.[17] Barbados, which has a double taxation treaty with Canada, accounts for a major portion of Canadian direct investment in the region, attracting investment valued at some US$38.4 billion in 2006. So, from the Canadian perspective, the Caribbean is obviously a good place to do business.

Unfortunately, the reverse does not seem to be the case. In fact, very few Caribbean firms are active in the Canadian marketplace. Various regional conglomerates (including Jamaica's Grace Kennedy Inc. and the Gleaner) have been operating in Canada for many years, albeit in a very small way. Some years ago, Trinidad and Tobago's Angostura Ltd. (a producer of bitters and rum) acquired a distillery in Manitoba, but with the collapse of the CL Financial Group which owns Angostura, it seems that the Canadian investment has also foundered. But CARICOM's stock of capital in Canada increased from US$531 million in 2000 to US$760 million in 2006. Investment from the Bahamas (US$136 million) and Barbados (US$471 million) has been the major inflow to Canada over this period.[18]

While there have been numerous Canadian trade missions to CARICOM states over the years,[19] very few missions by CARICOM businesspeople to Canada have taken place. Nevertheless, a Canada-Caribbean Business Council (CCBC) was established in 2006 by mainly West Indians in Toronto with the aim of linking the Caribbean and Canadian business communities, and representing and promoting the interest of businesses in Canada within the Caribbean Community. But this has apparently gone into suspended animation at worst or somnolence at best.

Interestingly, in an informal survey in 2010 by this author of government agencies and business associations in several Canadian provinces regarding the level of interest in the ongoing trade negotiations with CARICOM, most respondents expressed an interest in the Caribbean as a market for their products or services. But none could think of any joint-venture interest or collaborative initiatives or strategic partnerships that could be pursued with Caribbean firms or partners. In other words, Canadian small and medium-size firms were not interested in sourcing anything from the CARICOM region – only in selling their goods or services there. This is remarkable because the Caribbean is a very small market overall. On the other hand, firms in CARICOM also see the Canadian market as a distant third compared to the U.S. and Europe in terms of goods for export. In addition, business representatives indicate a perception that as a market Canada is difficult to do business with because of provincial differences, regulations, and shipping costs, among other issues. And on the services front, although Canada is a massive importer of services with an increasing propensity to import even more, the mainly small CARICOM firms do not see opportunities there. Some of this may stem from purely psychological barriers, but the real experience of a few businesspeople has not been particularly positive.

It was not surprising, then, that at the inaugural Canada-CARICOM Business Forum launched in November 2008 only a handful of CARICOM firms were in attendance. In fact, the Canadian High Commission in Port of Spain made most of the efforts to organize the Business Forum, and it was largely a tepid affair. Nonetheless, all the major Canadian banks and some mining companies were conspicuous by their presence.

Challenges Facing the Caribbean

Perhaps the biggest challenge facing most CARICOM countries nowadays is increasing crime (mainly related to the drug trade and sourcing in North America) and the resultant instability that it brings. What has long been an institutionalized problem in Jamaica is fast threatening to become so in tiny states like St Lucia and, more recently, sleepy, idyllic Dominica.[20] Trinidad and Tobago, the richest of the CARICOM group in terms of resources, now ranks significantly lower than it should in terms of quality of life because of the insecurity and instability of criminal activity due mainly to narco-trafficking. In fact, the recent destabilization of Kingston in May 2010 as a result of attempts to apprehend and extradite a famous, alleged drug lord – known as Christopher 'Dudus' Coke – is part of the push factor for educated, middle-class professionals to migrate to places like Canada. Similarly, the rampant kidnappings of businesspeople in Trinidad in the past four years has precipitated migration of numerous educated and enterprising persons to Canada and the United States. Indeed, the recent launching in Trinidad of Crime Stoppers International and the Caribbean's 'Most Wanted' website are all indications of this state of affairs – and of the impotence of national governments in the Caribbean to restrain the criminals and provide security to their citizens.

A 2007 report published by the World Bank and the United Nations Office on Drugs and Crime (UNODC) concluded that 'high rates of crime and violence in the Caribbean are undermining growth, threatening human welfare, and impeding social development.'[21] Indeed, per capita murder rates in the Caribbean are higher than in any other region of the world, and assault rates are significantly above the world average. There is little dispute that the illegal drug trade is at the core of these high rates. The narcotics trade also diverts criminal justice resources from other important activities, increases and embeds violence, undermines social cohesion, and contributes to the widespread availability of guns and the resultant insecurity in several capitals in the region.

Additionally, the narcotics business increasingly impacts negatively on youths, particularly males, who get caught up in violent gangs. Across the Caribbean, many people are concerned that there is currently a serious decline in role models to detract from the temptation of crime, suggesting that mechanisms and programs need to be developed to divert youth away from drug-related crime. Societies in CARICOM are very vulnerable because the region is a major transit point for narcotics from South America to the United States, Canada, and Europe.

In terms of bilateral relations with Canada, the deportation or repatriation of criminals to the Caribbean is a very controversial and difficult issue. In some instances, very seasoned and sophisticated criminals – with no contacts or legitimate prospects in their country of origin – wreak havoc on local communities and simply overwhelm law-enforcement authorities. Canadian officials argue that removing dangerous criminals from the country is integral to protecting Canadians and making communities safer; and the removal of inadmissible individuals is necessary to preserve the integrity of the immigration system for those who go to Canada lawfully. But the impact of deporting hard-core criminals to the Caribbean can be devastating on small communities.

Between 2001 and 2004, Jamaica received 2,700 deportees a year from the U.S., Britain, and Canada – an almost overwhelming number, especially given that Jamaica's prison population in 2003 was only 4,744.[22] Furthermore, as The Economist Intelligence Unit pointed out:

> The rising level of violence in the Caribbean is aggravated by a steady inflow of criminal deportees, many of whom have adopted criminal behaviour in major cities such as London and New York. An estimated 30,000 deportees were sent to Jamaica, Trinidad and Tobago and Guyana between 1990 and 2005. Of the 30,000, around 17,000 had been convicted for drug-trafficking, 600 for murder and 1,800 for illegal gun possession.[23]

The rich countries like Canada, the U.S., and the UK, which deport criminals to their country of birth, do not provide their criminal history to local authorities and often they do not notify them in sufficient time. Some Caribbean governments have asked the sending countries for funds to help deportees reintegrate in a land where they have little or no connections. The U.S. and UK have provided some funding, but Canada has apparently been less than forthcoming.[24] In principle, it is unfair that Canada and the U.S. are happy to receive the brightest and best from the Caribbean, but then send back the criminals (who learned their 'skills' in the North) to struggling CARICOM governments to deal with.

The UN/World Bank Report that analysed the economic costs of crime in the English-speaking Caribbean found that crime drives away both foreign and domestic investment and consequently slows growth. Because of the need to employ additional security measures to deal with rising crime, it increases the costs of doing business, and thereby diverts much-needed investment away from business expansion and productivity improvement. It also leads to business losses through theft, looting, arson, fraud, and extortion. Other intangible losses include the immeasurable cost of employee morale, productivity, and safety. The report suggests that if Caribbean countries were able to reduce crime levels to those similar to Costa Rica, their rates of economic growth would increase substantially. In the specific cases of Jamaica and Haiti, the report estimates that GDP growth would be boosted by 5.4 per cent annually.

A related issue is illegal immigrants from the Caribbean who overstay their welcome in Canada but are not really hardened criminals. Hardship and lack of economic opportunity in CARICOM states is often the reason for their actions. Guyana, Jamaica, and Trinidad and Tobago account for the greatest number of offenders in this regard. In March 2009, the Canadian High Commissioner to Guyana, Charles Court, said the waiting list of Guyanese to be deported was about 700 to 800, similar to the number pending deportation to Mexico, Iran, and other countries that have much larger populations.[25] It is, therefore, clearly in the interest of Canada to see economies in the region grow and prosper and thus increase employment opportunities there.

Negotiations toward a New Trade Agreement

In light of the economic and social issues discussed above, what bilateral mechanisms are needed to improve overall Canadian cooperation with the CARICOM group? For the most part, the only major forum is the current free trade negotiations – but that can only address a limited set of issues.[26] There is need for a broader framework to address crime and other socio-economic issues. But one should consider the economic issues at least.

The Framework for Economic Relations

Trade and economic relations between Canada and the Caribbean have a long history, dating back to the early eighteenth century when the British Northern Atlantic colonies exchanged fish, lumber, and other staples for West Indian rum, molasses, and spices. Currently, trade and economic relations are covered under a number of instruments – namely, the 1979 CARICOM-Canada Trade and Economic Co-operation Agreement and its Protocols, including the 1998 Protocol on Rum; and CARIBCAN, which grants unilateral duty-free access to eligible goods from beneficiary countries in the English-speaking Caribbean up to December 2011. There are also foreign investment protection agreements (bilateral investment treaties) with individual member states, namely Barbados and Trinidad and Tobago. In 2002, the Canadian government announced duty-free access for imports from the world's forty-eight least developed countries. But Haiti is the only country in the hemisphere to qualify for this category. All products imported from Haiti to Canada, then, are both duty-free and quota-free, with the exception of supply-managed agricultural products.

Canada also has memorandums of understanding (MOUs) with Jamaica, Trinidad and Tobago, Barbados, and the OECS countries under which farm workers are allowed to work in Canada on a seasonal basis each year. This special facility is protected by a most-favoured nation (MFN) exemption under the General Agreement on Trade in Services (GATS) in the World Trade Organization (WTO). Also, in recent years, hospitality workers from Barbados and a few other CARICOM states have been recruited on a temporary basis to work in the hotel sector in Canada and as household assistants.

Canada-CARICOM Trade Picture

In 2008, Canada celebrated the one-hundredth anniversary of its trade commissioner service in the Caribbean (in Barbados). However, the bilateral trade relationship is not particularly dynamic at the moment. Two-way merchandise trade between Canada and CARICOM has averaged just US$717 million over the last ten years.[27] CARICOM exports to Canada have averaged only US$ 393 million, and merchandise imports from Canada averaged US$324 million over this same period. Granted, positive growth trends were registered in both import and export flows, and overall trade surpluses were in CARICOM's favour.[28] But given the historical links, Caribbean diaspora in Canada, and CARIBCAN, the trade and investment activity between the two regions is not particularly impressive. And there is certainly room for significant growth.

The negotiation of a new comprehensive trade agreement between CARICOM and Canada is expected to result in a new treaty to govern the trade relations between both countries in the long run. And it is hoped that this will result in the conversion of the non-reciprocal CARIBCAN arrangement into a reciprocal and comprehensive trade agreement. The CARIBCAN Agreement, which deals with only trade in goods, will terminate in December 2011 unless Canada obtains another waiver from the WTO. In spite of preferences for many years, CARICOM has not diversified its goods export portfolio to Canada partly due to limited economies of scale and capacity constraints as well as restrictive rules of origin. It is anticipated, however, that CARICOM will benefit from a new trade and development agreement with Canada by improving market access for its goods and services and development support to address capacity constraints, among other things. But this is certainly not automatic. Since the new agreement will also cover investment, it could boost Canadian investment in CARICOM from the current low levels relative to the rest of the world. On the other hand, CARICOM will face a drop in trade revenue from the reduction of tariffs on goods which they currently import. The consequent adjustments are yet to be identified, and the overall event will depend on dynamic gains in other areas of the bilateral economic relationship. But this partly explains the lukewarm response to the agreement thus far by officials in various CARICOM countries.

Trade in Goods

CARICOM exports to Canada accounted for only 4 per cent of total regional exports over the period 2004–6. These exports comprised a narrow range of primary goods and basic manufactures such as alumina, petroleum, ferrous products, gold, rum, roots and tubers, beer, bakery products, liqueurs, sauces and condiments, nutmeg, and frozen fish. Jamaica, Trinidad and Tobago, Suriname, and Guyana dominated the basket of CARICOM merchandise exports to Canada. Collectively, these four countries accounted for 92 per cent of exports over the period 2004–6.[29] For Trinidad and Tobago, the biggest economy in CARICOM, trade with Canada is quite limited. Nevertheless, over the period 2004–6, Trinidad and Tobago accounted for 22 per cent of CARICOM exports and 34 per cent of imports from Canada on average; but this was a very tiny percentage of Trinidad and Tobago's total goods trade. The majority of its exports actually consisted of petroleum products, iron/steel products, and methanol.

From 2004–6, the top ten Canadian export products to CARICOM were a mix of manufactures, foodstuffs, and processed materials (newsprint, meslin/wheat, medicaments, telephone equipment, salt fish, copper wire, electrical equipment, potatoes). The top five products accounted for 21 per cent of total exports.

Negotiations on Rules of Origin

In the bilateral negotiations on trade in goods, the current rules of origin under CARIBCAN – which require that a minimum of 60 per cent of the inputs in manufactured products must originate in CARICOM – will have to be changed. This is to reflect the fact that most CARICOM economies are resource-deficient and that competitive manufacturing requires that inputs be sourced from the most cost-efficient sources. If more flexible rules of origin are not introduced, CARICOM manufacturers will never be able to take advantage of any market access granted by Canada.

Issues Regarding Market Access for Rum

Although it is the oldest manufactured import from the Caribbean, rum still faces complicated market access requirements in Canada. Apart from the highly controlled and inefficient system of provincial liquor board monopolies on the sale of alcohol, Caribbean rum faces two other obstacles. Under Bill S-38 of 2005,[30] rum may only be sold under the name 'Caribbean' if it has been made from sugarcane products of a Commonwealth Caribbean country or if it has been imported in bulk from such a country and subjected to blending either with other Caribbean rum or with Canadian rum 'in proportions that result in 1 to 1.5% Canadian rum by volume in the final product.' The Caribbean rum industry considers this legislation to be too restrictive and discriminatory since it prevents producers in CARICOM from making use of raw materials acquired from elsewhere (a practice that is becoming more crucial over time as the availability of molasses from the region's sugar industry declines). Furthermore, it does not accord with the treatment given to other spirits such as bourbon and cognac in Canada. The blending requirement is also particularly disadvantageous since in addition to it not being imposed on other spirits, it has been expressly prohibited under Canada's 2002 FTA with Costa Rica.

Trade in Services

In 2007, Canada imported CAD$88.6 billion and exported CAD$69.6 billion in services to the rest of the world. Due to its proximity to the United States and the integration of various markets in North America, Canada does not trade much with developing countries. Nevertheless, there are some developing countries which in recent years have been significantly increasing their services exports to Canada, apart from tourism/travel services. These include Bermuda, China, Hong Kong, India, and Singapore. Canada's bilateral services trade with CARICOM is minuscule (2 per cent) in comparison with the rest of the world. Of this percentage, Barbados accounts for the vast majority of services trade ($2.4 billion out of $3.3 billion in 2007) thanks to the bilateral tax treaty with Canada, which facilitates significant financial services activity. Trinidad and Tobago's services trade (imports and exports) with Canada is very small and amounted to only CAD$221 million in 2007. Nonetheless, Canada's services import propensity has been increasing substantially in recent years, and this could provide new and increased opportunities if a meaningful bilateral trade agreement can be concluded with CARICOM. (See table 8.5.)

Tourism is clearly the Caribbean's strong point and most famous

Table 8.5. Canada's trade in services with CARICOM states (CAD$ millions)

	2000	2001	2002	2003	2004	2005	2006	2007
Total services receipts (Exports)	919	937	1,540	1,832	1,477	1,140	1,433	1,551
Travel	81	86	106	86	102	106	118	128
Commercial services	771	762	1,344	1,671	1,259	913	1,178	1,290
Transportation and government services	68	89	90	75	116	121	137	133
Total services payments (Imports)	1,530	1,670	1,892	2,188	2,260	1,641	1,641	1,718
Travel	197	225	195	230	316	270	258	240
Commercial services	1,221	1,333	1,588	1,839	1,809	1,179	1,192	1,245
Transportation & government services	112	112	109	119	135	192	191	232
Services trade balance	−611	−733	−352	−356	−783	−501	−208	−167
Total bilateral services trade	2,449	2,607	3,432	4,020	3,737	2,781	3,074	3,269

Source: Statistics Canada.

industry. But even in this area, Canadian tourist arrivals in CARICOM states have been lethargic compared to other Caribbean destinations. In 2008, a total of only 565,275 Canadians visited all CARICOM states (except Haiti) compared to 818,246 in Cuba alone, and 635,933 in the Dominican Republic.[31] This was only a 47 per cent increase from 2000 for CARICOM, compared to 167 per cent for Cuba and a 160 per cent increase for the Dominican Republic. Furthermore, fewer and fewer Canadians are staying in hotels on land in the CARICOM region. The vast majority prefer to visit on day trips through the many cruise lines that traverse the region. So their local economic impact in the Caribbean is almost negligible.

Market Access Negotiations on Services

While Canada significantly liberalized its services market in the North American Free Trade Agreement (NAFTA), it has not done much on the services front with developing countries. The Canada-Costa Rica FTA mainly dealt with goods, and negotiations with Central America have not yet been concluded. In the Canada-Peru FTA, Canada did not grant significant market access at the sub-federal level to Peru. In fact, the provincial barriers were largely grandfathered. Canada actually included a most-favoured-nation (MFN) reservation for all current or future agreements for all sectors (Annex 11), as well as a sweeping reservation for MFN, national treatment, boards of management, local presence, and performance requirements that covers 'all existing non-conforming measures of all provinces and territories' (Annex 1). This may have been tolerable for Peru, which apparently has limited services interests, but will not be acceptable in a Canada-CARICOM trade agreement, since it will not lead to effective market access for Caribbean services suppliers.

The Canadian federal-provincial structure also involves a complicated situation regarding professional services. In Canada, all professions are regulated at the provincial level, as provinces have jurisdiction over all matters related to labour.[32] In many cases, provinces have delegated the responsibility for regulation to non-governmental professional bodies, often referred to as associations or colleges, by enacting laws that create professional regulatory bodies and confer on them the powers necessary to govern the professions.[33] This provincial delegation of power has resulted in most professions in Canada enjoying a self-regulated status. Therefore, to practise as a member of a regulated profession or use a professional designation, all applicants, whether Canadian-trained or international, must meet the requirements of the relevant provincial regulatory body (which often requires obtaining a licence to practise).[34] This has effectively resulted in multiple systems of registration and varying standards of qualifications across the country for the same profession. In order to gain effective market access in Canada in a bilateral agreement, it will be critical for CARICOM members to understand and navigate these barriers in the negotiations.

It should also be noted that it is extremely difficult for foreign professionals to practise in Canada. For instance, if an engineer is trained in Canada and has experience there, it is a relatively straightforward process to meet the licensing requirements. But if one's credentials are foreign, it is extremely difficult to do so. In fact, a survey of over 1,000 immigrants with engineering backgrounds drawn from 73 countries revealed that 'less than 5 per cent of immigrants with engineering backgrounds actually became licensed and even fewer are able to practice as Professional Engineers in Canada.'[35] This epitomizes the problems posed by qualification requirements at all levels, much more so for traders or service suppliers from the Caribbean.

In order for CARICOM companies, then, to take advantage of services opportunities in the Canadian market, they will require more than improved market access in a trade agreement. Local firms will have to form alliances with Canadian counterparts and try to fit into a global value chain in which Canada is involved. They will also have to look for complementarities between Caribbean firms and Canadian businesses in terms of outsourcing. But a comprehensive trade agreement can create a stimulus for greater investment and trade since non-reciprocal arrangements such as CARIBCAN are not a long-term incentive.

Considering the size of the Canadian services market, there should be opportunities in commercial services in Canada, particularly information and communication services, animation, energy, entertainment, and business services, among others. But given the small size of Caribbean firms, it would be necessary to first identify opportunities for joint-venturing with Canadian firms to supply their domestic market and third-country markets as well. There may be immediate possibilities in some modes of supply (in particular, Mode 1, or cross-border delivery of services), but it will require that an assessment be done of the sectors and modes in which CARICOM firms are competitive. In principle, CARICOM service suppliers are more competitive through

the presence of natural persons (Mode 4). Given the significant concessions granted to the Caribbean by the European Union (in twenty-nine
sectors for contractual service suppliers and eleven sectors for independent professionals), Canada will have to match the EU or do better. Indeed, CARICOM would like to see market access in Mode 4 not
limited to university graduates but include less highly skilled persons.
They would also expect that the Seasonal Agricultural Workers Program be extended to all CARICOM states; and it is not unreasonable
to expect that the region be given special access in tourism/hospitality
and other sectors such as oil and gas drilling and well servicing.

At the same time, it is critical to identify the sensitive sectors for
special treatment or shielding from Canadian competition. CARICOM
firms will also require provision of information on export opportunities
to Canada as well as information on import possibilities into CARI-
COM – particularly to address competitiveness issues in some domestic service sectors (especially in infrastructural services that are inputs
to other services and manufacturing). In other words, for a new trade
agreement to promote growth and employment in CARICOM, it will
need to have very significant and substantial trade facilitation and promotion measures.

Conclusion

In a volume dedicated to Canada's foreign policy in the Americas, it
is expected that the focus will be on government-to-government relations and the role of officials. However, in the case of the Caribbean, it
is clear that interactions purely at the political/official level have not
done enough to develop and enhance a key and historic relationship.[36]
First, what is needed to energize or reinvigorate Canada-Caribbean
relations may be less focus on officialdom and more on promotion of
greater interaction between ordinary citizens and companies from Canada and CARICOM states. It is evident that policy makers on both sides
should seek to engage and implement new ideas from the wider public
in order to refresh and revitalize the bilateral relationship.

Second, the Harper Conservatives should consider the private sector
as key to development of the region and thus should introduce programs for them. Third, Canada's approach to the region should not only
focus on the problems in the Caribbean, but it should seek to identify
and promote complementarities wherever they exist. In this regard, it
is advisable for CIDA and Foreign Affairs officials to consider broaden-

ing their consultations with the public and NGOs and supporting more NGO activities in CARICOM.

Fourth, the drug trade and resultant crime and insecurity in the region are a clear and present danger that must be addressed with greater emphasis and resources. While this is best done through collaboration with the United States, Caribbean governments, and others, it is important for Canada to provide more substantial and meaningful input in this area to address these needs in the region. Both Canada and the U.S. should also address the contradiction between wanting to help the Caribbean on the subject of crime and, at the same time, inadvertently contributing to crime through the injection of deportees who have perhaps become a channel for the 'internationalization' of criminal activity.

Finally, although aid and technical cooperation are supposed to be demand-driven, Canadian cooperation, to be effective in the medium term, should focus more on youth in the Caribbean. Most governments in CARICOM have failed miserably in this area, and there is a major disconnect with large segments of their populations.

With regard to the current trade negotiations in particular, if the Harper government really wants to assist CARICOM economies, it must recognize the idiosyncracies of the region and seek to cater to them. It would be worthwhile, for example, to be innovative and not work from the generic template of other trade bilaterals with Chile, Costa Rica, and Peru. If not, the greater beneficiary of the agreement will be Canada rather than the Caribbean – and this will do little to encourage serious CARICOM engagement.

More to the point, the negotiations (still ongoing as of mid-2012) should include a forward-looking and creative instrument on cultural cooperation that would harness the talents in the Caribbean and Canada to stimulate the development of cultural industries in CARICOM. In addition to granting permanent duty-free and quota-free market access for CARICOM goods in Canada, and solving the problem of market access for rum and rules of origin, CARICOM should be granted significant and meaningful market access for services so that Canadian firms can collaborate with firms and suppliers in the Caribbean to provide services to clients in Canada and other countries. Lastly, rules on investment in any new trade agreement will not be enough to attract significant new Canadian investment in CARICOM. As the late William Dymond pointed out in the case of the Canada-Chile FTA, the specific inclusion of a double taxation treaty had a positive impact on investment decisions:

Many of those interviewed also mentioned that these investment measures were positively enhanced by complementary agreements, and specifically the double taxation agreement negotiated by Canada and Chile,
and the regulatory reform effect of the implementation of the agreement.
It was this package of direct and indirect effects of the increased attention
on Chile as a result of the negotiation of the CCFTA that is one of the positive contributions of the agreement itself.[37]

If the Canada-CARICOM trade negotiations are to be successful, it
will be important to introduce a double taxation instrument to complement a new comprehensive agreement dealing with trade and investment.[38] In addition, Canadian investors in the CARICOM region should
be extended the same tax credit facilities granted to them for investing
in Canada. And funding should be provided to create a venture capital
fund that can be used to finance investment in CARICOM economies.

In closing, with the last major Canada-CARICOM initiative stretching back to the early 1990s, it is long past time for the two sides to fashion something significant and appropriate for the twenty-first century.
Whether it is a groundbreaking bilateral trade agreement or something
more comprehensive, it remains to be seen. But if no initiatives are
forthcoming in the short to medium term, the timeless cliché about a
'special relationship' will no longer be meaningful.

NOTES

1 After participating in the Fifth Summit of the Americas in Trinidad and
   Tobago in April 2009, Prime Minister Stephen Harper did go on to make
   an official visit to Jamaica, where he spoke before a joint session of the
   country's Parliament.
2 Antigua and Barbuda, Bahamas, Barbados, Belize, Dominica, Grenada,
   Guyana, Haiti, Jamaica, St Kitts and Nevis, St Lucia, St Vincent and the
   Grenadines, Suriname, and Trinidad and Tobago. Haiti joined CARICOM a
   few years ago but has not yet been able to implement the commitments of
   the Single Market. The Bahamas is also a member of CARICOM but not of
   the Single Market.
3 Sahadeo Basdeo, 'CARIBCAN: A Continuum in Canada-Commonwealth
   Caribbean Economic Relations,' *Canadian Foreign Policy* 1, no. 2 (Spring
   1993): 55–79, and Jerry Haar and Anthony T. Bryan (eds.), *Canadian-Carib-
   bean Relations in Transition: Trade, Sustainable Development and Security* (New

York: Palgrave-Macmillan, 1999). See also Trevor A. Carmichael, *Passport to the Heart: Reflections on Canada Caribbean Relations* (Kingston, Jamaica: Ian Randle Publishers, 2001).

4 Linda Hossie, '$182-Million Debt Forgiven, PM Informs Caribbean Leaders,' *Globe and Mail*, 20 March 1990, A15.

5 By April 2011 there had been only two negotiating sessions; the third session commenced in April but was postponed, and by the end of July it still had to be reconvened to be completed.

6 On 18–19 July 2007, a group of Caribbean and Canadian representatives met for the first Canada-Caribbean Ideas Forum in Bridgetown, Barbados. The event's purpose was to promote discussions on future public policy choices and directions in the region. The meeting brought together about forty eminent Caribbean individuals from a diverse range of backgrounds, including: police, academia, judicial, finance and business sectors, along with a smaller number of Canadian officials and private sector organizations. The discussions were primarily focused on the three interconnected themes of governance, prosperity, and security. This initiative was funded by the Canadian government.

7 CIDA disbursements to the Caribbean totalled $38.4 million for 2009–10. Government of Canada, *Caribbean Region: CIDA Report* (Gatineau: Canadian International Development Agency, 2011).

8 See Government of Canada, *Canadian International Development Agency, 2007–2008 Departmental Performance Report* (Gatineau, Quebec: Canadian International Development Agency, 2008), 48.

9 Note, for example, that in 2008–9 Canadian aid to Pakistan was only $32.14 million and Vietnam received $37.48 million.

10 See 'Immigrant Status and Place of Birth,' *2006 Census* (Ottawa: Statistics Canada, February 2009), 1.

11 Michael Lee Chin, a successful businessman and immigrant from Jamaica, donated CAD$30 million to the Royal Ontario Museum in 2006.

12 Quoted from Chambers's address to the Canada-Caribbean Ideas Forum II: Emerging Issues in Development Policy and Practice, University of the West Indies, Kingston, Jamaica, 23–4 June 2008.

13 F. Docquier and A. Marfouk, 'International Migration by Educational Attainment (1990–2000),' release 1.1 (Washington, DC: World Bank, 2005).

14 Government of Canada, *Canada-Caribbean Community (CARICOM) Free Trade Negotiations* (Ottawa: Department of Foreign Affairs and International Trade, 2009), 1. Canadian service exports were $1.5 billion in 2004, while imports amounted to some $2.3 billion – mostly involving commercial and travel services.

15 'The Canadian Connection: Providing Banking, Business and Policemen,' *The Economist*, 28 March 2008, 50. Also see Economic Commission for Latin America and the Caribbean, *Foreign Investment in Latin America and the Caribbean 2007* (Santiago, Chile: ECLAC, 2008) for Canadian investment by sector in the Caribbean. For example, IAM Gold is in Guyana and Suriname and Methanex is in Trinidad and Tobago.

16 See Joseph Schull and J. Douglas Gibson, *The Scotiabank Story: A History of the Bank of Nova Scotia, 1832–1982* (Toronto: Macmillan of Canada, 1982).

17 See Economic Commission for Latin America and the Caribbean, *Foreign Investment in Latin America and the Caribbean 2007* (Santiago, Chile: ECLAC, May 2008).

18 Ibid.

19 Note that Nova Scotia Inc. alone led ten trade missions to the Caribbean in the two years up to November 2010.

20 See John Briley, 'What to Know about Crime, Safety,' *Washington Post*, 1 March 2010, P1.

21 World Bank, *Crime, Violence and Development: Trends, Costs and Policy Options in the Caribbean* (Washington, DC: World Bank, May 2007).

22 Sandro Contenta, 'Jamaica Wants Canada to Help Look After 'Cons' It Sends Back.' *Toronto Star*, 23 November 2007, A1.

23 See Bronwen Brown, 'Economic Impact of Crime in Jamaica and Trinidad and Tobago,' in *Country Forecast Latin America: Regional Overview* (London: Economist Intelligence Unit, March 2008).

24 In a 2009 interview with a Guyanese newspaper, departing Canadian High Commissioner Charles Court noted that for the years 1996 to 2007, the U.S. returned some 1,500 criminal deportees (or roughly 150 per year), while Canada returned a similar number (148) in 2008. Staff, 'Interview with Canada's High Commissioner to Guyana,' Stabroeknews.com, 12 July 2009.

25 See Staff, 'Hundreds of Guyanese deported from Canada,' Caribbeannetnews.com, 28 January 2009.

26 See Ramesh Chaitoo and Ann Weston, 'Canada and the Caribbean Community: Prospects for an Enhanced Trade Arrangement,' *Canadian Foreign Policy Journal* 14, no. 3 (Fall 2008): 47–64.

27 For 2009, two-way trade between Canada and CARICOM countries reached $2.1 billion, marking a slight decrease from 2008. Government of Canada, *Canada-Caribbean Community (CARICOM) Free Trade Negotiations* (Ottawa: Department of Foreign Affairs and International Trade, June 2011). For 2010, two-way trade bumped up slightly to $2.4 billion, while trade figures for 2011 were not made available by DFAIT. See Government

of Canada, *Fact Sheet: Canada-Caricom Relations* (Ottawa: Department of Foreign Affairs and International Trade, July 2011).

28 However, this trade surplus was registered by Jamaica and Guyana, primarily through export of alumina and gold respectively.

29 See Caribbean Policy Development Centre, *The Future of CARICOM Trade Relations with the United States and Canada* (Bridgetown, Barbados: CPDC, 2008), 18.

30 Reference found in Canadian Legal Information Institute, *Spirit Drinks Trade Act, S.C. 2005*, 4.

31 See *Latest Statistics 2008* (Barbados: Caribbean Tourism Organization, 21 August 2009), 5.

32 This division of powers is set out in the Constitution Act, 1867.

33 See Government of Canada, *Agreement on Internal Trade* (Winnipeg, Manitoba: Internal Trade Secretariat, May 2007), 83–91.

34 For Ontario, see *Ontario's Regulated Professions* (Ontario Regulators for Access, 2004). There are also specific qualification requirements that appear more burdensome than in the Caribbean.

35 Quoted from a report by the Toronto-based Council for Access to the Profession of Engineering, *Engineering in Canada*, http://www.capeinfo.ca/eng_in_canada.php.

36 Then minister of foreign affairs for the Americas Peter Kent furthered government-to-government relations by visiting two CARICOM countries (St Lucia and Barbados) in mid-September 2010. Once again, he re-emphasized Canada's major aims in the region by observing: 'By strengthening relationships and working with countries such as Barbados and Saint Lucia, Canada continues to advance prosperity, security and democratic governance throughout the hemisphere.' Government of Canada, 'Minister of State Kent to Engage Caribbean Partners,' news release (Ottawa: Department of Foreign Affairs and International Trade, 15 September 2010).

37 William Dymond, *Canada-Chile Free Trade Agreement @ Ten: Beyond the Numbers* (Ottawa: Foreign Affairs and International Trade Canada, 2008), 10.

38 At the moment Barbados (1980), Guyana (1987), Jamaica (1981), and Trinidad and Tobago (1996) have bilateral tax treaties or double taxation agreements with Canada. Since 2010 some OECS governments signed tax information exchange agreements with Canada, but this is really to deal with tax evasion and to address OECD concerns about tax havens.

9 Canada and Central America: Citizen Action and International Policy

STEPHEN BARANYI AND JOHN W. FOSTER

Thirty years ago, Central America was in flames. In Nicaragua, the Frente Sandinista de Liberación Nacional (FSLN) had overthrown the Somoza dynasty and initiated deep reforms, yet it was mired in a war against the U.S.-backed *contras*. In El Salvador, an equally costly war pitted the U.S.-backed Armed Forces and Christian Democratic government against the Frente Farabundo Marti de Liberación Nacional (FMLN). In Guatemala, the Army had initiated a controlled democratic opening after crushing the Unidad Revolucionaria Nacional de Guatemala (URNG) and killing over 200,000 civilians. Honduras had become the regional platform for U.S. military activities, while Costa Rica harboured opposition forces from several countries' wars. In the U.S., the Reagan administration supported some of the most reprehensible allies in the region, giving birth to significant counter-currents in the U.S. public and in Congress.

Latin American middle powers sponsored innovative peace talks through the Contadora process, but by 1986, these negotiations were largely stalled. The spectre of an escalating war involving both super-powers loomed at this flashpoint of the Cold War. All this was unfolding in a region that had seen economic growth and democratic openings but was now plagued by state-sponsored torture and mass killing, recessions, democratic backsliding, and enduring socio-economic inequalities.[1]

Though the Canadian government had historically been wary about getting involved in this 'U.S. backyard,' relations between Canadian civil society and its Central American counterparts expanded from the late 1970s onwards. As development NGOs, churches, labour unions, parliamentarians, solidarity groups, academics, and artists flocked to the region, some pooled their efforts to persuade the Canadian government to play a more constructive role in the region.[2] And, for the most part, they did – albeit with varying degrees of commitment and success.

This chapter, however, is focused less on the specifics of Canadian government involvement in the region and more on one particular NGO initiative, the Canada-Caribbean-Central America Policy Alternatives (CAPA), which emerged in the 1980s. CAPA was a group of civil society activists and analysts who used policy research and multi-stakeholder dialogue to influence the practices of the Canadian government – and of other actors – in Central America. The chapter, then, explores three questions related to CAPA, its influence on government policy and on broader social change: What did CAPA and its allies do, and what influence did it have on Canadian policy/practice in Central America? Looked at some twenty-five years later, what long-term influence did CAPA have in Canada, on government policy, and civil society practices? Third, what can activists, analysts, and officials working in/on Canadian foreign policy, in Latin America, the Caribbean, and beyond, learn from these experiences today?

First we review CAPA's activities, offering an initial assessment of its influence at the time. Then we examine Canada and Central America almost thirty years on, considering whether CAPA's efforts had enduring influence on government policy and civil society practices. We conclude with thoughts on what might be learned from CAPA's experiences. It is worth emphasizing that this is not a traditional academic study of Canada-Central America relations. It is more of a retrospective analysis by two researchers with long experience in state–civil society policy dialogue processes, including participant observation in CAPA itself.[3] But we do provide a series of practical and pragmatic policy recommendations for the Canadian government to consider.

CAPA: An Experiment in 'Track Two' Diplomacy

In what soil did CAPA's response to the Central American conflicts take root? One locus of initiative was the Latin American Working Group (LAWG), one of the oldest Canadian research, solidarity, and action groups dealing with the region, which emerged in Toronto in the mid-1960s. This 'collective' was one of several international, feminist, and gay formations in Toronto at the time, carrying on public education, transnational exchange, and research activities.[4]

Equally important was the Inter-Church Committee on Human

Rights in Latin America (ICCHRLA), an ecumenical foundation created in 1973 in response to the military coup in Chile. Working with
church partners in the region on human rights and refugee issues, it
facilitated investigative missions to prisons and human rights bodies
in the Southern Cone and then to Central America. One of ICCHRLA's
members, the Jesuit Centre for Social Faith and Justice, also developed
expertise on Central America, benefiting from close links with Jesuits in
the region. A number of humanitarian NGOs including Development
and Peace, CUSO, and Oxfam-Canada, some of which had staff resi-
dent in Central America and all of which had a range of projects in the
region, contributed to regular traffic of Canadians as well as Central
American visitors. The churches, through Ten Days for World Development, sponsored visitors from the south who travelled beyond large
cities, taking the struggles for social justice in Central America to small
towns and regional media. A number of country-specific solidarity networks sprung up, several of which were spurred by the revolutionary
forces in Guatemala and El Salvador.

Several initiatives developed with the support of LAWG, the NGOs,
and churches, notably Tools for Peace – a community-based network
shipping everything from school supplies to bicycles to Nicaraguan
partners. LAWG also developed a campaign – Non-Intervention in
Central America (NICA) – opposing U.S. military interference. Under
the banner 'Mission for Peace,' LAWG sought to shift Canadian government policy and public opinion by sponsoring fact-finding missions
to the region. Clearly, all of this civil society and public interest in the
mid-1980s effectively put the issue of Central American civil wars on
both the political agenda in Ottawa and the bureaucratic radar of the
then Department of External Affairs (DEA).

The repressive nature of the Guatemalan and Salvadoran regimes,
the deadly conflicts in three of the republics, and the overt intervention
by the U.S. not only excited opposition among many Canadians but
convinced some that Canada could and should play a counter-balanc-
ing role for peace, human rights, and social justice, perhaps even for a
transformation of the region. What was missing, they concluded, was
the sort of citizen initiative to bring elements who might contribute to
a positive solution together: government officials, non-governmental
figures, establishment and revolutionary political tendencies, and even
military or business representatives. The objective: a deeper engagement about policy, as well as increased pressure for the implementation
of alternative approaches.

In 1983, Canada-Caribbean-Central America Policy Alternatives (CAPA) was formed involving figures from several of the elements mentioned above, the Jesuit Centre and Inter-Church Committee, LAWG, and others of an activist persuasion. What was new was participation by academics from York University and graduate students committed to serious research and to purposeful action. Around dining room tables in cooperative houses and professorial residences, CAPA participants met regularly – almost every Tuesday night for five years.

Repulsed by the horrors unfolding in Central America, participants invested in fashioning more positive visions for the region. Some found this in the initial results of the Nicaraguan revolution and the social mobilization which was apparent on the ground in the early 1980s. Many were moved by the visions and lives of figures like Ernesto Cardenal, Archishop Oscar Romero in El Salvador, and many lesser known but equally impressive religious and secular leaders. Some identified with the objectives of the political wings of the revolutionary movements, if not always with their armed partners.

What were the *key elements* in their working method? First of all, information sharing and common analysis were central. The flow of intelligence from investigative missions, published and informal sources was cross-sectoral and rich. Second, monitoring and reflecting on Canadian official policy, parliamentary debate, and media coverage was continual. Third, attempts were made to bring together diverse forces to dialogue about the region, Canadian policy, and potential proposals for initiatives for peace. These all spawned a number of contacts, visits, and investigative missions not only to gather information but to engage key figures in Central America, the United States, Mexico, and some European capitals. Fourth, there was regular publication of news and analysis, with the support of the Jesuit Centre, which gave CAPA a voice different in tone and emphasis from other solidarity-related newsletters and appeals.

The contribution of students merits attention as well. Through volunteer research, writing, editing, and publication assistance, as well as their logistical support, students' energies were vital to the project. None of this would have happened, of course, without the efforts of Professor Liisa North.

CAPA succeeded in gaining support for what became the central focus of its work, the Roundtable on Negotiations for Peace in Central America. The government's arm's-length Canadian Institute for International Peace and Security (CIIPS), led by diplomat Geoffrey Pearson, provided funding and a measure of legitimacy. On that basis, CAPA sponsored three roundtables over five years: the first, on Negotiations for Peace in Central America (September 1985); the Roundtable on Interim and Confidence-Building Measures (May 1987); and the last on Peace and Reconstruction in Central America (May 1989).

These events were designed to engage policy makers and implementers in official Ottawa. In fact, they were all held in Ottawa, on parliamentary premises. The *method* involved identifying key interlocutors among, for example, senior officials in the Mexican foreign ministry who had taken initiatives to recognize opposition forces in Central America, representatives of the political wings of those forces, as well as Washington Congressional offices and policy research institutes. Wherever possible, members of CAPA would engage participants directly, encourage participation, and elicit not just an exchange of analysis, but meaningful initiatives for peace or for interim elements like enhancing protection for refugees. The work benefited tremendously from the networks which each constituent brought to the table. Church links with key human rights and religious figures in the region, Jesuit links with academics and policy advisers in El Salvador and Nicaragua, academic and activist contacts with political spokespeople, coalitional relations with labour, NGO, and solidarity networks, all contributed to the high-level and diverse representatives who were brought together in the Ottawa roundtables.

Each roundtable produced a *publication*, encapsulating debates and detailing policy recommendations. The first two proceedings were published in English and French monographs. The third emerged in book form – *Between War and Peace in Central American: Choices for Canada*. This edited work was also based on the research of fact-finding missions to the region, Washington, Mexico, and Europe.

The work extended through two phases of Canadian foreign policy under a Liberal government – under foreign ministers Mark MacGuigan and Allan MacEachen – and during the Mulroney years with Joe Clark at External Affairs; from NGO responses to the Nicaraguan revolution of 1979 to Canada's becoming a member of the Organization of American States (OAS) in 1990; from the last phase of the Cold War to the final collapse of the 'iron curtain,' and a massive shift in geopolitical balances.

What were the key elements of CAPA's agenda? CAPA sought to inform and inspire citizen networks to spark Canadian intervention for peace, human rights, and social justice – for example, to encourage the

Canadian government to move from a posture of support and occasional prevarication regarding the Reagan administration approach, towards initiatives and coalitions in support of negotiations for peace. Canadian diplomacy was envisioned to be active at every level in the United States, with the White House but also with Congress, seeking allies for peace in an assertive advocacy role. Canadian parliamentarians were also urged to engage their U.S. counterparts, 'to spread the word about Canadian peace-promoting policies among the Washington policy community and the media.'[5] In addition, it worked to encourage the multilateralization of responses to the conflict to limit military interventions by the United States and support the engagement of other powers, whether Latin American or European, as well as the UN, in negotiations for peace. The Roundtable recommendations embody respect for human rights; the need for social transformation, non-intervention, and self-determination; respect for international law and the decisions of the International Court of Justice; and respect for the autonomy of Central American nations themselves.

Furthermore, CAPA attempted to facilitate conversations between Canadian officials and the insurrectionary movements in El Salvador and Guatemala. It tried to emphasize the situation of people on the ground, notably the large refugee populations, and respect for human rights at the community level. And this developed into support for national reconciliation commissions and, ultimately, for investigation into rights abuses. Internationally, it meant advocacy for UN initiatives against torture and disappearances. Lastly, it sought greater commitment to domestic policies that would ensure greater social justice as well as the international policies and conditions which would enable them to flourish in the region.

The preparation and conduct of the roundtables, with their focus on engaging officials and other actors, offered some chance, however infinitesimal, of multiplying energies for peace and the protection of fundamental rights. Diverse figures in the Canadian landscape, people like Major General Leonard Johnson or Gerald Caplan, visited the region and provided important support, testimony, and encouragement. Canadian parliamentarians such as Flora MacDonald and Walter McLean, Maurice Dupras, and Father Bob Ogle also provided key leadership. From the prevarications of MacGuigan to the interest of MacEachen and Clark, persistent advocacy eventually yielded some tangible advances.

Which CAPA initiatives might we link with policy or operational outcomes? Canada came to play a more active peace support role than may have been contemplated by External Affairs or its ministers in the early 1980s. Canada's diplomatic views became distinct from those of the U.S., particularly in encouraging the Contadora and Esquipulas peace initiatives. Canada also participated in the first UN peace observer mission (ONUCA) starting in 1989, with the primary mandate of monitoring the Honduran-Nicaraguan border, one of several efforts to end the deadly Contra war in Nicaragua.

In the late 1980s the U.S., then under George Bush Sr, distanced itself partially from the *contras* but continued its support of governments with a history of repression in Guatemala and El Salvador, working for and welcoming the electoral defeat of the FSLN in Nicaragua in 1990. Secret funding of covert activities and paramilitary groups continued. Peace negotiations, electoral processes, and some accountability for human rights violations did emerge in El Salvador and Guatemala as the Cold War evaporated. But peace was seldom the transition to a more just society and economy in Central America.

Equally telling, Canadian aid policy also changed – with civil society calls for assistance to be diverted from contra-supporting countries (Honduras, El Salvador and Guatemala) to the Sandinistas in Nicaragua. Aid to El Salvador was suspended for some time, and later initiatives in Nicaragua, Honduras, and El Salvador were more closely aligned with peace and reconstruction objectives. Canada supported a number of the initiatives in the UN human rights system, responding firmly to the egregious violations of human rights. In particular, the pioneering UN human rights monitoring effort at the community level in El Salvador (ONUSAL) seems to have been initiated in hallway conversations at one of the CAPA roundtables.

We will return to CAPA's contribution and significance in our concluding pages. However, it is fair to say that within the context of a diverse Canadian movement for justice and peace in Central America, CAPA played a role in organizing dialogue among key parties in the conflicts, developing more detailed policy recommendations, and prompting action by the Canadian state. It played a key role in legitimizing action for peace as distinct from what was clearly a counterproductive U.S. policy posture. It worked to these ends in collaboration with other non-governmental groupings dedicated to human rights; refugee, humanitarian, and development assistance; and solidarity. As CIIPS Executive Director Geoffrey Pearson noted in 1990, 'the principal influence on government policy will continue to be public concern.

CAPA can take some credit for the success achieved to date in stimulating this interest.'[6]

In the end, these efforts failed to meet CAPA's high expectations. Canada, in its view, could have done far more. As CAPA constituent Michael Czerny, S.J., concluded in May 1990: 'The 1980s demonstrated that Canada had not yet attained the maturity to promote its fundamental foreign policy tenets with as much energy and independence as the crisis required.' As we suggest in our conclusions, virtually the same statement could be made in late 2012.[7]

A Longer View, a Bigger Picture

By the end of the 1980s, one could already discern significant outcomes from CAPA's efforts – in terms of changes in government policy and in enhanced civil society capacities to blend research, partnership, and policy dialogue to promote policy change. Twenty-five years later, what enduring marks have CAPA's initiatives left on policy and practice?

In this section, we attempt to discern CAPA's longer-term legacy in two ways. First, we look at Canada's relations with Central America since the 1980s and compare these to CAPA's key policy recommendations. We do so by scanning four critical dimensions of Canada-Central America relations: diplomacy, development cooperation, trade, and security. Other important areas, like immigration and investment, are beyond the scope of this analysis. Then we broaden our focus to consider how CAPA's work influenced Canada's wider relations with Latin America and the Caribbean, as well as government–civil society relations on a range of foreign policy issues. This is a complicated exercise, since the more one lengthens the time frame and broadens the scope of one's analysis, the more difficult it is to determine with precision what influence civil society organizations (CSOs) may have had on Canada's policy framework. Nonetheless, let us proceed with this analysis for heuristic purposes.

Diplomacy

CAPA recommended increased Canadian diplomatic engagement in Central America, beyond the historic embassies in Costa Rica and Guatemala. In 1995, Canada modestly scaled up its diplomatic presence by establishing a diplomatic office in El Salvador, upgrading to a full embassy in 2004. Canada and the Central American governments have also held several high-level summits since the late 1990s. During the 1990s, Canada continued to push for the implementation of the Esquipulas II Accord across the region. It supported crucial United Nations peace mediation roles in El Salvador (deploying military assets on the ground) and Guatemala, and made major contributions to three UN peace operations in the region. Canada also continued to monitor respect for human rights in the region and expressed its concerns about ongoing or recurrent violations, particularly in Guatemala, Honduras, and Nicaragua. It did so bilaterally and through multilateral forums such as the then UN Commission on Human Rights in Geneva.

Canada's involvement in the peace processes of Central America was one factor that led to the expansion of its relations with Latin American middle powers such as Mexico and Colombia, and to Canada's finally joining the OAS in 1990. It also led to the development of a close diplomatic relationship with Costa Rica and ongoing cooperation on issues such as human rights, on which the two countries share perspectives. Canada's former Governor General, Michaëlle Jean, also visited the country in December 2009, and then minister of state for the Americas Peter Kent attended the inauguration of Costa Rica's new president, Laura Chinchilla, in early May 2010.

What is less clear is whether Canada has 'predicate[d] all diplomatic efforts on respect for human rights and the related need for social transformation as the sine qua non of durable peace in Central America.'[8] While Canadian diplomacy continues to highlight the need to promote human rights and economic development in the region, any understanding of the links between these goals and the need for major economic or social reforms, which crystallized among some DEA officials in the 1980s, appears to have been lost in the 2000s.

Development Cooperation

Do these tendencies hold for CIDA and its development cooperation in the region? Table 9.1 suggests that Canadian official development assistance (ODA) to Central America has almost doubled since the 1980s, though given inflation, this growth is less impressive in real terms. The distribution of Canadian ODA has shifted within the region: aid to Costa Rica and El Salvador has decreased; aid to Guatemala increased slightly; Honduras and Nicaragua have emerged as the main recipients of Canadian ODA. Indeed, Nicaragua has received some $19 million in development assistance for 2009–10, while Honduras has seen a huge

Table 9.1. Canadian ODA to Central America, 1980s and 2009–10*

Country	Average annual ODA disbursements, 1981–9 (CAD$millions)	ODA disbursements in 2009–10 (CAD$millions)
Guatemala	2.8	10.2
El Salvador	4.3	3.8
Honduras	8.7	26.0
Nicaragua	10.2	19.0
Costa Rica	10.2	1.7
Regional totals	36.2	60.7

* The averages of Canadian ODA to Central America in the 1980s, in actual Canadian dollars at the time, were calculated on the basis of the data in Liisa North, Between War and Peace in Central America: Choices for Canada (Toronto: Between the Lines, 1990), 100–1, table IV, itself drawing on CIDA documents. The ODA figures for 2009–10 were drawn from the country program pages on CIDA's website in June 2011.

increase from previous years – securing some $26 million for 2009–10. What are the stories behind these figures and how do these shifts compare to CAPA's recommendations?

CAPA had recommended that Costa Rica receive increased ODA in recognition for its role in the Esquipulas peace process and its own development needs, but by the mid-1990s both governments felt that high levels of Canadian ODA could not be justified given Costa Rica's growth and robust institutions. By the new millennium, it became even clearer that Costa Rica's major priorities were to gain increased access to Canadian markets, investment, and technology, rather than to continue relying on Canadian development assistance. The decrease in Canadian ODA to El Salvador since 2000 is also rooted in that country's economic growth and the priorities of its government and large businesses, namely negotiating a favourable trade agreement with Canada.

As mentioned, Honduras and Nicaragua emerged as the main recipients of Canadian ODA partly because these are the poorest countries in the hemisphere after Haiti. Canadian ODA was already relatively high when Hurricane Mitch devastated large parts of those countries in 1998. In Honduras, the post-Mitch reconstruction framework – resting on a poverty-reduction strategy supported by national stakeholders and international donors, and followed up with the Pro-Mesas multi-stakeholder platforms – provided an attractive basis for CIDA to increase its assistance even more. Against that backdrop, CIDA designated Honduras as one its nine focus countries in 2002, one of its twenty-five 'development partners' in 2005, and as one of its twenty 'countries of concentration' in 2009.[9]

In Nicaragua, fragile governance continued to hamper development efforts, but CIDA also designated that country as a development partner in 2005, in response to its enormous needs and the perception that there were opportunities to make a difference on the ground. CIDA's focus on fewer 'countries of concentration' in 2009 excluded Nicaragua, perhaps partly due to the re-election of a left-leaning Sandinista government, though Nicaragua still remains a significant partner.

In Guatemala, as per CAPA's recommendations, CIDA resumed bilateral ODA only in 1995, as an incentive for the government and URNG to complete peace negotiations. ODA was increased to assist the implementation of the peace accords during the late 1990s and tapered off afterwards. Guatemala was not identified as a CIDA priority partner in 2005 or 2009, yet ODA has remained steady in recognition of the country's humanitarian needs and its strategic position in Central America.

How are these funds actually being spent? An analysis of priorities in the largest recipients reveals interesting patterns. In Honduras and Nicaragua, CIDA's programming flows from the priorities established by each government, donors, and civil society through poverty-reduction strategy papers (PRSP). These generally emphasize macro-economic growth, fiscal prudence, support to geographically or socially marginalized populations, and sustainability.

In Honduras, and after the beginning of the new millennium, CIDA focused the bulk of its aid on multi-year support to agriculture and rural development, as well as on health and education, because it is in those sectors that multi-stakeholder coordination through the Pro-Mesas seemed most promising. In line with the thematic priorities announced by CIDA in 2009, Canada's current ODA programming in Honduras focuses on supporting child and maternal health as well as basic education. In those areas, CIDA channels its aid to discrete projects and to sector-wide approaches such as the implementation of the national health plan. CIDA also supports food security through increased agricultural productivity as well as through a major school meals program managed by the World Food Program.[10] To the extent that it is channelling considerable ODA through Honduran agencies (even after the June 2009 military ouster of the sitting president), in support of priorities and programs codified in national development strategies, CIDA seems to be walking the talk of 'aid effectiveness' in Honduras.

In contrast, the peace accords remained the stated basis for CIDA programming in Guatemala well into the twenty-first century. CIDA's last country development programming framework for Guatemala acknowledged the links between the thirty-six-year armed conflict, dramatic socio-economic inequalities, discrimination, exclusion, and weak governance. It recognized that the peace accords offered a basis for addressing those structural problems in an integrated manner and that CIDA should approach programming in Guatemala with a long-term perspective. Within that framework, CIDA focused on supporting marginalized sectors of the population like the rural poor, indigenous peoples, and women; basic social services; agriculture; as well as human rights, democracy, and good governance. Although CIDA's bilateral program has decreased since, its contributions in 2009 of CAD$5 million to the International Commission Against Impunity and of CAD$10 million to rural development in Sololá, reflect some continuity in this structural approach.[11]

If one compares current Canadian ODA in Central America to CAPA's recommendations two and a half decades ago, one sees that Canada increased levels of ODA to the region but not as dramatically as envisaged by CAPA. Canada did, however, make Nicaragua and Honduras priorities. In both countries, considerable Canadian aid has been aligned with national priorities and channelled through national institutions. In Guatemala, CIDA programming is still somewhat informed by an awareness of necessary structural reforms. Yet there, and particularly in Honduras – the only country of concentration remaining in the isthmus – this clearly falls short of CAPA's recommendation that Canada should 'provide major assistance for the implementation of redistributive policies ... agrarian reform, tax reform, the organization of productive and service co-operatives' as 'the essence of a distinctively Canadian approach in Central America.'[12]

Trade

Although the Canadian government explored some trade policy options mooted by CAPA in 1990 – such as extending CARIBCAN preferential trade agreements to cover Central American countries – those recommendations were sidelined by changing agendas. In the early 1990s, Canada's priority was to extend parts of the Canada-U.S. Free Trade Agreement to Mexico, then through the FTAA to the wider Americas. In 2000, CIDA approved a CAD$5 million project to provide trade-related capacity building to Central American govern-

Table 9.2. Two-way trade, Canada and Central America, 1990 and 2010*

Country	Two-way trade in 1989–90 (CAD$millions)	Two-way trade in 2009–10 (CAD$millions)
Guatemala	57	414
El Salvador	30	123
Honduras	21	191
Nicaragua	64	255
Costa Rica	73	544
Regional total	245	1,527

*These figures are two-way totals of merchandise trade. The 1989–90 numbers are drawn from United Nations, Canada's Trade and Investment with Latin America and the Caribbean (Washington, DC: Economic Commission for Latin America and the Caribbean, January 2003), 2. The 2009–10 numbers are drawn from the various "Fact Sheets" for each country made available on DFAIT's website, last updated for May 2011.

ments to strengthen their positions in the FTAA talks. Ironically, that same year the governments of Central America asked Canada to initiate talks on a sub-regional agreement when it became apparent that the FTAA would be delayed and ultimately killed. Talks with Costa Rica advanced quickly; by November 2001 Canada and Costa Rica had concluded a bilateral FTA with side agreements on labour and environmental standards.[13] Talks continue today on a multilateral FTA with the other four Central American governments (though a bilateral pact with Panama should come into force in late 2012 and trade negotiations with Honduras began in earnest in February 2011).[14] These talks are now in their twelfth round, having been stymied by market access issues. The fact that negotiations have dragged on for more than a decade does not signal great priority.[15]

It has certainly taken longer than CAPA anticipated to increase market access for Central American goods, but as shown in table 9.2, trade relations with the region have grown since the 1980s. Even before the FTA was signed with Costa Rica, the largest growth in two-way trade was with that country and Guatemala.[16] This reflects the dynamism of the former and the size and position of the latter – 'on the border with NAFTA,' as noted by Canadian representatives in Guatemala.[17]

As such, secular trends and the negotiation of bilateral trade liberalization agreements led to substantial increases in two-way trade between Canada and the region since the 1980s. Yet the poorest countries in the region have largely been left on the margins of these increases in merchandise trade. Moreover, as noted by the Canadian Council for

International Cooperation, negotiating the FTA with the remaining four Central American countries could undermine equitable development if it is not preceded by a social-impact assessment, if it does not include an enforceable agreement to protect and adjudicate on labour rights, if it extends NAFTA's chapter 11 one-sided protections for investors' rights, and if it does not make concessions on special and differential treatment as requested by Central American governments.[18] Since then an environmental impact assessment on the draft CAFTA accord has been conducted, but lack of follow-up on other issues could indeed undermine peace and development in the region. By March 2010, the first set of trade negotiations since 2004 had been held between Canadian officials and representatives of the Central America four. But much work still remains to be done in late 2012.

Security

With regards to more conventional security issues, the Canadian government provided significant assistance to the United Nations to plan and deploy the UN Observer Group in Central America (ONUCA) in 1989. Canada also provided senior officers to command the overall operation, to underpin some of its critical elements, and, at important moments, to bolster ONUCA throughout its lifespan. When Esquipulas II evolved into national peace processes in the early 1990s, Canada made significant contributions to UN peace support operations in El Salvador (ONUSAL) and Guatemala (MINUGUA). During the 1990s, ONUCA, ONUSAL, and MINUSAL were the main channels for growing Canadian military and police contacts with their counterparts in the region. This was consistent with CAPA's recommendation that Canada not provide security assistance bilaterally to any of the governments.

Important changes have occurred since. Most Central American security forces have gone through significant changes on the basis of the peace accords and related processes of democratic consolidation. In tandem with those changes on the ground, the Canadian Forces have deepened their interaction with senior Central American military personnel through the defence attaché located in Mexico, through annual Conferences of Ministers of Defense of the Americas (CDMA), and other channels. Several Central American governments were quite receptive to Canada's advocacy on 'human security' issues from the mid-1990s onward, since it converged with regional norms codified in the Framework Treaty on Democratic Security and other instruments.

This convergence also brought Canada and several of the region's governments together on the same side of the table in negotiations on major human security priorities such as the Landmines Treaty. Central American and Canadian military personnel also began serving side by side in peace support operations, including the UN Stabilization Mission in Haiti (MINUSTAH).

Against that backdrop, Canada has expanded its training to Central American forces through two main channels. At the Banff CDMA in 2008, it announced that Guatemala and Honduras would become partners in Canada's Military Training Assistance Program (MTAP). Through MTAP, Central American military personnel receive training in staff command and the management of peace operations.[19] The second channel is the Regional Training Command for Peacekeeping Operations (CREOMPAZ) in Guatemala. In 2009, Ottawa made a CAD$250,000 grant to CREOMPAZ to enhance Central American armed forces' capacity to participate in UN peace operations.[20]

The opening of MTAP to Guatemalan and Honduran forces, like the support to CREOMPAZ, also seems consistent with CAPA's views on how Canada should engage with Central American forces. Canada now provides and supports training that should foster the professionalism of those forces and their participation in multilateral peace operations, not in offensive operations against their own or others' citizens. Yet the complexity of civil-military relations in the region (highlighted by the role of the armed forces in the Honduran coup of 2009) and the ambiguity of 'peace operations' in theatres like Afghanistan, remind us that this cooperation should be monitored to ensure that it does not undermine fragile progress on human security in the isthmus or elsewhere.[21]

Beyond Central America

The dilemmas associated with training Central American military personnel reflect wider tensions in Canada–Central American relations since the 1980s. Canada has supported peace implementation, democratization, and human rights in the region. It has augmented and carefully targeted development cooperation. It is also increasing market access. Canadian investment, particularly in resource extraction, has expanded as well. However, Canada has not consistently promoted the structural reforms that CAPA and others advocated aimed at removing the key drivers of conflict in Central America. Some of Canada's initiatives, especially in the realms of trade and security cooperation, could even erode advances made on peacebuilding in recent decades.

These problems certainly reflect larger hemispheric and global tendencies. Four of these are salient to understanding CAPA's long-term influence on Canada's international policies and practices. First, it is important to situate Canada–Central American relations within Canada's wider relations with Latin America and the Caribbean. Ottawa's increasing involvement in Central America's peace processes is one factor that led it to revive relations with middle powers like Mexico and to join the OAS in 1990. As recently noted by a senior Foreign Affairs official:

> Our motivations have not changed greatly since Canada joined the Organization of American States (OAS) in 1990 prompted in large part by changes in the region ... But an even more significant factor was the activism of Canadian civil society and NGOs particularly in Central America, whose message was heard loud and clear at the political level.[22]

Obviously, the priority of economic interests became more pronounced in the 1990s, with NAFTA and the FTAA talks. Diplomatic ties were strengthened with countries like Costa Rica and Chile, while Central America faded into the background in the larger canvas of relations with Latin America and the Caribbean. From our vantage point, Canada's interest in independent initiatives in the region has faded.

Canadian civil society and the interests of activists have changed as well. Initially, the alliance between Canadian, U.S., and Mexican civil society organizations opposed to NAFTA broadened into the Hemispheric Social Alliance (HSA) and opposition to the proposed Free Trade Area of the Americas (FTAA). Instrumental in this and subsequent campaigns is Common Frontiers, an alliance of major trade unions, ecumenical, student, and nationalist groups. Opposition to the FTAA and to the NAFTA itself was taken to the streets around the site of the 2001 Summit of the Americas in Quebec City, in which arguably one of the largest demonstrations on a hemispheric issue in Canadian history involved tens of thousands of unionists, students, and various other civil society representatives.[23] The HSA continued to engage each hemispheric summit and trade ministers' meeting, opposition deepened, and the defeat of the FTAA project was celebrated at the Mar del Plata Summit in 2005. Official initiatives to create a 'NAFTA plus,' as well as the development of an exclusive business-friendly trilateral

Security and Prosperity Partnership (SPP) among the 'three Amigos' has also stimulated a revival of tri-national civil society collaboration. With the Obama administration, the SPP has faded to a series of bilateral initiatives.

On the NGO front, the Americas Policy Group of CCIC continues to monitor and influence Canadian policy towards the region. The APG cites 'rights-based approaches to trade and investment,' including human rights impact assessments of FTAs and public debate based on transparency of negotiating texts. They have thus monitored and intervened regarding the negotiation of the Central America (CA-4) trade and investment agreement. The NGOs also cite the need to support human rights defenders, as well as specific action to ensure a return to democratic governance and rights in post-coup Honduras. In addition, the APG monitors security policy in the Americas, including the influence of the U.S. on Canada, and evaluating the impact of this policy on human rights and democracy.[24] Groups like MiningWatch focus on the extractive sector, on which they provide analysis and advocacy. Ottawa-based FOCAL once provided some space for a more officially oriented policy dialogue. However, in general, and particularly with regard to Central America, the groundswell of activism that characterized the Canada-Central American constituency in the 1980s is largely absent today.[25]

Second, from the 1990s onward, Canada's diplomatic attention was largely drawn away from the hemisphere, to conflict, genocide, and humanitarian urgencies in Africa, the Balkan wars, the focus on terrorism provoked by 11 September 2001, and the resulting invasions of Iraq and Afghanistan. Haiti, of course, has been the major exception to this trend.

While discourse has developed in Canada regarding 'fragile states' and the 'war on terror,' producing some serious thinking in CIDA and among other donors about the reforms required to prevent or reverse state fragility, these analyses have been overshadowed by the tendency of chief executives and foreign ministries to focus on a few 'crisis states,' to channel huge amounts of ODA to those countries, and to ignore donors' lessons about the need for deeper, longer-term reforms to prevent conflict or promote development.[26] Recent governments have allocated the lion's share of ODA increases to Afghanistan, Haiti, and Iraq, dwarfing the combined allocations to Central America.[27] The 'war on terror' has shaped Ottawa's priorities in this regard. Increasing U.S. counter-terrorism assistance to the region's security forces, within the war on terror paradigm, may have more sinister impacts on democratic governance in Central America.[28]

Third, Canada's pursuit of trade and investment agreements, the continuation of the 'Washington Consensus' economic policies, and the increasing predominance of a U.S.-centred security framework have all increased fears that Canada's commitment to human rights and its willingness to combine with progressive, like-minded governments in offsetting superpower intervention has evaporated. The destabilization of the Montreal-based Rights and Democracy international centre and the defunding of KAIROS and other active advocacy women's and development groups weaken the potential for progressive civil society initiatives.

Finally, CAPA's pioneering experiences in government–civil society policy dialogue initially dovetailed nicely with increasing policy engagement efforts embodied in the Foreign Affairs–based Centre for Foreign Policy Development and CIDA's Development Days and other consultative engagements. The Chrétien government initiated a wide-ranging and highly consultative Voluntary Sector Strategy, which developed guidelines for policy dialogue and CSO-government relations across departments. Yet as a major assessment of these relations in the field of peacebuilding concluded in 2002, these exercises are limited by several tendencies: the difficulty of engaging senior officials and broadly representative CSO leaders; the challenge of moving from one-off events to ongoing dialogue, recognized by many stakeholders as essential for policy change; the difficulty of preparing CSO participants to dialogue with officials, who often have access to much more information on the issues under discussion; and the difficulty of linking Canadian policy dialogue to dialogues on the ground in countries of concern.[29] But as of 2001, the Centre for Foreign Policy Development is no more. The Voluntary Sector Strategy has faded into oblivion. And access to government ministers and government MPs has become increasingly more difficult.

The current government's Americas Strategy was developed without the sort of wide-ranging consultative processes which characterized the foreign policy reviews of the 1990s, and has been termed by an experienced NGO advocate 'to be too focused on gaining advantage for Canadian investors in the Americas – also [there is] enormous shock at how human rights/democratic processes are so utterly disregarded in favour of trade and investment agendas.'[30]

CAPA did not reach its ultimate objective of reorienting Canadian policy towards support for a more transformative agenda in Central America, but interest in civil society was revived with the emergence of the so-called 'pink tide' governments in Bolivia, Ecuador, and Venezuela. The vibrant exchanges facilitated by the Hemispheric Social Alliance and sectoral networks like Via Campesina sustained civil society solidarity. It is important to explore what combination of CSO strategies and contextual developments might bring such transformative ideas back onto agendas in official Ottawa.

But this will require a great deal of imagination because Ottawa, post-9/11, has become more concerned about international security and much less about the links between insecurity and social injustice abroad, aligning itself with more conservative governments like that in Colombia. As such, it seems timely to reflect on how one might apply insights from CAPA's efforts in the 1980s to struggles for social justice, in Central America and elsewhere, at the beginning of the new millennium.

Conclusion

If Canada could really promote human rights throughout the isthmus; if Canada could help Central Americans demilitarize their societies and let civilian institutions emerge; if Canada could support democratic steps towards greater social justice; if Canada could privilege the poor in development and show leadership in protecting the environment – these steps would be a fitting tribute to Saint Romero of the Americas, to Ellacu and Elba and Héctor and all their fellow martyrs of Central America. (Michael Czerny, SJ)[31]

The thought that Canada might take up a *transformative* agenda in Central America presupposes the convergence of coherent demands for transformation on the ground and a government in Ottawa with the political will to support such a transformative approach. Though certain Liberal ministers championed human security in the late 1990s, no government has taken a clear, integrated approach to promoting social justice abroad. Instead, the Harper government has promoted liberal democratic institutions, market-oriented economic policies, and social development, while carefully balancing its partnerships with emerging regional powers and its special relationship with Washington.

Yet from a historical standpoint, one can see that CAPA and other civil society initiatives contributed to important changes in Central America. These included profound reforms in Nicaragua, negotiated approaches to peace as well as on-site UN human rights monitoring in El Salvador and Guatemala. This influence reached beyond the isthmus, as noted by a senior diplomat in 2006:

> Unpacking Canada's engagement ... reveals not unexpected preoccupations with the advancement of governance, the rule of law, human rights/human security, and trade liberalization ... These goals can be traced in the keen focus of Canadian NGOs in the 70s and 80s on governance, human rights, and socioeconomic inequities in the Hemisphere, as well as in a history of Canadian Prime Ministers' and Foreign Ministers' contributions to regional peace processes.[32]

CAPA was part of an approach to public participation in foreign policy which was encouraged by the government-supported CIIPS and later by the Centre for Foreign Policy Development. Yet neither body has survived. CAPA was part of a flourishing Canadian civil society which invited, supported, and encouraged the growth of credible interlocutors in the region. Yet this constituency has dwindled. The Jesuit Centre is no more, the Latin American Working Group has ceased operations, and CUSO is less active on Canadian policy engagement. OXFAM remains active in Central America, with radically reduced resources and staff, but ecumenical and denominational church engagement continues. The Canadian Labour Congress (CLC) and other parts of the labour movement retain strong links in the hemisphere. The Americas Policy Group of CCIC has become a focal point for civil society initiatives on social justice in the hemisphere, but CCIC itself has suffered CIDA cuts. Many of the individuals involved in CAPA have gone on to distinguished roles in academe, NGO leadership, and in other fields, where they apply the skills acquired in the 1980s. The approaches pioneered by CAPA are now part of diverse international civil society engagements.

The CAPA experience suggests that policy influence rests on three major factors: the agency of civil society organizations themselves; the willingness of Canadian governments to listen and engage; and the ability of a critical mass of actors on the ground, in this case in Central America, to push for clear alternatives to failed policies.

Although Canadian civil society organizations active in Latin America seem diminished, many remain active and some are adapting to new conditions. Although the actors pushing for transformation in Latin America have become more ideologically diverse, they are converging around a broad consensus on the need for greater equity, sub-stantive democracy, and self-determination. The major missing piece is political change in Canada, perhaps akin to the changes that have taken place in the United States. Given that such changes do not appear on the horizon, civil society organizations will have to be extremely crea-tive with modest resources to put equity-oriented structural reforms back on official government agendas in Canada.

In terms of specific policy recommendations for both politicians and officialdom in Ottawa, a few key areas are worth highlighting.[33] First, the Harper Conservatives should place the promotion of the full spec-trum of human rights at the centre of its policies in Central America. Active support for the work of human rights defenders should be a pillar of this approach. With reference to Honduras, Canada could begin by calling on the authorities to repeal all legislation and execu-tive orders issued by the de facto authorities, investigate all reports of violations (including the killing of journalists), and ensure that all those responsible, including security forces, are duly brought to justice.

In Honduras (the only 'country of concentration' in the isthmus), Canada should continue supporting sector-wide approaches in areas like health and food security, while building the capacity of civil society to strengthen democratic governance. In Guatemala, Canada should renew its engagement by supporting key justice sector instruments like the International Commission Against Impunity. It should also com-plement its support for rural development projects with support for broader fiscal and other reforms required to address the dramatic struc-tural inequities in today's Honduras.

On the trade front, Canada should impose a moratorium on negotia-tion and ratification of NAFTA-style bilateral agreements including the proposed Canada-CA4 agreement. In fact, it should negotiate any fur-ther agreements in a transparent, democratic manner based on interna-tional human rights standards, with fixed time periods for review and independent human rights impact assessments. Furthermore, Ottawa should implement the recommendation of the Standing Committee on International Trade that all draft texts and Canadian negotiating pro-posals should be disclosed to the public.

Similarly, the Harper government should regularly report to Parlia-ment on its military training and other forms of security cooperation with Central American governments. Ottawa should avoid any secu-rity cooperation that could reverse the fragile advance of civilian con-trol over the long-entrenched power of the military and police forces in the isthmus. Lastly, given the limited resources that Canadian NGOs have for policy analysis and advocacy on Central America, CCIC's Americas Policy Working Group should creatively engage academics, interested think tanks, and parliamentarians from all sides of the House to expand awareness and influence on Central American policy issues.

CAPA demonstrated where the heady combination of academic skills, youthful enthusiasm, commitment to social justice, and the exciting sense of forging new trails and relationships can lead. Meeting almost every Tuesday night for five years builds effective working relationships and deep mutual understandings. It was a lively and productive model of engagement. The times in which we find ourselves today require – and we hope inspire – many more such initiatives.

NOTES

1 Victor Thomas-Bulmer, *The Political Economy of Central America Since 1920* (Cambridge: Cambridge University Press, 1987); Tom Barry, *Roots of Rebellion: Land and Hunger in Central America* (Boston: South End Press, 1987); Jack Child, *Conflict in Central America: Approaches to Peace and Security* (London: C. Hurst Publishers, 1986).
2 Peter McFarlane, *Northern Shadows: Canadians in Central America* (Toronto: Between the Lines, 1989) and James Rochlin, *Discovering the Americas: The Evolution of Canadian Foreign Policy Towards Latin America* (Vancouver: UBC Press, 1994).
3 An earlier draft of this paper was presented at the Annual Congress of the Canadian Political Science Association at York University in Toronto, Canada, on 3 June 2006.
4 See for example John Saul, *Revolutionary Traveller: Freeze Frames from a Life* (Winnipeg: Arbeiter Ring Publishing, 2009).
5 Liisa North, with CAPA, *Between War and Peace in Central America: Choices for Canada* (Toronto: Between the Lines, 1990), 244.
6 Geoffrey Pearson, 'Foreword,' in North, *Between War and Peace in Central America*, 12.
7 Michael Czerny, S.J., 'Afterword,' in North, *Between War and Peace in Central America*, 262.
8 North, *Between War and Peace in Central America*, 250.
9 It is worth noting that both Canada and Honduras have now embarked on negotiations to conclude a bilateral free trade agreement. Government of

Canada, 'Canada Pursuing Free Trade Agreement with Honduras,' news release (Ottawa: Department of Foreign Affairs and International Trade, 11 February 2011).

10 Government of Canada, *Honduras* (Gatineau: Canadian International Development Agency, February 2012), http://www.acdi-cida.gc.ca/acdi-cida/ACDI-CIDA.nsf/eng/JUD-129123554-NN3.

11 Government of Canada, 'Minister of State Kent visit to Central America—January 13-16, 2009,' news release (Ottawa: Department of Foreign Affairs and International Trade, January 2009).

12 North, *Between War and Peace in Central America*, 127. From 1999 to 2002, one of the authors worked for IDRC, funding research by Guatemalan institutes that fed directly into policy processes on agrarian reform, tax reform, and security sector reform – all rooted in the peace accords. The Canadian Embassy in Guatemala recognized the strategic importance of IDRC support for these processes, yet CIDA was unable to co-fund any of these initiatives or support follow-up efforts.

13 This agreement has been updated and modernized in 2010 with an eye toward lowering tariffs, expanding market access, and removing trade barriers in a host of economic sectors. Government of Canada, 'Canada and Costa Rica Set to Enhance Free Trade Agreement,' news release (Ottawa: Department of Foreign Affairs and International Trade, 28 August 2010).

14 Government of Canada, 'Update and Canada-Central America Four Trade Agreement Negotiations,' news release (Ottawa: Department of International Trade, 2006), and Government of Canada, 'Canada-Costa Rica Free Trade Agreement Enters Into Force,' news release (Ottawa: Department of Foreign Affairs and International Trade, 2002).

15 Government of Canada, 'Canada-Central America Four (CA4) Free Trade Agreement Negotiations,' news release (Ottawa: Department of Foreign Affairs and International Trade, June 2011). By late 2011, these negotiations, which have been ongoing for some nine years, have hit a rough patch – spurring the bilateral track that Canada has now adopted with Honduras.

16 Canadian foreign investment in the region is focused mostly on Nicaragua's mining sector, which reached almost $970 million in 2011. See Nicolas Johnson, 'Nicaragua Holds Out New Promise for Foreign Investors,' *Globe and Mail*, 5 April 2012, B9.

17 Background briefing with Canadian officials in Guatemala, 6 October 2005.

18 'Canada in Guatemala: An Agenda for Justice and Peace. A Statement by the Americas Policy Group of CCIC,' briefing note (Ottawa: Canadian Council for International Cooperation, 2005), 1–6.

19 MTAP fosters the interoperability of Canadian and partner forces for peace

operations and promotes Canadian values such as democratic control over the armed forces, the rule of law, and respect for human rights. See Government of Canada, *Directorate of Military Training Assistance Programme: 2008–2009 Report* (Ottawa: Department of National Defence, 2009).

20 'Canada Contributes to Training in Peacekeeping Operations,' news release (Ottawa: Government of Canada, August 2009). For more information on CREOMPAZ, see: http://www.mindef.mil.gt/ftierra/cespeciales/entrenamiento/historia_eng.html.

21 On the ambiguities of international engagement in 'fragile states' since 9/11, see Stephen Baranyi (ed.), *The Paradoxes of Peacebuilding Post-9/11* (Vancouver: UBC Press, 2008).

22 Peter Boehm, 'Notes for an Address by Peter M. Boehm, Assistant Deputy Minister, North America, Department of Foreign Affairs and International Trade, at the FOCAL/CIIA Conference, Where Can Canada Really Make a Difference?' (Ottawa: Department of Foreign Affairs and International Trade, 2006), 4.

23 Some police estimates put the number of demonstrators at the Quebec City Summit of the Americas at over 25,000. See Mark MacKinnon, 'Breaking the Barriers,' *Globe and Mail*, 23 April 2001, A10–11.

24 Fiona Meyer Cook, memo to authors, December 2009.

25 Several participants at the FOCAL-CIIA seminar noted that few NGOs were at the table. Former foreign minister Joe Clark suggested that politicians and officials had also failed to nurture a constituency in the post-1990 period.

Several factors help to explain this decline in activism since the 1980s: structural change in the demography of groups (the decline in ecumenical capacity, the end of ICCHRLA and the Jesuit Centre, and the endangering of a much-reduced KAIROS) and a change in activism (still oriented to Central America) as groups focus primarily on investment/resource extraction (MiningWatch, Common Frontiers, and others concerned with Honduras, Guatemala, and Salvador) and trade (APG, unions, etc). One could also add a short list of other explanatory variables: a decrease in the drama of revolution/counter-revolution and repression/resistance on the ground and in the U.S.; the broadening of Canadian governmental and civil society engagement in other parts of Latin America (particularly Mexico and Colombia); the emergence of new causes célèbres in Africa, the Balkans, and Afghanistan; decreased CIDA funding for development education; and less governmental openness to, and support for, dialogue with civil society organizations on contentious international policy issues, particularly in recent years.

26 See Martin Doorbos, Susan Woodward, and Silvia Roque, *Failing States or Failed States? The Role of Development Models: Collected Works*, working paper (Madrid: Fundacion para la Relaciones Internacionales y el Dialogo Exterior, 2006), 1–20.
27 For more analysis of these trends in Canada, see Baranyi, *The Paradoxes of Peacebuilding*.
28 For a detailed analysis of U.S. security cooperation with Latin American forces, see Lisa Haugaard et al., *Erasing the Lines: Trends in U.S. Military Programs with Latin America* (Washington, DC: Washington Office on Latin America, 2005).
29 See Paul H. Chapin and John W. Foster, 'Peacebuilding Policy: Consultations and Dialogues: A Study of the Canadian Experience,' *Canadian Foreign Policy*, 9, no.1 (Fall 2001): 103–42.
30 Fiona Meyer Cook, memo to authors, 2009.
31 Czerny, 'Afterword,' in North, *Between War and Peace in Central America*, 262.
32 Boehm, 'Notes for an Address,' 8.
33 In 2009, the Americas Policy Group of the Canadian Council for International Cooperation (CCIC) tabled a comprehensive series of recommendations for Canadian policy in the Americas. Our recommendations are informed by this document, by other CCIC briefs, as well as by the analysis in this chapter. See especially CCIC, *What Role for Canada in the Americas?* (Ottawa: Canadian Council for International Cooperation, 15 April 2009), 1–12, and *Honduras: Democracy Denied: A Report from the CCIC's Americas Policy Group with Recommendations to the Government of Canada* (Ottawa: Canadian Council for International Cooperation, April 2010), 1–28.

10 Canada and Colombia: A Rhetorical Relationship?

MARIA TERESA AYA SMITMANS

Although Canada's foreign policy is, in part, built upon international cooperation and respect for human rights, from the Colombian perspective, these Canadian pillars ring more as hollow words than as solid commitments. The purpose of this chapter is to focus on Canadian foreign policy initiatives in Colombia: including its cooperation activities and its foreign aid, both its economic/trade and social/human rights initiatives. Additionally, it is important to situate these issue areas within an analytical framework that takes into account historic and current developments. One of the key questions is: how has Canada addressed the central problem affecting Colombia – namely, its violent internal conflict?

Another important question has to do with the trade agreement signed between Colombia and Canada in November 2008 (which finally came into force on 15 August 2011). The ratification of this agreement became a cornerstone of the relationship between the two countries, especially for Colombia, which saw in the agreement not only the Canadian recognition of former president Álvaro Uribe's effort to position the country as an important investment destination but also as a sign of respect towards the country.[1] However, policy makers in Ottawa did not seem as interested in ratifying the commercial agreement, and this led Colombian officials to perceive them as mostly talkers 'without serious and sustained commitment.'[2] It also makes Canada's Colombia policy vulnerable to criticism from those who want to believe in a liberal foreign policy and see only empty words coming out of Canada.

Canada's traditional idea of liberalism involves democratic values and human rights as a staple of its foreign policy focus. In addition, Canadian liberalism believes in the importance of multilateralism as the way to solve global conflicts and to promote international peace and security as opposed to the idea of bilateral talks and agreements – an idea sponsored by the U.S. in the region. (A Washington-sponsored approach is seen as an imposition most of the time by Latin American countries.) Nevertheless, it is an idea that should have given the Canadians a natural advantage in their relationship with Colombia, but it did not, for Canadians have been, once again, hesitant to get involved in the solution of the country's internal conflict outside the realm of multilateral initiatives, which are seen by many Colombians as futile and short-lived.

From a Colombian perspective, Canada's strict emphasis on multilateralism is not its only shortcoming in its approach to the region. The 'northern country' is also seen as being caught between the notion of human security as an international ideal and the idea of a classical realpolitik-type security. The latter has become important in the international arena not only because of the 11 September 2001 attacks but also because it is the one which Prime Minister Stephen Harper most subscribes to. In addition, Canada is also perceived as a country caught in the middle between the U.S. government's pragmatic vision of the world and its own much more liberal vision and, as such, as a country that hesitates to act forcefully, especially when it comes to Latin America, which is viewed as Washington's own backyard. This hesitation, though, manifests itself in actions (or non-actions) that can seem confusing and even perplexing to Colombians.

Furthermore, it can be argued that the Colombian-Canadian relationship offers a divided view of the Canadian approach to the region. That is, it has elements that are associated with human security and, at the same time, aspects that are consistent with more traditional security issues. Put another way, Canada has exhibited elements associated with previous Liberal governments and components that are important to the current governing Conservatives, who have been in power since early 2006. Consequently, it is a complex relationship and, as a result, given to frequent misunderstandings. This fact can be seen, for example, in the efforts to combat the scourge of drug trafficking, where issues such as minorities at risk appear simultaneously with matters such as border control. Likewise, trade issues involve both these kinds of security concerns for they encompass minorities' human rights questions while discussing economic and political rights. As Stephen Randall points out: 'Traditional and non-traditional threats to national security tend to overlap' in Colombia.[3]

Historical Background

Even though Canada gained autonomy in its foreign relations in 1931, under the Statute of Westminster, it was not until 1953 that Ottawa established formal diplomatic relations with Colombia. Before 1953, the bilateral relationship was limited and based solely on trade and investment issues. However, after the Second World War, both Canada and Colombia became members of the San Francisco Charter, the first step in the formal creation of the United Nations, a fact that brought them closer together. Colombia admired Canada's commitment to the creation of the organization as well as its idealism, while 'Canadians regarded Colombia as one of the most democratic and enlightened of the South American Republics.'[4]

Colombia's Eduardo Zuleta Angel became the first president of the First Commission that set the stage for the first UN General Assembly and, as such, met Canadian diplomat L.D. Wilgress, with whom he worked closely on the 1946 London preparatory meetings for that first assembly. Ambassador Zuleta was so impressed with the Canadian representation that when he became foreign minister in 1948, he organized the first official visit by a Colombian diplomat to Canada in 1949.[5] He met with Lester B. Pearson, then Canada's external affairs minister, which put in place the cornerstone for the establishment of formal diplomatic relations.

During the 1950s, the Canadian presence in Colombia increased because of the involvement of Halifax-native Lauchlin Currie.[6] His economic mission was designed to promote development through the study of rural versus urban alternatives. Furthermore, during the Korean War, both Canada and Colombia participated with troops in an effort to support UN participation. In regards to trade, the exchange of goods between both countries rose from $33 million annually in the 1930s to close to $600 million by 1952.[7] As such, ties between the two countries were important enough to warrant the formal establishment of diplomatic relations in 1953.[8]

During this period, both Canada and Colombia shared a view of the world that included democracy, free trade, and a strong belief in international law and multilateral organizations.[9] They also shared an ambivalent and complicated relationship with the U.S. For both countries, the U.S. represented an important force and influence over its foreign policies – a force that Canada has tried to overcome by leaning towards multilateralism. Colombia, in striking contrast, responded by mostly aligning itself with Washington in its foreign policy decision-making process.

Canada's effort to separate itself from the U.S. in the foreign policy arena led, in part, to their postponing the decision on whether to join the Organization of American States (OAS), an organization it viewed as a peon of Washington's interests in the hemisphere. In Colombia, this paved the way for Canada to be perceived as aloof, remote, and not particularly interested in the region. At the same time, Colombia's interests became increasingly more and more fused with those of Washington's.

This divergence in its interests was a constant fact during the following decades and helps explain, for example, why during the late nineties, when Plan Colombia came into effect in Colombia, Ottawa objected to its military characteristics and decided to support instead a peace process with the guerrillas. Moreover, Canada's trust and belief in civil society and in NGOs as a driving force of politics have also led to a distancing with Colombia, a country where governments distrust NGOs and where civil society and government are seen as rivals.

It is instructive, then, to note that Canada and Colombia began a formal diplomatic relationship in 1953, when, as Adam Chapnick suggests, Canadians were forced 'to abandon their ambivalence toward the world outside of North America ... [reinventing] themselves as concerned and responsible global citizens.'[10] Furthermore, it needs to be noted that the formal establishment of the bilateral relationship took place between 1947 and 1957, a period that Canadians call their first internationalization. This phase is remembered as a time when Canadians actively participated in international institutions and promoted Canada as a country active in global affairs. Moreover, during this time most of Canada's foreign and national security policies could be defended in terms that would satisfy not only the advocates of narrow national interests but also those who believed in Canada's altruistic foreign interests.[11]

This fact has changed under the current Conservative government and it is one of the many problems faced by Prime Minister Harper – namely, that his national security proposals do not always match the views of those who believe Canada should advance more altruistic interests in the world. For Harper, trying to match the long-standing domestic ideals of Canada to his view and the needs of the international system has become a difficult task, and one that threatens the electoral constituency that brought him to power. For the Canadian prime minister, 'no nation [should adopt] a foreign policy from altruistic motives alone,"[12] yet Canada seems entrenched in internationalizing its own altruism despite Harper's own limited view of the world.

Canada's altruism, though, is seen from Colombia as a crusade that seeks to impose its own agenda and liberal point of view of the international system. This altruism explains why throughout the years Canada has been involved in finding ways to end the conflict in Colombia through negotiations and peace initiatives as opposed to military cooperation. Such an idea works fine for a country that last experienced war in its territory in 1812, but what about a country like Colombia where violence has been a daily affair for the last two centuries?[13] As some argue, Colombians have lost the capacity to be astonished by violence and, from the security point of view, have become selfish, interested only in their own well-being. Being at war for so many years has eroded their social foundations. And this is a critical fact that is misunderstood by most Canadians, who largely perceive life as having no value in Colombia.

Pacifism is also seen in Colombia as a staple of Canadian foreign policy. Consequently, it can be argued that Colombians view Canada as a utopian state that still lives under the parameters of idealism and that embraces its different characteristics. Canadians believe in disarmament as a way to decrease violence, a fact that can be seen in the promotion of the Ottawa Convention (on anti-personnel landmines) and the Small Arms treaties. Colombians, on the other hand, think of disarmament as futile; for when violence is endemic, anything can be used as a weapon: gas canisters used to attack police stations and villages; plain, old-fashioned TNT used to bomb the oil pipeline and thus interrupt the flow of oil and create havoc; and, finally, empty canisters filled with excrement and used as biological weapons.[14]

Nevertheless, Colombia respects Canada's position and struggles to make peace with it. As such, they have ratified the Ottawa Convention, although they do not think that to ratify it means eradicating all landmines but simply working towards that overarching goal. Colombia also participates in the UN Disarmament Committee, while continuing to heavily arm its military. This is one of the many examples where the dichotomy that permeates the bilateral relationship between the two countries can be seen most vividly.

Canada believes in an open agenda as a way to promote trust between parties in conflict. From the Colombian perspective, military strategy in combat situations calls for surprise as one of its most important tactics. In addition, Canada has faith in a supranational system to secure international peace and world order. But a country like Colombia still thinks of sovereignty as a Westphalian concept, where domestic affairs are not to be questioned by anyone, including supranational entities. The 'intermesticity' implied by Canada's support of various UN interventions in the last ten years is something that Colombia disapproves of, because it sees this as setting the stage for outside interference. In Colombia, human rights are perceived as a strictly domestic affair, and, to that extent, humanitarian/rights recommendations are seen as a tool or pretext for intervention. Furthermore, in Colombia, people have learned to 'accept that security has a necessary cost in terms of freedom [that it] seems reasonable to accept all sorts of limitations on civil liberties [and that] making the citizen less free means making the policeman and government ... freer and less accountable'[15] – an idea that clashes with Canada's liberal ideals.

Canada's actions in Colombia also include programs designed to combat poverty through 'the alleviation of poverty, advancing human rights, improving the condition of women, children, and youth, strengthening justice systems,'[16] as well as establishing educational and basic infrastructure development programs. This approach to Colombia's problems differs strikingly from that of its neighbour, and yet while it is very much appreciated by all in Colombia it is also dismissed as secondary in importance. To be sure, a short-term approach to solving the internal struggles that is favoured by Colombians clashes sharply with Canada's all-encompassing, long-term strategy of cooperation and reconciliation, which is something that in Colombia is perceived as a dangerous and naive approach to the realities of intra-state war.

It is viewed as ineffective because it essentially leaves the door open for the insurgents to continue with their deadly attacks. And it is naive because it is based on the needs of people (i.e., the guerrillas) who do not understand peace and other Colombians who have not experienced tranquillity on their land for close to two centuries. When faced with daily threats to their survival, Colombians do not understand cooperation in developmental matters as something that solves their immediate security needs. The very notion that this assistance will somehow help in planting the seeds for a non-violent country in the future is something that most Colombians do not have the time to think about, let alone understand, for much of their time is spent on daily survival. As such, it can be said that Canadian objectives do not match up well with the Colombian reality on the ground – although they are theoretically understood as part of a real solution to the country's internal violence. Again, there is an obvious dichotomy in the bilateral relationship.

Still, it is important to note that since Stephen Harper became prime minister, the Canadian discourse has noticeably changed. This shift in foreign policy was welcomed by Colombia and especially by President Uribe, who shared with Harper a conservative-minded view of the world. Yet, the domestic division in Canada, a federal Parliament of three opposition political parties, and a minority government situation for the governing Conservatives converted the prime minister's speeches regarding Colombia into largely rhetorical discourses. (Whether this changes with Harper's majority government remains to be seen.) And this fact only reinforces the view in Bogotá of Canada as an ambivalent bilateral partner that preaches one thing and does something entirely different.

To Canadians, at least according to a 1995 government report, 'Colombia [still] represents [one of] the most significant challenge[s] in the hemisphere to such Canadian values as human rights and good governance.'[17] Even today, it is a challenge that can be seen in the fact that in 2009, 26,011 Colombians died a violent death out of a population of 45 million, which means there are 57 deaths per 100,000 inhabitants. In Canada, 730 people died violently in 2005 in a population of 32.2 million, or 2.2 violent deaths per 100,000 inhabitants – 26 times less than in Colombia.[18] For a non-violent country like Canada, these startling numbers are an outrage, as it can be argued that anything above 1,000 sounds like continuous massacres. How to resolve this internal crisis is a question that lies at the heart of a sometimes misunderstood bilateral relationship.[19]

The Colombian Conflict and Canada

Canada has traditionally viewed the Colombian conflict as an internal problem for Colombia and, until recently, interpreted it as the result of mostly social and economic injustices in the country.[20] However, after 9/11 and especially after the election of Prime Minister Harper in 2006, the Canadian government has become far more willing to accept the conflict not only as a political one, but as a phenomenon that is permeated by drug trafficking, unorthodox violence, and terrorism. This change in perspective has been confusing and perplexing for Colombians. For while Canada accepts the fact that the conflict is no longer the idealistic guerrilla war of the seventies, officials in Ottawa still rely on human rights issues and reconciliation strategies as the main pillars on which to base a solution to Colombia's internal troubles.

For instance, Canada was involved in the Mesa de Amigos, a group that began in the 1990s to find a negotiated solution to the conflict. Likewise, it was a member of the Group of 24 (G24) [21] donor countries as Chair of the G24 from January to June, 2005, where it helped to manage international participation in the International Coordination and Cooperation agenda for Colombia.[22] This was a policy agenda, moreover, that stressed cooperation and the strengthening of democracy and basic human needs as a way to solve the conflict rather than strictly military assistance.

Canadian involvement here was consistent with a previous human security policy agenda endorsed by Ottawa (especially under the Jean Chrétien Liberals), which included such measures as protection of civilians and human rights; preventing the use of children in armed conflict; conflict deterrence; rule of law and accountability; and public safety.[23] In the case of Colombia, the protection of civilians can be seen in the strengthening of women's rights through education and technical cooperation. Canada has also been active for many years in dealing with the problem posed by the internally displaced – namely, through the establishment of centres designed to work towards the reintegration of these displaced people. As such, Canada's most important participation in Colombia is through cooperation initiatives funded by the Canadian International Development Agency (CIDA) and managed mostly by NGOs operating in Colombia.[24]

As for children and armed conflict, Canada has been active in funding the operations that prevent the recruiting of minors by the terrorist/guerrilla organizations FARC and ELN.[25] Ottawa supported those Colombian state policies geared towards putting a stop to the use of minors as combatants and to the reinsertion of those minors who left the terrorist groups after being captured. It also funded private initiatives sponsored by NGOs, such as Save the Children, that protect minors in combat zones and in areas infiltrated by guerrillas who are trying to recruit minors. It is important to note that Canada prefers to fund private NGO initiatives as opposed to the specific proposals put forward by the Colombian government itself.[26] Indeed, this fact makes the Colombian government suspicious of Canadian help and also creates distrust with the Colombians – who would prefer that Canada fund more government-sanctioned initiatives.

Canada's policy regarding minors and the armed conflict is just one of the many ways in which Ottawa has been involved in the Colombian conflict. For the past twenty years or so, Canada has been a friendly participant in the Colombian peace process.[27] But it has been an inconsistent participant, responding to the Colombian political environment and not necessarily to the needs of the Colombian people.[28]As Stephen Randall and Jillian Dowding explain: 'Canadian policy has consistently, albeit to varying degrees of commitment, concentrated on negotiated settlements of conflict ...'[29] Still, Canada's participation in activities that promote peace in Colombia have been somewhat diminished recently due to the fact that former president Uribe did not believe in a negotiated solution to the conflict. Nevertheless, he made important advances in strengthening the rule of law throughout Colombia's territory. However, there are still unanswered questions in matters such as the demobilization of thousands of paramilitary forces and the involvement of congressmen in these unsavoury movements. A number of elected officials, most of them members of the former president's own party (LA U), have been arrested in recent years because of their links to paramilitary funding, a fact that undermines both the credibility and accountability of the government. While Canada has observed the rupture in the Colombian social fabric, it has kept a mostly guarded distance in accordance with its preference for a modest diplomatic profile in the country. From the Colombian perspective, though, Canada has acted not so much as a diplomatic observer but as a distant ally. This in spite of Prime Minister Harper's assurances of friendship and his flattering remarks about 'President Uribe's commitment to resolving the decades-old civil strife, and his successes in demobilizing thousands of paramilitary combatants whose violations of human rights have placed such an indelible stain on the Colombian record.'[30]

This detached attitude has also permeated the way Canada understands Colombia's public safety problem – that is, as a deadly internal problem that includes terrorism and drug trafficking. In 2003 the Canadian government labelled both FARC and ELN terrorist organizations, a determination that proved to be a major turning point in the relationship between the two countries. Since that time, former President Uribe recognized Canada as a true partner and friend of Colombia as opposed to the previous Canadian governments that he encountered during his term in office.[31] Nevertheless, questions still remain as to whether or not Canada views the conflict as the result of socio-economic injustices or of terrorist activities. Furthermore, Canada insists on talking about the social drivers of internal violence/conflict, whereas President Uribe stated that Colombia is a country that faces internal terrorism problems and a counterinsurgency struggle.

As for the intractable problem with drug traffickers, Canada believes that 'coordinated international action is the only effective way to restrain the trade'[32] in illicit substances, while the Colombian government insists that bilateral cooperation and military action are required to curtail the trafficking in drugs. Nevertheless, and largely because of Prime Minister Harper, Ottawa has been shifting its attention to areas such as the financial relationship between insurgent groups and the drug trade. For this reason, Canada has increased its military presence in the Miami-based U.S. Southern Command (SOUTHCOM), and 'Canadian authorities in Ottawa as well as Bogotá in recent years have also been working in a number of other security areas, including aviation and maritime security, which pertain as much to the counter-narcotics agenda as to threats of terrorism.'[33]

While these moves by Ottawa constitute an integral part of the strategy towards the wider region, they are still associated more with U.S. interests than with strictly Canadian policy objectives:

The high profile and controversial military role played by the United States under Plan Colombia, which began as a counter-narcotics initiative and evolved after 9/11 into one that combines counter-narcotics with counter-insurgency, would in itself make Canadian involvement politically non-viable domestically, even were such a military contribution acceptable to the Colombians.[34]

Consequently, the Canadian government faces significant domestic political problems whenever it contemplates a shift in tactics regarding drug trafficking. Nevertheless, this apparent shift in attitude by the governing Conservatives is confusing for those in the South, who have almost always believed that Canada was substantially different from the U.S. To others, though, the Harper government's approach to the Americas is 'more focused, practical and articulate than the public position of previous Canadian governments on Latin American relations and Colombia specifically,'[35] a shift more in accordance with the so-called 'war on terror' and with the shift in the global security paradigm led by Washington. But it is a shift, nonetheless, that Colombia views as more the result of Canada's quest for balance after a few turbulent years in its relationship with the U.S. rather than the result of some renewed interest in South America, long-term 're-engagement'[36] in the region, or a desire to help the Colombian people.

This shift in attitude was initially undermined by the fact that Prime

Minister Harper faced a tenuous minority in Parliament (altered substantially by his majority win in May 2011), one that could unravel politically at any given moment. Therefore, it can be argued that the change in Canada's strategy is rhetorical rather than practical. Although such a shift may in fact contribute to Canada's standing throughout the Americas, it only reinforces the ambiguity of Canadian foreign policy in the eyes of Colombian officials. Canada presents itself as a humanitarian partner for Colombia, but evidence of this is difficult to detect. In 2003, France actually became the speaker for humanitarian concerns in Colombia, but that engagement waned a few years later, triggered in part by the 2008 rescue from FARC guerrillas of high-profile politician Ingrid Betancur (who held French citizenship), leaving no friendly country to champion these important concerns. The Canadian government has certainly not moved in to fill that gap.

Prime Minister Harper's Visits to Colombia

On a one-day visit to Colombia in mid-August 2011, marking his second visit to the South American country in four years (with a third taking place during the April 2012 Summit of the Americas in Cartagena, Colombia), Prime Minister Stephen Harper met with senior Colombian officials in Bogotá – including President Juan Manuel Santos.[37] Besides celebrating the entry into force of the Canada-Colombia FTA, the Canadian government announced increased development assistance for Colombian children and at-risk youth and the promotion of human rights in the country, and indicated Colombia's accession to Canada's Military Training and Cooperation Program (2011–14).[38] Harper mostly defended the trade agreement with Colombia – even characterizing opponents (who single out the country's poor treatment of union officials and rights violations by paramilitary forces) of the deal as protectionists in disguise. (Interestingly, just days before Harper's visit, suspected FARC guerrillas attacked a small Canadian oil company, Alange Energy, setting fire to one of its oil reservoirs that contained 1,000 barrels of oil.)[39] 'No good purpose is served in this country or in the United States by anybody who is standing in the way of the development of the prosperity of Colombia,' Harper said. 'We can't sit around; we can't block progress of a country like this for protectionist reasons and try to use human rights as a front for doing that.'[40]

Harper's visit to Colombia in July 2007 was actually the first time that a Canadian prime minister had visited the country. The official visit came as a result of Ottawa's renewed interest in Latin America; however, it was also the result of pragmatic interests in the region and in Colombia itself. For instance, it was important to launch bilateral trade negotiations and to support President Uribe, a president whose conservative ideals were close to Harper's (as were their views of the world), to add their support for the ongoing conflict in Afghanistan, and to confirm their understanding of the United States as an important hemispheric partner. Consequently, the meeting was significant because it was the first by a top Canadian leader held in Colombia. But it was not as significant as it could have been since topics such as democracy, corporate social responsibility, and human rights were secondary to the overall visit.[41]

Trade

Two-way trade, on the other hand, has continued to grow since 1953. Colombia signed its first trade agreement with the Canadian government in 1968, following the visit of Jean Luc Pépin, minister of trade and industry. By 1980, bilateral trade had increased by almost 90 per cent – with coffee being an important product in the bilateral exchange. In 1995, after Colombian president César Gaviria (1990–4) called for an 'aperture' or lessening of the trade restrictions in the country, Colombia positioned itself as an attractive partner for Canada in Latin America, where trade between the two countries approached $280 million.[42] Commercial exchange continued to increase, with free trade becoming the pillar of both countries' exports and imports, so that trade between Canada and Colombia totalled more than $1.3 billion by 2008.[43]

Similarly, the financial relationship between the two countries grew as Canadian investments in Colombia increased to roughly $740 million in 2007,[44] especially in the mining, oil, and telecommunications sectors (where more than seventy Canadian companies operate). Furthermore, in 2009, Pacific Rubiales Energy, a Canadian-owned company, became the first international company to be listed in the Colombian Stock Exchange. As one of the largest independent oil and gas exploration and production companies in Colombia, it has substantial operations in the country's Piriri oil fields and has identified lucrative growth opportunities within the Eastern Llanos Basin.

While political and security issues have tended to dominate the bilateral relationship, trade and investment considerations are now taking on greater policy significance.[45] (Two-way trade between Canada and

Colombia reached $1.4 billion in 2009–10, with literally hundreds of Canadian businesses operating in the country.) To be sure, Canada's then minister of international trade, David Emerson, announced the launch of free trade negotiations between Canada and Colombia (as well as Peru) in early June 2007.[46] This was done after Colombia had made several requests to the Canadian government in order to start bilateral negotiations geared towards a comprehensive free trade agreement. In the beginning, Canada wanted to negotiate with the Andean countries as a whole, but changes in the internal politics (i.e., a leftward tilt as part of the so-called 'Pink Tide' in the Americas) of both Bolivia and Ecuador, and the fact that neither Peru nor Colombia shared the same economic and labour conditions, prompted Canada to consider a pact with each country individually. In addition, it was not until Stephen Harper came to power that the decision to launch the negotiations with Colombia was given added impetus, a fact that can be attributed to the closeness in personal relations and philosophical outlook between former President Uribe and Prime Minister Harper.

To Prime Minister Harper, the free trade agreement with Colombia is 'in Canada's own strategic trade interests … Colombia needs its democratic friends to lean forward and give them a chance at partnership and trade with North America.'[47] This key statement underlies not only Harper's willingness to negotiate with Colombia, but also Canada's desire to balance off its hemispheric relations in light of historic U.S. dominance. Stated differently, if Washington refused to ratify a free trade agreement with Colombia (doing so in mid-2012), as the Democratic Party–controlled Congress that came to power in 2006 has indicated, then Canada could provide a viable alternative to the United States. As a result, it was in both Canada's and the governing Harper Conservatives' interest to finally give in to Colombia's request for formal bilateral negotiations on free trade.

Even after Prime Minister Harper signed a trade agreement with Colombia in November 2008, the treaty needed to go through Parliament for ratification, and the opposition parties (especially the federal Liberal Party) were not initially willing to ratify it on human rights grounds (the Liberals would later back away from this position and eventually support the trade pact). In fact, while preaching the pragmatic good behind the free trade agreement, Harper decided in early 2009 to remove the treaty from Parliament's agenda (via his prorogation request in late December) so as not to compromise further his minority government situation. But as 2010 came to a close, the trade pact was finally approved – in large part because the Liberals (and not the NDP) and governing Conservatives agreed to an amendment to have Colombia and Canada jointly produce annual reports on the human rights implications of the deal for the two countries.[48] From the Colombian perspective, the years of open waffling only exemplified the double standard that underscored Canadian policies towards Colombia, policies that talk about lofty support for Colombian institutions and insist that peace stems from social and economic justice and opportunities but then, in the crunch, seem to come up short in terms of tangible socio-economic results.

Importance of Free Trade to Colombia

To President Uribe, the signing of a free trade agreement with Canada was also important in order to show the United States that other countries, more specifically a NAFTA country, were willing to negotiate and sign trade pacts with Colombia. The free trade agreement between Colombia and the United States had been at the top of former President Uribe's agenda since the moment he took office in 2002. Negotiations were initiated in May 2004 and ratified by the Colombian Congress in September 2007; nevertheless, it has not been ratified by the U.S. Congress (held up by concerns over human rights violations and the targeted killings of prominent trade union leaders). Moreover, the administration of Barack Obama (and the Democratic Party in general), does not view the trade deal as important as it was under the previous Bush administration. As a result, the treaty has encountered many obstacles to its ratification in Washington (right up to its actual implementation in May 2012), mainly because of human rights concerns and labour issues.

Consequently, and because the U.S. trade agreement became a personal matter and a veritable crusade for President Uribe, Colombia had developed a strategy by which negotiating alternate free trade agreements with others would highlight for the U.S. its own error in not ratifying the Colombian agreement.[49] Among the alternatives, Canada was the most important one for it is the number-one trade partner of the United States. Therefore, signing a treaty with Canada would, in the eyes of Uribe, send a message to Washington: a message that he believed would prompt the U.S. to review its ratification objections. As such, signing the free trade agreement with Canada became instrumental for Uribe, his foreign policy goals, and his relationship with the United States. For the Colombians, the short-term fate of their relations with Canada were very much tied to the passage of that trade deal.

CIDA in Colombia

The Canadian International Development Agency (CIDA) has been active in Colombia since 1972 and has invested close to $355 million in aid funds in the country.[50] Canadian cooperation has been oriented towards humanitarian projects, especially those designed to empower minorities and victims of internal violence. Among these, children and minors in the war are a key Canadian priority. Since 1998, when Canada got involved in the peace process launched by President Andres Pastrana (1998–2002), CIDA's contribution to the country's development programs increased from an average of $2.5 million per year to over $20 million in 2009–10 (as Colombia became a 'country of focus' for CIDA disbursement funds).[51] In light of the peace negotiations, and the endemic violence in the country, CIDA's awareness and involvement have increased accordingly. Canada is currently Colombia's third-largest donor after the European Union (EU) and USAID.[52]

Policy Recommendations for Canada-Colombia Relations

To secure more substantive policy outcomes from the Canada-Colombia relationship, it may be worth considering the following policy suggestions. To begin, Colombia is in the midst of a decades-long conflict (though it has waned considerably in recent years as the FARC has diminished in strength), and while it is true that it is a humanitarian disaster, it is also true that the country tries to follow Canada's humanitarian guidelines, limited in part because of a lack of resources. Consequently, Canada should offer increased support (both financially and in terms of technical assistance) for Colombia's institutional structures on a more regular basis. From a Colombian standpoint, one of the major problems facing the Canadian government is its unconditional support of NGO initiatives, while putting conditions on its support of government-backed institutional initiatives in Colombia. Although this is due to the problems associated with these same Colombian institutions – such as corruption, paramilitary infiltrations, and the restriction of basic freedoms and rights – there are other, official, institutions such as La Defensoria del Pueblo (the People's Ombudsman) and La Procuraduria General de la Nacion (The Office of the Attorney General)[53] that are one step removed from the corruption and infiltration that permeates others. Indeed, these institutions have programs in line with Canada's own agenda, and thus cooperating with them would probably serve to heal some of the bilateral relationship's sharp differences.

It is instructive to note that Colombia has a presidential regime and a decidedly classic view of state sovereignty. As a result, it sees Canada's relations with civil society in the country – human rights groups, other NGOs, and UN agencies – as a way to bypass the national government's legitimate authority. Therefore, it is strongly suggested that communications with the Colombian government by Canadian officials be reinforced, and that Bogotá be informed of most of Canada's societal interactions in the country. It is understandable that the Canadian government might be reluctant to do this for it can compromise the safety of many of its interlocutors. But to continually bypass the Colombian government will only serve to create bilateral tensions and to foment criticisms of Canada. An effort should be made, therefore, to find a balance between satisfying the Colombian government's sense of integrity and sovereignty and strengthening Canada's relations with civil society in Colombia.

Moreover, Colombia is a country that envisions security as a survival matter, while Canada tends to view it as more of a human rights question. There is an acute dichotomy in both countries' views. This being the case, the country that can afford a wider vision of security – that is, Canada – should concentrate on humanitarian or human rights training not only of the endangered minorities but also of institutional forces. Initiatives such as the financing of the Pearson Peacekeeping Centre's courses (or similar ones from other institutions) for Colombian government employees and military officials would help make the government in Bogotá understand that Canada is on their side and not that of the guerrillas.

Canada's involvement in Colombia, while constant from a rights perspective, tends to be seen as erratic and reactive to the local political environment as opposed to steady and consistent over time. But Canada's often low and unassuming profile might not always be the best approach to dealing with a country that is used to politicians who are loud and to countries that boast of their assistance. Again, taking care not to endanger those who work with the Canadian government in Colombia, it could participate in foreign policy forums and academic debates locally and thus help to erase the view of Canada as a hesitant or mostly rhetorical partner.

More important, Canada's rhetoric could be balanced if it were to develop a strategy to work not only with NGOs on the ground but also with the private entrepreneurial sector in Colombia, with the provincial governments, with opinion leaders, and with Latin American academics in order to bring about a more well-rounded view of the country. This, in turn, would help diminish Colombia's criticism of Canada as a country that promises one thing but is incapable of delivering the goods. It is true that Ottawa did single out Colombia for initial commercial, political, and diplomatic attention. Still, Canadian governments would do well to commit themselves over the longer term and live up to their own words, instead of leaving the Canada-Colombia relationship to languish without sustained and focused attention and nourishment.

Conclusion

In one sense, the Canada-Colombia relationship is hampered by long-standing flaws in the actual wider formulation and implementation of Canadian foreign policy. Indeed, former Canadian diplomats Bill Dymond and Michael Hart have recently argued that 'Canadian foreign policy suffers from inherent weaknesses [and] chief among these is the predominance of sentiment … and a propensity for [a] declaratory foreign policy.'[54] This is true today as Prime Minister Harper and the Canadian Parliament each seem to have their own conflicting agendas towards Colombia. Furthermore, Harper's approach to foreign affairs is based largely on a domestic political agenda (especially during the minority government years), with no serious attempt to chart an independent or forward-looking foreign policy. It has created, in effect, an 'intermesticity' that only serves to confuse officialdom in Colombia.

Prime Minister Harper's relationship with former President Uribe was excellent and his understanding of Colombia's challenges is generally good, and will likely remain so during the tenure of President Juan Manuel Santos.[55] However, the view of Colombia that is put forward by his Conservative government is quite different from Santos's, and is tainted by its own domestic humanitarian/human rights priorities, as well as by the input of local NGOs. As such, the intermesticity of Canadian foreign policy has become a problem not only within Canada, as Peter McKenna has argued in a newspaper op-ed piece about Harper's unabashed 'politicization' of Canada's external relations, but outside the country as well.[56] For Colombians, then, Canada has become a country whose foreign policy has had to take into account the wishes of a host of competing political parties (mostly of a left-leaning hue) rather than an external policy that reflects a true interest in Colombia or in Latin America as a whole. Should it continue in the short term, such domestication of Canadian foreign policy can only hobble the cultivation of a more constructive Canada-Colombia relationship.

Regardless of the continuing problems in Colombia and the wide differences in the well-being and expectations of individuals in both countries, Canada is still perceived by Colombians as a friend. But it is a friend that tends to push its own interests on Colombia, albeit not through the imposition of national security matters as in the case of the U.S., but through the admonition for a more robust human rights agenda. While it appears to be a calling that is largely grounded in domestic political considerations rather than a genuine interest-based Colombia policy, it is a calling that makes human rights rhetoric both the centre of, and an impediment to, a more productive bilateral relationship going forward.

NOTES

1 As a sign of improving bilateral relations, President Uribe visited Canada on two occasions: in June 2009 and during the special session of the G8 Summit in June 2010.
2 Drew Fagan, 'Canada in the World: Heading Back Up?' *Globe and Mail*, 15 April 2003, A17.
3 Stephen Randall, 'Canada's National Security Challenges in the Caribbean and Latin America,' in *Strategic Datalink* (Toronto: Canadian International Council, 2009).
4 A.R. Menzies, 'Memorandum by Acting Head, American and Far Eastern Division,' *Documents on Canadian External Relations*, no. 15 (Ottawa, 21 July 1949).
5 Ambassador Zuleta's objective for the trip was to get Canadian cooperation in the design of a new identity card for Colombians. Canada was chosen over Belgium, Switzerland, Holland, and the United States because of the positive impression Canada made during the creation of the United Nations.
6 Lauchlin Currie was a Canadian economist who headed what is considered in Colombia to be the most important development initiative. Professor Currie was also the father of Colombia's National Planning Agency. He became the country's most influential economist in the 1970s.

7 Department of Foreign Affairs, 'Canadian Goodwill Trade Mission to Latin America' *External Affairs* (Ottawa, March 1953).

8 It has been said that one of the reasons Canada was interested in increasing its ties with South America in the early fifties was that Newfoundland and Labrador, which had just joined Canada as the tenth province, needed a market for its fishing industry and Ottawa believed that the Catholic Latin countries that ate fish on Fridays could be a promising market. In the case of Colombia, Bogotá, its capital, is located 8,000 feet in the Andes, and in the 1950s, fresh fish were not available, but salted dehydrated cod proved an interesting alternative.

9 This is not to suggest that there were no significant differences between the two middle power countries during these years, only to point out that they shared some wider objectives vis-à-vis the international system.

10 Adam Chapnick, *The Middle Power Project: Canada and the Founding of the United Nations* (Vancouver: University of British Columbia Press, 2005), 16.

11 Peter Dobell, 'The Management of Foreign Policy for Canadians,' *International Journal* 26, no. 1 (Winter 1971): 218–19.

12 Angus M. Brown, *The Military Implications of Canada's New Latin American Policy*, study project (Carlisle, PA: U.S. Army War College, March 1991), 1–41.

13 It started with the Wars of Independence in the early nineteenth century, a number of civil wars that lasted until 1886, the War of the Thousand Days at the start of the twentieth century, and the Violencia of the 1950s, which has been extended in many ways into the twenty-first century. Among the more important wars of the nineteenth century were the War of the Supremos, the War of 1851, the Melo Revolution in 1854, the War in Cauca throughout the 1850s, the 1876–7 War, and the violent outbursts associated with the Radical movement between 1855 and 1886. For more information, see Alfredo Rangel, 'Las Farc-Ep Una Mirada Actual,' in Malcolm Deas and Maria Victoria Llorente (eds.), *Reconocer la guerra para construir la paz* (Bogotá: Editorial Norma S.A., 1999), 23.

14 Paul Richter, 'U.S. Debating Wider Assault on Colombia Rebels,' *Los Angeles Times*, 23 February 2002, A1.

15 Mauricio Perez, 'Security Is about Defending Freedom,' *Revista Zero* (October 2003): 12.

16 Stephen Randall and Jillian Dowding,'Canada, Latin America, Colombia and the Evolving Policy Agenda,' *Canadian Foreign Policy* 14, no. 3 (Fall 2008): 34.

17 Government of Canada, *Colombian Conflict* (Ottawa, 1995).

18 Data taken from: Dane Colombia, *El censo es confiable* (Bogotá, 2007) and

Reloj de poblacion (Bogotá, 2010); *Forensis datos para la vida* (Bogotá: Medicina Legal, 2008), *Medicina Legal y ciencias forenses* (Bogotá: Medicina Legal, 2010); Statistics Canada, *Homicides by Method* (Ottawa, 2009); Statistics Canada, *Population by Year, by Province and Territory* (Ottawa, 2009); and Statistics Canada, *Canada's Population Clock* (Ottawa, 2010).

19 2005 is the last year for which statistics are available from Statistics Canada as of the writing of this chapter. It should be stated that violent deaths for both countries included suicides and traffic accidents. For homicide rates in 2008, the last year for which statistics are available for Canada, there were 611 people killed in Canada versus 16,140 in Colombia, or 1.8 violent deaths per 100,000 in Canada versus 39 per 100,000 in Colombia, 21.6 times the rate in Canada. During his last visit to Ottawa in June 2009, President Uribe claimed that there had been a decrease in the number of violent deaths in Colombia from 28,546 in 2007 to 26,958 in 2008. Notwithstanding such a decrease, the numbers are still high and quite unimaginable for Canadians.

20 It should be noted that Colombia has internal insurgency problems but no continuous conflict and definitely not an unending war. Many Canadians, however, insist that there is almost uninterrupted violent conflict in Colombia.

21 The G24 is a group of twenty-four nations created to facilitate appropriate humanitarian agreements and peace conditions in the country. Its members include Canada and a number of European countries.

22 Department of Foreign Affairs and International Trade (DFAIT), *Canada-Colombia Relations* (Ottawa: Department of Foreign Affairs and International Trade, 2009).

23 DFAIT, *Human Security* (Ottawa: Department of Foreign Affairs and International Trade, 2009).

24 CIDA invested CAD$13.93 million in Colombia in the fiscal year 2007–8. See Canadian International Development Agency (CIDA), *Colombia* (Ottawa, 2009).

25 FARC stands for Fuerzas Armadas Revolucionarias de Colombia, a group that for nearly fifty years has been fighting to attain political power. It started out fighting against social and economic injustices but has evolved into a group that deals with, among other things, drug trafficking and money laundering.

26 Personal interview with Beatriz Linares Cantillo, consultant for the International Organization for Migrations (IOM) and adviser to the Office of the Vice President for matters regarding the design and execution of public policy regarding minors and the conflict (Bogotá, 30 October 2009).

27 Colombia has undertaken a series of negotiations with both FARC and

ELN in recent years and Canada has supported the Colombian government in these endeavours, most notably from 1999 to 2002, when Canada
was an active participant in the process during the administration of
Andres Pastrana in Colombia.

28 When the political climate in Colombia calls for negotiations, the Canadians move in, and then, when it does not, they quickly move away. The
U.S., on the other hand, is always an active partner whether the political
scene calls for military actions or peace processes. Consequently, Colombia
tends to view the U.S. as a constant partner and Canada as a fluctuating or
casual partner.

29 Stephen Randall and Jillian Dowding, 'Canada, Latin America, Colombia
and the Evolving Policy Agenda,' 34.

30 Ibid., 38–9.

31 Personal interview with Camilo Reyes, former deputy minister of foreign
affairs and member of the VII Mechanism of Political and Economic Consultations at vice-ministerial level between Colombia and Canada (Bogotá,
3 November 2009).

32 Diane Leduc and James Lee, *Illegal Drugs and Drug Trafficking* (Ottawa:
Parliamentary Research Branch, Political and Social Affairs Division, 2003).

33 Stephen Randall and Jillian Dowding, 'Canada, Latin America, Colombia
and the Evolving Policy Agenda,' 37.

34 Ibid., 36.

35 Ibid., 32.

36 Stephen Harper delivered a major speech on Canadian-Latin American
relations in mid-July 2007 in Santiago, Chile. See 'Prime Minister Harper
Signals Canada's Renewed Engagement in the Americas,' news release
(Ottawa: Office of the Prime Minister, July 2007).

37 Interestingly, at the VI Summit of the Americas in Colombia in mid-April
2012, Prime Minister Harper (along with U.S. President Barack Obama)
stood alone from his hemispheric counterparts on how best to combat the
scourge of narcotrafficking. While President Santos of Colombia called
for a discussion of legalizing the drug trade in Latin America, Harper was
adamantly opposed to the idea. See Campbell Clark and Marina Jimenez,
'Rethinking the War on Drugs,' *Globe and Mail*, 14 April 2012, A3.

38 Government of Canada, 'PM Wraps Up Successful Visit to Latin America,'
news release (Ottawa: Office of the Prime Minister, 12 August 2011), 2.

39 Mark Kennedy, 'Harper Defends Trade Deal with Strife-Plagued Colombia,' *Calgary Herald*, 11 August 2011, A4.

40 Quoted in Steven Chase, 'PM Defends Colombia Trade Deal,' *Globe and
Mail*, 11 August 2011, A11.

41 With Air Canada flying direct to Colombia, more and more Canadian tourists are visiting the country, with almost half of them staying in Bogotá. This is obviously one area of the bilateral relationship in which the Colombian government would like to see some growth.

42 'Relaciones comerciales Canada – Colombia,' http://www.tlc.gov.co/econtent/documentos/negociaciones/canada/relacionescomercanada.pdf (accessed 15 January 2010).

43 Government of Canada, *Canada–Colombia Free Trade Agreement* (Ottawa: Department of Foreign Affairs and International Trade Canada, 2009).

44 Ibid.

45 With well over $3 billion in direct investment in Colombia, some of Canada's leading companies (especially energy and mining companies) have a stake in the country's marketplace, including SNC-Lavalin, Greystar Resources, Talisman, and Brookfield. For a recent discussion of Canada's economic stake in Colombia, see Paul Christopher Webster, 'Hello Canada! Bienvenido a Colombia, Your New Best Friend,' *Globe and Mail Report on Business*, May 2012, 40–52, and Eric Hoesgen and Dennis Hoesgen, 'For Good Reason, Gold Explorers, Producers, and Investors Have Their Eye on Colombia,' *Globe and Mail*, 5 March 2012, B14.

46 DFAIT, *Canada-Andean Countries – Free Trade Discussions: Background* (Ottawa: Department of Foreign Affairs and International Trade, 2009).

47 Stephen Harper, 'A Conversation with Stephen Harper' (Council on Foreign Relations, 25 September 2007).

48 See Tavia Grant, 'Commons Approves Free-Trade Deal with Colombia,' *Globe and Mail*, 15 June 2010, A8. Amnesty International Canada was less than impressed with the overall pact and the human rights amendment: 'This was an opportunity to show leadership and set a meaningful precedent in terms of a human-rights approach to trade and investment and that's why we called for an independent human-rights impact assessment,' a spokesperson said. Also see Jane Taber, 'Dining, Dancing, Free-Trade Deal Making,' *Globe and Mail*, 27 March 2010, A10, and Bill Curry and Campbell Clark, 'Deal Amends Colombia Free Trade Pact,' *Globe and Mail*, 25 March 2010, A4.

49 A free trade agreement is also being negotiated with the European Union but has not been ratified by the Europeans as of the writing of this chapter. A U.S.–Colombia free trade agreement was eventually ratified and put into force in May 2012.

50 Government of Canada, *Canada–Colombia Fact Sheet: Canada's Engagement on Human Rights in Colombia* (Ottawa: Department of Foreign Affairs and International Trade Canada, 2009).

51 Gobierno de Colombia, *Agencia presidencial para la accion social y la cooperacion internacional* (Bogotá: 2009).The $20 million figure is taken from Government of Canada, *Colombia: Country Profile* (Gatineau: Canadian International Development Agency, 2011).

52 For the years 2010–15, CIDA intends to focus its development assistance on children and youth, food security, and sustainable economic development. CIDA will be initiating a series of projects in the country, including inclusive and quality education in schools, environmentally sustainable agricultural programs, and community-level sustainable development projects. Government of Canada, *Colombia: CIDA Report* (Gatineau: Canadian International Development Agency, 2011), 2.

53 In Colombia, 'The Office of the Attorney General (Procuraduria General de la Nacion) is [not an office that prosecutes, instead, it is an office] appointed by the Senate from a list of candidates selected by the President and the highest courts. The Attorney General acts as guardian of constitutional rights and liberties, democratic principles, public interests, and the rule of law in general. The Attorney General shall also file any appropriate action to hold liable public officials who have incurred civil, labor, military, criminal, administrative or disciplinary liability in the course of their official duties.' Antonio Ramirez, 'An Introduction to Colombian Governmental Institutions and Primary Legal Sources,' in *GlobaLex* (New York: New York University School of Law, May 2007).

54 Drew Fagan, 'Canada in the World: Heading Back Up?' *Globe and Mail*, 15 April 2003, A1.

55 One would expect that to remain the same under the tenure of President Juan Manuel Santos, a former Colombian defence minister, who was the hand-picked successor of Uribe. Chris Kraul, 'Former Defense Minister Wins Colombian Presidential Election,' *Los Angeles Times*, 21 June 2010, A3. A senior member of Harper's cabinet, Citizenship and Immigration Minister Jason Kenney attended Santos's presidential inauguration in early August 2010.

56 Peter McKenna, 'Harper's "Politicization" of Canada's Foreign Policy,' *The Chronicle Herald*, 17 October 2009, A15.

11 Between Rhetoric and Reality: Canada-Venezuela Relations

LESLEY M. BURNS

This chapter on Venezuela comes at a pivotal moment when Canada seeks to solidify relations with its Latin American neighbours. To do so, the Stephen Harper Conservatives have designated the Americas as a core foreign policy priority. This chapter explores the nature, extent, and scope of Canada's wide-ranging, though sometimes less than cordial, relationship with Venezuela. It will focus predominantly on Canada-Venezuela relations since the end of the Cold War period. In 1990, Canada finally asserted its role in the hemisphere, independent of Great Britain and the United States, by joining the Organization of American States (OAS) – a regional organization that promotes inter-American cooperation – showing not only that it sought to strengthen ties with the hemisphere, but also that it believed in multilateral diplomacy. Over the last twenty years, Venezuela has established itself as a key player in the region, and the often controversial President Hugo Chávez's openly critical position on Western engagement has Canadian officials and analysts concerned about future relations with the country.

In 1989, Venezuela's seemingly stable democracy was severely shaken when street riots erupted in violence and protest over neoliberal reforms and government policy. The 1990s also saw continued political instability with two coup attempts in 1992 and the impeachment of President Carlos Andres Pérez in 1993. Chávez was elected in 1998 on a platform of fundamental change, vowing to break from past elite-dominated political institutions and deliver an improved, citizen-centric democracy to the Venezuelan people. His populist rhetoric struck a responsive nerve with the country's impoverished masses.

But the current Venezuelan conception of democracy and its notion of multilateralism differ significantly from Canada's. This chapter provides a brief overview of both Canada's and Venezuela's current understanding of multilateralism that underpins their involvement in the hemisphere and each country's attempts to strengthen and uphold democracy in the region. It will then discuss increased challenges posed by this new form of multilateralism in the hemisphere and by Venezuela's conception of 'participatory' democracy.

This chapter will also survey the Canada-Venezuela political, economic, diplomatic, and security relationship, and underline how Canada's understanding of prosperity, security, and democracy has been challenged in the case of Venezuela for the years 1990 to 2012. It intends to be useful in building a better understanding of the key issues that dictate the Canada-Venezuela relationship and in highlighting issues of future concern and importance. The chapter concludes by offering some practical policy recommendations for official Ottawa.

Canada's Engagement in Latin America, 1990–2012: Two Decades of Interaction

It is important to begin by focusing on three significant stages in Canadian-Latin American relations: 1) Canada's joining the OAS in 1989–90; 2) the Summit of the Americas in Quebec City in 2001 (a major component of which was the agreement to develop an Inter-American Democratic Charter; and 3) the Harper government's 2007 Americas strategy. These three phases represent the most recent stages of Canada-Latin American relations. But as Jean Daudelin states pointedly, 'every twenty years or so, it seems, Canada rediscovers the Americas.'[1]

As a sign of Canada's commitment to multilateral participation and one of the first major moves to engage more directly in the hemisphere, Canada decided to join the OAS, becoming a full member in 1990.[2] Prior to 1990, reluctance in Washington, chiefly based on a concern that Canadian foreign policy was dominated by the British, combined with serious reservations on the part of Ottawa about the OAS's effectiveness and belief that it was a U.S.-dominated organization, deterred Canada from joining the hemispheric body sooner.[3] Any U.S. uncertainty over Canada's membership, though, would eventually evaporate, as Washington recognized the value of having another 'friendly' country sitting around the OAS table.

Canada's decision to join the OAS came at a unique historical moment when the fall of the Soviet Union and the end of the Cold War marked a notable turning point in hemispheric relations. Of greatest significance in the region was the move away from ideology-based struggles between communism and capitalism.[4] Canada's membership in the OAS also positioned it to participate in the post–Cold War world as a full member of the inter-American community and signalled where Canadian foreign policy might go in the coming years.[5]

Canada was among the last countries in the hemisphere to join,[6] and its decision to do so was a significant milestone in hemispheric relations. In the words of then prime minister Brian Mulroney: 'Our decision to join the OAS symbolizes our determination to be full and constructive citizens of the Americas.'[7] And as Brian Stevenson explained: 'Once Canada had become a full member of the OAS, its multilateral policies would have to be more responsive to the hemisphere.'[8] Underlying Ottawa's decision to join the OAS was the perception of former prime minister Joe Clark – who was then secretary of state for external affairs (1984–91) – that the world was coalescing into three main regions: Europe, the Pacific, and the Americas.[9]

Twenty years later, one of Canada's major contributions to the inter-American system has been its role in promoting, building capacity for, and upholding democracy in the hemisphere. This was demonstrated through one of Canada's first initiatives – namely, when it proposed and funded the Unit for the Promotion of Democracy (UPD). The promotion of democracy still remains today a component of the OAS's mandate, though related activities are currently housed under the Secretariat for Political Affairs. However, budget constraints within the organization and political differences in the hemisphere have limited its mandate.

Another concrete expression of Canada's support for a hemisphere-wide mechanism to support democracy was evidenced by its backing for Resolution 1080, which was tabled at the 1991 OAS General Assembly in Santiago, Chile. Resolution 1080 was a joint recognition of the importance of representative democracy and gave member countries the ability to react to an 'irregular interruption of the democratic political institutional process' in member states. In other words, it laid the foundation for building a democratic norm in the Americas.

Ten years on, when it hosted the 2001 Quebec City Summit of hemispheric political leaders, Canada championed the inclusion of a democracy clause in the final documentation.[10] The inclusion of this clause, spearheaded by Canada's Mark Lortie, essentially meant that democracy was a necessary pre-condition for participation in the Summit of the Americas process. And as the Summit of the Americas was the only meeting where political leaders across the hemisphere gathered, this was another strong expression of the importance member states placed on democratic pluralism.

This support for democracy, even at its earliest stages, was not without reservation, and leading up to the Quebec City Summit, Venezuela objected to the inclusion of representative democracy, advocating instead to include the term 'participatory democracy.'[11] Following a process of diplomatic negotiation, Venezuela withdrew its objections to the terminology: 'after having lobbied successfully for the insertion of references to citizen participation,' Venezuela essentially agreed to support the inclusion of representative democracy.[12] Nevertheless, Venezuelan officials continued to advocate that participatory democracy was a superior form of democracy.

This support-for-democracy clause was important because it laid the foundation for the subsequent Inter-American Democracy Charter (IADC) signed in September 2001, which outlines what democracy is and asserts that the OAS can help defend it. The IADC established that democracy and social and economic development are interdependent and are mutually reinforcing (article 11), and that article 18 gave the secretary general of the OAS the right to, 'with prior consent of the government concerned,' investigate the situation and under article 20 to take the necessary diplomatic measures to restore democracy. In the words of Maxwell A. Cameron, 'Making the Charter work as an effective instrument for the defence and promotion of democracy must be a priority in the Summit process.'[13] Previous agreements within the OAS had set representative democracy as the foundation for stability, endorsed peace and development, and promoted the consolidation of democracy in the region.

The IADC formalized previous agreements that had laid the foundation for a collective defence of representative democracy, establishing a joint hemispheric reaction to democratic crises, while respecting the principle of non-intervention. The Charter made specific reference to representative democracy, but this did not emerge without significant debate. Indeed, Legler, Lean, and Boniface remind us that 'the discursive struggle between Chávez and his allies in the region and the proponents of representative democracy in the Inter-American system highlights the social construction of the meaning of democratization and the contested nature of the concept.'[14] Where the Venezuelan model of participatory democracy and Canadian ideas about representative democracy diverge in practice will be discussed in a later section.

The theme of democracy would continue through the Jean Chrétien and Paul Martin years and into the Stephen Harper era. To adapt to changing hemispheric developments and to redirect Canada's position in the Americas, Prime Minister Stephen Harper stated in 2007: 'We believe [that] security, democratic governance and economic prosperity are mutually reinforcing.'[15] Harper proceeded to recognize in his throne speech that the separation between different economic and political structures was not as sharp as it was during the Cold War when he noted that the division 'is not simply between unfettered capitalism and Cold War socialism. The Canadian model of democratic freedom and economic openness, combined with effective regional and social support, offers a middle course for countries seeking democratic institutions, free markets and social equality.'[16] This implies that Canadian best practices could be used as a positive example in various political institutional settings in the region.

The understanding that security, economy, and democratic governance are related and mutually reinforcing is reflected in the government's 2007 strategy to re-engage in the Americas. The Canadian government's America's Strategy identifies Latin America and the Caribbean as a central foreign policy priority. This re-engagement in Latin America was driven by the realization that what happens in the hemisphere deeply impacts Canada. For this reason, the strategy is based on three main pillars: democratic governance, economic prosperity, and regional security. To achieve these goals, the government expressed its intent to 'reinforce bilateral relations, strengthen regional organizations, bolster Canadian partnerships and expand Canada's presence.'[17]

The economic agenda of trade integration – namely, the Free Trade Area of the Americas (FTAA) – that emerged from the Quebec City Summit would later collapse. While the FTAA agenda has been the focus of hemispheric integration, the economic policies that came to be known as the 'Washington Consensus' were driven by the idea that trade and investment liberalization would increase the overall standard of living for the majority of the population throughout the Americas. When such policies failed to reduce economic inequalities, objection to these policies grew and culminated in their outright rejection by several Latin American governments. This period marked a division in hemispheric relations and witnessed an increased push by Venezuela's leadership for an alternative development path.

The Canadian government, for its part, continued with its policy of neoliberal trade promotion. In Harper's own words, the driving purpose was as follows: 'Though the FTAA negotiations have stalled in recent years, Canada remains steadfast in our commitment to liberalize trade and investment with our partners in the hemisphere.'[18] This emphasis on trade and investment is seen as a necessary piece of a mutually reinforcing puzzle: 'We believe that security, democratic governance and economic prosperity are mutually reinforcing.'[19] According to this thinking, trade and investment can help improve economic conditions, reduce poverty, and, in turn, improve the security of societies – a security that is best maintained, protected, and preserved through democratic governance.

Since the beginning of the 1990s, Canada has continued to have a successful and, in fact, growing economic relationship with Venezuela. However, a look at the current Venezuelan economic development plan, which sees the unfettered capitalist system as nothing short of evil, does not suggest that a formal bilateral trade agreement is likely under the current circumstances. So while bilateral relations with Caracas are a tad frosty in late 2012, there is no threat of any irreparable break with the country.

Examining the Important Aspects of the Canadian-Venezuela Relationship

To begin, Venezuela and Canada have had formal diplomatic relations since 1948. In 1953, motivated mostly by commercial interests, Canada opened its first embassy in Caracas.[20] One measure of gauging the state of diplomatic relations between the two countries can be found in the number and frequency of official visits. One of Canada's first notable visits to Venezuela was Prime Minister Pierre Elliott Trudeau's trip in early 1976. (This visit was overshadowed by his far more controversial visit to Cuba.) This was followed by visits from Venezuelan ministers in 1981 and a visit by Canadian secretary of state for external affairs Mark MacGuigan in 1982.

Over the lasts two decades, there have been a number of high-level visits by officials and politicians from Canada and Venezuela, though many of them have been unofficial in nature. In 1991 then president of Venezuela Carlos Andrés Pérez visited Canada, and Canadian diplomats reported that they had good access to the Venezuelan government during this period.[21] In addition to Joe Clark and Governor General Jeanne Sauvé, Prime Minister Brian Mulroney also visited Caracas in 1992. (Both Mulroney and Pérez worked closely on the restoration of democracy to Haiti in the early 1990s.) In 1998, secretary of state for Latin America David Kilgour and minister of foreign affairs Lloyd Axworthy visited Venezuela for an OAS meeting, but there was no extensive bilateral program for the gathering.

President Hugo Chávez visited Canada in 1999 as president-elect (prior to his February inauguration) and three times in 2001: attendance at a meeting for the Summit of the Americas in Quebec City, a private trip to Whitehorse, Yukon, and an unofficial visit to Ottawa. It is important to note that these visits were not official state visits. In 2002, secretary of state (Latin America and Africa) Denis Paradis visited Venezuela to discuss a host of bilateral matters. To promote both trade and tourism, Venezuelan deputy minister Maria Pilar Hernandez visited Canada in 2005. On this visit, Hernandez also took the opportunity to inform audiences about the specifics of the Venezuelan revolution. Following these meetings, she was quoted as stating that 'Venezuela's relationship with Canada, was cold ... not a bad relationship, but a cold one. We need to warm it up.'[22]

Perhaps an indication that Canada was willing to do its part to warm its bilateral relationship with Venezuela, deputy minister of foreign affairs Peter Harder made an official visit to Venezuela in 2006 with the purpose of enhancing diplomatic relations between the two countries. Although the visit was driven largely by trade interests, the deputy minister also met with representatives from academia and civil society. Moreover, the relationship between Caracas and Ottawa is complicated by the fact that, except for a brief period of time, there had not been an ambassador representing the Bolivarian Republic of Venezuela in Ottawa since 2006 (as is still the case in late 2012). Analysts of international affairs assert that this lack of high-level representation not only indicates a coolness in political relations, but also contributes to an inability to get the bilateral relationship back on more solid diplomatic footing.

To further promote the relationship between the two countries, vice-minister Jorge Valero came to Canada for bilateral meetings in 2007. Also in 2007 a member of Venezuela's parliament, Augusto Montiel, visited Ottawa for discussions. In describing this visit, Jim Creskey, who covered foreign affairs for *Embassy*, reported that 'the only Canadian politician the Venezuelan MP was able to meet was a Mulroney-appointed Independent Senator Marcel Prud'homme'[23] Creskey proceeded to note that Montiel did meet with Department of Foreign Affairs and International Trade officials, trade unionists, and 'others sympathetic to his government.'[24] Finally, in 2008 Chávez led a Venezuelan delegation to the World Heavy Oil congress in Edmonton. Taken together, these visits may have contributed to maintaining a diplomatic relationship between the two countries. But Canadian diplomats of various stripes report that over the years it has become more difficult to get meetings with government officials.[25] Some political analysts note a marked downturn in the professionalism of the Venezuelan foreign service.

To show dedication to the region, then minister of state for the Americas Peter Kent visited Venezuela in early 2010. His visit was intended to promote democratic governance, security, and prosperity, as outlined in the Harper government's Americas strategy. Although the timing of his visit prevented him from meeting with representatives from the Ministry of External Relations, Kent did manage to make his government's concern for the political situation in Venezuela public. Kent released a statement expressing concerns over shrinking democratic space following the failure of the Venezuelan government to renew broadcast licences for several opposition television stations.

Not surprisingly, this statement provoked a backlash from the Venezuelan government, and the Venezuelan ambassador to the OAS, Roy Chaderton Matos, accused the Canadian government of being ultra-right-wing, of supporting the coup in Honduras, and of violating the norm of non-intervention.[26] Prior to this, Canada had largely avoided being demonized as the United States has been, but in a televised speech Chávez directly accused Canada of trying to harm his government. Such accusations could lead to Canada's being considered an extension of the U.S. and thus undermine the Canadian government's attempt to promote democratic best practices in Venezuela and the wider hemisphere. Although frequently accused of undermining the Chávez administration, the United States has, for the most part, not publicly responded to Chávez's rhetoric. Provided that the economic relationship continues, there is little evidence to suggest that this will change in the short term.

The diplomatic relationship between Canada and Venezuela, then, has been unbroken for almost sixty-five years. But the impact of Canadian diplomats in Caracas has clearly decreased, which does little to serve Canadian interests. Previously, diplomats had better access to government officials than is characteristic under the Chávez administration. Although direct access to government officials is by no means the only way to evaluate diplomatic relations, it is an important instrumental and symbolic indicator. For this reason, work remains to be done to get bilateral relations on a more productive diplomatic track. Canada still remains committed to multilateral diplomacy through the OAS. The Canadian government has recognized that there are imperfections in the current inter-American system and has sought to improve it through internal reform rather than cast away the institution in its entirety. Canada and Venezuela have differing views, however, on how democracy impacts their respective countries' conception of multilateral institutions like the OAS. Prior to examining multilateralism, though, this section will first discuss the different concepts of democracy and the implications that these concepts have.

As the Cold War ended, American political philosopher Francis Fukuyama concluded that it was the 'end of history' and that liberal democracy had prevailed.[27] No longer would there be the ideological struggle that characterized much of the Cold War. When the 'Washington Consensus,' underpinned by free trade and open markets, failed to deliver an improved standard of living to the majority of people in the Americas, a backlash, often referred to as the 'left turn' or 'pink tide,' emerged in the wider hemisphere. This resurgent wave of criticism against liberal democracy and neoliberalism took on new life under the leadership of Venezuelan president Hugo Chávez. Fuelled by high oil prices, Venezuela propelled itself into a leadership role by questioning the hemispheric equilibrium, the neoliberal agenda of free trade, and Western-style representative democracy.

A vibrant debate has emerged regarding the merits of different forms of democracy outside of liberal democracy. Some analysts believe that democracies that are not fully liberal are still in transition and will someday reach full consolidated liberal democracies.[28] Other analysts believe that these countries have been in transition for such a long period that they actually constitute alternative forms of democracy and are not on track to become liberal democracies at all. Instead, theorists in this group suggest that these countries have created unique forms of democracy that should be analysed based on their own merit.[29]

A new, and very different, form of democracy is what Chávez is seeking to construct.[30] He did not set a clear path toward achieving this goal at the outset, however, and fluidity in his policy has made it difficult to judge advances against a set of specific end goals. Tellingly, Chávez blames representative democracy as having kept over half of his population in poverty and sees a more participatory form as superior.[31] (He did not publicly identify his Bolivarian revolution with socialism until the beginning of 2007.) Chávez has regularly stated that this form of participatory democracy is not Marxist but is a uniquely Venezuelan creation that has given the poor hope for a more prosperous future.

A large component of participatory democracy is to increase the population's role in the political process by revamping the political structure. Chávez announced that 'five motors' would drive the revolution forward. These included:

1 enabling laws, which gave the executive the ability to rule without constraint of Congress;
2 constitutional change, which allowed the 1999 constitution to be revamped;
3 education that includes social values;[32]
4 a new geometry of power to allow for political decentralization to replace the existing federal-state-municipal division and permit a 'socialist reordering' of the nation;
5 an increase in communal power, which was spearheaded through the creation of communal councils to give communities greater say in their own development.

Theoretically speaking, this form of democracy could empower the population. In practice, however, the attendant concentration of power in the executive branch of government has left governing institutions ineffective in restraining the power of the president. In turn, sceptics and critics have diminished hope that this form of participatory democracy will materialize into a sustainable political system, pointing to serious concerns around gerrymandering and the stacking of the Venezuelan electoral commission with friends of the government. Supporters, on the other hand, often cite a highly unequal past and hope for greater equality in the future as part of their main justifications for continued support of President Chávez.

The Venezuelan revolution is obviously a work in progress. The fact that this process has taken more than a decade has conditioned the Canadian government's reaction thus far. Canada's foreign policy is, historically at least, open to respecting forms of democracy that are not strictly classified as liberal democracies. Canada's continued engagement in Cuba is one example, and increasing bilateral relations with China is another. As one official policy document states: 'Canada's democracy support will strengthen democratic processes that give citizens a greater say in the decisions that affect their lives with a focus on elections, parliaments, independent media, political parties and civil society.[33] In theory, this suggests that there may be few problems with the emerging form of democracy in Venezuela. In practice, though, the Canadian government has kept a close eye on these reforms:

> Canada is monitoring the process closely and paying particular attention to the impact these reforms may have on standards of democracy and human rights that have been endorsed by all OAS Member States, particularly in the Inter-American Democratic Charter. It is also Canadian policy to support civil society and foster its contribution to the democratic process in many countries around the world. Thus, Canada continues to support civil society organizations that are working in the areas of democracy and human rights in Venezuela.[34]

When the Canadian government looks for more typical components of liberal democracy, however, it is finding these openings rather limited. The reason could, in part, be that Venezuela does not fit the mould of Western liberal democracy. Nor does it have any intention to do so. But if Ottawa wants to respect non-liberal forms of democracy, it needs to consider Venezuela for its unique merits.[35]

The support for democratic organizations is a sensitive and complicated subject in this context, which could potentially aggravate diplomatic relations between the two countries. The Venezuelan government looks unfavourably upon foreign involvement with civil society groups (including Canadian government support for critical NGOs in the country), deeming it to be a violation of state sovereignty. Many political parties were centralized into the United Socialist Party of Venezuela, and, following an election boycott, opposition parties were largely shut out of the formal political system in 2005 and attempted to rebuild for the 2010 parliamentary elections. Still, politics in Venezuela remains highly personalized, and the political structure that Chávez is building has not been fully institutionalized. For policy makers in Ottawa, these factors combine to pose challenges to easy classification by government officials and make the situation in Venezuela unique, necessitating close attention to the rapidly changing political environment.[36]

Nevertheless, the Canadian government continues to foster its relationship with the Government of the Bolivarian Republic of Venezuela. According to official statements, the Canadian government maintains 'dialogue with the government of President Chávez, particularly on the issues of democratic governance and economic and social development. Canada is also promoting constructive dialogue with Venezuela on a multilateral level, notably within the Organization of American States (OAS).'[37] Similarly, the international community has engaged Chávez's government on the issue of democracy several times through electoral observation missions and the Inter-American Democracy Charter. And this multilateral approach to Venezuela continues today as a viable mechanism for officialdom in Ottawa.

Multilateral Exchanges

Clearly, Canada has worked within the OAS to address shared hemispheric concerns, including the 'crises' of democracy in Venezuela. Thomas Legler reports that the OAS has had mixed results in its attempts to defend democracy in Venezuela.[38] The OAS's pro-democracy activities have included its attempts to promote dialogue surrounding the 2002 coup attempt against Chávez, technical assistance and monitoring for the 2004 presidential elections, and subsequent electoral observation missions.[39] Despite repeated threats to pull out of the OAS, and expressions of public frustration with the body, Venezuela still remains a full member. Venezuela's efforts to get secretary general José Miguel Insulza elected in 2005 (and support for his re-election in 2010) suggest that it sees some value in the hemispheric institution. In fact, Chávez's critics have often accused him of using PetroCaribe, a program that brought subsidized oil to struggling Caribbean nations, as a tool to build political allies in the OAS.

In April 2002, Chávez was briefly removed from power. Directly following this, then OAS secretary general César Gaviria convened a meeting of the Permanent Council[40] and undertook a fact-finding mission. Such a mission was permitted under the IADC, which evolved, in large part, from the democracy clause at the 2001 Quebec Summit. Chávez was quickly restored to power because the coup planners made a series of undemocratic decisions and because Chávez's supporters took to the streets to demand his reinstatement. The OAS was subsequently criticized for not being able to prevent the coup, and the Chávez government refused support for greater OAS assistance until the situation had deteriorated further.

In the ensuing months, a tripartite mission of the OAS, the Carter Center, and the United Nations Development Program (UNDP) facilitated a roundtable negotiation. Finally, after an economically debilitating general strike, the government and opposition agreed to hold a recall referendum. (A unique clause in the Venezuelan constitution of 1999 set out criteria to recall a sitting president.) The OAS participated in the referendum as an observer, much like it had in many elections in the region. (Such missions can contribute to the strengthening of democracy, increasing the perception of legitimacy, and decreasing the likelihood of fraud.)[41] Although imperfect, electoral observation missions contribute to strengthening multilateral support for democracy while recognizing the principles of sovereignty and non-intervention in the hemisphere. Not only does Canada support electoral observation missions, but, according to one former high-level government official, it is one of only a few, if not the only country, to give sufficient money in advance of the mission to allow for preplanning.[42]

The institutional framework which allowed for these kinds of missions is found in the IADC, the foundation for which was laid at the Quebec Summit. Implementation of the IADC was effective in Peru (2000) and Haiti (2001–4), yet it may prove ineffective for future crises of democracy associated with Venezuela's variant of Bolivarian democracy. For one, it does not take into account the possibility that 'the concentration of executive power, the erosion of checks and balances, the persistent violations of the rule of law – might occur within a more or less constitutional framework, or might even be given legitimacy by constitutional change.'[43] Opposition groups and critics accuse Chávez of changing the constitution to undermine democracy, concentrating power in the executive and stifling the power of other branches of government and political actors. Additionally, the current norm is that only the executive branch of government can request that the OAS get involved in a country.[44]

Additionally, on a sub-regional level Canada has extended its attempts to foster democracy through the Andean Unit for Democratic Governance, which will oversee democracy programming in the region – including Venezuela. As a complement to work that Canada does through the OAS, this unit positions Canadian diplomats to better understand the unique situation in each country. In turn, the Canadian government will be well positioned to tailor its programming more directly to local factors.

In another vein, Venezuela initiated a different form of multilateralism when it created the Alternativa Bolivariana para las Americas (ALBA) in 2007. This group emerged in opposition to the FTAA – that is, as a citizen-led alternative to the 'Washington Consensus' and neoliberalism. Gott notes that Chávez implied that this union would be especially political in nature.[45] Chávez's 'aim was nothing less than the Bolivarian dream of the union of the peoples of Latin America.'[46]

In fact, the member countries acted as a unified bloc on several occasions, including at the December 2009 United Nations Climate Change conference in Copenhagen, arguing that capitalism and a serious dedication to combating climate change were clearly incompatible. This does not mean, however, that Chávez ignores the economic aspect of the union. Indeed, ALBA has moved toward a virtual currency – the SUCRE (short for Unified System of Compensation of Reciprocal Payments) – which uses products for barter, in place of monetary currency. This new currency is designed to reduce dependence on the U.S. dollar, the currency in which most Latin American countries hold their reserves. As a notable shift in hemispheric relations, this could have a large impact on future inter-American integration.

Enhancing Economic Relations

Although Venezuela has made recent attempts to move away from a strictly capitalist economic system, to date those efforts have not had a sizeable impact on external trade. Over the past several decades, Venezuela has grown to become Canada's fourth-largest trading partner in Latin America and the Caribbean (excluding Mexico), with exports reaching $890 million in 2008.[47] Those exports include primarily cereals, paper and paperboard, automobiles, mineral ores, and vegetables. Notwithstanding increasing difficulties in terms of exports, gas turbines, newsprint, vegetables, and preserved foods saw an increase in totals for 2009.[48] For the most part, the trade relationship is dominated by the oil and gas extraction industry; petroleum refineries; alumina and aluminum production and processing; other basic chemical manufacturing; tire manufacturing; as well as iron and steel mills and ferro-alloy manufacturing.

According to Industry Canada, nearly 90 per cent of Canadian imports from Venezuela come from the oil sector.[49] In 2009, imports from Venezuela totalled $1.4 billion and included mineral fuel and oils, fertilizers, inorganic chemicals, organic chemicals, and rubber.[50] Not surprisingly, Canada continues to import substantively more from Venezuela than it exports to the country. As Figure 11.1 illustrates, imports have been growing since 1992, with the exception of the period 2002–3, when Venezuelan production was seriously damaged by a national strike. This strike affected the national oil company and had a major impact on the country's economic output. Imports from Canada peaked in 2005 and have fallen since but remain greater than the level of trade in the

Figure 11.1. Venezuela-Canada Trade, 1992–2009

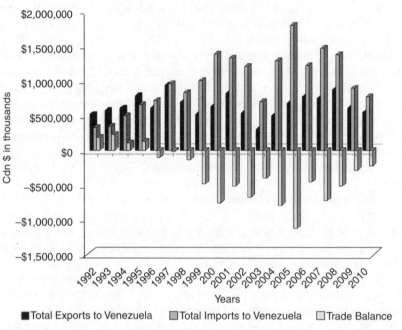

■Total Exports to Venezuela   ▦Total Imports to Venezuela   □Trade Balance

early 1990s. The most striking impact on the overall trade relationship is Canada's balance of trade deficits with Venezuela.

Canada and Venezuela made recent attempts to improve cooperation in relation to trade and investment as demonstrated through a double taxation agreement which came into effect in 1998 and a Foreign Investment Protection Agreement (FIPA) that went into force in 2005.[51] Double taxation agreements are in place to reduce the tax burden of individuals who reside outside of their country of citizenship. Taxation agreements also ease the burden for Canadians who want to conduct business in Venezuela. FIPAs can be interpreted as a sign of bilateral cooperation because they 'seek to ensure that foreign investors will not be treated worse than similarly situated domestic investors or other foreign investors; they will not have their investments expropriated without prompt and adequate compensation; and, in any case, they will not be subject to treatment lower than the minimum standard established in customary international law.'[52]

The agreements in place may help reduce the formal cost of business, but Canadians doing business in Venezuela expressed concern about a number of newly emerging obstacles to doing business in Venezuela, many of which they report deviate from the formal procedure.[53] For example, it is difficult to get business permits, and several business commentators believe that preferential treatment is being given to companies from countries that share the Venezuelan government's ideology.[54] This has deterred some investors, while others have chosen to leave the country altogether. According to the Department of Foreign Affairs and International Trade, 'one of Canada's priorities for Venezuela will be to continue representations aimed at eliminating discretionary import licensing. Venezuela's lack of transparency in the issuance of import permits for certain food products'[55] is an ongoing concern as well.

Transnational corporations fear what the media have termed a wave of nationalizations. More accurately, the Venezuelan government has taken majority ownership in several companies. A lack of consistency in application and compliance to the law has heightened the fear that foreign companies could be targeted for takeover. Several private sector representatives in Canada have expressed concerns about the government seemingly making legislation as it saw fit, and without being held accountable for its actions.

Further complicating the situation, the Venezuelan government has a fixed exchange rate on currency, which has led to the creation of a black, or parallel, currency market.[56] In March 2003 the government introduced a currency control and exchange system to reduce capital flight by regulating the purchase and sale of foreign currency. These restrictions have led to the development of a parallel market to buy and sell currency, where U.S. dollars and Euros can fetch double or two-thirds their value compared to the fixed exchange rate set by the government. Some foreign companies doing business in Venezuela have also had to face longer waiting periods to receive their proper payments. Furthermore, Export Development Canada (EDC) expects that the Foreign Exchange Administration Commission's (CADIVI for its acronym in Spanish) recent tightening of remuneration will 'continue to cause further delays on import payments and capital outflows from the country.'[57] Although formal agreements have been reached, conducting business in Venezuela can still be risky.

The difficulty that monetary control causes in exchanging money has complicated business among private companies. It makes foreign currency difficult to get and more expensive. In an attempt to ameliorate problems with access to currency, the Venezuelan government set one rate for necessary and priority goods and another for non-essential goods.[58] Private sector representatives report that difficulties receiving payment from Venezuelan business partners are a deterrent to further investment.[59] Overall, this has discouraged some would-be Canadian investors, while other companies prefer to ride out the rough times in hopes of maintaining an advantage in the future.[60]

Some business observers fear that access to foreign currency will be used as a political tool. Representatives from Canadian businesses operating in Venezuela maintain that individuals and companies (from China) are given preference based on their country of origin.[61] Former Venezuelan ambassador to the United Nations, Milos Alcalay, in the course of an interview, stated that while Venezuela is seeking a relationship along ideological lines, China is looking for a more practical and 'non-ideologically based' relationship.[62] The same does not appear, however, to be true for other countries with which Venezuela has sought to increase trade relations, including Russia and Iran.[63]

Security Considerations

Canada's dedication to enhancing security in the hemisphere is not a new preoccupation. In fact, in 1992 it created a Special Committee on Hemispheric Security to explore cooperative security and address proliferation issues.[64] It has remained on Canada's inter-American agenda ever since. Further hemispheric engagement is secured through the Canada Border Services Agency's sixteen border officers posted throughout the region and through five defence attachés. In addition, improving security does not come only from direct programs to address security and defence. In the words of Stephen Harper: 'Canada believes the principal challenges to security and stability in the Americas stem from weak democratic institutions and profound socioeconomic inequalities. Though ongoing violence is present in some countries, the principal threats to security in the region derive from crime and corruption … Canada will continue to work with our partners and regional institutions to address these concerns.'[65]

For Canada, then, security concerns regarding Venezuela have been largely indirect in nature. Simply put, there has been no reason to see Venezuela as a direct threat to Canada's national security. But there are those in Ottawa who have started to express some reservations about the size and nature of defence expenditures in Venezuela. And an increase in amicable relations between Venezuela and Iran has become a security concern less for their shared anti-U.S. rhetoric and more for Venezuela's support of the Iranian nuclear program, along with the fear that this capability may be used against Israel or to otherwise exacerbate already tense problems in the Middle East. Iran is now subject to United Nations Security Council sanctions for its uranium enrichment program. Some security analysts also fear that Venezuela is seeking to create its own nuclear program, despite being a signatory to the non-proliferation treaty (NPT).

In addition to concerns about closer relations with Iran, Venezuela's acquisition of weapons from Russia has been a source of preoccupation for neighbouring countries and Canadian officialdom. Though some security experts argue that these weapons do not give Venezuela any tactical advantage, they do contribute to an environment of insecurity within the hemisphere.[66] There is a growing fear that an armed militia has been created to protect President Chávez and that it could be turned against the country's political opposition. Moreover, there is circumstantial evidence that suggests the Venezuelan government may be supporting the Colombian rebel group FARC. Canadian officials are also cognizant of increasing disputes along the Colombian-Venezuelan border that have worsened relations between those two countries. When the Colombian army crossed into Ecuador in pursuit of rebel fighters in 2008, the Chávez administration demonstrated its solidarity with Ecuador and disapproval of Colombia by closing its embassy in the Colombian capital of Bogotá. The two governments rectified this disagreement, but the Venezuelan government was vociferously opposed to the opening of seven U.S. bases on Colombian soil. In response, Venezuela moved to sever Colombian imports. These sorts of disagreements can have spillover effects on hemispheric relations, drawing in Canada whether it likes it or not.[67]

Conclusion

Since taking our seat at the OAS in 1990, Canada has been a strong advocate for democracy in the hemisphere and has been successful in maintaining respect for the principles of non-intervention. Over the last twenty years, successive Canadian governments have increased their engagement in the Americas. On the bilateral front, Canada and Venezuela have never been close allies; but neither have they been irreparably estranged. It is true that, despite the domestic economic environment, which has made conducting business in Venezuela more challenging, several Canadian companies prefer to continue doing business there. Still, different understandings of democracy and Venezuelan attempts to revamp the multilateral architecture in the hemisphere mark important divergent perspectives. At times, it has led to tension in the bilateral relationship – witness then minister of state for the Americas Peter Kent's visit to Caracas in January 2010, which highlighted the challenging nature of bilateral relations. It could be more productive in the future if meetings could be set up in advance with ranking ministerial counterparts.

To strengthen Canada-Venezuela relations, the Harper government could remain committed to improving the basic tenants of democratic governance, whether representative or participative or, most productively, where the two overlap. It could also do so in Venezuela by contributing to the capacity of individual citizens to make informed choices and to hold their government accountable for its actions. But it would be well advised to be mindful of Venezuelan sovereignty and sensitivities – making sure not to galvanize Chávez supporters in the country against Canada. Such strategies could contribute to the opening of dialogue between divergent interests in Venezuela and not exacerbate tensions in an already polarized society. Through the Andean Unit for Democratic Governance, Canada is well positioned to tailor its democracy-related programming to local conditions.

To recast bilateral relations, officials and politicians in Ottawa need to ensure that Canada has a clear understanding of the political situation and to seek political space to promote open democratic exchange and improved access to information. Venezuela is presently seeking to establish a form of democracy based on a fundamentally different set of principles than liberal democracy. But programs and initiatives that aggravate societal polarization will only damage rather than improve the political situation on the ground or enhance Canada-Venezuela relations. This could be implemented through programs and measures that seek to improve aspects of democracy that are valued in both representative and participatory democracies – such as aspects that improve participation including access to information from numerous perspectives, freedom of the press, and accountability.

The Harper government's Americas strategy makes note of the mutually reinforcing relationship between democratic governance, prosperity, and security. Canadian companies have continued to trade with both the Venezuelan government and members of the private sector. Over the past two decades, imports have grown even with government policies that have been unfriendly to the private sector. To further enhance ways to fortify business/commercial interaction, Ottawa could push for the transparent application of trade rules, adherence to the rule of law, and the reduction of corruption to ensure that Canadian companies are treated in a fair and just manner. Beyond having an impact in the commercial domain, an improved commitment to the rule of law could help to cut through ideological divides and to provide a more solid institutional foundation for interested Canadians.

As a market economy with a social safety net, Canada can act as an important example or model and share best practices with the Venezuelans on regulatory frameworks, public-private partnerships, and the role of the state. Both the Canadian government and non-governmental organizations (NGOs) with links to their counterparts on the ground in Venezuela could also take into account the legal definition of a civil society organization, which has been under serious consideration by the Venezuelan courts.

Since the Bolivarian Revolution is still under way, we cannot measure its final results or impact. Sympathizers and supporters feel that the drastic change is necessary to reach a more equitable distribution of wealth and resources, and that greater prosperity will come from the reforms of the Bolivarian Revolution. Chávez has indicated that his changes are driven by a new form of socialist revolution – though details have been few. Critics, on the other hand, refer to the absence of the rule of law, corruption, economic mismanagement, the lack of checks on the power of the president, and the revolution's threats to democracy in the country and the wider region. Any improvement in the bilateral relationship, then, must begin with a clear understanding of these social, economic, and geopolitical realities in Venezuela. This all suggests that there is an opportunity for Canada to skilfully bring forth best practices in trying to bridge the gap between the two sides. To be sure, looking beyond the rhetoric, many of the goals Venezuelans strive for are compatible with Canada's vision of democratic development. But a constructive bilateral relationship must begin with mutual respect, pragmatic (and non-ideological) dialogue, and a belief that engagement is more profitable than estrangement.

NOTES

1 Jean Daudelin, 'Canada and the Americas: A Time for Modesty,' *Behind the Headlines*, 64, no. 3 (2007): 2.

308   Canada Looks South

2 Canada had been a Permanent Observer since 1972. See D.R. Murray, 'The Bilateral Road: Canada and Latin America in the 1980s,' *International Journal* 37, no. 1 (Winter 1981–2): 108–31.
3 Peter McKenna, *Canada and the OAS: From Dilettante to Full Partner* (Ottawa: Carleton University Press, 1995), 163.
4 For an analysis of Canadian-Latin American events prior to this period, see Gordon Mace, 'Explaining Canada's Decision to Join the OAS: An Interpretation,' in Nelson Michaud and Kim Richard Nossal (eds.), *Diplomatic Departures: The Conservative Era in Canadian Foreign Policy, 1984–93* (Vancouver: UBC Press, 2001); James Rochlin, *Discovering the Americas: The Evolution of Canadian Foreign Policy towards Latin America* (Vancouver: UBC Press, 1994); Brian J.R. Stevenson, *Canada, Latin America, and the New Internationalism: A Foreign Policy Analysis, 1968–1990* (Montreal: McGill-Queen's University Press, 2000); Jerry Haar and Ed Dosman (eds.), *A Dynamic Partnership: Canada's Changing Role in the Americas* (Miami: University of Miami, North-South Center, 1993); J.C.M. Ogelsby, *Gringos from the Far North: Essays in the History of Canadian-Latin American Relations, 1866–1968* (Toronto: Macmillan, 1976).
5 Hal Klepak, 'What's in It for Us? Canada's Relationship with Latin America,' *Ottawa: Fondation canadienne pour les Amériques, section Québec* (FOCAL-Québec, 1994), 6.
6 The OAS was established in 1948 as the successor to the 1910 Pan American Union (PAU).
7 Brian Mulroney, 'Prime Minister Announces Canada's Intent to Join the Organization of American States,' Prime Minister's Office, news release, San José, Costa Rica (27 October 1989), 5.
8 Stevenson, *Canada, Latin America, and the New Internationalism,* 182. For a more detailed overview of Canada's changing role in Latin America and the debates surrounding its decision to join the OAS, see McKenna, *Canada and the OAS*; Rochlin, *Discovering the Americas;* Stevenson, *Canada, Latin America, and the New Internationalism*; Murray, 'The Bilateral Road.'
9 McKenna, *Canada and the OAS,* 134.
10 John Graham, *A Magna Carta for the Americas. The Inter-American Democratic Charter: Genesis, Challenges and Canadian Connections?* policy document (Ottawa: The Canadian Foundation for the Americas, 2002).
11 Ibid., 4.
12 Barry S Levitt, 'A Desultory Defense of Democracy: The Organization of American States, Resolution 1080 and the Inter-American Democratic Charter,' *Latin American Politics and Society* 48, no. 3 (2006): 95.
13 Maxwell A. Cameron, 'The Inter-American Democratic Charter: Challeng-

es and Opportunities for the Collective Defence and Promotion of Democracy in the Americas,' *FocalPoint Spotlight on the Americas* 2, no. 3 (Ottawa: The Canadian Foundation for the Americas, March 2003): 4.

14 Thomas Legler, Sharon Lean, and Dexter Boniface (eds.), *Promoting Democracy in the Americas* (Baltimore: Johns Hopkins University Press, 2007), 11.

15 Stephen Harper, 'Interview,' *Americas Quarterly* (Fall 2007): 10.

16 Government of Canada, 'Prime Minister Stephen Harper Addresses the House of Commons in a Reply to the Speech from the Throne' (17 October 2007) http://www.sft-ddt.gc.ca/eng/media.asp?id=1373 (accessed 15 January 2010).

17 Government of Canada, *Canada and the Americas: Priorities and Progress* (Ottawa: Government of Canada, 2009), 6.

18 Harper, 'Interview,' 10.

19 Ibid.

20 For a historical overview of diplomatic relations see Alejandro Coutreras Ramírez, *Canadá-Venezuela 143 años de amistad*, Gobierno Bolivariano de Venezuela (Caracas: Dirección General de Archivos y Bibliotecas, División de Investigación Histórica, División de Biblioteca, 2007).

21 Conversation with a former Canadian diplomat on a not-for-attribution basis, 11 February 2010; interview with a senior representative of the Canadian government on a not-for-attribution basis, 19 January 2010.

22 Jim Creskey, 'The Bolivarian Revolution Touches Down in Ottawa,' *Embassy Magazine*, 13 July 2005, 19.

23 Jim Creskey, 'Selling 21st Century Socialism,' *Embassy Magazine*, 17 September 2007, 2.

24 Ibid.

25 Conversations with current and former Embassy of Canada in Caracas employees and diplomats on a not-for-attribution basis, November 2009–March 2010.

26 Roy Chaderton Matos, 'Intervención del Representante Permanente de la Republica Bolivariana de Venezuela ante la Organización de los estados Americanos' (Washington DC, 3 February 2010).

27 Francis Fukuyama, *The End of History and the Last Man* (New York: Avon, 1992).

28 For more detail see Juan Linz, *The Breakdown of Democratic Regimes* (Baltimore: Johns Hopkins University Press, 1978); Adam Przeworski et al., *Democracy and Development: Political Institutions and Well-Being in the World 1950–1990* (Cambridge: Cambridge University Press, 2000); Samuel Huntington, *The Third Wave* (Norman: University of Oklahoma Press, 1991).

29 Thomas Carothers, 'The End of the Transition Paradigm,' *Journal of*

Democracy 13, no. 1 (2002): 5–21; Larry Diamond, 'Thinking about Hybrid Regimes,' *Journal of Democracy* 13, no. 2 (2002): 21–35; Fareed Zakaria, *The Future of Freedom: Illiberal Democracy at Home and Abroad* (New York: Norton, 2004).

30 For a critique of Chávez's 'participatory democracy,' see Roberta Rice, 'Venezuela: Pacts, Populism, and Poverty,' in Katherine Isbester (ed.), *The Paradox of Democracy in Latin America: Ten Country Studies of Division and Resilience* (Toronto: University of Toronto Press, 2011), 229–49.

31 For an assessment of Venezuelan democracy see: Michael Coppedge, 'Prospects for Democratic Governability in Venezuela,' *Journal of Interamerican Studies and World Affairs* 36, no. 2 (1994): 39–64; Jennifer McCoy and David Myers, *The Unraveling of Representative Democracy in Venezuela* (Baltimore: Johns Hopkins University Press, 2003); Julia Buxton, 'The Deepening of Venezuela's Bolivarian Revolution, Why Most People Don't Get It,' Open Democracy Net (2007), http://www.opendemocracy.net/democracy-protest/deepening-revolution-4592.jsp.

32 A new education law was passed in August 2009. Critics of the law argue that it is intended to indoctrinate children. The education minister, Hector Navarro, defends the law as a means of bringing greater equality to the nation and as a way to help build participatory democracy. For example, Article 15 says that one of the basic purposes of education is 'to develop a new political culturé based on protagonist participation and the strengthening of popular power, the democratization of knowledge, and the promotion of the school as a space for the formation of citizenship and community participation, for the reconstruction of the public spirit.' See Brian Thompson, 'Venezuela's Polarized Society Split by Another Issue: Chávez's Robust Educational Reform Roils the Political Waters' (Washington, DC: Council on Hemispheric Affairs, 10 September 2009), http://www.coha.org/venezuela%E2%80%99s-polarized-society-split-by-another-issue-chavez%E2%80%99s.

33 Department of Foreign Affairs and International Trade Canada, *A New Focus on Democracy Support. Government Response to the Eighth Report of the Standing Committee on Foreign Affairs and International Development: Advancing Canada's Role in International Support for Democratic Development* (Ottawa, 2 November 2007), http://www.international.gc.ca/democracy_support.aspx (accessed 15 December 2009), 5–6.

34 Government of Canada, *Canada-Venezuelan Relations*, http://www.canadainternational.gc.ca/venezuela/bilateral_relations_bilaterales/canada_venezuela.aspx?menu_id=7&menu=L (accessed 23 December 2009).

35 The Venezuelan government expressed its concern over the state of democ-

racy in Canada and, in response to concerns expressed by Canada over freedom of expression in Venezuela, questioned the Harper government's prorogation of Canada's Parliament in December 2008 (in the face of a non-confidence vote) and its December 2009 prorogation for reasons of recalibration.

36 With the July 2011 news of a cancerous tumour being removed from Chávez, it remains to be seen what impact that will have on the scheduled October 2012 presidential elections. Mery Mogollon and Chris Kraul, 'Venezuela says Hugo Chavez Will Remain in Charge,' *Los Angeles Times*, 2 July 2011, A4. It is worth noting that at the time of this writing, Chávez and his administration had publicly professed that he would be a candidate.

37 Government of Canada, *Canada-Venezuelan Relations* (2009). CIDA disbursements to Venezuela for 2009–10 were a paltry $1.3 million. For all intents and purposes, though, there is very little in the way of real dialogue – as of this writing in mid-2012 – between the two countries.

38 Legler, Lean, and Boniface (eds.), *Promoting Democracy in the Americas*, 205.

39 Ibid. In this chapter, Legler, recounting his personal experience as a member of the observation team, states that there were several democratic backslides that the OAS was unable to prevent despite being present in Venezuela, including the controversial Supreme Court expansion. Ibid., 216–17.

40 This was also done based on instruction from the influential Rio Group (a group developed to encourage dialogue between Latin American countries), which had coincidently been meeting at the same time.

41 It is worth noting that electoral observation missions from both the OAS and the European Union identified problems with the use of state resources to support Chávez's campaign, coercion against public employees, and biased media coverage. But observation missions reported that the voting occurred in a manner that was both free and fair. As Paul Durand, the Canadian ambassador to the OAS at the time of the 2006 presidential election, noted, 'there was not a large enough team or enough time or resources to validate the electoral process beyond reasonable doubt. The OAS confined its opinion to the actual election day, rather than providing a broader view of how the electoral process had developed. What we did see was acceptable – we just weren't allowed to see enough to eliminate all doubts.' In Paul Durand, 'The OAS and Democracy in the Americas' (Ottawa: Foreign Affairs and International Development Canada), http://www.dfait-maeci.gc.ca/cip-pic/features-manchettes/democracy-democratie/paul_durand.aspx (accessed 14 December 2009).

42 Conversation with a former high-ranking representative of the Canadian government on a not-for-attribution basis.

43 Maxwell A. Cameron and Catherine Hecht, 'Canada's Engagement with Democracy in the Americas,' *Canadian Foreign Policy* 14, no. 3 (October 2008): 9–10, http://works.bepress.com/maxwell_a_cameron/4/ (accessed 14 December 2009).

44 At the time of writing several governments in the hemisphere and non-government actors were seeking to expand the channels to involve the OAS, including by the request of legislatures and judiciaries. The political climate in the hemisphere at this time suggests that such a change is unlikely in the short term.

45 Richard Gott, *In the Shadow of the Liberator: Hugo Chávez and the Transformation of Venezuela* (London: Verso, 2000), 192.

46 Ibid., 190.

47 Department of Foreign Affairs and International Trade, Government of Canada. Canada-Venezuelan Relations, http://www.canadainternational.gc.ca/venezuela/bilateral_relations_bilaterales/canada_venezuela.aspx?menu_id=7&menu=L (accessed 23 December 2009).

48 'The Canadian Trade Commissioner Service,' *Commerce and Economic Quarterly Newsletter* (December 2009).

49 Industry Canada, http://www.ic.gc.ca/eic/site/tdo-dcd.nsf/eng/home (accessed May 2010).

50 Two-way trade for 2010–11 declined slightly, totalling $1.3 billion. Total Canadian direct investment in Venezuela is comparatively small at $700 million. Figures drawn from Government of Canada, *Fact Sheet: Canada-Venezuela Relations* (Ottawa: Department of Foreign Affairs and International Trade, April 2012).

51 Government of Canada, *Negotiations and Agreements* (Ottawa: Department of Foreign Affairs and International Trade, 2010), http://www.international.gc.ca/trade-agreements-accords-commerciaux/agr-acc/index.aspx?view=d.

52 Department of Foreign Affairs and International Trade Canada, *Canada's Foreign Investment Promotion and Protection Agreements (FIPAs)*, http://www.international.gc.ca/trade-agreements-accords-commerciaux/agr-acc/fipa-apie/index.aspx (accessed 23 December 2009).

53 Conversation with a high-level business official who has spent several years in the Venezuelan market, on a not-for-attribution basis, 16 December 2009.

54 Telephone conversation with the chief executive officer of a Canadian company operating in Venezuela, on a not for attribution basis, 4 January 2010.

55 Department of Foreign Affairs and International Trade Canada, *Canada's International Market Access Report* (Ottawa, 2008), http://www.international.

gc.ca/trade-agreements-accords-commerciaux/cimar-rcami/2008_09_08. aspx?lang=eng (accessed 21 December 2009).

56 In May 2010, trading in currency at private brokerage companies in Venezuela had been frozen.

57 Veronica Lares, *Venezuela Economics* (Ottawa: Export Development Canada (EDC), December 2009).

58 The national oil company (PDVSA) has special rules and can hold currency abroad, meaning it is not as constrained as companies in the private sector. Venezuela used a foreign exchange control in the mid-1990s as a temporary measure to avoid capital flight. Economic analysts suggest that this will again be a temporary measure, but how long it is in place will largely depend on the health of the Venezuelan economy.

59 Telephone conversation with the chief executive officer of a Canadian company operating in Venezuela, on a not-for-attribution basis, 4 January 2010.

60 Conversation with a Latin American economic analyst on a not-for-attribution basis, January 2011.

61 Ibid.

62 W. Ratliff, 'Pragmatism over Ideology: China's Relations with Venezuela,' *China Brief* 6, no. 6 (14 March 2006), http://www.jamestown.org/programs/chinabrief/single/?tx_ttnews[tt_news]=3936&tx_ttnews[backPid]=196&no_cache=1 (accessed 4 January 2010).

63 Some business analysts fear that allocating contracts based on ideological background and not skill level has damaged the capacity, most notably, of the state-owned oil company in Venezuela.

64 Graeme Clark, 'Some Thoughts on Canada and Hemispheric Security' in H.P. Klepack (ed.), *Canada and Latin American Security* (Laval: Méridien, 1998), 91.

65 Harper, 'Interview,' 8.

66 Conversation with a security analyst on a not-for-attribution basis, February 2009.

67 Chávez has recommended that Latin America form a military alliance that excludes the U.S., which he often accuses of preparing for an imminent attack on Venezuela.

12 The Current Paradox in Brazil-Canada Relations and the Path Forward

W.E. (TED) HEWITT

The bilateral relationship between Canada and Brazil has improved markedly since the days nearly a decade ago when the Bombardier-Embraer and mad cow debacles largely defined the diplomatic space between the two countries. Until very recently, however, and despite efforts at the highest political and bureaucratic levels within both Ottawa and Brasilia, progress in defining and acting upon a unique Brazil-Canada bilateral agenda has been very slow indeed.[1]

Scholarly commentary on the state of Brazil-Canada relations is surprisingly sparse.[2] In fact, little has been offered on this front since the publication by the Canadian Foundation for the Americas (FOCAL), nearly a decade ago, of two important position papers describing the past, present, and future of relations between the two countries: Florencia Jubany's *Getting Over the Jet-Lag: Canada Brazil Relations 2001* and Edgar Dosman and Kenneth Frankel's *Brazil and Canada: What Is to Be Done.*[3] Of the two, Dosman and Frankel offered the most prescriptive recipe for 'building an agenda for change' in the Canada-Brazil relationship. Specifically, they recommended: a joint Eminent Persons Group to review the overall relationship and reach out to stakeholders; a joint Ministerial Committee and engagement with the private sector; a Brazilian studies network in Canada and increased student mobility; joint development assistance opportunities; media scholarships to enhance mutual understanding; and the promotion of trade and investment linkages.

Based upon the observations made by Jubany, this chapter revisits this debate but takes a somewhat different approach than seen previously with respect to understanding the current impasse and the bilateral road forward. Its primary observation is that traditional and diplomatic efforts to get the Canada-Brazil relationship on track – often focusing on high-level political interaction and the definition of joint agendas – has had minimal effect and has accomplished little in terms of kick-starting productive interchange between the two countries. What has been obvious to those directly involved, and is only now attracting the attention of key stakeholders in the foreign affairs community in Canada, is the potential for building the relationship between the two countries from the bottom up, effectively taking advantage of the positive interaction that is already occurring within the economy and some sectors of civil society.

Although there may well be a number of instances where this can be demonstrated, this chapter focuses on just three, as signalled by: 1) the recent and dramatic increase in Brazilian investment in Canada in several key sectors of the Canadian economy; 2) enhanced interchange among Canadian and Brazilian academics and scientists in areas ranging from Brazilian studies to alternative energy; and 3) the significant opening of the cultural space between the two countries forged as a result of the Canadian Governor General's visit to Brazil in 2007 (and Governor General David Johnson's visit in April 2012). In the sections that follow, this chapter explores the contours of the apparent paradox between official and community 'diplomacy' in each of these respects with an eye to understanding its implications for the prospective development of a more meaningful bilateral relationship that can offer lasting benefits to the citizens of both countries.

The Importance of the Brazil Factor in Canada

For much of their history to the end of the twentieth century, Canada and Brazil existed largely in sociopolitical, economic, and diplomatic isolation from each other. Within the Americas, their relatively infrequent interactions were largely conditioned by a mutual economic and political relationship with the United States. For Brazil, Canada was essentially viewed as an extension of the American frontier. For Canada, Brazil was, for the most part, an unknown, one of thirteen South American nations operating within the U.S. sphere of influence. By the end of the century, bilateral trade appeared to have plateaued at some $3–5 billion per year, equivalent to about twice the value of goods and services crossing the border between Canada and the U.S every single day.[4] Tourism was largely inconsequential, outside of a few exclusive jetsetters on both sides of the equator.

This situation began to change during the 1990s, but in some respects perhaps for all the wrong reasons. A growing array of very public international disputes effectively put the two countries on each other's radar, but more as a contest of wills as opposed to peaceful cooperation and productive relationship building. In 1992, two Canadians – Christine Spencer and David Lamont – were arrested in Brazil and subsequently convicted for their role in orchestrating the kidnapping of Brazilian supermarket magnate Abílio dos Santos Diniz. In response to growing public pressure to act on behalf of the pair, whom many in Canada believed to be innocent of the crime, the Canadian government openly took up their cause and pressured the Brazilian government to intervene in the case. The apparent lack of faith in Canada in the Brazilian justice system was enough of an irritant, but the situation was further aggravated in 1995 when, during a state visit to Ottawa by then president Fernando Henrique Cardoso, Prime Minister Jean Chrétien halted a diplomatic motorcade on Parliament Hill in order to speak personally to the parents of one of the jailed Canadians. Brazil was later vindicated as evidence from an arrest and search of documents found in Nicaragua firmly established the Canadians' guilt as major players in the abduction and sequestration of Mr Diniz.

In 1997, tensions escalated again when Canada's preoccupation with protection of its aerospace industry led to a petition to the World Trade Organization (WTO) claiming that unfair government subsidies of Brazil's formidable aircraft manufacturer Embraer were eating into the profitability of Quebec's Bombardier Inc. Brazil responded in kind, and following sequential WTO rulings interpreted alternately in each country's favour, the dispute has quietly simmered for years, with the two nations agreeing to disagree and to forge pragmatic solutions which have essentially allowed current subsidization practices to continue while ensuring a more level playing field for each other's business and passenger aircraft.[5] The most visible outcome of this détente is Air Canada's growing fleet of Embraer regional jets and the awarding of a major contract for the extension of the São Paulo subway to Bombardier rail division.

A new low point eventually appeared, however, during the year 2001 when Canada arbitrarily halted imports of Brazilian beef out of fear that it might carry the serious mad cow disease – despite the fact that not one case had been reported by Brazilian authorities. It was later revealed that the incident had been precipitated by Brazil's apparent failure to file an import document with Canadian health authorities within the prescribed time frame. This action subsequently spawned widespread public outrage in Brazil that included demonstrations at the Canadian mission in Brasilia and the dumping of Canadian whisky in the streets of São Paulo.

For the Brazilian government, the story may well have ended there, especially as it has moved in recent years to establish its presence as the regional powerhouse in South America and to develop stronger ties with other emerging economic powers such as India, China, and Russia.[6] In this scenario, Canada did and does not now figure prominently. For its part, however, amid growing realization of Brazil's increasing importance as an economic power and potential receptor for Canadian exports, the Canadian government after 2002 slowly began to search for ways to build more productive relations with its hemispheric neighbour. This resulted in a series of actions designed to forge better linkages at the diplomatic level with the Brazilian government. These included the setting aside or compartmentalization of the long-simmering Bombardier-Embraer dispute, the creation of a Senior Interdepartmental Committee within DFAIT to focus on the relationship with Brazil; the initiation of bilateral consultations at the deputy-ministerial level[7]; meetings and visits of senior ministers and their delegations[8]; discussions regarding potential military cooperation; collaboration in international development assistance between the Canadian International Development Agency (CIDA) and the Agência Brasileira de Cooperação;[9] and the recent formation of a Canada-Brazil steering committee to manage the Science and Technology agreement signed between the two countries in 2008. Canada and Brazil have also engaged together in peacekeeping activities and state building in Haiti.

Despite such efforts to develop a joint understanding and agenda between the two countries, no one can seriously argue that Canada's current relationship with Brazil has achieved anything close to its full potential. Ironically, where most successes have been recorded in the Brazil-Canada relationship is on the ground, through various forms of economic and community engagement occurring at the grassroots level: through economic interchange and investment, academic cooperation, and exchanges in the arts and cultural realm, each of which is discussed below.

Financed in Brazil, Made in Canada

Between 2004 and 2009, Canadian imports of Brazilian goods remained fairly steady at about $2.5–3 billion, over twice the value of Canadian goods exported to Brazil. In 2008, however, largely as a result of strong growth in the Brazilian economy, Canadian exports climbed dramatically to an all-time high of $2.6 billion, effectively eliminating a trade imbalance that had for many years favoured Brazil.[10] In the following year, this slipped back to historic levels, effectively leaving Brazil as Canada's twelfth-largest export market[11] and signalling that total trade remains relatively small – certainly far less than Canada has managed to secure with other economic powerhouses of the so-called BRIC countries, notably China.[12]

Significantly, however, and with much stronger implications for the relationship between the two countries, direct foreign investment by Brazil in Canada has literally exploded since the turn of the century. Currently, Brazil has nearly $14 billion invested in Canada, now surpassing by a wide margin the $9.5 billion that Canadian companies have invested in Brazil. Indeed, Brazil is now the seventh-largest source of foreign investment in Canada, a keystone upon which to build a mutually beneficial Canada-Brazil relationship.

Readers of any of the business pages in prominent Canadian newspapers are undoubtedly aware of the Brazilian appetite for buying up local companies. The march effectively began in 2001, when Votorantim of Brazil purchased St Mary's Cement, with operations throughout southern Ontario and in eastern Michigan. Then in 2002, Gerdau Steel of Brazil made an intial foray into the North American market through its purchase of Ameristeel operations in Ontario. From its humble beginnings in Cambridge, Ontario, the new company, GerdauAmeristeel, has established a foothold in virtually every part of the production line. Two year later, Brazil's Ambev, which had earlier merged with Interbrew of Belgium to create a global brewing giant, assumed control of Labatt's. The most recent major acquisition by the Brazilians was the purchase of nickel mining and refining firm Inco by the Companhia Vale do Rio Doce (CVRD) in 2006.

Virtually all such takeovers produced an in-migration of Brazilian management teams in cities and towns throughout much of southern and central Ontario with the sole mission of reorganizing and ensuring maximum profitability of these new ventures. For the most part, however, the newcomers went unnoticed in their new host communities. In fact, despite the fact that many even fly the Brazilian flag at their corporate offices, there seems to be little recognition of the Brazilians' presence or even efforts to capitalize upon it through attempts to attract additional Brazilian investment. This is in stark contrast to efforts by local economic development agencies to promote investment by German, South Korean, and other international firms through active recruitment.

Even more remarkable is the almost complete lack of positive recognition on the part of the government of Canada of this new wave of investment. In fact, one may argue that just the opposite is true. Certainly this is the case where CVRD ownership of INCO is concerned, given recent criticism of that company's putative failure to live up to agreements it had made regarding maintenance of employment levels, despite the worst downturn in thirty years. And although the federal government has since backed off of this position, the perceived role of CVRD in prolonging a strike by its unionized personnel during the second half of 2009 has drawn similar criticism from both government sources and NGOs.

A Scholarly Approach

Relationships between scholars in Brazil and Canada have a long history, and in a variety of disciplines.[13] Some of the relationships have given structure through membership of Canadian and Brazilian academics in scholarly networks, such as the Canadian Association of Latin American and Caribbean Studies, and even U.S.-based groups such as the Latin American Studies Association, and especially the Brazilian Studies Association. More recently, Canadian government support for the Association of Canadian Studies in Brazil (ABECAN) has seen broader collaboration emerge, including major growth in attendance at ABECAN conferences in Brazil, such as the one held in Goiania in November of 2009.[14]

In terms of scholarly interest and publication, the numbers of theses produced by Canadian graduate students on topics related to Brazil has grown substantially over the years, from one or two per year in the 1970s to ten to twelve by the turn of this century. In addition, publications (monographs, refereed articles, book chapters) produced by Canadian authors on Brazil have increased from six per year to nine on average in this decade.[15]

In recognition of the work they have done and their contribution to scholarship in Brazil, many Canadian academics have been awarded prestigious prizes. For example, Edgar Dosman (York University) and Hendrik Kraay (University of Calgary) were awarded the Order of

Rio Branco by the Brazilian Ministry of Foreign Relations in 2003. This award specifically recognized the work of both in enhancing diplomatic relations between Brazil and Canada through their development of the Canadian Visiting Research Chair in Brazilian Studies program. In recognition of his longtime collaborations in Brazil and especially the role he has played in training Brazilian graduate students in computer science and software engineering, Waterloo University professor Don Cowan received in 2006 the Brazilian National Order of Scientific Merit's Grand Cross, presented to him by the president of the republic in a ceremony in Brasilia. By contrast, it would appear that no Brazilian scholars have been accorded similar honours by the government of Canada.

Other than membership in associations, academic programs designed exclusively to promote scholarly interchange between Canada and Brazil are few and far between.[16] One notable exception is the Centre for Research on Brazil (CERB), formed at the Université du Québec à Montréal (UQAM) in the late 1990s. Over the past decade, CERB has served as a lightning rod for study, research, and interaction for Brazilianist research in Canada, although its influence has largely been restricted to the province of Quebec.

By far the most comprehensive academic program oriented towards bilateral collaboration in research is the Canada Visiting Research Program in Brazilian Studies.[17] The Brazil Chair was established in 2003 by a consortium of four Canadian institutions – the University of Calgary, the University of Western Ontario, York University, and UQAM – with support from the Canadian government's Department of Foreign Affairs and International Trade, the International Development Research Centre, and the Brazilian Embassy in Ottawa. In 2006, Saint Mary's University in Halifax joined the consortium.

Historically, the primary objectives of the Chair have been to accelerate constituency building and knowledge sharing between Canada and Brazil among universities, government, and business. By agreement among the partners, distinguished Brazilian scholars are invited to Canada each year for a period of at least two weeks. Typically, Chairs are expected to deliver at least one major address at each of the participating universities, meet with faculty, students, and representatives from both government and the private sector, and participate in organized events such as conferences or workshops.

Brazil Chairs to date have included some of Brazil's leading authorities in a wide variety of sectors and disciplines, from agriculture to steel, the environment, urban development and alternative energy. They include Marcos Jank, formerly of Universidade de São Paulo and now president of UNICA (the Brazilian cane producers association), Germano de Paula (Universidade Federal de Uberlândia), Lucio Kowarick (Universidade de São Paulo), Antonio Brand and Cleonice Le Bourlegat (Universidade Católica Don Bosco – Campo Grande), Rafael Villa (Universidade de São Paulo), Fernando Henrique Cardoso (world-renowned sociologist and former president of Brazil), and Roberto Schaeffer (Universidade Federal do Rio de Janeiro).

In conjunction with the Chair program, a number of events have been held across Canada focusing on critical issues of importance to Brazilians and Canadians. The inaugural Chair event, held at the University of Calgary in 2003, focused on the role of Canada and Brazil in international agricultural trade. The following year, the Lawrence National Centre for Management and Policy at the Ivey School of Business, University of Western Ontario, hosted a day-long conference on world trade in steel. This event was attended by senior federal politicians; administrators from both federal and provincial levels; academics from Western, the University of Toronto, and the University of Calgary; and business leaders. In 2005, York University, with the support of a number of agencies, including IDRC, Industry Canada, CIDA, the Forum of Federations, and DFAIT, hosted an international conference on urban planning and development in Brazil. The following year, Saint Mary's University hosted a workshop focusing on contemporary Brazilian foreign policy. Invited speakers included Guillermo Rishchynski, then Canadian ambassador to Brazil, and Valdemar Carneiro Leão, then Brazilian ambassador to Canada.

In 2007, the University of Western Ontario organized a one-day seminar featuring Dr Fernando Henrique Cardoso, who spoke on democracy and development in Brazil. Finally, the Brazil Chair program, in collaboration with the Department of Foreign Affairs and International Trade, was instrumental in organizing a bilateral conference on Canada-Brazil Scientific Cooperation in Renewable Energy in 2008. The conference attracted over one hundred participants from a large number of agencies and ministries of both the Canadian and Brazilian governments, businesspeople and entrepreneurs in the energy sector, and academics and scientists from both countries. Guests included scientist, academic, and politician Jose Goldemberg, former minister of science and technology in the Brazilian government; Mme Marie-Lucie Morin, Canada's deputy minister of international trade; as well as the

Brazilian ambassador to Canada (Paulo Cordeiro) and the Canadian ambassador to Brazil (Paul Hunt).

The impact of these various initiatives lives on through a number of publications. These include *Trade Negotiations in Agriculture: A Future Common Agenda for Brazil and Canada*, a collection of articles emerging from the University of Calgary event and published by the University of Calgary Press. Another collection, *Brazil and Canada in the Americas*, was edited by Rosana Barbosa of Saint Mary's University and distributed by the Gorsebrook Research Institute. And finally *The Canada-Brazil Round Table on International Trade in Steel* was published by the Ivey School of Business as a record of the Brazil Chair conference on steel held at Western.

It is fair to say that the Brazil Chair initiative has now opened the door to a number of more recent academic initiatives that are providing unparalleled opportunities for collaboration among Canadian and Brazilian scientists. The newly minted Canada-Brazil Science and Technology Agreement will provide equal contributions from both countries (up to $3 million) to support collaborative research in key areas of importance to both countries, including the environment and energy, nanotechnology, and the life sciences. Although the bulk of the funding is unlikely to become available until 2012 at the earliest, a number of collaborations – particularly in the energy sector – have already emerged involving biomass conversion and wastewater treatment from the ethanol production process. These and other programs have been funded by the International Science and Technology Partnerships Canada program, which has pulled together funding from a variety of sources to fund incipient research and start the ball rolling on significant academic and industry collaborations. In addition, in partnership with Brazil, the Department of Foreign Affairs and International Trade has initiated a small-scale funding program (the Canada-Brazil Awards) to enhance mobility for graduate students in the two countries and to allow them to participate in ongoing research projects.

Citizen Diplomacy

Another door that has been opened widely – if tentatively – falls within the realm of what might be called citizen diplomacy. This was essentially the theme of the visit to Brazil made by former Governor General Michaëlle Jean in July 2007. In her own words, the trip represented an opportunity to 'strengthen an old and natural relationship between Brazil and Canada, as Brazil has many similarities with Canada. This trip will also be an opportunity to strengthen the ties that exist in many different sectors, as Brazil is one of Canada's most important partners in the Americas.'[18] Through the visit, the Governor General sought to exercise 'diplomacy at the human level' with various sectors of civil society, as part of a novel effort to strengthen people-to-people relationships between Brazil and Canada. This approach was made manifest from the start in the broad array of individuals chosen to accompany her on the visit. Government representatives constituted only a small minority of participants and included the National Science Advisor, the president of the International Development Research Centre, and a DFAIT official. For the most part, delegates were chosen to represent the full spectrum of the Canadian artistic, cultural, and social activist communities: the director-general of Alternatives; the international programmer for the Toronto film festival; the director of Winnipeg's Grafitti Gallery; the head of Development and Peace; the co-founder of TakingITGlobal; an aboriginal youth leader; an AIDS activist; a representative of the La Francophonie; as well as artists and filmmakers, including the Governor General's own husband, Jean-Daniel Lafond.

Arriving aboard a Canadian Air Force transport aircraft, the delegation spent over a week meeting with various cultural and activist groups in Brazil. Beginning in Salvador, the group was hosted by Olodum, the musical percussion group that has made a name for itself worldwide not only for its music but for its engagement with the poor of that city. Some members of the delegation also visited GAPA-Bahia, a non-governmental organization working on AIDS prevention, while others participated in a public forum entitled 'Film as a Force for Social Change: Accommodating Diversity in Canada and Brazil.' In São Paulo, the next stop, the group participated in a similar dialogue on arts and new technologies. The same day, the Governor General addressed a sell-out crowd at a luncheon event sponsored by the Brazil-Canada Chamber of Commerce. Her message, reiterated the next day in her speech at her elaborate welcoming ceremony in Brasilia – hosted by President Lula – focused almost exclusively on the human dimension of the ties between the two countries: respect for ecological and human diversity; a commitment to peacekeeping, social inclusion, respect for human rights, and poverty reduction; and, lastly, education and the arts.

By all accounts, the visit was a huge success. The level of interaction between Canadian delegates and their hosts was indeed remarkable, with much praise on both sides for the work that they had accomplished, particularly in the sphere of community activism. Moreover, their own accounts pointed to a number of opportunities for follow-up activities. For example, a representative from the São Paulo State Secretary of Culture offered space to a Canadian delegate to mount an exhibition at the state's Museum of Image and Sound. In addition, the forum on film in Canada and Brazil, as well as the two Canadian films exhibited – Jean-Daniel Lafond's *Tropic North* and Martine Chartrand's *Black Soul* – were broadcast by one of Brazil's national television networks. Perhaps most importantly, President Lula, in his response to the governor general's comments in Brasilia, pledged publicly to a commitment 'to furthering initiatives to bring our two countries closer together.' He ended his speech by affirming his intention 'to make my first official trip to Canada, possibly in the first half of 2008.'[19] Although that proposed visit did not occur, another opportunity was nevertheless created to further build the bilateral relationship through a promising 'grass-roots' initiative. But for whatever reason, until August 2011 (and not much since), there has been little in the way of follow-up from both sides.

Carpe Diem: A Canadian Diplomatic Non Sequitur

The question of the hour, of course, is why the Canadian government has not managed to effectively leverage the considerable impact of increasing Brazilian investment and growing scholarly and cultural ties to firmly establish a stronger political partnership and trading relationship between the two countries. There is no single answer to this question, but rather a series of clues explaining this outcome.

To begin with, there has been a failure on the part of Canadian political leaders and policy makers to clearly articulate a unique set of clear, focused objectives with respect to the relationship with Brazil. Up until the end of the 1990s, in fact, Brazil was considered by many within DFAIT as simply one of thirteen – that is, just one of the countries making up the South American continent. Where the United States government clearly considered, and treated, Brazil as its key South American ally and partner, no such special status has been accorded Brazil by Canada. And while it is true that Canada has certainly rethought and further developed its Americas position, as reflected in its decision to participate fully within the framework of the Organization of American States (OAS), it has been careful to strike a balance in relations with individual countries in the region. Clearly, such an exclusively bilateral approach does not jibe with Brazil's own aspirations as a regional superpower and stands as one potential block in the furtherance of the Brazil-Canada relationship. This seems especially odd given the Harper government's pledge in 2007 to make the Americas the centrepiece of its foreign policy universe.

As part of its broader innovation strategy, though, DFAIT has pushed to 'leverage international linkages and intelligence to enhance private sector commercialization through proactive partnerships.' This strategy has actively engaged various sectors, including government departments, universities, and researchers, as well as the private sector. In the case of Brazil, it has led to the successful negotiation of a science and technology agreement between the two countries. Signed in São Paulo in November 2008, the agreement will see the establishment of a joint committee to oversee the development of ancillary agreements on intellectual property and to establish priority sectors for collaboration. Both countries have agreed to invest $1.5 million (for a total of $3 million) to fund joint projects and thus stimulate interchange in research and development among researchers and industry. While the agreement has been ratified by Canada, and approved later by the Brazilian Congress, it did not come into effect until April 2010.[20]

One of the concerns expressed by Brazilian diplomats regarding the agreement, however, is that it is simply not focused enough on both areas of collaboration and outcomes. Moreover, the agreement comes on the heels of similar, previously negotiated agreements with India and China, and to which the Canadian government had already committed many times the amount allocated for Brazil. While an important first step, then, the Brazil-Canada Science and Technology agreement will likely not have the impact desired until additional investments can be leveraged and clear foci emerge – foci which unequivocally benefit both Canada's and Brazil's economic interests.

Just as Canada has struggled to define its own policy objectives for engagement, the methods that have been employed for securing what has been articulated to date have been somewhat misguided. In its diplomatic dialogue with Brazil, Canada has consistently emphasized this country's similarities with Brazil in a variety of respects: our joint commitment to global peace and peacekeeping; our frequently challenging relationship with the United States, the ethnic and racial diversity of our peoples, our commitment to education, and so forth. In fact, it can be argued that the two countries are not really that similar at all. Brazil is one of the world's most populous countries, and one that has taken a relatively non-linear path over the past century to democratic governance and economic development. Culturally, it is far more a melting pot than a mosaic. Its geopolitical aspirations and desire for major power influence are not confined to the South American continent but increasingly extend to the global theatre. And despite remarkable advances in recent years in the social realm, educational attainment for its citizens is still modest and social inequality pervasive. Economically, we are increasingly competitors in the global marketplace, in sectors from aerospace to forestry products, mining, automobile manufacturing, and other areas. Clearly, the 'we share similar values and aspirations' argument cannot be the sole building block for closer relations between the two countries.

In fact, by not recognizing the inherent differences between the two countries, Canada has often adopted a subtly patronizing approach to Brazil which has done little to aid in building a stronger bilateral relationship. In the wake of the Bombardier and tainted beef incidents, it was Canada that actually sought to test the waters of improved bilateral relations. But the fact that Brazil did not jump at the opportunity to re-engage puzzled many within the Canadian foreign policy community. What they failed to recognize and appreciate then – and is arguably still the case today – is that for Brazil, Canada largely remains a question mark and is far less important to its future development and international aspirations than Canadians would like to believe.

This gap in mutual perception and understanding has been continually reinforced over the years by the pervasive Canadian view that somehow Canada has much to 'offer' Brazil – much as it would to any other 'developing' nation or area. Frequently cited is our system of educational institutions, government legislation protecting the rights of minorities, regional development programming, and even English-language training. To Brazilian ears, such offers of 'assistance' not only appear to be antiquated but often frustratingly patronizing. To add insult to injury, such an approach comes on the heels of the war of words and actions that defined the period of the late 1990s, when Canada, in effect, undertook fairly aggressive and unbending steps to diminish the competitiveness of Brazil's aerospace sector and sought to close the door to Brazilian beef imports. At the time, a senior Canadian diplomat justified this approach to the author with reference to the need for Canada to stand up for once and eliminate the Brazilian manufacturing threat (after all, he added condescendingly: 'That is all they have going for them'). He concluded, wrongly as it turned out, that once the war was won, Canada would have no difficulty in 'making nice' and restoring the relationship between the two countries to a more productive state of affairs.

Conclusion

If we are to move forward in developing a long-term and mutually productive relationship with Brazil, we need a fresh approach and a clear set of high-level objectives that recognize Brazil for what it is: an economic powerhouse with a rapidly expanding global presence and status. We also need to recognize and accept the fact that in developing closer relations with Brazil, Canada is essentially beginning from a conspicuous deficit position. This does not just refer to the need to redress diplomatic hard feelings accruing from the Bombardier/tainted beef affairs of past years. It is more fundamental than that. Hard feelings and tainted memories aside, the fundamental reality is that just because we are interested in engaging Brazil does not mean that Brazil will automatically reciprocate. Brazil will engage, but only to the extent that clear benefit will accrue – benefit that will assist and reinforce its overarching goals of economic and social development, and regional/global influence.

There is now at least some evidence that, on the diplomatic front at least, a change in tactics and perceptions is occurring. Although long overdue, Prime Minister Stephen Harper (joined by four cabinet ministers) undertook a high-profile, two-day visit to Brazil in early August 2011 (in the wake of U.S. President Barack Obama's visit in March). Clearly, Canada is now recognizing that as an emerging economic powerhouse (though still only Canada's tenth-largest trading partner), Brazil is important for Canada's foray into the wider hemisphere and that Brazil needs to be at the centre of Harper's Americas strategy.[21] In large part, Harper's official visit was about bridge building and fence mending (given the irritants of the late 1990s and early 2000s mentioned at the outset of this chapter). According to one Canadian official, the central objective was to 'thicken the relationship to the point where little things don't screw everything up.'[22]

Accordingly, both Harper and Brazilian President Dilma Rousseff announced a series of relatively minor, but encouraging, economic, diplomatic, and investment-related initiatives. Included among these was a new air transport agreement (which is expected to lower the costs of flights), a Canada-Brazil Strategic Dialogue, a memorandum of understanding (MOU) on international development cooperation, and an agreement by both leaders to have their foreign ministers meet annually. A key measure was the highly touted creation of a CEO forum that would utilize executive talent from both countries to offer ways to expand Canada-Brazil trade. (Murilo Ferreira, the CEO of Brazil's mining giant Vale SA, which bought Canada's Inco several years back, was the first person to be named to the forum along with Canada's Rick Waugh, CEO of Scotiabank.) In addition to inviting President Rousseff to visit Canada soon, Harper offered to share with the Brazilians, who will be hosting the Summer Olympics in 2016, Canada's expertise in hosting three previous Olympic Games. Harper also indicated his commitment to visit the region more often: 'So, although this is my first visit to this magnificent country, I don't intend it to be my last. Indeed, I anticipate spending more time on this continent as we continue to pursue our Americas strategy.'[23]

In a major speech in São Paulo to a largely Canadian and Brazilian business audience, Harper reiterated the theme of placing Canada on Brazil's radar screen and improving bilateral commercial relations. In an obvious pitch to placate the Brazilians, and in a radical departure from the Conservative government's previous posturing, Harper pointed to the country's status as a major world power: 'For, when the world looks at Brazil, what does it see? It sees a new industrial power, forging ahead with information and communication technologies, justly proud of its aircraft industry and well on the way to becoming a space-faring nation with its own orbital launch capacity ... For these and many other reasons, Canadians applaud as Brazil takes its rightful place on the world stage.'[24] He even acknowledged that Ottawa has ignored Brazil for far too long and indicated his willingness to remedy this situation. He declared pointedly that 'too much grass grows in the cracks on the road between our two great countries. It is time for increased ambition and that is why I am here today.'[25] Equally important, the prime minister highlighted the fact that previous trade irritants and diplomatic disputes were a thing of the past, and that it was time to place Canada-Brazil relations on a much stronger bilateral footing. 'Ladies and gentlemen, I began by talking about how as nations we had travelled parallel roads in the past. But parallel roads never bring you together. But I suggest to you that it is not good enough any more. My earnest hope is that, in the days and months to come, we will make good decisions for the decades that follow: decisions that will put us, not on parallel tracks, but on a common highway to a great destiny together,' he said.[26]

To build on this incipient momentum, the areas of engagement identified earlier in this chapter – economic activity, collaboration in research and development, and cultural exchange – stand as at least three key areas to prioritize in building an effective and productive relationship with Brazil. For example, instead of complaining about the presumed business and labour practices of Brazilian mining giant Vale, Canada should be recognizing and celebrating the increasing tide of Brazilian investment and, in fact, working to expand it – within, of course, the framework of existing foreign investment legislation. Why is Brazil different from India or China in this respect, where investment is routinely greeted as good for the Canadian economy? Along with a concerted effort to encourage Canadian investment in Brazil, such a strategy can have no other effect but to enhance the level of productive interchange between the two countries, enhance levels of mutual understanding among key economic players, and lead to a greater appreciation among citizens of both countries of the investment realities in each other's economy.

In addition, and to the same end, serious future investment must be made to enhance interchange and collaboration among researchers, scientists, government, and the private sector in matters that both countries recognize as priority areas. Here again, the benefits of joint research and development work in areas such as ethanol production, biomass conversion, neuroscience, and nanotechnology can feed innovation across borders to the benefit of key industries. This is already occurring – particularly in areas related to the conversion of biomass residues to bio-oil (e.g., from the ethanol production process) – but more needs to be done in this regard. As joint programs of research reach maturity, they also attract additional researchers and trainees from both countries, leading to a broader exchange of personnel, information, and best practices between the two countries.

To date, very little funding has been invested in this type of activity, and with only $3 million allocated as stimulus for activities related to the Brazil-Canada Science and Technology agreement, this is not likely to increase significantly in the short term. To truly achieve impact, federal investments must be supplemented by targeting joint programming led by the Canadian research granting councils and their counterparts in Brazil, the Conselho Nacional de Desenvolvimento Científico e Tecnológico (CNPq) and the Coordenação de Aperfeiçoamento de Pessoal de Nível Superior (CAPES). To the extent that this has occurred to date at all, it has been led by post-secondary institutions themselves. For example, the University of Western Ontario, together with the University of Toronto, established in 2011 an agreement directly with the Fundacao de Ampara a Pesquisa do Estado de Sao Paulo (FAPESP) to provide $200,000 in seed money for joint projects involving the two Canadian institutions and prospective partner institutions in São Paulo.

Similarly, the value of artistic and cultural interchange to the Brazil-Canada relationship cannot be underestimated, given the importance of this sector (economically and strategically) within both countries. This is perhaps one reason why, within Canada at least, Quebec has long had a far more active and productive interchange with partners in Brazil. Some structures, such as the Brazilian Association of Canadian Studies, already exist and can help lead future collaborative activity focusing on exchange between Brazilian and Canadian artists, filmmakers, and authors. Given that ABECAN attracts hundreds of scholars from both Brazil and Canada to its bi-annual conferences, there would seem to be a logical opening here to expand upon such activity. Other formal programs might be established between institutions and arts councils to ensure that Canadian and Brazilian artists and musicians are regularly appearing in each other's countries and at important cultural events, such as film festivals. Here again, however, strategic investments on the part of governments, at both the federal and provincial level in Canada, would be required.

Such efforts are certainly not meant to, nor should they, supplant traditional diplomacy aimed at improving political relations with Brazil. Although Canada failed to secure a visit by President Lula before he left office in 2010, senior government officials have become frequent visitors to Brazil. By prioritizing and encouraging interchange among key sectors of the economy and civil society, however – and by investing serious resources in such activity – Canada could add effectively to its more traditional diplomatic efforts and send a much clearer signal that it wishes to engage Brazil on a priority basis, as an equal partner, and in recognition of Brazil's own national interests and global aspirations. It would also signal that the Harper government is willing to invest considerable resources to do so, much as other countries – notably the United States, France, and Germany – have already done.

For the Brazilians, the situation is somewhat more complex. The Brazilian government has historically been cool to the notion – perhaps related to a widespread assumption that Canada is little more than an extension of the United States, or at least geographically and geopolitically close enough such that Canada is widely perceived to offer little value to Brazilian aspirations. This may very well change under the presidency of Dilma Rousseff, but the Lamont-Spencer/ Bombardier/mad cow debacles have done nothing to dislodge such notions, or to form the basis for a new and 'special' relationship between the two countries. Justified or not, it is time for Brazil to move beyond the current frame and to put its relationship with Canada in higher gear. The potential benefits to Brazilians in terms of expanded trade, investment, tourism, and educational and cultural interchange are clear, as is the value of Canada's prospective support for the Brazilian diplomatic and geopolitical agenda – in at least some key respects. Moving in this direction will require closer attention and much more timely responses to Canadian advances and initiatives at the level of both high diplomacy and civil society. A good example is the Canada-Brazil Science and Technology Agreement. Brazil must also move to take full advantage of its burgeoning investments in Canada and the toehold it has gained in the Canadian market to enhance its presence in the mind of the Canadian consumer – much as Germany has done through clever merchandizing of it high-end products in the automotive, clothing, appliance, and other sectors. Until then, the two countries at opposite ends of the Americas will likely continue to persist as two 'solitudes.'

NOTES

1 The failure of Prime Minister Stephen Harper to hold a bilateral meeting with Brazil's former president, Luiz Inácio 'Lula' da Silva, at the April 2009 Summit of the Americas in Trinidad was emblematic of the need for a more salient and formal framework of engagement for Canada.
2 For a recent treatment, see Paul Alexander Haslam and Edison Rodrigues Barreto, Jr, 'Worlds Apart: Canadian and Brazilian Multilateralism in Comparative Perspective,' *Canadian Foreign Policy* 15, no. 1 (Spring 2009): 1–20; also see Annette Hester, 'Canada and Brazil: Confrontation or Cooperation?' in Andrew F. Cooper and Dane Rowlands (eds.), *Canada among Nations 2005: Split Images* (Montreal: McGill-Queen's University Press, 2005), 203–21.

3 Florencia Jubany, *Getting Over the Jet-Lag: Canada-Brazil Relations 2001* (Ottawa: FOCAL, 2001), 1–12; Edgar J. Dosman and Kenneth N. Frankel, *Brazil and Canada: What Is to Be Done?* (Ottawa: FOCAL, 2002), 1–8.

4 For a thoughtful discussion of Canada-Brazil relations in the early 2000s and how each country parted company on the Free Trade Area of the Americas (FTAA), see Hester, 'Canada and Brazil: Confrontation or Cooperation?' 213–14.

5 See Jean Daudelin, 'Trapped: Brazil, Canada, and the Aircraft Dispute,' in Norman Hillmer and Maureen Appel Molot (eds.), *Canada Among Nations 2002: A Fading Power* (Toronto: Oxford University Press, 2003), 256–70.

6 See Tavia Grant and Brian Milner, 'Why Brazil Stands Out,' *Globe and Mail*, 10 June 2010, B1.

7 In early 2010, some twelve federal deputy ministers from Canada met with their Brazilian counterparts in Brasilia, ostensibly to reciprocate for a November visit to Canada by some fifty Brazilian officials.

8 In June 2011, Ottawa launched a major trade mission to Brazil to seek out commercial opportunities in infrastructure-related projects, transportation systems, green building technologies, and security systems for crowd control.

9 Dosman and Frankel, *Brazil and Canada*, 7. CIDA disbursements for Brazil totalled $9.4 million for 2009–10. Government of Canada, *Brazil: Country Profile* (Gatineau: Canadian International Development Agency, June 2011).

10 Canada, Department of Foreign Affairs and International Trade, http://www.international.gc.ca/commerce/strategy-strategie/r5.aspx. Two-way trade between Canada and Brazil reached almost $7 billion for 2010–11, marking a noticeable increase from the $4 billion of 2008–9. Government of Canada, *Fact Sheet: Canada-Brazil Relations* (Ottawa: Department of Foreign Affairs and International Trade, April 2012). It is worth noting that several high-profile Canadian companies have operations/investments in Brazil: Ivanhoe Cambridge, Bombardier, Brookfield, Scotiabank, Dorel, and the Canada Pension Plan Board. See Steve Ladurantaye, 'Canadian Developers Go Shopping in Brazil,' *Globe and Mail*, 10 February 2011, B11.

11 These figures were drawn from David Akin, 'Day Seeks "Buy American" Solution,' *Calgary Herald*, 25 August 2009, A6.

12 Although some 400 Canadian companies operate in Brazil, the country still remains in late 2012 as Canada's tenth-largest trading partner (though the largest in South America). Brazil was the eighth-largest foreign investor in Canada for 2010, and two-way investment reached $23 billion in that same year. Government of Canada, 'Statement by the Prime Minister of Canada

while in Sao Paulo, Brazil' (Ottawa: Office of the Prime Minister, 9 August 2011), 4.

13 It is also worth emphasizing that Canada is now the number one study-abroad destination for Brazilian students – numbering over 17,000 in 2008. Government of Canada, *Canada-Brazil Relations* (Ottawa: Department of Foreign Affairs and International Trade, January 2010). See also Government of Canada, 'Canada and Brazil Strengthen Higher-Education Ties,' news release (Ottawa: Department of Foreign Affairs and International Trade, 22 October 2010).

14 For a summary of academic relations involving Brazil and Canada, see W.E. Hewitt, 'Brazilian Studies in Canada: Dawn of a New Era?' *Interthesis* (May 2006): 1–15.

15 Ibid.

16 Some 20,000 Brazilian students were studying in Canada in 2012, and there are plans for this program to continue into the future.

17 See www.brazilianchair.ca for a summary of the program and related activities.

18 Michaëlle Jean, 'We're Listening Brazil,' *State Visit to Brazil* (Ottawa: Office of the Secretary to the Governor General, 2007), 4–5.

19 Luiz Inácio da Silva, 'Statement on the Occasion of the State Visit to the Federative Republic of Brazil,' in *State Visit to Brazil*, 29–30.

20 Government of Canada, *Innovation, Science and Technology Partnership with Brazil* (Ottawa: Department of Foreign Affairs and International Trade, June 2009), http://www.international.gc.ca/trade-agreements-accords-commerciaux/cimar-rcami/2009/12.aspx?view=d.

21 Barbara Yaffe, 'Harper Looks beyond the U.S., to Brazil,' *Vancouver Sun*, 9 August 2011, B2. One of the potential problems with enhancing trade relations between the two countries is the intracies of Mercosur (a South American common market involving Brazil, Argentina, Uruguay, and Paraguay). While Canada has begun exploratory talks with Mercosur on cementing a wider trade deal, the three other partners, under the terms of the economic arrangement, have veto power over any proposed Canada-Brazil trade pact. In the past, the two smaller members, Paraguay and Uruguay, have expressed serious reservations about removing their protectionist agricultural policies. See Carl Meyer, 'Small Agreements Sign of Bigger Things with Brazil,' *Embassy Magazine*, 10 August 2011, 11.

22 Quoted in Steven Chase, 'Brazil Trip Aims to "Thicken" Relationship,' *Globe and Mail*, 6 August 2011, A4. According to a survey by the Ottawa-based FOCAL, Canadians in general have a favourable opinion of Brazil

compared with Mexico and Argentina. See Marina Jimenez, 'Canada Embraces Brazil as New Preferred Partner,' *Globe and Mail*, 8 August 2011, A4.

23 Quoted in Steven Chase, 'PM Seeks Stronger Business Ties with Brazil,' *Globe and Mail*, 9 August 2011, A6.

24 Quoted from Government of Canada, 'Statement by the Prime Minister of Canada while in Sao Paulo, Brazil' (Ottawa: Office of the Prime Minister, 9 August 2011), 2.

25 Ibid., 4.

26 Ibid., 9.

13 Canada-Chile Relations: Assessing a Key Bilateral Relationship

ROBERTO DURÁN

It certainly looks like Chile – and not Brazil (as advocated in the previous chapter) – is the centrepiece of Canada's Americas strategy. Indeed, it was no coincidence that Stephen Harper's government launched its foray into the Americas during a high-profile visit to Chile in July 2007.[1] As Harper noted at the beginning of his prepared speech: 'Ten years ago this month, the Free Trade Agreement linking our two countries came into force ... It is especially ironic that our initiative ten years ago has been an overwhelming success, opening doors to friendship, prosperity, growth and cooperation between Canada and Chile that have exceeded all of our expectations.'[2] It is obvious that Ottawa sees Chile – with its firm embrace of market liberalism and democratic pluralism – as a key link in its Latin American and Caribbean policy thrust. Given Canada's openness to thousands of Chilean refugees in the early 1970s, its significant mining stake in Chile, the Canada-Chile free trade pact of 1997, and a shared concern about diminishing U.S. dominance in the region, Harper was clearly trying to build on that record and historical experience.[3]

Accordingly, it is worth noting that Chile and Canada have had uninterrupted diplomatic relations for over seventy years – beginning officially in 1941. Ottawa clearly views the Canada-Chile relationship in terms of shared values such as respect for international human rights, the rule of law, the Inter-American Democratic Charter, and a similar world view of international and hemispheric affairs. 'Canada and Chile also cooperate closely on a range of issues at the United Nations (UN), the Organization of American States (OAS), the Asia-Pacific Economic Cooperation forum (APEC) and within the Summit of the Americas process,' declares a Canadian fact sheet on the overall relationship.[4] From a Chilean standpoint, they tend to see Canada mostly in terms of economic exchange, direct investment, and business compatibilities (with expanding security or military ties). But the Chilean government also views relations with Canada as generally trouble-free, as a like-minded partner and as a source of practical and innovative ideas.[5] Put simply, both countries share many common interests, approaches to hemispheric challenges, and a determination to strengthen bilateral linkages.

The above reflections are quite pertinent in terms of clearly under-standing the various dimensions of Chile's relations with Canada.[6] At the moment, Chile possesses the necessary characteristics in terms of structure (a positive rate of economic growth and financial and politi-cal stability) and a stable socio-political entity over the past ten years to be considered an expanding society, or a 'medium-growth country' for certain observers, and an 'emerging country' in the eyes of others.[7] In this sense, this chapter aims to clarify the nature or types of links that have been established between this 'medium-growth country' of Latin America and a developed country that has enjoyed worldwide politi-cal and commercial power from the 1950s up to the end of the first half of the 1990s in the twentieth century. The idea is to analyse how com-mercial and diplomatic links have built up between Chile and Canada, taking into account the asymmetry of their bilateral relations. It bears repeating that Chile is clearly a country that has changed considerably over the last thirty years, which has led to enhanced contacts with Can-ada in terms of people-to-people exchanges and military linkages. The chapter concludes with some useful policy recommendations on how best to sustain a profitable bilateral relationship, along with some final observations.

A Conceptual Framework

In order to grapple with Chile's interest in expanding contacts with Canada across a wide range of policy areas, one has to first understand the country's position in the international hierarchy of states. Stated differently, to undertake an analysis of the participation of developing countries in the different spheres of international politics is as complex as it is to do for the developed countries of the world. As far back as the early 1950s, attempts have been made to understand the nature and consequences of the increasing incorporation of the countries of Latin America, Africa, and Asia into the affairs of global and region-al politics. The numerous countries making up the so-called 'Third World' tried to gain access to the international political system by way of agreements with the major hubs of the developed world or by entering into ideological or political alliances either with Western societies or with the 'real' socialist countries. The studies prepared by sociologists and developmental anthropologists toward the end of the 1950s represented a first effort to try to understand and describe the challenges that underdeveloped nations faced in a deeply polarized international context. However, the gigantic wave of political and social changes in the 1960s and 1970s would bring these paradigms into serious question.[8]

The results of these changes radically transformed the underdeveloped world, to the extent that the previous 'Third World' generalizations were no longer valid. A large number of African states would plunge into a structural crisis that continues to this very day. The Asian countries, also deeply affected by wars controlled by outside foreign powers, would make efforts to improve the living conditions of their societies. Some of these countries would be successful toward the end of the 1980s, but others are still awaiting their turn at improved economic prospects. For their part, Latin American countries like Chile underwent extensive authoritarian experiences during the turbulent 1970s. Indeed, the generalized re-democratization of the 1980s affected many of these countries in the region, with the exception of the Cuban regime. During the 1980s and the first half of the 1990s, then, a sizeable group of South American nations adhered to the globalization process and embraced the neoliberal ideas of the market economy and a smaller state structure. Because these countries, including Chile, were deeply affected by the implications of economic growth and social modernization, their status within a hierarchical structure of international politics tended to improve.[9] However, the effects of globalization of the market economy in economically emerging countries like Chile have clearly been far from equal.[10]

Yet, from the time that states like Chile succeeded in maintaining an increasing rate of economic growth from the 1980s onward, along with improving the living conditions of disadvantaged social groups as well as the competitiveness of their economies, two key phenomena began to occur. On the one hand, the countries with more rapidly growing economies such as Chile felt comfortable approaching the developed countries of the world with greater ease – and this included Canada. On the other hand, this increasing closeness resulted in unexpected costs, in large part because of the fading away of old diplomatic and political loyalties that the poorer countries previously enjoyed. This occurred, for example, in those countries that enjoyed financial advantages following the oil crisis of the early 1970s, and also at the time of the Yom Kippur war. A totally different phenomenon thus arose, and one which triggered a process that basically separated the 'medium-growth countries' like Chile from the 'poor countries.'[11] In this situation, it was the first and only occasion on which a group of developing countries (such as Brazil, Argentina, Colombia, and Cuba) had successfully challenged the stability of the international economic system – by pressing for fundamental structural reforms to the existing international economic and financial architecture.

But the lingering asymmetries between and among developing countries still made it impossible to set in motion a common outline in terms of foreign policy – leading some Latin American nations such as Chile to distance itself progressively from its African and Asian counterparts in the major multilateral forums of the world. This trend lasted throughout the entire decade of the 1980s and became even stronger in the 1990s. At the end of the day, and paradoxically, the lessons derived from those occurrences were mostly taken advantage of by the developed nations like Canada, which have subsequently tried to establish a new style of rapprochement with developing countries like Chile. Indeed, the wave of political re-democratization that took place in Latin America in the 1980s and 1990s – in lock step with the end of the Cold War period – made it possible for the developing world to establish renewed relations within the sphere of multilateral and bilateral diplomacy, and to do so in the face of a more pragmatic and less confrontational international terrain.

The Canada-Chile Setting

For the years 1935–73, Chile was part of an economically impoverished and politically unstable continent, and thus Canadian governments studiously kept their distance. Nonetheless, Chile was in many ways a notable exception in the political sphere, given the long-standing consolidation of its democratic regime. But linkages with Canada, whether of the economic or diplomatic variety, were still kept to a minimum. (On the other hand, in the socio-economic sphere, Argentina was obviously the exception, although its political stability was far removed from that of Chile and closer to the rest of the Latin American countries.) This reality changed dramatically in the 1950s and 1960s, most particularly in Chile. The complex process of socio-economic reforms that began toward 1966–7 ended with a violent coup d'état in 1973, giving rise to a long military dictatorship that was to last for approximately seventeen years. And as a result of the massive violations of basic human rights and democratic rights in general, the military regime was strongly isolated between 1973 and 1990, especially in the diplomatic realm. Interestingly, at no time did Canada seriously consider severing diplomatic relations with the highly repressive Augusto Pinochet government.[12]

During this same time frame, though, international trade intensified remarkably, giving rise to increased economic and commercial links between advanced economies like Canada and the 'the emerging economies' like Chile – a trend that continues unabated to this day. The military regime in Chile benefited from this new context, and shortly after the financial crisis of 1981–2, the country sought to diversify its international trade posture. Thus, in spite of dictatorial Chile's political and diplomatic isolation, its economic and commercial relations with the developed nations continued and prospered, including exchanges with Canada and Canadian mining companies.

The recovery of political democracy at the beginning of the 1990s marked a new phase in Chile's foreign policy outlook. This was known as 'a period of international reinsertion' in every sense of the phrase. Accordingly, bilateral relations with other Latin American countries were intensified and strengthened, as were contacts with the Canadian government (in part through Jean Chrétien's 'Team Canada' trade missions to the region in the 1990s). In fact, toward the middle of 1991, a preliminary commercial negotiation was initiated with the government of Brian Mulroney. Between 1992 and 1996, four agreements of this type were signed with a group of Latin American countries, in addition to a similar agreement entered into in 1997 with Canada. (With regard to relations with Europe, Chile established a 'third generation agreement' with the European Community in 1991, and in 1996 initial negotiations were launched to establish an association agreement with the European Union, which was eventually signed in 2002.) Clearly, Chile's bilateral relations with Canada were enhanced and cultivated in the commercial, political, and diplomatic spheres during the period of the 1990s.

This deeper cooperation between Canada and Chile on the diplomatic level also extended to the region's principal political institution – the Washington-based Organization of American States (OAS). Not only do the two countries share similar or common objectives within the body, but they also coordinate their governmental actions on many of the region's critical policy challenges.[13] (It is worth mentioning that Canada strongly backed former Chilean foreign minister José Miguel

Insulza's selection as the OAS secretary general in both 2005 and 2010.) Within the OAS, both the ambassadors from Canada and Chile (and their respective mission staffs) work together on a host of inter-American issues, such as hemispheric security (drugs and organized gangs), democratization and human rights, economic issues and trade competitiveness, and the strengthening of the OAS itself (especially around managing the OAS budget and sustainability). The ambassadors themselves have informal exchanges or discussions on a wide range of issues and challenges confronting the Americas – oftentimes a function of the fact that the respective ambassadors sit next to one another around the OAS Permanent Council table.[14]

This is not to suggest that the two countries invariably see eye to eye on every single issue of hemispheric significance. There are obvious differences of opinion – depending on the issue in question – but the differences are certainly not grounds for precipitating a major rift between the two governments. Take, for example, the democratic crisis of legitimacy that engulfed Peru and then president Alberto Fujimori in the early 2000s. In fact, Canada played a pivotal role in trying to defuse the crisis by forcing Fujimori to step aside and thus restore some semblance of democratic normalcy to Peru. But the Chileans, for their part, were less than enthusiastic about the Canadian intervention. Unlike officials in Ottawa, Chile was adamant about respecting principles of state sovereignty and non-intervention, and both sides effectively 'agreed to disagree' on this issue.

Canada-Chile Trade and Investment Relations

There is little disputing that the Canada-Chile Free Trade Agreement (FTA), in force now since 1997, has been the most significant milestone of bilateral relations since representative democracy was reinstated in Chile in 1990.[15] It became for Canada the template from which other bilateral deals would be signed with a host of other Latin American and Caribbean countries. But such a trade arrangement was the first to be signed by Chile, though it was certainly consistent with the 1994 Marrakech Agreement, which established a new trend in liberalized world trade, along with the creation of the World Trade Organization (WTO). The trade pact with Canada would be supplemented by two other agreements: one was about environmental collaboration, and the other about labour cooperation. Both were ratified and acted upon along with the broader Canada-Chile FTA.

These three agreements put Chile's economy and foreign trade in touch with a member of the G8, marking an important departure in the conduct of Chilean foreign policy. It was also a central milestone in bringing Canada closer to the countries of Latin America, pointedly demonstrating a more hemispheric thrust to its diplomacy, instead of one limited to its long-standing ties with the English-speaking Caribbean countries of the Commonwealth. To be sure, the trade deal served to fortify Canada's presence in the Americas – and obviously its future outlook.

The environmental agreement was designed to achieve effective control over ecological/biodiversity legislation and to promote bilateral cooperation in this subject area. The labour agreement closely resembles the model established by the 1994 North American Free Trade Agreement (NAFTA). In fact, there is a bilateral commitment to implement a transparent process in the creation of environmental norms, compelling the Chilean government to maintain high standards in this area.

The agreement, for instance, reaffirms both countries' right to establish their own environmental regulations, as well as their own policy priorities. But it does not allow for the authorities of one country to undertake environmental law enforcement in the other country's territory. The agreement also promotes transparency and public participation in the debate and approval and implementation of the decisions agreed upon. Moreover, both governments have access to consulting mechanisms and conflict resolution strategies in the environmental field.

Returning to trade flows, these have obviously increased since the treaty entered into force in 1997. Over 99 per cent of trade has been entirely liberalized since 2008 – truly resembling a free trade zone. And the bilateral relationship has continued to intensify over the years: witness the Chapter on Financial Services that was ratified in 2007. There is now a new chapter on public purchasing, which has been added to the FTA since January 2009.

With respect to specific trade policies, there have also been some important developments. The two countries share fairly common positions in the negotiations within the WTO, APEC, and the Organisation for Economic Co-operation and Development (OECD). In addition, the signing of the Chile-Canada framework partnership agreement in July 2007 reinforced a solid relationship after ten years of the initial FTA. It is important to highlight that the framework agreement has the purpose of enhancing bilateral ties, in the sense of being privileged partners and interlocutors on hemispheric issues, and working closely together on such issues as climate change and international energy matters.

These subjects, and others linked to production and trade of metals and minerals, along with the intensification of bilateral cooperation in science and technology, have all been included in several memoranda of understanding (MOUs) approved in June 2008. One of these documents, which was dedicated specifically to the promotion of bilateral investments, was particularly useful as an innovative measure in free trade arrangements.

When analysing recent trends in Canada-Chile bilateral trade, it is worth noting that during 2008 – the year of the last international financial crisis – the inclusion of Chilean exports in Canada's total imports was just 0.44 per cent. In 2008–9, Chile ranked twenty-eighth as a source for Canadian imported goods, but with a 13.8 per cent growth rate since 2004. Judging from Canadian exports over that same period, they amounted to just 0.14 per cent of the Chilean economy. It is important to point out here that in spite of this fact, during the period 2004–8, an average growth of 24.9 per cent can be observed in Chilean imports.[16]

Leaving copper exports aside, bilateral trade expanded five times during this same period, totalling US$699 million (with an average yearly expansion rate of 30 per cent). The imports from Canada between 1996 and 2006 have maintained an average of approximately US$400 million. Still, these figures have increased significantly since then, accumulating an average of US$971 million annually.[17]

Between 1997 and 2002, the Chilean trade balance was actually negative with Canada, becoming positive and increasing its levels from 2003 until 2006. In 2007, the trade was more balanced due to a small decrease in Chilean exports and a strong increase in Canadian imports. Nevertheless, by the end of 2008, the trade balance experienced an improvement compared to the previous year of US$452 million in Chile's favour (with a notable increase in the export of fresh fruits).

In 2008, Chile exported a total of 549 products to the Canadian market. Despite a certain variety in the products, there is only a handful of key exports. In fact, during 2008, the twenty-five main exported products comprised 89 per cent of the total amount. These correspond mainly to the mining sector, as copper is the most important export (46.2 per cent). Following copper are methanol exports (9.9 per cent) and copper ores and concentrates (6.7 per cent).[18]

On the other hand, gold in its various forms was an important export to Canada between January and March 2009, with shipments totalling US$48.4 million (less than the US$126 million in 2007). This can be explained by the lower international price of copper and the significant decrease in Canada's purchasing power, due to the international financial crisis in 2008–9.

Obviously, the Canada-Chile FTA has created a positive evolution in bilateral trade, along with an important expansion in commercial interaction in general. Two-way trade reached US$585 million in 2002, rising to US$2.38 billion in 2008. In the meantime, exports have increased by an annual average of 32.2 per cent between 2002 and 2008. Non-copper exports expanded over five times during this period, with an average annual rate of 30 per cent. Notable examples include the food sector, beverages and alcohol, chemical products, rubber, plastic, forestry and furniture, and fruits.[19] Two-way trade figures for 2009 come in at just over $2.3 billion – impressive still given a period of global sluggishness and retrenchment.[20]

To be sure, the FTA has favoured bilateral relations for Chile, as Canada grants tax preferences for almost all of its exports. The rebate is currently 98.7 per cent, applied to all products negotiated with Canada. In the area of imports from Canada, these have practically tripled between 2002 and 2008, totalling US$964 million. It is also important to point out that between 1974 and 1989 the total accumulated amount of foreign direct investment (FDI) coming from Canada only reached US$500 million.[21] But today, Canada ranks third among countries in terms of FDI in Chile between 1974 and 2008, following only the United States and Spain.

During this period, accumulated FDI reached US$12.9 billion, representing 18 per cent of the total FDI earmarked for Chile. Of this amount, US$9.4 billion (or 72 per cent) was invested since the year the Canada-Chile FTA entered into force. (Canada was actually the largest source of new direct investment in Chile for the years 2006–8.) As in 2006, there is a strong concentration of Canadian investment in important projects in the areas of mining, electricity, gas, and water.[22] According to figures for 2009, Canadian direct investment in Chile now stands at roughly $8.34 billion – mostly in the northern part of Chile and the austral region.[23]

Canada-Chile Expanding Military Contacts

When it comes to the military in Chile, its reputation has been less than stellar from a democratic standpoint, long known for its authoritarian streak, substantial human rights abuses and torture, and its exercise of inordinate power in Chilean society.[24] Today, however, Chile has one of the most modern and professional armed forces in South America. It would appear to be an obvious area where both Canada and Chile would be able to cooperate within the OAS, to exchange notes and strategic thinking, and to work collaboratively on various military-related missions. Peacekeeping, joint military training operations, and military officer exchanges have already strengthened this growing component of the bilateral relationship.

In fact, the armed forces from both countries worked very closely together while helping to restore stability and some semblance of normalcy to impoverished Haiti in the 2000s. Along with Canada, Chile contributed over 500 soldiers to the United Nations peacekeeping operation in Haiti since 2004 – known by its acronym MINUSTAH. Both countries actually share a number of reasons for working in the area of regional security – not the least of which is to curry favour with official Washington. Their participation in peacekeeping operations like MINUSTAH also serve both of their respective national interests; increase their presence on the international stage; enhance global stability and order, which are inextricably linked to increased international trade flows; and demonstrate that the two countries are not indifferent to regional security problems (where Chile is often accused of focusing exclusively on commercial matters). It is also important to note that the Pearson Peacekeeping Centre and the Centro Conjunto Para operaciones de Paz of Chile hosted a joint seminar to discuss ways of enhancing peace operations training within the MINUSTAH in May 2009.

Furthermore, on the human security front, both countries have also exhibited early signs of bilateral cooperation. Though largely a Canadian initiative in the late 1990s, and spearheaded by Canada's then foreign minister Lloyd Axworthy, among others, it focused on broadening the definition of security and putting human interests ahead of traditional national interests. For the Chileans, they have looked at this conception of building new international security norms in a positive light, and thus opportunities for cooperation between the two countries have opened up. Indeed, and in light of the country's extensive use of mine fields along its borders with Bolivia, Peru, and Argentina, Chile expressed an early interest in reducing the human costs from anti-personnel landmines. Accordingly, both Chile and Canada played important roles in fashioning the Land Mines Treaty Initiative of the late 1990s – symptomatic of how military linkages could be strengthened and fortified in the overall bilateral relationship.

Opportunities for Enhanced People-to-People Contacts

When he visited Chile in July 2007, Prime Minister Harper and then president Michelle Bachelet initialled an important bilateral document: the Canada-Chile Partnership Framework (CCPF). Ostensibly, the agreement was intended to facilitate people-to-people exchanges in the cultural, educational, youth, and scientific fields, among others. (It was subsequently enhanced in June 2008 to include university-level scholarships and youth mobility.) To date, the level of exchange has been rather limited, though there are signs of some improvement in this area. In October 2009, well-known Chilean artists/musicians Cecilia Echenique and Eduardo Peralta appeared in the auditorium of Ottawa's main city library to share their experiences. And under the banner of 'Culture Unites Us in the Bicentenary,' cultural acts from Chile were set to participate in a host of local gatherings in various Canadian cities. Chilean writer/poet Julio Torres-Recinos read from some of his books in June 2009 in Saskatoon, and the Chilean film *Chile Can Do It* was exhibited in the Latin American Cinema Festival in Ottawa in March 2009. Lastly, a group of Chilean Canadians took part in a Workshop of Cultural Promoters in Ottawa in November 2009.

In a reciprocal four-day visit, President Bachelet came to Ottawa to sign a series of agreements with Canada's Stephen Harper in June 2008. At the top of the agenda were several memoranda of understanding (five in total) intended to enhance relations between the two countries, especially in the areas of science and technology and in investment and mining ventures. (To signify the importance of bilateral relations, Bachelet was accompanied by three members of her inner cabinet: Foreign Affairs, Economy, and Energy.) As Prime Minister Harper indicated at the signing ceremony, 'the Canada-Chile relationship is a model of successful partnership in our hemisphere.'[25] The two leaders also spoke about a host of wider global issues such as climate change, the peace support operation in Haiti, and international energy pricing and supply. In a rather effusive tone, Harper commented: 'The Canada-Chile partnership sets the standard with Chile as well as with other countries of our hemisphere.'[26]

In terms of overseas development assistance (ODA), Canada has been involved in Chile for several years, providing $8.6 million in loans to the country in the mid-1960s. Even during the repressive Pinochet years, the Canadian government continued to allocate small sums of economic assistance to Chile, including $5 million in credit from Canada's Export Development Corporation (EDC) to purchase six Twin Otter aircraft from De Havilland.[27] For the years 1997–2007, and though admittedly not a key part of the overall bilateral relationship, Canadian aid initiatives focused on securing sustainable development through various partnership arrangements, including technology transfers through the Canada-Southern Cone Technology Transfer Fund. The 2008–9 disbursement to Chile from the Canadian International Development Agency (CIDA) amounted to roughly $2.4 million and was earmarked primarily for projects and initiatives like the Indigenous Peoples Partnership Program.[28] According to CIDA, these initiatives have led to Chile's adoption of Canadian forest management practices and models to better manage its natural resources, meet safety challenges, and regulate pesticides.

After a devastating earthquake struck parts of Chile's Pacific coastline in late February 2010, the Canadian government was quick to respond with offers of financial, technical, and medical assistance. By early March, Ottawa had offered to provide $2 million in humanitarian assistance to aid in the country's relief efforts and promised to increase that amount if need be. Canada did, however, rule out sending its military disaster response team (DART) to deal with the catastrophe in Chile. But a number of Canadian relief organizations, including the Canadian Red Cross and Global medic, committed themselves to restoring access to clean drinking water through water purification units and the distribution of water purification tablets. Some Canadian companies operating in Chile also agreed to provide donations, relief supplies, and logistical support. But one Canadian newspaper editorial raised a critical voice by highlighting Canada's leadership role when a massive quake devastated Haiti in January 2010 and its less-than-generous response to the Chilean earthquake. As it noted pointedly: 'As of yet, there are no federal matching funds for Canadians who donate to Chilean earthquake relief efforts. No Canadian warship is steaming south, loaded with supplies. There's no talk of waiving immigration rules for Chileans wanting to live in Canada.'[29]

Some Policy Recommendations

There is no disputing that Chile is one of Canada's chief allies in the Americas. But if the Canada-Chile relationship is to remain on a solid economic and political footing, it cannot be allowed to drift on diplomatic autopilot.[30] It will need regular cultivation, engagement, and reassessment from the political leadership, government officials, and civil society groups in the two countries. They have too much in common – and share so many identical approaches, responses, and perspectives to hemispheric issues – to permit the relationship to be weakened because of neglect or indifference. So as in any relationship, adjustments and modifications can always be made to bolster the goodwill that is already there.

For instance, if a revitalized Canada-Chile relationship is to flourish well into the future, it will most assuredly need to be nurtured by the two countries' top political leaders. Both the prime minister of Canada and the president of Chile – irrespective of political party stripe – will need to commit themselves to making the bilateral relationship an important foreign policy priority. This, in turn, will necessarily involve more regularized official state visits to each of the countries and perhaps even the use of more 'telephone diplomacy.' (Perhaps Prime Minister Harper missed an opportunity to extend a diplomatic hand to Chile by failing to invite President Sebastian Pinera as part of an outreach session to the June 2010 G8 Summit in Ontario.) These top-level meetings could also be supplemented by more regularized gatherings of senior cabinet ministers to give added impetus to the bilateral agenda.

Furthermore, there is plenty of room for greater policy cooperation, consultation, and coordination when it comes to inter-American affairs. Both sides could make more of an effort to work together in a more formal, rather than ad hoc, basis to confront the hemisphere's major challenges. There is certainly no reason why Canada's ambassador to the OAS could not seek to establish more regularized meetings (perhaps monthly) with his or her Chilean counterpart to exchange notes and to plot strategy. This more collaborative ethic could also be applied at the official level as well, not only between the respective OAS mission staffs, but also between the senior mandarinate in their professional foreign ministries. Put simply, both countries should take full advantage of the many available opportunities to align themselves as like-minded partners and confidantes.

Additionally, much work remains to be done to foster enhanced people-to-people contacts between the two countries. It is instructive to note that approximately 30,000 Chileans are already living in Canada, and there is great potential for that number to grow. Not only should cultural and artistic groups in each country be encouraged to work more closely together, but scientific and educational linkages should also be pushed. Indeed, the template in some ways already exists given the extensive ties between the two countries' academic communities and institutions. From a business standpoint, obvious areas of exchange exist in agriculture, fishing, forestry, renewable energy, and resource extraction. There are also many opportunities yet to be tapped in tourism promotion, the NGO sector, and military exchanges and training.

One area in particular where the two countries could explore greater collaboration is their respective aboriginal populations. With each country having an indigenous population of over one million, it would seem an obvious area in which bridges could be built and exchanges could be enhanced. As the government responsible for First Nations in Canada, Ottawa could take the lead in opening the door to stronger linkages with Chile's indigenous peoples, especially given CIDA's existing Indigenous Peoples Partnership Program. Furthermore, Canada's Assembly of First Nations already has positive contacts with indigenous groups in Mexico, Bolivia, and Guatemala and thus could easily establish stronger links with Chile's representative organizations (for the Mapuche, Aymará, and Rapa Nui). Both countries could then build upon these people-to-people ties to advocate – perhaps through the institutional machinery of the OAS – the promotion of the rights of indigenous peoples throughout the Americas.

Conclusion

It bears repeating that the Canada-Chile relationship is already on a fairly sound diplomatic footing, but there does exist room for improvement and a need to guard against complacency.[31] Officialdom in Ottawa would do well to remind themselves, as one foreign newspaper correspondent once remarked, that Chile is 'the country other Latin Americans would like to be when they grow up.'[32] We should also remember that Chile remains a bastion of democratic and institutional stability in South America, dovetailing nicely with the Harper government's focus on democracy, security, and prosperity in the region. In fact, Chile has already signed some fifty-four free trade pacts, including agreements with the European Union (EU) and China, and a preferential trade arrangement with India. Like Canada, Chile is a major exporting country, an attractive destination for foreign investment, and has chalked up fiscal surpluses in recent years. There is no disputing, then, that both countries can learn a great deal from each other, and can benefit from closer cooperation and interchange.

It is important to point out here that greater Canada-Chile cooperation in the military field can only have positive benefits for both
countries. To be sure, the presence of the Chilean military in UN peacekeeping missions like MINUSTAH can only serve to incorporate these
central actors into the wider international political system – a welcome
development given its past record of brutal repression. Of course, the
long experience of the Canadian armed forces in numerous peacekeeping and peacemaking operations can have a tremendously important
influence and impact on the Chilean armed forces as well. This has
the potential to contribute to a further modernization or awakening of
the Chilean military in terms of their international participation and is
essential for their incorporation into Chilean society itself, especially
given the psychological scarring from the Pinochet dictatorship. The
continuation of this process of military interaction obviously brings
new expectations and thus can serve to shape the very contours of the
Canada-Chile bilateral relationship down the road.

Another important point that Chileans can learn from the Canadian experience is the need for the government in Santiago to permit social actors to engage more in foreign relations and thereby give
them greater legitimacy and more transparency. This statement does
not contradict or undermine the essence of autonomous state policy
making, a key Chilean concern, as long as the approval is extended
to a greater number of citizens who are properly informed and fully
aware of the importance of international politics. In other words, since
foreign policy crucially affects almost every sector of society, Chile
can benefit from creating space for citizen participation in this policy
domain.

Moreover, the operationalization of the 1997 FTA has allowed for the
incorporation of ecological and environmental issues into the Chilean
political debate. These subjects are now of widespread interest and are
no longer limited to specialized groups. It is also a pattern that is beginning to permeate the perceptions and behaviour of other larger civil
society groups in Chile, especially in the area of labour supply. This
may be due to the improvement of standards in this area, manifested
throughout the different professions in the development of technical
requirements, which various sources of employment now demand.
Additionally, the FTA and recent educational agreements between
Chile and Canada have fostered higher qualitative standards in labour
supply and demand. This can be appreciated most visibly in Canadian
and other foreign mining activities in the north of Chile.

Economic ties between Chile and Canada have, in effect, created a different reality on the ground. The presence of new elements and challenges for competitive advantage in the Chilean economy have forced its exporters to reconsider quality standards in the production of its exports. For example, mining, fruit, fisheries, aquaculture, and forestry exports have to meet certain requirements, which immediately affect the volume of their earnings. This has, in turn, not only sensitized a large number of companies, but also mobilized important social standards. Through its commercial exchanges with Canada and other countries, Chilean foreign trade is assuming the cost of its permanent entrenchment in a globalized world economy. That is, Chile is adopting new forms of commercial transactions and using new techniques to boost productivity and exports. And this trend seems to be firmly established, notwithstanding the consequences of the 2008–9 world financial crisis.

On the other hand, the preparation of the Canada-Chile policy agenda has emphasized the importance of achieving practical and feasible agreements. These must be able to adapt to the needs and changes that frequently emerge abruptly in the international marketplace. Bilateral economic ties between Chile and Canada, then, have helped in terms of adjusting to the rapidity of change taking place in the international economic environment. And these very real changes also include new challenges in the design and execution of their respective foreign trade and external policies.

But the compatibility of the two countries in how they deal with the most pressing issues of inter-American affairs bodes well for the future. Both countries can advance their national interests by applying similar approaches and strategies to such issues as strengthening economic development and trade competitiveness; fostering democratic openness and respect for human rights; encouraging hemispheric security; and putting the OAS on a stronger financial footing. And they both share the same goal of trying to constrain the dominance of the United States and to modify U.S. behaviour in the Americas (especially in terms of confronting the region's major challenges from more of an inter-American standpoint). As natural allies and like-minded partners, there is a great deal that the two countries can do hemispherically by working together as opposed to hanging separately. In short, it only makes sense to further strengthen, expand, and deepen this bilateral relationship in the coming years.

NOTES

1 Though it was not the only stop for Harper, it did signify his government's commitment to countries like Chile that are democratic, capitalist, and moderate.

2 See Government of Canada, 'Prime Minister Harper Signals Canada's Renewed Engagement in the Americas,' *Speeches* (Ottawa: Office of the Prime Minister, 17 July 2007), 1.

3 After the VI Summit of the Americas in Colombia in mid-April 2012, Stephen Harper made a point of visiting Chile to mark the fifteenth anniversary of the Canada-Chile Free Trade Agreement and to announce – along with Chile's president Sebastián Pinera – the expansion of the trade pact. He also thanked President Pinera for endorsing Canada's bid to join critical trade talks that involve the countries of the Trans Pacific Partnership (TPP). Government of Canada, *Fact Sheet: Canada-Chile Relations* (Ottawa: Department of Foreign Affairs and International Trade, April 2012). Symptomatic of a desire to strengthen bilateral relations, the Canadian government was also quick to respond to the February 2010 earthquake in Chile by offering $2 million for urgent humanitarian assistance. Government of Canada, 'Government of Canada Announces Assistance to Chile,' news release, 2 March 2010. CIDA also disbursed some $3 million in aid to Chile for 2009–10.

4 Government of Canada, *Fact Sheet: Canada-Chile Relations* (Ottawa: Department of Foreign Affairs and International Trade, 2009), 1.

5 See Philip Oxhorn, 'The Lagos Presidency: An Assessment of the Elections and Its Impact on Canada-Chile Relations,' *Policy Paper* (Ottawa: Canadian Foundation for the Americas, 2001), 8.

6 See Christopher K. Ansell and Steven Weber, 'Organizing International Politics: Sovereignty and Open Systems,' *International Political Science Review* 20, no. 1 (1999): 95–115.

7 Two-way trade for the period 2010–11 amounted to roughly $2.7 billion, marking a slight increase from the previous year. Canadian direct investment in Chile is also substantial, and much of it is concentrated in the mining and resource extraction sectors – totalling over $13 billion. Government of Canada, *Fact Sheet: Canada-Chile Relations* (Ottawa: Department of Foreign Affairs and International Trade, April 2012).

8 See Celso Furtado, *La economía latinoamericana desde la conquista ibérica hasta la revolución cubana* (Santiago: Editorial Universitaria, Universidad de Chile, Colección Estudios Internacionales, Santiago, 1969), 138–227. Franz

Hinkelammert et al., *Dialéctica del desarrollo desigual: El caso latinoamericano* (Santiago, Chile: Centro de Estudios de la Realidad Nacional (CEREN), Université Catholique du Chile, 1970), 17–220.

9 See Hollis Chenery et al., *Redistribution with Growth. Policies to Improve Distribution in Developing Countries in the Context of Economic Growth* (New York: Oxford University Press, 1974), 3–72, and Guy F. Erb and Valeriana Kallab (eds.), *Beyond Dependency: The Developing World Speaks Out* (Washington, DC: The Charles F. Kettering Foundation, 1975), 3–164.

10 See Peadar Kirby, 'Tackling Global Inequality: Latin America and the Limits of Liberal Internationalism,' *Irish Studies in International Affairs* 12 (2001): 7–19.

11 See Roberto Russell and Teresa Carballal, 'El nuevo orden económico internacional: tendencias observables en el norte y en los países mayores de América Latina,' *Estudios Internacionales* 14, no. 53 (1981): 55–88; Celso Lafer, 'Reflexiones sobre el tema del nuevo orden mundial en un orden internacional en transformación,' *Estudios Internacionales* 15, no. 58 (1982): 127–65.

12 It is true that Canada, at least historically speaking, maintains relations with countries and not necessarily specific regimes or governments, however detestable. In fact, three weeks after the September 1973 military coup, official Ottawa moved to recognize the Pinochet regime. There is not much evidence to suggest that the Trudeau government was overly critical of Pinochet's reprehensible record on human rights and democratic freedoms. For a critical treatment of this period, see Yves Engler, *The Black Book of Canadian Foreign Policy* (Black Point, NS: Fernwood, 2009), 99–103.

13 One area where the two countries did part company was on how best to handle the reintegration of Honduras into the OAS family. While Canada did favour a facilitation of Honduras's re-entry, the Chileans – largely because of a history of military coups in their own country – were reluctant to be seen as endorsing the June 2009 coup in Honduras or as sending out the wrong message to the rest of the hemisphere about the acceptability of coups.

14 Interview with a Canadian official at the OAS mission in Washington, 6 July 2010.

15 The initial agreement itself was signed officially in November 1996 and came into force in early 1997.

16 Ministerio de Relaciones Exteriores de Chile, Dirección General de Relaciones Económicas Internacionales (DIRECON), *Evaluación de las relaciones comerciales entre Chile y Canadá a doce años de la entrada en vigencia del TLC* (Julio 2009), 9–11.

17 Ibid., 20–4.
18 Ibid., 30–3.
19 Ibid., 40.
20 Government of Canada, *Fact Sheet: Canada and Chile* (Ottawa: Department of Foreign Affairs and International Trade, 2010), 1.
21 Ministerio de Ralaciones Exteriores de Chile, *Evaluación*, 44.
22 Ibid., 56–63. A host of major Canadian firms are involved in the Chilean marketplace: Scotiabank, Barrick Gold, Brookfield Asset Management, and Teck Cominco Limited. See also, Gordon Pitts, 'Tech Rounds Up Chile's Copper,' *Globe and Mail*, 30 April 2012, B1.
23 Government of Canada, *Fact Sheet: Canada and Chile* (Ottawa: Department of Foreign Affairs and International Trade, 2010), 1.
24 For more on this, see Adrian J. English, *Armed Forces of Latin America* (New York: Jane's Publishing, 1984), 132–63.
25 Government of Canada, 'Prime Minister Harper and Chilean President Michelle Bachelet Strengthen Canada-Chile Relations,' press release (Ottawa: Office of the Prime Minister, 2008), 1.
26 Ibid.
27 See Engler, *The Black Book of Canadian Foreign Policy*, 99–100.
28 Government of Canada, *Chile* (Gatineau, Quebec: Canadian International Development Agency, 2010), 1.
29 See Editorial, 'Answer the Call,' *Globe and Mail*, 3 March 2010, A16. One could argue, of course, that Haiti's earthquake was more of a country-wide catastrophe and Chile's was more localized in scope.
30 Some of these suggestions are drawn from Philip Oxhorn, 'The Lagos Presidency: An Assessment of the Elections and Its Impact on Canada-Chile Relations,' 10–11.
31 While visiting Chile in August 2010, then international trade minister Peter Van Loan recognized this point, noting that 'in many different sectors, and for many different reasons, Canada views Chile as an important and strategic regional partner, now and in the future.' Government of Canada, 'Address by Minister Van Loan to Chile-Canada Chamber of Commerce,' *Speeches* (Ottawa: Department of Foreign Affairs and International Trade, 24 August 2010), 4.
32 Quoted in Jorge Heine, 'Pay Attention to Chile,' *Ottawa Citizen*, 11 June 2009, A15.

Conclusion

Prime Minister Stephen Harper has obviously placed important emphasis on Canada's relations with the Americas. In part, this is because much of the region has embraced democratic pluralism and free market liberalism, and has exhibited signs of a growing middle class among its 600 million people (many of them young). As the Harper government's 2009 core statement on the region explains: 'The Americas are and will remain a foreign policy priority for Canada. Canadians have much to gain by being involved in the region, and they also have much to contribute.'[1] The document goes on to state: 'Canada is a country of the Americas. By geography, history and multi-faceted relationships between states, in terms of trade, immigration and cultural and social exchanges, the Americas is a region of strategic, domestic and international interest for Canada.'[2] As this collection has amply demonstrated, Canada's core foreign policy interests are clearly at stake in the region and thus deserving of intense and sustained government attention. The country stands to reap huge benefits from a political/diplomatic, economic, strategic, and people-to-people standpoint.[3]

We should not forget that the various countries of Latin America and the Caribbean also stand to benefit from their engagement with Canada. Through our development assistance programs, universities and colleges, and job-skills training programs to fight extreme poverty, countries in the region could benefit in each of these areas. From a political/diplomatic perspective, countries in the Americas can take advantage of important links with an advanced, industrialized country (and member of the G8 and key player in the OAS) other than the United States. Canada could also be a useful ally in their official interactions with Washington (for example, as a bridge builder in the U.S.-

Cuba stalemate). In terms of military-security relations, countries in the Americas will be in a position to tap into Canadian expertise in peace-keeping and peacebuilding through officer exchanges, joint exercises and training, and workshops/seminars (like the one on protecting civil-ians in peacekeeping operations held in Asuncion, Paraguay in June 2011). Through Canadian financial, policing (e.g., RCMP liaison and training), and legal (mentoring judges) resources, LAC countries get additional help in dealing with organized crime (narcotics trafficking) and gangs, strengthening political institutions, and fortifying judicial structures. By utilizing Canadian assistance, these countries can work to strengthen the rule of law and to improve the quality of democratic pluralism (by accessing Elections Canada expertise) in their region.

Our Latin American friends can also take advantage of growing com-mercial and investment ties with Canada, especially when these coun-tries are reducing their reliance on the U.S. marketplace. There are other benefits to countries in the region: they get access to high-tech Cana-dian goods and equipment, agricultural worker programs (and remit-tances), increased numbers of Canadian tourists, and a fairly lucrative export market for their food products. Indeed, by forming partnerships with Canadian companies, people in the region can see the influx of much-needed jobs, investment, and expertise (e.g., in the energy sec-tor). Countries can also tap into Canadian expertise with respect to governance and accountability structures, regulatory frameworks, and the collection of income tax and customs duties/tariffs. Simply put, enhanced relations with Canada can offer important economic advan-tages for the region.

But the problem, as is always the case for Canada and the Ameri-cas, is joining these obvious LAC benefits and acknowledged Canadian interests with sufficient financial and bureaucratic resources, a menu of practical and meaningful policy prescriptions, and, most important, the requisite political will and follow-through.[4] It is instructive to note that the Conservative government has not earmarked any new budget-ary resources to DFAIT to properly implement this foreign policy focus on the Americas (seeing as Afghanistan took up a good portion of the department's resource allocation and now budget cuts have become the norm in official Ottawa).[5]

Harper, of course, is certainly not the first prime minister to over-promise and underfund when it comes to the Americas. Prime Minis-ter Pierre Trudeau singled out Latin America in his only foreign policy review, *Foreign Policy for Canadians*. Brian Mulroney crafted a strategy for the region – largely under the tutelage of then foreign affairs minister Joe Clark – and finally brought Canada to the OAS table as a full-fledged member. Jean Chrétien, though lukewarm about the Americas, did bring his Team Canada concept to the region in search of new trade markets and a counterweight to the United States. But there has been no major breakthrough that would entrench Canada in this hemisphere for the foreseeable future. While there has been much talk and declaratory policy about enhancing Canada's engagement with the region, it has mostly been empty words, with little follow-through.[6] That situation will have to change in the twenty-first century.

Why have Canadian governments in the past failed to sustain their interest in the Americas? Other foreign policy priorities (for example, Afghanistan, border security, and a European Union trade pact) have diverted political attention and consumed a fair amount of the oxygen in the foreign policy tank. Part of the problem also stems from the fact that successive Canadian foreign ministers have had little foreign policy experience and even less interest in inter-American affairs. A lack of personal or political interest in the region – especially at the prime ministerial level – spells neglect and only sporadic flashes of engagement and involvement. Moreover, there is no substantive domestic political constituency – besides a handful of interested NGOs – pushing hard for sustained participation in the Americas, and thus few votes to be had. Not even the Canadian business community has deigned to look much farther than the nearby, lucrative U.S. market. It has not lobbied aggressively for a comprehensive Americas strategy. While the mining sector (not always viewed fondly by those in the region or even in Canada) has had long-standing interests in the region, corporate Canada has been slow to jump on the Americas bandwagon.[7]

That is not to say that no Canadian companies are active in the region. Major firms like Brookfield Asset Management, Research in Motion (RIM), McCain Foods Limited, Bombardier, SNC-Lavalin, and Scotiabank all have a solid presence in the Americas. But as Scotiabank's chief executive officer Rick Waugh observed: 'Canadians do have to be pushed on this issue.'[8] As Canadian companies still retain outdated perceptions of the business/political climate in the region and are not picking up the correct signals from official Ottawa, they continue to fall behind their U.S., Chinese, and Asian counterparts. It bears remembering that Latin America and the Caribbean are slated to register economic growth rates of over 4 per cent annually for the next five years – well ahead of projections for the advanced economies of the world.[9] If we are going to take advantage of the promise of the Americas, at least according to Scotiabank's Waugh, 'the window for Canadians is open, but in three or four years, it's going to close. It won't close completely, but opportunities are presenting themselves and it would be a shame for us not to take part.'[10] The economic realities of our neighbourhood are likely to compel Canadian business leaders to change direction and to embrace the region from a commercial standpoint. But when? This question will undoubtedly require some vision and leadership from the governing Conservatives.

Any past efforts to expand and strengthen our links with the region have often foundered on the shoals of Canada-U.S. relations. There is no disputing the fact that Canadian overtures toward the Americas are inevitably complicated by our relationship with our closest neighbour and ally. In part, there are concerns in Ottawa's political circles, and within the foreign policy establishment in the Pearson Building, about getting 'off-side' with our American friends. As past experience has shown, our cordial relations with some countries in the region (notably Cuba, Guyana, and Jamaica) have raised hackles in official Washington. Similarly, there have always been reservations about the prospect of Canada ending up as the proverbial 'ham-in-the-sandwich' vis-à-vis Washington and various Latin American capitals.[11] Simply put, our Americas policy is at risk of being sidelined if we upset our Latino friends, frustrate our U.S. colleagues, and take positions at variance with what they expect from us. The thought of pleasing no one and annoying just about everyone else has dampened enthusiasm within the political class about embracing the region wholeheartedly.

Jim Rochlin's advocacy for a twenty-first-century version of the 1972 'Third Option' organizing principle for Canada's America's strategy is instructive here. After all, Trudeau's intellectual framework for the Options paper was essentially to find counterweights to balance the disparity in power and economic vulnerability in our relations with Washington. To that end, the Liberal government of the early 1970s thought about Latin America and the Caribbean as a logical place to diversify Canada's trade and investment relations. And when one considers the present- and even medium-term state of the U.S. economy (to say nothing of its striking deficit and overall long-term debt situation), it would be prudent for Canadian governments to think seriously about reducing our reliance on the U.S. marketplace. When this is combined with persistent voices for 'Buy American' in the U.S. Congress and the more pernicious protectionism (and talk of tariffs on 'dirty oil' from Alberta) via regulation that confronts Canadian businesses at the border, carving out a larger commercial stake in the Americas takes on even greater urgency.

Part of the problem with the 1970s Third Option concept was that it lacked sufficient bureaucratic buy-in and corporate endorsement. This was absolutely deadly in terms of the actual implementation and viability of the initiative. To secure wider support, one could recast the actual third option of the Options Paper itself to read as follows: To fashion a comprehensive, long-term strategy to develop and strengthen the Canadian-Latin American relationship and other aspects of its hemispheric thrust and in the process to reduce the present Canadian vulnerability to the U.S. Any new reformulation of the Options Paper, though, would need to begin with the required governmental and business support before embarking on such an endeavour. But if the senior ranks of the bureaucracy, key business leaders, ambassadors in the field, and NGO representatives do not take ownership of this policy framework, then governments in Latin America will not take it seriously either. Successive governments in Ottawa, along with their respective cabinets, will need to say it loudly and often that the Americas are an integral component of Canada's foreign policy – and then back it up with concrete evidence and action.

Unlike Trudeau's short-lived emphasis on the Third Option, current and future Canadian governments – irrespective of party political stripe – will need persistent and sustained political will and commitment over a multi-decade period. Clearly, a key element in maintaining this political will could come from sub-national governments as well. Provinces should be encouraged to make hemispheric affairs a policy priority as well – perhaps by also incorporating them into any Team Canada missions to countries in the region. Quebec, in particular, which has historical, cultural, and linguistic linkages to the Americas, could prove to be a useful partner in strengthening Canadian–Latin American relations. The point here is to put in place as many policy takers as possible to ensure and sustain an Americas focus over a long period of time that will not change with each new federal government.

But if Canada's revised and contemporary version of the Third Option is going to have the expected policy impact and outcome, it will need to avoid the pitfalls of the early 1970s gambit. First, it will require far more staying power than Trudeau's passing infatuation with diversifying Canada's external relations away from an overwhelming reliance on the United States. Second, it will need an institutional structure and memory entrenched in Ottawa and in policy-making circles. Third, rather than focus almost exclusively on trade expansion – which was really at the heart of the Trudeau initiative – Canadian governments may wish to apply former Prime Minister Jean Chrétien's Team Canada approach to political, diplomatic, security, people-to-people, and trade relations to several key countries – and not simply to the region as a whole. Finally, if the 'whole-of-government' approach (with the attendant dollops of development assistance) to earthquake-ravaged Haiti in early 2010 was applied to Canada's relations with the Americas, good things would come of it.

Perhaps it is too early to properly assess Harper's Americas strategy – particularly in light of his May 2011 majority government victory. Clearly, some steps have been taken to strengthen Canada's standing in the region – including visits to the region by the PM and Governor General, senior ministers and deputy ministers, and representatives from civil society. The centrepiece thus far appears to be the signing of free trade deals and investment pacts with a handful of countries, with some still in the works. On the downside, our response to the 2009 Honduran crisis, our frosty relations with countries like Cuba and Venezuela, the imposition of a visa requirement for Mexicans, and a less than vigorous posture within the OAS all point to an Americas strategy tainted by ideological blindness, overly commercial interests, and overarching Canada-U.S. considerations.

Like Mr Trudeau's early 1970s strategy, the Harper approach lacks sufficient financial resources and staff allocations, the necessary political will and staying power, and a nuanced approach to the region. The Harper government has tended to create needless divides in the region (like free traders versus non–free traders or democrats versus non-democrats), deliberately igniting petty diplomatic fires with the Cubans or Venezuelans, and seeming to be unwilling to listen to regional specialists, civil society groups throughout the area, and prominent business leaders like Ian Delaney and Rick Waugh and those pushing for fairly traded products. Indeed, it would be difficult to say that Canada's image, profile, and prestige have been substantially elevated under the Harper policy thrust.[12] It is hard to argue convincingly that Canada has succeeded in making itself a part of the Americas firmament any more than it has under previous Canadian governments going back to the 1970s. And as the title of this volume suggests, a considerable amount of work still remains to be done on the Americas file.

As all of the contributors to this volume have indicated, there are pragmatic and constructive initiatives that Canada can do from a policy standpoint to bolster our standing in Latin America and the Caribbean. These are outlined in capsule form here. On the trade and investment front, Grinspun and Mills argue that pushing bilateral trade pacts (the so-called 'prosperity' pillar) using the NAFTA model and highlighting investor rights should be rethought. They urge the Canadian government to embrace more than just a one-dimensional commercial-investment focus – that is, by grafting on a people-centred or trade-plus agenda to its Americas thrust. Rather than imposing an investors' bill of rights, Ottawa would be well advised to seek mutual socio-economic benefits for peoples in Canada and in Latin America and the Caribbean. By placing human rights considerations at or near the top, issues around health, safety, and environmental and community protections will be given more prominence. In addition, opening up or democratizing the trade dispute settlement process would create space for civil society participation and thus bolster our reputation throughout the Americas as a fair and trusted economic partner.

In terms of democracy promotion and consolidation, the advice of Max Cameron and Jason Tockman is worth recalling. The Canadian government – particularly in light of the Honduran debacle – should seek to have the OAS involved in advancing democratic reforms in Honduras and those member states in similar circumstances. Democratic institutions, from the constitutional ground up, will need to be strengthened to ensure that there is no repeat performance of the 'Honduran effect'; Ottawa should be leading the charge here. It is now also clear that the OAS Democratic Charter is in need of revision, and Canadian officials are well placed to advocate for some type of early-warning mechanism within the OAS – where other branches of government can make representations about alarming developments – so as to stave off future democratic crises in the region. Similarly, Canada should be at the forefront of composing new language in the Charter to prevent illegitimate caretaker governments from taking power illegally and then subsequently validating a coup by holding presidential elections.

From a hemispheric security standpoint, Hal Klepak has offered up several gems of policy-oriented wisdom. He maintains that Canada needs to realize that hemispheric security, and our role in advancing it, are the foundation for broadening our relations and linkages in the Americas. Drawing on our past experience as a bridge builder and 'helpful fixer,' officials in Ottawa should work with the many left-leaning governments in the region to keep them engaged in the inter-American security fold. Accordingly, Klepak's suggestion for Canada to strengthen its defence contacts with the Cuban armed forces would be a good place to start. Finally, we should enhance our Military Training and Assistance Programme (MTAP) assistance to militaries in the Americas, make our expertise available to those countries opting to host the Conference of Defense Ministers, and encourage our navy to display the Canadian flag at port calls in the region.

As for specific bilateral interaction, Duncan Wood rightly singles out the centrality of the Canada-Mexico relationship. To this end, he reminds Canadian politicians and policy makers to stop looking at Mexico as a complicating factor in our bilateral relations with the United States rather than as a valuable ally at the negotiating table with Washington. The importance of widening and deepening people-to-people contacts between Canadians and Mexicans cannot be overemphasized as a means of getting past U.S. dominance at the discussion table. Wood points out that the two countries have similar or compatible foreign policy objectives in the Americas, opening up possibilities to work assiduously and collaboratively within multilateral fora like the OAS and the UN, to create a stable Central America, and to cooperate on security matters like peace building and military integration in the region. They should also give serious consideration to working in tandem on fashioning a persuasive response to U.S. carbon regulations and on developing continental climate change measures. In addition, there are other areas – such as security cooperation (especially in fighting the drug cartels), health care, education, energy, and indigenous affairs – where the two countries could benefit from a frank exchange of ideas and best practices.

The always fascinating Canada-Cuba relationship, as McKenna and Kirk explain, is an important barometer of the health of Canada's overall engagement with the Americas. This is why officialdom in Ottawa needs to discard the shrill and hard-line rhetoric and engage the Cubans in a respectful and constructive manner. It is also important for the Canadian government not to allow legitimate human rights concerns to dominate the entire bilateral relationship to the point of nullifying areas of potential advancement. Lecturing the Cubans will only leave Canada spinning its wheels. In fact, if Canada says that it is concerned about human rights, the treatment of political prisoners, and a democratic opening in Cuba, the best way to promote this agenda is to take a page out the Chrétien handbook by building up trust and credibility via serious diplomatic dialogue, a targeted aid program, ongoing commercial exchange, and enhanced people-to-people contacts. Perhaps it is time for Canada to use its good offices to encourage the Obama administration to modify its still-lingering isolationist thrust, to speak out more forcefully against the U.S. embargo, and, more controversially, to put out feelers about whether the Cubans would be interested in an official state visit in the near future. As McKenna and Kirk argue, it is extremely important that Ottawa not be perceived by Havana as having bad intentions with respect to Cuba, doing Washington's bidding in the Americas, or acting as a mouthpiece for the U.S. in the OAS.

With respect to Canada-Haiti relations, Yasmine Shamsie makes some key recommendations about this politically and historically significant relationship. By adopting the 'fragile state' framework or policy lens, Canadian policy makers – especially those involved in ODA decisions – need to be mindful of security and stability aims squeezing out the critical objective of poverty reduction. At the same time, officials at CIDA and DFAIT should not forget about agricultural and rural development initiatives – the place where most of Haiti's poor reside – in their haste to promote urban-based development strategies. As Shamsie indicates, the Canadian government must implement a development strategy that places the long-term interest of Haitians first – through capacity-building, small-scale agriculture, good governance, and the reduction of socio-economic inequities. Simply put, the poorest country in the Americas needs a policy organizing principle that is based more on the vulnerabilities and daily challenges of Haitians themselves.

In the area of Canada-Caribbean relations, Ramesh Chaitoo strongly advises Ottawa to return to the days when Canada's voice actually carried some weight in the region. To do that, he argues convincingly that enhanced diplomatic or political engagement will not be sufficient – far greater emphasis should be placed on people-to-people exchanges. CIDA and Foreign Affairs are specifically singled out as governmental bodies that need to work more cooperatively and purposefully with CARICOM NGOs (with a more intense focus on youth and the private sector). Furthermore, it would be pure folly, Chaitoo warns, for Canada to ignore the attendant crime and instability of narco-trafficking; it will need to allocate substantial resources in the areas of drug interdiction, policing and justice, and economic development. Accordingly, on the bilateral trade front, officials in Ottawa must take into account Caribbean vulnerabilities, its core economic objectives, and the need for transition assistance – in contrast to what it has done in the cases of Peru,

Chile and Costa Rica – if it hopes to conclude a comprehensive agreement with the region.

Stephen Baranyi and John Foster, in their analysis of Canada–Central America relations, pick up on some of the same policy themes discussed in the chapters on Haiti and the Caribbean: promoting human rights and capacity-building; targeting development assistance toward health care, food security, and good governance; and addressing the crippling structural inequities in the isthmus through support for rural development. With respect to Honduras, they urge Canadian officials to adopt a more forceful position – pressing the Lobo government to investigate serious human rights abuses and improper executive orders during the 2009 crisis. The authors also call for a moratorium on any Canada-CA4 trade and investment negotiations and the need for a comprehensive assessment of the impact on human rights. Lastly, Ottawa should seek to ensure that its military training program reinforces civilian control over the armed forces and police in most of the Central American countries.

In her evaluation of Canada-Colombia relations, Maria Teresa Aya Smitmans maintains that Ottawa needs to provide more in the way of financial and developmental assistance to the erstwhile strife-torn country. While she suggests that Canadian funding for NGOs should continue, this disbursement of funds should not be at the expense of governmental institutions like the People's Ombudsman or the Attorney General's Office. Colombian sensitivity and autonomy should also be respected and taken into account – preferably through direct communications with Bogotá – whenever the Canadian government wishes to support civil society groups in Colombia. She also recommends that Canada concentrate some of that same funding on training Colombian security forces in various military-related courses (including civil-military relations) organized by the Pearson Peacekeeping Centre in Ottawa. Of course, the passage of the Canada-Colombia trade agreement will go some way toward revitalizing the bilateral relationship and reconfirming Canada's bona fides when it comes to recognizing Colombian interests.[13]

Overall, Lesley Burns posits that Canada should strive for engagement over estrangement in its bilateral relationship with Venezuela. She acknowledges that Canada can indeed play a role in fostering democratic governance in Venezuela but that it should do so in a respectful, non-ideological, and tactful manner. It should refrain from putting stringent demands or conditions on the Chávez government. But there are opportunities that take into account representative and participatory democracy – namely, governmental accountability and respect for the rule of law, freedom of the press, and greater access to information. We should also be more willing to work with Venezuelan authorities to create a more favourable trade and investment environment for both countries. In this regard, Burns recommends that officials in Ottawa seek to work with their Venezuelan counterparts in terms of implementing best practices in a whole range of issue areas.

From the standpoint of Canada-Brazil relations, Ted Hewitt is understandably puzzled by the neglect of Brazil in Canada's Americas thrust. To begin, officialdom in Ottawa needs to situate Brazil in the proper context of being not only a major power in the Americas, but a serious economic and political actor on the world stage. In doing so, Canada could then inject the necessary political and diplomatic energy into the bilateral relationship, by intensifying ministerial exchanges, visits by senior Canadian officials, collaboration within the OAS and other multilateral forums (such as the Union of South American Nations and the Rio Group), and military linkages, and by securing a presidential visit from Brazil. Priority areas need to be singled out for special attention – such as commercial interactions, R&D collaboration, and a wide variety of people-to-people exchanges – and given the requisite resources to do the job properly. The federal government should also encourage provincial governments, and not just Quebec, to establish more productive interchanges with the Brazilians on resource development, alternative energy sources, and climate change.

As far as Canada's relationship with Chile is concerned, Roberto Durán makes the case that productive relations require a sustained commitment at all levels of the Canadian and Chilean governments – from the prime minister/president down to their ambassadors in Santiago and Ottawa. He also advocates a stronger relationship between the respective ambassadors and staffs of both countries at the OAS in Washington, calling for a more structured process of consultation and interchange. He takes a similar approach with respect to people-to-people contacts, placing particular emphasis on military linkages; educational, scientific, and cultural exchanges; business ties; and NGO interaction. To this end, closer cooperation between indigenous peoples in both countries is posited as a means of adding an important layer to an enhanced bilateral relationship going forward.

Ottawa will need to work assiduously and purposefully at cultivating and strengthening the Canadian–Latin American relationship. Trust, rapport, and good faith – all integral to building positive relations with governments and peoples in the Americas – require more than fine words, good intentions, and the occasional state visit. Such objectives need to be carefully cultivated and calibrated over time and with great care and patience. Canada should not adopt the historically damaging U.S. approach of looking at the Americas as our 'own back-yard.' A sustained effort, genuine commitment, and tangible accomplishments or achievements on the ground are required.

Canada's politicians, policy makers and businesspeople have to do more to establish a firm and lasting footprint in Latin America.[14] There must be sufficient resources, personnel, active foreign service officers, and, most important, political will. Ministerial exchanges, visits involving senior Canadian officials, and increased engagement in community events from Canada's diplomatic corps are required. And there can never be enough people-to-people exchanges – from tourism to serious academic meetings – which Ottawa should be actively encouraging. Simply put, we need to ensure that the Canadian flag is being regularly shown throughout the region.[15]

At the same time, the Department of Foreign Affairs and International Trade (DFAIT) needs to do its part. It can begin by strengthening the bureaucratic enclaves dedicated to the Americas with more financial resources, personnel, and Spanish-speaking foreign service officers. They would be far better off retaining people with expertise and experience of Latin America for longer periods of time instead of rotating staff from the Asia-Pacific or European divisions every few years. These officials should then concentrate on building links to the small NGO community in Canada with an interest in Latin America, hold regular exchanges with interested academics across the country, and participate regularly in workshops, study groups, and conferences that focus on the Americas. The Canadian Foundation for the Americas (FOCAL) made some strides in this regard, but it was ideologically rigid and could not survive the Conservative budget cutters (it was disbanded in September 2011). It makes sense for Ottawa policy makers to resurrect a similar forum but make it a non-partisan centre or institute for thoughtful policy discussions and advice.

Furthermore, Canada needs to take a much higher profile within the corridors of the OAS headquarters in Washington. To do this, our diplomats must have clear policy direction from Ottawa politicians and policy makers, which has not always been the case. As Hal Klepak rightly points out, delegations from other member states want to know and hear what Canada thinks and has to say. And if we want to be taken seriously as a dedicated inter-American partner (instead of as a dilet-tante), we need to make our presence felt within the corridors of the hemispheric body. As the second-largest financial contributor to the OAS, we should not shy away from flexing our not insignificant dip-lomatic muscle. The time is overdue for Canada to be recognized as a major player in the region's principal political institution.

In addition, Canada should initiate more state visits (like Harper's August 2011 foray into the Americas) to countries throughout the region (and not just those with which we have trade agreements), bear-ing in mind the Latino preference for getting to know each other before building a productive friendship.[16] Ottawa should also consider estab-lishing regular meetings (perhaps every four months or so) with vari-ous foreign ministers throughout the Americas and even advancing the idea of having exchanges involving officials from Canada's foreign pol-icy establishment and other foreign ministries in the region. Indeed, the only way for the people of the Americas to truly discover Canada is to make a long-term commitment – to make it 'our home,' in the prescient words of former prime minister and foreign minister Joe Clark. And we should not shy away from using 'public diplomacy' in an aggressive fashion to get the word out that Canada is committed to making each country in Latin America and the Caribbean a policy priority.

At the same time, we may wish to focus our energies, at least initially, on five or six major countries in the region – including Mexico, Brazil, Cuba, Argentina, and Chile. If we really want to have a meaningful pres-ence in the region, we need to be ready to play with the hemisphere's major political and economic players. As John Kirk has said on many occasions, the key to opening the door to enhanced relations with the Americas must include a productive Canada-Cuba relationship. The Canadian government does not have to break new policy ground here – Trudeau fashioned a solid bilateral relationship with Havana and even talked about a strategy of 'concentrated bilateralism' with respect to the Americas in the early 1980s. Nor do the traditional aspects of Canada's Americas diplomacy need to be radically changed from democratiza-tion, order, stability, and responsible trade and investment.

But official Ottawa needs to be careful about making human rights considerations a decisive element in shaping its policy toward the wider region. This is not to say that human rights should be down-played or sacrificed for long-term economic/trade benefits – only that it should not dominate the discourse of our bilateral relationships or exhibit selective bias or indignation. This would seem to be the case in our relations with Colombia, Cuba, Venezuela, Bolivia, and the countries of Central America. Isolating these and other countries on the basis of rights concerns is not likely to further the above-mentioned agenda. But through engagement, confidence building, and mutual respect, Canada will be in a far better position to seriously advance and address these thorny and complex issues.

We may not always be totally comfortable with all of the countries that we engage with in the hemisphere. It is difficult to determine which countries are worth engaging and which are not (and for what reasons). Engagement in the Americas, then, should be responsible, genuine, multi-faceted, and geared toward positive policy outcomes. As is the case with Cuba today, talking is always better than not talking – as the United States is surely coming to realize.

The contributors to this book have all sought to put down some substantive markers along the path to a robust Americas strategy. In part, Canada needs to get back to doing what it does best – applying middle-power diplomacy to the Americas by talking less and listening more, fashioning pragmatic and well-conceived policy ideas, finding a consensus or middle ground, and striving to build bridges around common themes. The last thing that Canada needs is an Americas policy driven primarily by rigid ideological considerations. That said, we are now paying the price of policy neglect over the decades. Surely it is time to put an end to triumphantly 'discovering' the Americas every ten years or so. Canada must – for reasons of national interest and community building – become a permanent fixture in our own hemispheric neighbourhood. An Americas strategy should not just be a bunch of fine words and breathless intentions cobbled together in a glossy brochure. What really talks is money and political will – and it is not there yet. But as the Latinos are fond of saying, it is never too late to come to the fiesta.

NOTES

1 Government of Canada, *Canada and the Americas: Priorities and Progress* (Ottawa: Her Majesty the Queen in Right of Canada, 2009), 3.
2 Ibid., 4.
3 The key assumptions underpinning why Canada has moved to embrace the Americas is covered, though in critical tones, in Jean Daudelin, 'Foreign Policy at the Fringe: Canada and Latin America,' *International Journal* 58, no. 4 (Autumn 2003): 638–9.

4 For criticism of Harper's Americas strategy, see Jennifer Ditchburn, 'Harper's Americas Strategy Falling Short: Internal Review,' *Waterloo Region Record*, 17 March 2011, A12. Officials from DFAIT's office of the inspector general go so far as to suggest that 'there is evidence to suggest Canada's credibility in the region could decline.' Also, see 'Loss of Focus,' editorial, *Globe and Mail*, 1 June 2011, A16.

5 Confidential interview with a senior Canadian foreign service officer, 16 March 2010. With the exception of increased Canadian International Development Assistance (CIDA) aid for earthquake-ravaged Haiti, our development assistance has barely budged – increasing by some $20 million in the first two years after the 2007 launch of Harper's Americas strategy. See Campbell Clark, 'Solid Americas Strategy Promises Big Rewards,' *Globe and Mail*, 24 May 2011, A11.

6 This comment is not intended to disparage the work of previous Canadian foreign affairs ministers like Allan MacEachen, Barbara McDougall, Lloyd Axworthy, and Bill Graham on hemispheric affairs. The fact remains that they did not make the Americas a top priority deserving of sustained foreign policy attention.

7 See Kevin Carmichael and Tavia Grant, 'Missed Opportunities,' *Globe and Mail*, 26 March 2011, B1. On Canada's mining presence, see the critical perspective of Liisa L. North, 'Bad Neighbours,' *Canadian Dimension* 45, no. 1 (Jan./Feb. 2011): 19–23.

8 Ibid.

9 Tavia Grant, 'Stage Set for "Latin America's decade,"' *Globe and Mail*, 28 March 2011, B3.

10 Carmichael and Grant, 'Missed Opportunities.'

11 Canada's lacklustre response to the 2009 Honduran crisis was an obvious example of how not to build credibility in the Americas. As Max Cameron and Jason Tockman argue, the perception in the region – rightly or wrongly – was that Canada largely emulated the tepid U.S. response to the coup. Maxwell A. Cameron and Jason Tockman, 'A Diplomatic Theater of the Absurd: Canada, the OAS, and the Honduran Coup,' *NACLA Report on the Americas* 43, no. 3 (May/June 2010): 18–22.

12 When the new grouping of countries – the so-called Community of Latin American and Caribbean States – met for its February 2010 inaugural gathering in Mexico, only Canada and the United States were not invited to attend. Perhaps it was nothing. But perhaps it was a sign that Canada needs to make its presence more widely felt in the region. See also Jeff Davis, 'Two Years into the Americas Strategy,' *Embassy Magazine*, 29 April 2010, 13.

13 Needless to say, there existed strong opposition to this pact in Canada, with several NGOs criticizing the deal primarily on human rights grounds. See Sheila Katz and Gauri Screenivasan, 'Against the Odds: Fighting Canada's Free Trade Deal with Colombia,' *NACLA Report on the Americas* 43, no. 3 (May/June 2010): 23–8.

14 There are even possibilities of working cooperatively together on issues around federalism. Canada could easily utilize its experience in intergovernmental relations, regional economic development, and fiscal federalism and share it with such countries as Brazil, Argentina, Venezuela, and Mexico.

15 This point was made by Carlo Dade, the then executive director of the Canadian Foundation for the Americas (which was shut down in September 2011 by the Harper government), in an op-ed piece in the *Globe and Mail* after Harper's five-day visit to the region in August 2011. As he argued: 'The country needs to become known in the hemisphere and to become a player once again.' Carlo Dade, 'Latin America: The Glass Is Half ...,' *Globe and Mail*, 17 August 2011, A11. Also see his 'We Need Latin America More Than It Needs Us,' *Globe and Mail*, 13 April 2012, A13.

16 While other previous opportunities were missed, it is worth noting that Prime Minister Harper did manage to hold a bilateral meeting with Brazil's Lula da Silva during the 15 April 2010 Nuclear Summit Meeting in Washington.

Contributors

Stephen Baranyi is an associate professor with the School of International Development and Global Studies at the University of Ottawa. He researches and teaches on development challenges in fragile states – particularly on the reform of security agencies and Canadian policies in such contexts. Recent publications include a special issue of the *Journal of Peacebuilding and Development* on Haiti (2011), and a chapter on the development dimension of Canadian engagement in high-priority fragile states, in a book on Canadian aid edited by Stephen Brown (2012).

Lesley M. Burns is a political analyst with a Doctorate in Political Science and International Relations from the University of British Columbia. Her work focuses on strengthening governance institutions and enabling responsive government. She has lived, worked, and travelled extensively throughout Latin America.

Maxwell A. Cameron teaches at the University of British Columbia in the Department of Political Science, where he directs the Centre for the Study of Democratic Institutions. His research and teaching focuses on problems of democracy and constitutionalism, with a concentration on the separation of powers. At the Centre for the Study of Democratic Institutions, Cameron is working on democratic reform and citizen engagement. In 2011–12 he was a Distinguished Scholar in Residence at the Peter Wall Institute for Advanced Studies.

Ramesh Chaitoo is a doctoral candidate at the University of Ghent in Belgium and an international trade consultant. He was previously

Head of the Services Trade Unit at the Caribbean Regional Negotiating Machinery. Prior to that, he was a senior associate at the Centre for Trade Policy and Law at Carleton University in Ottawa.

Roberto Durán is professor of International Politics at the Catholic University of Chile in Santiago. He is also a former professor at the Chilean Diplomatic Academy. He is currently leading a research project examining the diplomacy of countries in the Southern-Cone.

John W. Foster teaches human rights and globalization at Carleton University and the University of Regina, having spent a lifetime in domestic social justice and international development. His most recent publications are 'Making Room for Democracy: Three Moments in the Struggle against Trade and Investment Regimes in the Americas,' in Julian Castor-Rea, ed., *Our North America: Social and Political Issues Beyond NAFTA* (2012), and 'NAFTA and After: The Triumph of Bilateralism,' in *The USA and Canada 2012* (2011).

Ricardo Grinspun teaches economics and is a Fellow of the Centre for Research on Latin America and the Caribbean (CERLAC) at York University in Toronto. He is a former director of CERLAC and has directed several large-scale international development projects, including a six-year CIDA-funded linkage project with Chilean partners on agro-ecology and sustainable rural development. His publications are on issues of development and international trade, hemispheric integration, and Canada's role in the Americas.

W.E. (Ted) Hewitt is currently Public Policy Scholar in the Brazil Institute at the Woodrow Wilson International Center for Scholars in Washington, DC, and professor of sociology at the University of Western Ontario in London, Canada. He has published extensively on issues related to social movements and population health, local government, and international cooperation for urban development in Latin America. He is a leading Canadian authority on Brazil whose work has appeared in monographs, edited works, and a range of academic journals including *Cities, Journal of Latin American Studies, Journal of Developing Areas, Third World Quarterly*, and *Habitat International*.

John M. Kirk is professor of Latin American Studies at Dalhousie University. He is the author/co-editor of 13 books on Cuba, and his most recent works are *A Contemporary Cuba Reader* (2008), *Cuban Medical Internationalism* (2009), and *José Martí, Mentor of the Cuban Revolution* (2012). He is currently writing a new book on lessons to be learned from Cuban medical cooperation abroad. He is the editor of the Contemporary Cuba series at the University Press of Florida and a member of the editorial boards of the *International Journal of Cuban Studies* and *Cuban Studies/Estudios Cubanos*.

Hal Klepak is professor emeritus of History and Strategy at the Royal Military College of Canada. He has written extensively on foreign and defence policy issues in Latin America and is Special Adviser to the Commander of the Canadian Army on Inter-American Affairs. His latest book is entitled *Raúl Castro and Cuba: A Military Story*, which is to be published in 2012 by Palgrave/Macmillan.

Peter McKenna is chair and professor of political science at the University of Prince Edward Island in Charlottetown. He is the co-author of *Fighting Words: Competing Voices from Revolutionary Cuba* (2009), the co-author of *Canada-Cuba Relations: The Other Good Neighbor Policy* (1997), and the author of *Canada and the OAS: From Dilettante to Full Partner* (1995).

Jennifer Mills is a doctoral student in the Faculty of Environmental Studies at York University. She completed her Master's degree in Development Studies at York University and is a Research Associate of the Centre for Research on Latin America and the Caribbean (CERLAC).

James Rochlin is professor of political science at the University of British Columbia–Okanagan. He conducts research in the areas of critical security and political economy vis-à-vis Mexico, Venezuela, Colombia, Ecuador, and Bolivia. He is the author of *Social Forces and the Revolution in Military Affairs: The Cases of Colombia and Mexico* (2007), and *Discovering the Americas: The Evolution of Canadian Foreign Policy towards Latin America* (1994).

Yasmine Shamsie is an associate professor in the Department of Political Science at Wilfrid Laurier University and a Fellow at the Centre for Research on Latin America and the Caribbean (CERLAC) at York University. Her research focuses on the peacebuilding efforts of bilateral and multilateral actors in Haiti and Central America.

Maria Teresa Aya Smitmans is an international affairs specialist at the Universidad Externado de Colombia in Bogotá. She is also the Director of the San Carlos Diplomatic Academy in Colombia.

Jason Tockman is a doctoral candidate in the Department of Political Science at the University of British Columbia. He is a researcher with UBC's Centre for the Study of Democratic Institutions, and a regular contributor to the North American Congress on Latin America. His research focuses on questions of citizenship, democratic participation, and indigenous rights in Latin America.

Duncan Wood is profesor numerario and Director of the International Relations Degree at the Instituto Tecnologico Autonomo de Mexico (ITAM). He is also a Senior Consultant for the Mexico Institute at the Woodrow Wilson International Center for Scholars and a Senior Associate with the Americas Program at the Center for Strategic and International Studies (CSIS), both in Washington, DC. His main area of research focuses on Mexican democracy and energy politics.

Index

285n.37; drug trafficking in Haiti,
185, 186; effects in Canada of the
Latin American drug trade, 13, 19;
as inter-American security prob-
lem, 48–9; Merida Initiative (MI),
130; Mexican drug war, xi, 15, 19,
130, 139–40, 143, 148n.44, 361
Duarte, Jaime, 70
Duffield, Mark, 184, 188, 189, 200
Dupras, Maurice, 245
Durán, Roberto, 364
Durand, Paul, 311n.41
Duvalier, Jean-Claude, 35–6, 193
Dymond, William, 235–6
Dymond, William (Bill), and Michael
Hart, 281

Echenique, Cecilia, 345
Ecuador, 12, 16, 20, 40, 44, 76, 89, 98,
108, 258, 305; Canada's relations
with, xviin.3, 72, 277
Eizenstat, Stuart, et al., 187
Ejército de Liberación Nacional
(ELN), 9, 272, 273, 284–5n.27
El Salvador, 5, 12, 40, 98, 99, 243, 244;
Canada's relations with, 7–8, 35,
36, 68, 82n.48, 242, 245, 246, 247–8,
252 table 9.2, 253, 259; Canadian
ODA to, 248–9; Frente Farabundo
Marti de Liberación Nacional
(FMLN), 240; and Pacific Rim
mining company, 73; relations
with the U.S., 28, 240, 242, 246
Emerson, David, 70, 277
Entwistle, Mark, 165–6
environmentalism: and Canadian
policy towards the Americas, 58,
59, 62, 67, 77, 92; environmental
agreement between Canada and
Chile, 341, 342; regulation of Mexi-

co's energy sector, 141–2, 148n.44;
petro-related ecocide, 20
Erikson, Daniel, 182
Escobar, Arturo, 14
European Union (EU), 7, 99, 106,
118, 195, 234, 279, 286n.49, 311n.41,
339, 348, 356

Farrar, Jonathan, 176n.18
Fast, Ed, 148n.43
Fearon, James, and David Laitin, 199
Ferrari, Bruno, 148n.43
Ferreira, Murilo, 328
Fox, Vicente, 124, 125–6, 129
Fukuda-Parr, Sakiko, 195, 199
Fukuyama, Francis, 23n.6, 199, 296
Fuerzas Armadas Revolucionarias
de Colombia (FARC), 9, 272, 273,
275, 279, 284n.25, 284–5n.27, 305
Fujimori, Alberto, 91, 108, 340
Funes, Mauricio, 12
fragile-state concept, 187–8, 189–90,
200, 256; Haiti as 'fragile state,'
180–1, 186–92, 193, 196, 197–201,
362
François, Monika, and Inder Sud,
197
free trade agreements. *See under*
trade and investment
Free Trade Area of the Americas
(FTAA), 58, 59, 60–5, 70, 71, 76, 77,
87, 90, 101, 251–2, 255, 292–3, 300
Frente Farabundo Marti de Liberación Nacional (FMLN), 240
Frente Sandinista de Liberación
Nacional (FSLN), 240, 246, 250
Fuentes-Berain, Sandra, 123

García, Alan, 85n.92, 93
Gaviria, César, 91, 276, 299